International Ethics

International Ethics

Concepts, Theories, and Cases in Global Politics

FOURTH EDITION

Mark R. Amstutz

ROWMAN & LITTLEFIELD PUBLISHERS, INC.
Lanham • Boulder • New York • Toronto • Plymouth, UK

Published by Rowman & Littlefield Publishers, Inc.
A wholly owned subsidiary of The Rowman & Littlefield Publishing Group, Inc.
4501 Forbes Boulevard, Suite 200, Lanham, Maryland 20706
www.rowman.com

10 Thornbury Road, Plymouth PL6 7PP, United Kingdom

British Library Cataloguing in Publication Information Available

Library of Congress Cataloging-in-Publication Data

Amstutz, Mark R.
   International ethics : concepts, theories, and cases in global politics / Mark R. Amstutz.—Fourth edition.
      pages cm
   Includes bibliographical references and index.
   ISBN 978-1-4422-2095-9 (cloth : alk. paper)
   ISBN 978-1-4422-2096-6 (pbk. : alk. paper)
   ISBN 978-1-4422-2097-3 (electronic)
   1. International relations—Moral and ethical aspects.   I. Title.
JZ1306.A67   2013
172'.4—dc23

                                                        2012044978

♾ ™The paper used in this publication meets the minimum requirements of American National Standard for Information Sciences—Permanence of Paper for Printed Library Materials, ANSI/NISO Z39.48-1992.

Printed in the United States of America

Contents

PART TWO: Global Issues

Cases

Introduction

The place of morality in international politics is the most obscure and difficult problem in the whole range of international studies.[1]
—EDWARD HALLETT CARR

A FUNDAMENTAL AIM of this study is to demonstrate, through arguments and illustrations, that moral values are an essential element of international relations and that international ethics are foundational to global politics. Although international relations scholars have increasingly recognized the importance of moral values and ethical reasoning in international affairs, political realism continues to serve as the dominant paradigm in international relations. Even though realism does not deny international ethics, it allows little room for moral reasoning, focusing instead on the quest for national security and the promotion of economic and social well-being.

In this book, I argue that the realist notion that international politics is fundamentally a quest for political power and economic interests is false and untenable. Instead, I suggest that international politics is rooted in ethics and that states and other nonstate actors share a basic moral vocabulary that influences the individual and collective choices of states. To be sure, the ethical analysis of foreign policies and global structures is fraught with major epistemological and methodological challenges. However, the difficulty of applying moral principles to concrete issues and problems does not invalidate the possibility of or the responsibility for morally assessing political actions and institutional structures.

Realists assert that international society is a realm of power and necessity, not morality and choice. Because no common authority exists in the international system to protect states and to resolve disputes, some political thinkers have suggested that states' overriding interests are national security and material well-being. These interests, it is suggested, automatically displace morality. George Kennan, for example, argues that because a statesman's primary duty is to secure the vital interests of states, foreign affairs are essentially amoral. He writes,

> Government is an agent, not a principal. Its primary obligation is to the interests of the national society it represents . . . its military security, the integrity of its political life and the well-being of its people. These needs have no moral quality. They are

the unavoidable necessities of national existence and therefore are subject to classification neither as "good" or "bad."[2]

Kennan thinks that because interests such as security, political independence, and national well-being are essential to the survival and economic viability of states, they have no moral quality. But why should vital interests be amoral? Are not human interests rooted partly in morality? And does not the pursuit of foreign policy goals involve moral judgment? As Arnold Wolfers has wisely observed, international relations are not beyond the scope of morality but are themselves based on moral norms.[3]

A brief perusal of contemporary international developments illustrates the pervasive and influential role of moral values in the foreign policy debates, if not actions, of government officials. Consider the following events, each of them involving important moral norms:

1. On September 11, 2001, Muslim fanatics commandeered four large passenger airplanes, flying two of them into the World Trade Center in New York City and another into the Pentagon in Washington, D.C. These attacks, which led to the collapse of the World Trade Center's twin towers and major destruction to a section of the Pentagon, caused the death of more than three thousand persons. They were the single most destructive act of aggression against the territory of the United States, eclipsing the destruction caused by the Japanese attack on Pearl Harbor in 1941. The U.S. government responded to the 9/11 attacks with a "war on terror." When Afghanistan's ruling authorities, the Taliban, refused to turn over Osama bin Laden and other Al Qaeda operatives that were partly responsible for the 9/11 terrorist attack, U.S. military forces intervened and toppled the Taliban regime. In view of the danger posed by contemporary terrorism, was the U.S. military action against Afghanistan justified? Is war against states harboring terrorist organizations morally legitimate, even if they are not directly responsible for terror?

2. From 2003 until 2007 an intense war took place in Darfur, Sudan, between rebels demanding greater political autonomy and government-backed militia (*janjaweed*). The Darfur rebels were African tribesmen who survived as farmers, while the militia were mainly nomadic Arab herdsmen. When the Darfur rebellion began, Sudan's government responded by arming and supporting the *janjaweed* and carrying out periodic military operations on land and from the air. The war is estimated to have resulted in the deaths of more than two hundred thousand Darfurians and the forced displacement of more than two million other persons. Although the U.S. government charged Sudan's regime with genocide, the international community was unwilling to use military force to protect the innocent. In 2005 a small, ineffective African peacekeeping force was introduced into the territory, but it was unable to halt atrocities. Finally, a UN peacekeeping force was established in 2007 that significantly reduced violence in Darfur. When domestic conflicts like the Darfur war occur, resulting in widespread killing and suffering among innocent civilians, should the international community intervene to restore order? When fighters target civilians directly, who should rescue them?

3. Following the 9/11 attacks on the United States, Pakistan cooperated with the U.S. military in the campaign against Al Qaeda and the Taliban, receiving close to $30

billion in foreign aid from America. But in time cooperation dwindled, and the bilateral ties became increasingly strained after the U.S. military increased attacks on militant groups in the semiautonomous tribal areas of Western Pakistan in the 2009–2011 period. Although most of these attacks were carried out against specific targets with highly accurate drone missiles, the attacks posed numerous legal and moral challenges, including the violation of Pakistan's sovereignty and the inevitable deaths of civilians. Two events in 2011 increased tensions significantly. First, U.S. special forces located and killed Al Qaeda founder Osama bin Laden in a covert mission deep in Pakistani territory in May 2011, embarrassing Pakistan's armed forces both with the revelation that the most sought-after terrorist had been living in their land for more than five years and also with their failure to detect the American violation of Pakistani airspace. The second event was the inadvertent killing of twenty-four Pakistani soldiers along the Afghanistan–Pakistan border in November 2011. When NATO soldiers were fired upon, NATO responded by bombing a border target, resulting in the soldiers' deaths. This act angered Pakistani authorities, who then closed the supply road for U.S. forces in Afghanistan for more than six months. Given the ongoing military operations against the Taliban in Afghanistan, how should the United States pursue its immediate security interests as well as its long-term goals of maintaining a stable, coherent Pakistani state? Should U.S. forces continue to target militants in the tribal territories?

4. Ever since Iran began to expand its nuclear enrichment program, Western powers have been deeply concerned about nuclear proliferation in the Middle East. As a result, the United States has imposed a variety of sanctions to influence Iranian nuclear ambitions. Although Iran denies that it is seeking to acquire nuclear weapons, a 2011 International Atomic Energy Agency (IAEA) report suggests that the country's uranium enrichment program is not solely pacific in nature. As of mid-2012, however, Russia and China—both of which have significant economic interests in Iran—have opposed comprehensive sanctions against Iran. The United States along with the European Union have imposed significant sanctions that have reduced petroleum exports and banned transmission of advanced Western technology. In view of the ongoing dispute over Iran's nuclear program, how should the West approach the problem of nuclear proliferation? What moral values should guide American coercive diplomacy?

5. After rebellions broke out in Tunisia in December 2010, the political awakening spread rapidly to other Arab countries, including Egypt, Yemen, and Libya. When rebel forces succeeded in taking control of various territories of Libya, including the eastern port city of Benghazi, Colonel Muammar Qaddafi, the country's longtime dictator, vowed to carry out mass killings against rebel-held territories. In view of Qaddafi's threat, the major powers adopted a UN Security Council resolution that authorized military force to protect civilians in the Libyan civil war. NATO began military operations in mid-March 2011, destroying most of Libya's air defense system, communications centers, and air forces. After six months of intermittent fighting, the rebel forces eventually took control of most of the country, and when Qaddafi was captured and killed, the rebel forces took control of Tripoli and the institutions of government. Although Qaddafi had committed much evil in his four decades of autocratic rule, when NATO began its military operations, fewer than five hundred persons had been

killed in the fighting. From an ethical perspective, was the decision to intervene militarily against a sovereign state morally defensible? How much suffering must a country endure before foreign powers should rescue civilians in a foreign land? Finally, was the shift in strategy—from protecting civilians to supporting rebel forces—morally justified?

6. The Arab political awakening influenced Syria as well. Beginning in March 2011, antiregime forces began to challenge the longtime Baathist regime, currently headed by Bashar al-Assad. As the rebel forces increased their attacks on the state, the Syrian government's military and security forces responded with brutal force. As of mid-2012, the political revolt was still ongoing, with more than twenty-five thousand deaths attributed to the fighting. Interestingly, whereas the UN Security Council authorized military action in Libya, there was less international support for military action in Syria, even though the level of deaths and human suffering was much greater in Syria than had been the case in Libya. To a significant degree, the inability of the United Nations to get involved stemmed from Russia's continued support of the Assad regime.[4] U.S. government and EU officials have called for regime change. As with the Libyan rebellion, Western powers have imposed significant economic sanctions on Syria, but unlike Libya, the international community has not challenged the Syrian state militarily. In view of the widespread suffering in Syria, does the international community have a responsibility to protect civilians from the ongoing revolution?

As these multilateral issues suggest, contemporary international relations involve fundamental moral choices. Although not all international relations issues involve moral values, most foreign policy decisions are based in part on ethical judgment. Moreover, the development of the international community's rules, procedures, and structures will similarly depend on values and norms that are partly moral.

This study explores two distinct dimensions of international political morality: the role of moral values in foreign policy and the ethical foundation of the rules and structures of global society. Some scholars and decision makers have suggested that moral values have no place in foreign policy because each sovereign state is entitled to its own moral norms. Additionally, some theorists have argued that in view of the international community's cultural diversity, there is, and can be, no common international political morality. This conclusion, however, is untenable for two reasons. First, although cultural diversity is a feature of global society, state and nonstate actors share a common moral vocabulary that influences international relations. These shared basic norms provide the basis for moral claims on issues such as self-determination, human rights, the use of force, and humanitarian relief. Second, and more importantly, despite the reality of cultural pluralism, there is no necessary or logical connection between the empirical fact of cultural pluralism and the normative belief that there is no morality in global society. The normative belief in moral relativism does not and cannot follow necessarily and logically from the fact of cultural diversity. Morality, after all, is based not on consensus but on perceived moral obligations.

This is a study in applied international political ethics. Although I address important philosophic issues, such as the epistemological and substantive challenges posed by cultural pluralism, the major aim of this book is to describe and assess the nature, role, and impact of international political morality on the individual and collective conduct of foreign relations. This task is undertaken by examining the nature and legitimacy of moral values and the role of ethical strategies and traditions in applying moral values to such issues as human rights, war, and foreign intervention.

This study also examines the ethical nature of the rules, structures, and informal patterns of the international system itself. Whereas the morality of foreign policy focuses on the role of moral norms in international relations, international ethics is concerned with the justice of global society, including the moral legitimacy of the nation-state and the structures and dominant patterns of the international community. For example, are territorial boundaries morally important? Is the norm of nonintervention a principal ethical rule of international society? If it is, can the norm be violated to protect other moral norms, such as basic human rights? Is humanitarian intervention morally defensible? Are the egregious economic and political disparities among states morally acceptable? Do high-income states have a moral obligation to admit a large number of refugees?

This book comprises two distinct dimensions. The first part, chapters 1 through 4, analyzes conceptual and theoretical issues. Chapter 1 explores the nature of morality and ethics and the role of moral values in foreign policy. Chapter 2 examines different ethical conceptions of the international community and how these alternative world-views influence how theorists conceive of justice in global society. Chapter 3 analyzes the nature and role of ethical traditions in structuring moral analysis, focusing on three major traditions: realism, idealism, and principled realism. Chapter 4 describes different methodologies for applying moral reasoning to political action, focusing on rule-based analysis and ends-based analysis. It also includes a new section dealing with the process of moral decision making in public life. The remaining chapters (chapters 5–12) focus on eight important ethical issues in global politics. The first six chapters (5–10) examine the following foreign policy issues: human rights, political reconciliation, war, irregular war, foreign intervention, and international economic relations. The last two chapters (11 and 12) examine the quest for justice in the international community, with chapter 11 addressing justice among states and chapter 12 exploring justice within global society.

Throughout this study, I use case studies to illuminate and apply moral norms to specific international relations issues and problems. To encourage ethical analysis, each case study concludes with a brief discussion of relevant moral questions and concerns raised by a particular conflict or problem. Because the test of political morality is whether it contributes to a more just global society, the challenge in international ethics is not simply to identify appropriate moral values but to apply them to specific global issues and problems. The aim of this book is thus to encourage ethical analysis that contributes to political judgments resulting in a more just, humane world.

This book involves several major changes from the third edition. To begin with, the book has added one new chapter. Whereas the previous edition devoted two chapters (10 and 11) to justice and the international community, the current edition has added a new chapter (2) to supplement chapters 11 and 12. The new chapter presents alternative conceptions of global society—communitarianism and cosmopolitanism—and their distinct ethical approaches.

A second important change is the addition of a chapter on asymmetric or irregular war. The chapter focuses on two major moral dilemmas posed by unconventional warfare—coercive interrogation and targeted killing.

Third, the new edition devotes a full chapter (10) to international economic relations, focusing on the challenges of financial globalization and the role of economic statecraft. To further highlight international economic affairs, chapter 2 includes a case study on global poverty.

Fourth, the chapter on foreign intervention (chapter 9) has been revised significantly by eliminating the analysis of strategic and political intervention and expanding the analysis of humanitarian intervention. The chapter gives increased emphasis to the responsibility-to-protect (R2P) principle.

Fifth, the new edition has six new case studies. These include global poverty (chapter 2), coercive interrogation (chapter 8), targeted killing with drones (chapter 8), protecting civilians in Libya (chapter 9), the euro crisis (chapter 10), and U.S. assistance to HIV/AIDS victims (chapter 11).

Finally, I have updated the data in the case studies and the moral analysis to incorporate insights from the growing and evolving scholarship on international political ethics.

As with earlier editions, I have benefited from the assistance and encouragement of numerous persons in preparing this book. I am grateful to my parents, the late Mahlon and Ruth Amstutz, for teaching me as a young boy the value of personal integrity and the importance of moral reflection. I also acknowledge with gratitude the opportunity to teach at Wheaton College (IL), a Christian liberal arts college that places a premium on character development and the skills of rational and moral analysis. I am grateful, too, for the financial assistance of the college's Aldeen Development Fund, which helped get the original study under way. Additionally, I thank my students—especially those in my Ethics and Foreign Policy course—for encouraging and challenging my thinking on many of the issues examined in this book. Finally, I gratefully acknowledge the editorial assistance of Stephanie Hagen, a former student of mine.

PART ONE

Ethical Foundations

Chapter One

Morality and Foreign Policy

The "necessities" in international politics, and for that matter in all spheres of life, do not push decision and action beyond the realm of moral judgment; they rest on moral choice themselves.[1]

—ARNOLD WOLFERS

Man's moral sense is not a strong beacon light, radiating outward to illuminate in sharp outline all that it touches. It is, rather, a small candle flame, casting vague and multiple shadows, flickering and sputtering in the strong winds of power and passion, greed and ideology. But brought close to the heart and cupped in one's hands, it dispels the darkness and warms the soul.[2]

—JAMES Q. WILSON

There does not exist such a thing as international morality.[3]

—SIR HAROLD NICOLSON

What passes for ethical standards for governmental policies in foreign affairs is a collection of moralisms, maxims, and slogans, which neither help nor guide, but only confuse, decision.[4]

—DEAN ACHESON

THIS CHAPTER examines the nature and role of moral values and ethical reasoning in international relations. It begins by identifying distinctive features of the terms *morality* and *ethics* and then explores the nature and bases of international political morality, addressing the challenge posed by cultural pluralism to the conceptualization and application of such morality in global society. It then examines the role of moral norms in foreign policy, giving special emphasis to the goals, methods, and problems of applying international morality. The chapter illustrates the role of international political morality with a case study on the 1999 NATO intervention in Kosovo.

MORALITY AND ETHICS

The word *morality* derives from the Latin *mores*, meaning custom, habit, and way of life. It typically describes what is good, right, or proper. These concepts, in turn, are often associated with such notions as virtue, integrity, goodness, righteousness, and justice. The term *ethics* is rooted in the Greek *ethos*, meaning custom or common practice. Because its root meaning is similar to that of *morality*, the two concepts are often used interchangeably. Strictly speaking, however, the two terms represent distinct elements of normative analysis: *morality* referring to values and beliefs about what is right and wrong, good and bad, just and unjust, and *ethics* referring to the examination, justification, and critical analysis of morality. Because of the significance of these elements in international ethics, I explore each of them more fully below.

The Nature of Morality

Moral values have at least three important distinguishing features: they command universal allegiance, they demand impartiality, and they are largely self-enforcing. The claims of universality mean that moral norms are binding on all peoples. Immanuel Kant articulated this requirement in his famous *categorical imperative*, which calls on persons to treat others as having intrinsic value and to act in accordance with principles that are valid for others.[5] As one scholar has explained, universalization means that if "I ought to do X, then I am committed to maintaining that morally anyone else ought to do X unless there are relevant differences between the other person and myself and/or between his situation and mine."[6]

The second dimension of morality—the impartiality of norms—helps to ensure that morality is not simply a means to clothe and advance self-interest. Because of the propensity for human selfishness, philosophers have emphasized the need for dispassion and disinterest. As a result, they have argued that morality must be defined and applied in terms of perspectives and interests other than those of the actor. For example, in his classic work *A Theory of Justice*, John Rawls argues that moral principles should be based on impartiality by requiring that they be selected through a "veil of ignorance," that is, defining and selecting norms without knowledge of who will benefit from them.[7]

A third important feature of morality is its self-enforcing quality. Unlike law, which is enforced by government, morality is applied mainly through the voluntary actions of persons. The decision to abide by moral obligations is rooted in the beliefs and values that people hold. In a short article titled "Law and Manners," which was published in 1924 in the *Atlantic Monthly*, English jurist John Fletcher Moulton defined the moral domain as "obedience to the unenforceable." According to Moulton, human affairs involve actions in three different realms: legal, moral, and voluntary. In the domain of the law, compliance is assured because of the government's capacity to enforce rules. In the third domain, the realm of free choice, persons are free to do as they wish. Between these two realms is the area of morality, or what Moulton termed "manners," by which people behave in accord with "consciousness of duty" rather than the coercive rules of public authority. Moulton describes this domain as follows: "It is the domain of obedience to the unenforceable. That obedience is the obedience of a man to that which he cannot be forced to obey. He is the enforcer of the law himself."[8] Morality, whether private or public, individual or collective, involves a duty to obey moral precepts that are accepted as inherently binding because of their claims to rightness or justice.

Although morality is pervasive in human life, it is concerned mainly with a particular dimension of human affairs, namely, individual and collective judgments involving moral values. It is not concerned with choices and actions in the nonmoral realm.[9] Because government policies have a society-wide impact, most political affairs, whether domestic or international, involve some level of moral judgment. For some decisions, such as military intervention to halt genocide or the development of a weapon of mass destruction, moral considerations are primary; for others, such as selecting the UN secretary-general or determining the level of foreign economic assistance to a particular country, the role of moral norms will be limited. However, regardless of the issues, foreign policy will generally involve moral values.

The Nature of Ethics

Fundamentally, ethics involves choosing or doing what is right and good and refraining from choosing or doing what is bad or evil. From an ethical perspective, the good is realized by the application of appropriate moral norms to private and public affairs. This is no easy task, especially in domestic and international politics, in which government decisions do not lend themselves to simple moral verdicts. This difficulty is partly due to the complexity of public affairs as well as to overlapping and even competing moral values that are often involved in specific political issues and policy dilemmas. As a result, decision makers must select the most desirable action from a number of available alternatives, each involving moral limitations. Thus, if political decisions are to be developed and implemented on the basis of morality, *ethical reasoning* will be required. At a minimum, this process will entail identifying the moral dimensions of issues (a process sometimes called moral imagination), selecting relevant moral norms, critically assessing the issue or problem in the light of morality, applying morality to the potential alternatives, and then implementing the preferred action. Thus, ethical reasoning in international relations will involve the identification, illumination, and application of relevant moral norms to the conduct of states' foreign relations.

Another important dimension of international ethics involves the assessment of rules, practices, and institutions of global society in light of relevant moral norms. In effect, international ethics is concerned with the moral architecture of the international system, that is, the moral legitimacy of the patterns and structures of global society. For example, international ethics addresses such issues as the fairness of the existing international economic order, the justice of global institutions, and the moral legitimacy of international regimes (rules and semi-institutionalized patterns of decision making in specific issue areas) in shared areas of global concern, including the care of refugees, protection of human rights, energy conservation, protection of biodiversity, and safe waste disposal. The aim of such moral reflection is to assess the justice of the existing world system. In addition, international ethics is concerned with the implementation of the rules and structures of global society. Are the rules applied fairly and impartially? For example, are the international rules governing the management of fisheries, waste disposal, and pollution reduction applied equitably? Are the judgments of the World Trade Organization or the International Court of Justice fair and consistent?

4, part 1 of the book, present foundational principles and con-
~~~ask of integrating moral values into international relations. Chap-
~~~ature and sources of international political morality and then
~~~ship of moral norms to the development and implementation of
~~~e specifically, it explores some of the major aims, methods, and
~~~in integrating moral values with foreign policy decision making.
~~~es different ethical conceptions of the international community and
how ~~~ative views influence the pursuit of global political justice. Chapter 3
describes three major moral traditions—realism, idealism, and principled realism—that
help to structure the analysis of global issues and problems. In effect, traditions are
like paradigms that guide analysis and moral reasoning. Finally, chapter 4 describes
different ways of integrating political morality into the foreign policy decision-making
process. These alternative strategies, which are based on major philosophical perspectives, emphasize either moral rules or moral outcomes. Throughout each of these theoretical chapters I illustrate the ideas and concepts with case studies.

THE NATURE AND BASES OF POLITICAL MORALITY

Personal morality is frequently identified with political morality. Although the two are
related, they are not identical. Individual morality consists of moral values and norms
(i.e., principles, rules, prohibitions, and duties) that are applicable to the conduct of
persons in their personal or private relations. The Ten Commandments, the admonition
to "love your neighbor as yourself," and the obligation of truth telling are examples of
personal morality. Political morality, by contrast, consists of moral values and norms
that are applicable to the political life of communities, including neighborhoods, cities,
states, and the international community itself. Examples of political morality include
such norms as the equality of persons, freedom of conscience, equal treatment under
the law, the right of self-defense, and nonintervention. Although political morality is
rooted in personal morality, the former differs from the latter both in the nature of its
norms and in the sphere in which moral norms are applied. Whereas individual morality
governs the actions of individuals, political morality applies to the public decisions of
political or government officials.

Fundamentally, a political community is one in which a government exists with the
authority to make society-wide decisions. It is a society based on a hierarchical distribution of power, with rulers and subjects having different levels of authority and thus
different types of political responsibilities. It is a mistake to assume that the responsibilities of citizens and rulers are identical; individual and political moralities are not symmetrical. Although citizens and government officials share similar moral obligations as
human beings, their different roles in political society place different moral obligations
on them. As Lea Brilmayer observes, "The prohibitions found in interpersonal morality
cannot be mechanically transplanted into a code of conduct for public officials."[10]
Political morality may allow some actions that are prohibited by personal morality. For
example, a soldier may kill in wartime, or a state may carry out capital punishment, but

such actions are not synonymous with murder. Similarly, a state may tax its citizens, but an individual may not steal or extort resources from another person. Political morality thus provides norms for the just and effective use of legitimate power in political society. Although it is beyond the scope of this study to describe the nature and bases of legitimate political authority, it is noteworthy that political morality not only helps justify government authority but also provides norms for judging political action.[11]

Domestic and international politics are qualitatively different. Although scholars differ in their explanations of these differences, one widely accepted comparison characterizes domestic politics as a hierarchical system in which sovereign authority exists to make society-wide decisions and international politics as a nonhierarchical system without common authority to make and enforce decisions. Domestic society is the realm of authority, whereas international society is the realm of anarchy (i.e., no authority to impose order). In view of the structural differences in domestic and international politics, some scholars argue that the political moralities of domestic and international communities are also qualitatively different.

Some realists, for example, argue that in domestic society moral judgments are possible because typically cultural and moral values are widely shared, whereas in global politics, in which cultural and moral pluralism is prevalent, few moral judgments are possible. According to this perspective, whereas domestic society provides a rich and substantive political morality, international society provides a limited moral menu. Indeed, for some realists the only morality is that which promotes and protects the territorial security and economic well-being of a state. However, other scholars argue that differences between domestic and international politics have been greatly exaggerated and that moral values are far more significant in global society than realists suggest.[12]

There are two groups of thinkers that acknowledge an important role of political morality in international affairs: communitarians, who believe that states are significant moral actors in global society, and cosmopolitans, who regard the individual, not the state, as the major moral actor. Michael Walzer, a communitarian, gives a prominent place to international political morality by deriving states' international obligations from the "domestic analogy," that is, by arguing that states have rights and duties in global society analogous to the rights and duties of individuals in domestic political society.[13] For Walzer, international political morality entails such norms as the prohibition against aggression, the right of political sovereignty and the corollary right of self-defense, the duty of nonintervention in other states' domestic affairs, the protection of human rights, and the duty to settle disputes peacefully. By contrast, Charles Beitz, a cosmopolitanist, develops a global morality based on the rights and well-being of persons, challenging the morality of the existing Westphalian political order of sovereign states.[14] Because territorial boundaries are not morally significant in his cosmopolitan ethic, the autonomy of states can be qualified by the moral claims of individuals. In effect, since the rights of states ultimately depend on the rights of persons, human rights must take precedence over state sovereignty.

In assessing the role of political morality in foreign policy, scholars have periodically made two errors. First, some have simply denied the relevance of morality to international affairs. For them, although moral norms might be relevant to interpersonal relations or even to domestic political affairs, they have little to do with interstate political affairs. Global politics is the realm of necessity, and there can be no right and wrong when the survival of the state is at stake. However, as Arnold Wolfers noted at the outset of this chapter, the fundamental choices of statesmen are rooted in moral values. Thus, international politics is not divorced from ethical judgment but rests on morality.

The second error, frequently related to the first, is the tendency to deny the existence of political morality altogether. Here, morality consists solely of norms governing individual private behavior. George Kennan illustrates both of these errors in the following passage:

> Moral principles have their place in the heart of the individual and in the shaping of his own conduct, whether as a citizen or as a government official. . . . But when the individual's behavior passes through the machinery of political organization and merges with that of millions of other individuals to find its expression in the actions of a government, then it undergoes a general transmutation, and the same moral concepts are no longer relevant to it. A government is an agent, not a principal; and no more than any other agent may it attempt to be the conscience of its principal. In particular, it may not subject itself to those supreme laws of renunciation and self-sacrifice that represent the culmination of individual moral growth.[15]

Although Kennan is correct in his claim that personal morality should not govern the behavior of diplomats, his failure to recognize that political morality is an essential element of all normative decision making in global politics is a serious error. To be sure, the political morality applicable to interstate relations is not the same as personal morality. Thus, the challenge in bringing moral norms to bear on global political relations is to identify and then apply relevant norms of international political morality.

Before exploring the role of morality in foreign affairs, it will be helpful to briefly address the validity of political morality. Because of the growing influence of postmodern subjectivism, there has been a growing skepticism in the contemporary world about the legitimacy of moral claims in public life. This has been the case especially for political morality in global society, in which cultural pluralism is much more pronounced than in domestic society.

Sources of Political Morality

Because philosophers hold a number of theories about the source of moral values, political theorists have offered a variety of justifications for political morality. Three of the most important theories include foundationalism, constructivism, and consensualism. The foundationalist approach assumes that international morality is rooted in universal, unchanging first principles that are apprehended by reason. The constructivist approach, by contrast, derives moral values from general conceptions of justice (or the common good) through deductive arguments based on hypothetical cases. Finally, the consensual approach derives political morality from existing agreements among member states.

The foundationalist perspective assumes that transcendent moral norms exist and that such universal standards can be apprehended by rational reflection. Foundationalist thinkers such as Thomas Aquinas, John Locke, and Immanuel Kant believed that morality was valid and true not because it made the world better or more humane (pragmatism) or because it increased the happiness and well-being of persons (utilitarianism) but because it was divinely ordained by a transcendent Creator. An example of international morality from a foundationalist perspective is the belief that universal human rights exist and that they are rooted in a transcendent moral law (natural law) that is universal and unchanging. Another illustration is the just war doctrine, which provides moral principles for specifying when and how force can be utilized in pursuing just international relations. Foundationalists recognize that the international community is comprised of a large number of nations, each with its own cultural norms and social patterns; and, although such cultural and social diversity results in different value systems, there is nonetheless substantial consensus among moral value systems at a foundational level.

The constructivist thesis assumes that moral values are derived from hypothetical arguments. Whereas foundationalists assert that the basis of morality consists of transcendent norms whose truth and validity are inherent in the created order, constructivists ground morality in instrumental, deductive reasoning. For example, constructivists might deduce moral values from political and normative premises (e.g., political liberalism, justice as fairness, or some related normative proposition) through hypothetical arguments guided by logic and impartiality. Rawls illustrates this moral theory in his book *The Law of Peoples*, which extends his domestic theory of justice to international society.[16] Rawls imagines an "original position," in which representatives from different societies gather to impartially develop norms of international justice. He argues that a just "law of peoples" can be developed only if the societies themselves have achieved a minimal level of justice. Rawls specifies three minimal conditions for well-ordered societies, whether liberal or not: they must be peaceful, they must be perceived as legitimate by their own people, and they must honor basic human rights. Rawls assumes that when representatives from liberal and nonliberal societies meet to develop a just "law of peoples," they will be able to define minimal norms that will advance justice within international society. Some of these rights and duties of "peoples" include a right to freedom and independence, the equality of peoples, the right of self-defense, the duty of nonintervention, the obligation to fulfill treaties, and the responsibility to honor human rights. I explore Rawls's theory more fully in the next chapter.

A third view of political morality is consensual theory, sometimes called ethical positivism.[17] According to this approach, political morality is rooted in binding norms expressed by the formal and informal rules of domestic society, whereas international political morality is rooted in the shared norms embodied in the conventions, informal agreements, and declarations that states accept as obligatory in their international relations. These shared norms are obligatory because they are part of international law and morally obligatory because they specify norms conducive to order, justice, or the perceived common good. Some thinkers have argued that, because it is impossible to derive "ought" from "is," it is similarly impossible to derive international ethical obligations from existing interstate legal conventions. However, scholars such as Terry Nardin have convincingly demonstrated that to the extent that law establishes binding obligations on individuals, groups, and states, it fulfills the criteria of an ethical framework.[18]

In her seminal study on twentieth-century international legal and political ethics, Dorothy Jones has illuminated how international law has produced an authoritative and widely accepted framework, or "code," of international peace. This framework, she argues, is a normative system because it prescribes behavior that is conducive to global order and international harmony. Jones's study thus reinforces the claim that international morality can be based on consensual norms and multilateral declarations.[19]

It is significant that international law has established a category of law that is binding apart from the consent of states, thereby recognizing the limitations of consent as a basis of political morality. This type of international law—known as the *jus cogens*—refers to peremptory norms that are authoritative because the norms are inherently valid. Such norms, rooted in the values and practices of civilized society, include prohibitions against piracy, slavery, terrorism, and genocide. To some extent, the Tokyo and Nuremburg tribunals that prosecuted Japanese and German military officials for crimes against peace and humanity were based on this tradition of international law.

Although moral intuition, rational construction, and consent can each contribute to the development and articulation of international political morality, political morality must ultimately be grounded in norms that transcend human experience. Thus, this study proceeds from the belief that political morality, however it is justified, is based on normative principles of right and wrong, justice and injustice.

The Challenge of Cultural Pluralism

One of the major challenges in defending international political morality is the absence of a shared, universal morality. Because the international system is comprised of many different nation-states, each with its own social patterns and values, cultural pluralism is a prevalent feature of the international community. Moreover, not only do peoples from different cultures hold different political moralities, but their moral systems have also evolved over time. Because of the evident variability and pluralism of global morality, some thinkers have concluded that there is no universal morality applicable to the international community. In their view, the only morals in international society are the subjective, relativistic values associated with each society. This perspective, known as the doctrine of *cultural relativism*, holds that because notions of right and wrong, justice and injustice, are rooted in each society's cultural mores, there is no universal moral code.

Although competing and conflicting moralities can inhibit the development of moral consensus and call into question the role of moral values in international politics, they do not necessarily substantiate the cynic's conviction that morality is nothing more than the subjective preferences of the powerful. To begin with, morality is concerned with what "ought" to be, not with what "is." Because the diversity of cultural norms and social practices is a manifestation of what "is," the existence of cultural pluralism does not threaten the notion of moral obligation. Moreover, it is important to emphasize that cultural and social pluralism is generally concerned with secondary norms, not basic principles. Although peoples from different cultures do not normally share particular beliefs about women's rights, government structures, and policies of distributive justice, there is generally widespread commitment to such notions as truth and justice as well as agreement about such fundamental norms as the dignity of human persons, freedom from torture, impartial application of the law, and freedom of conscience. Walzer calls this shared morality "minimal" to differentiate it from the particular, more developed "maximal" moralities found in each society.[20] Moral minimalism is a "thin" morality not because it is unimportant or makes few claims on human beings but because its claims are general and diffuse. Because of this shared minimal morality, Walzer claims that human beings from different societies "can acknowledge each other's different ways, respond to each other's cries for help, learn from each other and march (sometimes) in each other's parades."[21]

In light of the distinction between minimal and maximal moralities, the claim that all morality is subjective and relative is not empirically sustainable. Although maximal norms vary from culture to culture, there is also a high level of global consensus about thin morality, namely, those norms that are essential to social and political life. Thus, although humans often disagree about many issues and social and economic values, there is also consensus about the need for such foundational principles as truth telling, beneficence, promise keeping, courage, self-control, and justice.[22] A. J. M. Milne has argued that moral diversity in global society cannot be total because some moral values are necessary to sustain social life. According to him, the international community's common morality includes such norms as respect for human life, pursuit of justice, fellowship, social responsibility, freedom from arbitrary interference, honorable treatment, and civility.[23]

One way of illustrating the existence of common morality is to imagine the likely response to the arbitrary denial of property in different cultures. For example, if a number of persons were to visit various remote regions of the world and, on arriving in these distant, isolated areas, were to walk up to strangers and take some of their possessions, how would these strangers respond? What would mothers do if the visitors were to take their children from their arms? In all likelihood, they would oppose the arbitrary deprivation of their property and, most assuredly, resist the removal of their children. In addition, they would do so because of the universality of social values regarding friendship, family bonding, self-control, and property.

The pervasiveness of political morality has been convincingly demonstrated by Walzer's study of the ethics of war, *Just and Unjust Wars*, in which he argues that throughout history human judgments and arguments in wartime demonstrate a consistency and continuity in moral reasoning. According to Walzer, the structure of moral reasoning is revealed not by the fact that soldiers and statesmen come to the same conclusions but by the fact that they acknowledge common difficulties, face similar problems, and talk the same language. "The clearest evidence for the stability of our values over time," writes Walzer, "is the unchanging character of the lies soldiers and statesmen tell. They lie in order to justify themselves, and so they describe for us the lineaments of justice."[24]

In the final analysis, cultural relativism is a wholly unacceptable ethical theory because it is impossible to live with the doctrine's severe consequences. If there are no standards, everything is possible, and if everything is possible, torture, forced expulsion, systematic violation of human rights, denial of freedom, and religious persecution are not wrong. Although moral values and cultural patterns vary across societies, there is broad consensus about core values. For example, most human beings have a basic moral intuition that gross violations against other human beings are wrong. Thus, it does not follow, as cultural relativists assert, that there are no universal norms. Despite the existence of moral and cultural pluralism among secondary and tertiary norms, most thinkers reject cultural relativism. They do so, as Thomas Donaldson has noted, not because of compelling evidence for moral absolutism (i.e., the notion that eternal, universal ethical norms exist and are applicable to human actions) but because relativism is itself intellectually indefensible.[25]

THE DEVELOPMENT OF A MORAL FOREIGN POLICY

What role do moral principles play in the conduct of foreign relations? First, morality helps define the goals and purposes of states and other actors. Moral norms do not provide policy directives, but they can offer a general vision and broad direction and provide the moral norms by which to illuminate and define a country's vital interests. As theologian John C. Bennett once noted, moral values contribute to public policy debates on foreign policy goals by providing "ultimate perspectives, broad criteria, motives, inspirations, sensitivities, warnings, moral limits."[26] In effect, moral norms can establish the boundaries for policy deliberation and execution.

Moral norms also provide a basis for judgment. Without standards, evaluation is impossible. Moral norms thus provide an ethical foundation for assessing the foreign policies of states as well as for judging the rules and structures of international society. For example, the widely accepted norms of international human rights provided the basis for the widespread condemnation of Serb "ethnic cleansing" carried out against Muslims during the 1992–1995 Bosnian war. Moreover, the growing recognition of ecological interdependence has resulted in an increasing international acceptance of principles and practices that seek to protect the earth's environment. Thus, when Saddam Hussein deliberately sought to destroy Kuwait's environment during the Persian Gulf War (by dumping oil into the sea and setting hundreds of oil wells on fire), his destructive actions were condemned worldwide.

Finally, moral norms provide the inspiration and motivation for policy development and implementation. Morality, in effect, provides the "fuel" for the government "engine." For example, the U.S. government's decision to intervene in Somalia in December 1992 to permit humanitarian relief was inspired in great measure by the humane concerns of leaders to alleviate starvation and keep hundreds of thousands of people from dying. And the NATO decision to intervene in Kosovo in 1999, a case examined below, was similarly inspired by humanitarian norms. In his important study of foreign aid, David Lumsdaine shows that the principal motivation for Western countries' substantial postwar foreign economic assistance to poor nations was morality. Although many factors and motivations influenced the giving of economic aid, the major inspiration and motivation was donor countries' "sense of justice and compassion."[27] Lumsdaine argues that international political morality, or what he terms "moral vision," shapes international relations. Contrary to realist claims that global politics is simply a realm of necessity, he claims that international relations involve freedom of action based on moral choice. As a result, international politics is an environment in which "conceptions of fairness and compassion, human dignity and human sympathy, justice and mercy" can be applied to the reform of global society.[28]

As will be made clear in chapter 2, there is no simple, easy method of applying political morality to foreign policy. One reason that international political action is generally morally ambiguous is that foreign policy issues and problems typically involve multiple and frequently clashing moral obligations. Thus, the process of moral reasoning must identify and apply the relevant moral criteria and, where moral conflict occurs, make the necessary tradeoffs among the relevant criteria. Moreover, developing a moral foreign policy is a challenging task because an ethical decision-making strategy requires that morality be applied to the goals, means, and results of political action. However, because moral norms rarely result in ethical action at all three levels, tradeoffs among the goals, means, and potential outcomes are generally inevitable.

Methods

How are moral norms applied in global politics? Among the different ways that moral norms affect international relations, three instruments are especially noteworthy: (1) the conscience of decision makers, (2) the influence of domestic public opinion, and (3) the role of international reputation.[29] William Wilberforce, the early-nineteenth-century British parliamentarian, illustrates the first approach. After becoming a Christian, Wilberforce concluded that slavery was immoral and contrary to the will of God. For three decades he led the fight in the House of Commons against this inhuman practice, first seeking to abolish the slave trade and then attempting to abolish slavery altogether.[30] President Jimmy Carter also demonstrates the importance of leaders' moral values. As a result of his strong convictions about human rights, his administration pursued an activist human rights policy, leading U.S. officials to publicly condemn repression and the abuse of basic rights and to halt foreign assistance to repressive military regimes.

The role of domestic public opinion in foreign relations—the second method by which morality is applied to foreign policy—is applicable only in democratic societies, in which a government's continuing authority and influence depend on its perceived legitimacy. To be sure, public opinion is not an automatic by-product of the thinking and analysis of the masses. Rather, public opinion is developed, organized, and mobilized by elites, including the media, interest groups, professional associations, and political parties. The important role of public opinion in foreign affairs in democratic societies is illustrated by the inability of the government of the Netherlands to accept deployment of NATO nuclear missiles in the early 1980s. Although the Dutch government was committed to such a deployment, the mass opposition to such action delayed the Netherlands' acceptance of cruise missiles for several years. In the United States, the role of mobilized public opinion was especially influential in the imposition of economic sanctions against South Africa. As a result of mass mobilization against South Africa's apartheid policies, many corporations halted their operations in South Africa, and universities and local and state governments adopted policies requiring divestment of stock from companies continuing their South African operations. The growing public opposition to apartheid also resulted in government action. In 1985, congressional debate forced the Reagan administration to adopt modest sanctions, and a year later Congress imposed, over presidential objections, much more substantial sanctions.

Finally, global public opinion influences the application of international political morality. Because public opinion is comparatively weak in the international community, its impact on government decision making is limited. Still, dominant international perceptions of power and morality do affect the foreign policy behavior of states. Just as an individual's reputation is based on other people's perceptions, so too the reputation of states is derived largely from people's perceptions of international actions. For example, in the late 1990s, Switzerland tarnished its financial reputation when it failed to acknowledge that its banks had held large assets of Holocaust victims and that they had failed to compensate families following World War II. Only after the U.S. government threatened economic sanctions did Swiss authorities agree to a major program of financial reparations. According to the 1998 U.S.-brokered accord, leading Swiss banks agreed to pay $1.25 billion into a fund that would cover financial aid and medical services to hundreds of thousands of survivors.[31]

Foreign policy behavior can contribute to a state's reputation as a reliable, credible, and moral actor, or it can damage such a reputation. Because a state's influence is rooted to a great extent in public perceptions, governments continuously assess the impact of their decisions on global public opinion. For example, during the Cuban missile crisis of 1962, U.S. officials considered numerous options in responding to the Soviet Union's installation of medium-range ballistic missiles. According to Robert Kennedy, the main reason direct military intervention was deemed unacceptable is that it would have harmed the international reputation of the United States.[32] Moreover, although some military officials advocated the limited use of nuclear arms in the Vietnam War, this action was never seriously contemplated by government leaders, in part because of the loss of prestige and influence that the United States would have suffered from such action.

Problems

Scholars and statesmen have called attention to a number of important challenges to the effective integration of morality into the fabric of foreign relations. One of the most common criticisms of international ethics is the belief that the decentralized structure of global society allows little room for moral judgment. Although the decentralized, anarchic structure of global society places a premium on national security and the promotion of national well-being, the priority of national interest does not obliterate the moral claims of other actors in the international community. Politics, after all, is the means by which actors pursue the common good in light of competing and conflicting individual and group interests. If actors pursued only self-interest in domestic or international politics, there would be no place for moral action. However, international politics, like domestic politics, involves the quest for order and justice based on the cooperative actions of actors.

Scholars and statesmen have also questioned the role of morality in foreign affairs because moral norms have been repeatedly misused in global politics. Rather than guiding and judging policies, morality has been used to clothe and justify national interests, resulting in rigid, moralistic foreign policies. In addition, rather than contributing to the process of moral reflection, morality has been used as an ideological and moralistic instrument, fashioning a self-righteous and hypocritical policy that has contributed to cynicism rather than public justice. In effect, morality has not contributed to justice because of the absence of impartiality.

The dangers of moralism are clearly illustrated in American history, especially during the late nineteenth and early twentieth centuries, when political leaders sought to define and justify U.S. foreign policy through morality. For example, President William McKinley supposedly relied on divine guidance in using military force to end Spanish colonial rule in Cuba and the Philippines, and when President Woodrow Wilson intervened in Veracruz, Mexico, he did so on the basis of the moral conviction that such action would foster greater democracy in Mexico. More recently, the Carter administration used foreign aid to reward states that improved human rights and to punish those that violated basic human rights. Because the use of moral language in foreign policy has often led to moralism, self-righteousness, inflexibility, and utopianism—qualities that are inimical to orderly international relations—some scholars, including historian Arthur Schlesinger Jr. and diplomatic historian George F. Kennan, argue that foreign policy should be based on national interests, not morality. Schlesinger writes, "Saints can be pure, but statesmen must be responsible. As trustees for others, they must defend interests and compromise principles. In politics, practical and prudential judgment must have priority over moral verdicts."[33] Both Schlesinger and Kennan note that when moral values dictate foreign policy, foreign policy becomes simplistic, utopian, and fanatical, perverting, if not eliminating, the process of prudential reasoning.

Although the misuse of morality can lead to cynicism and the denial of moral values, moral duplicity and hypocrisy do not justify the removal of moral values from international politics. Indeed, because human choices involve morality, domestic and international politics are inescapably moral enterprises. At the same time, it is essential to recognize that the integration of morality into the fabric of decision making and judgment poses challenges and dangers. For example, because political action is partly an exercise in self-interest, public officials may misuse moral rhetoric by justifying foreign policy decisions even when actions are chiefly motivated by national interests. Moreover, reliance on political morality can result in a self-righteous and arrogant foreign policy, especially when leaders are unmindful of their own national shortcomings. And since the conception and pursuit of the common good always involves partiality, the application of political morality must always be undertaken with humility and self-criticism. This is why Stanley Hoffmann has observed that an essential norm of the international system is the virtue of moderation, or what he calls "the morality of self-restraint."[34]

In the following section, I illustrate the important, though ambiguous, role of moral values in one case study—the 1999 NATO war against Serbia. This case is important because it shows the complex and at times contradictory role of political morality in the design and execution of foreign policy. As I argue below, while the use of force brought to an end the Serb abuse of human rights in Kosovo, the resort to war dramatically increased the immediate suffering of the victims for whom the war was being waged. In the end, Serbia consented to the introduction of NATO forces in Kosovo, thereby allowing the UN to assume governmental responsibilities in the territory.

BACKGROUND

Kosovo, a poor, small province of Serbia, is a multiethnic community of two peoples. Of its two million inhabitants, the vast majority (about 80 percent) are Albanian Muslims, or Kosovars; the dominant minority (about 10 percent) are Orthodox Christian Serbs. Ever since the medieval era, political and religious animosity has existed among major ethnic groups throughout the Balkans, and especially within this small territory, where Kosovars and Serbs have historically competed for power. In 1912, as Turkey's influence in the Balkans was waning, Serbs conquered Kosovo, effectively imposing imperial control over the territory.[35] Despite the cultural and political cleavages between these two ethnic groups, Joseph Tito, Yugoslavia's postwar dictator, managed to pacify Kosovo by granting its people significant governmental autonomy within the Serb Republic. This action, which was formalized in the 1974 Federal Constitution of Yugoslavia, allowed the majority Albanians to develop and celebrate their distinctive cultural and national interests.

The unraveling of the multiethnic status quo can be attributed to several political events in the latter phase of the Cold War. First, the death of Tito, Yugoslavia's charismatic communist leader, marked the beginning of the end of the modern state of Yugoslavia. With his death in 1980, the authority of the federal government declined, leading to increased ethnic and political fragmentation among Yugoslavia's distinct republics.

Second, in 1988 the government of Serbia suspended Kosovo's political autonomy and imposed direct rule from Belgrade. This action by Serbian president Slobodan Milosevic was undertaken to foment Serb nationalism and to consolidate Serb power within Kosovo, presaging future Serb actions in other parts of Yugoslavia. While the lifting of Kosovo's autonomous status pleased the minority Serbs in Kosovo and fueled the nationalistic ambitions of Serbs elsewhere, Albanians responded with rage. Ethnic animosity toward Serbs greatly intensified in the early 1990s when they halted the public financing of Albanian schools and began replacing institutions and policies established by Kosovars. Warren Zimmerman, the last U.S. ambassador to Yugoslavia before the country fell apart in the early 1990s, noted that "under Milosevic, Kosovo took on all the attributes of a colony."[36] And Misha Glenny, one of the most astute observers of Balkan politics, wrote that the reimposition of Serb rule "transformed Kosovo into a squalid outpost of putrefying colonialism."[37]

Finally, the collapse of communist rule in the Soviet Union and Eastern Europe in 1989–1991 undermined the authority of the Yugoslavian government. With the loss of Communist Party authority, ethnopolitical tensions began to rise throughout Yugoslavia, eventually leading to the collapse of the federal state as various republics (Slovenia, Croatia, Bosnia, and Macedonia) demanded political independence from the central government in Belgrade. As different republics pressed for political self-rule, the ethnic animosities within and among these political communities greatly intensified, fueling the tensions in autonomous provinces like Kosovo.

However important these events may have been in the growing ethnic tensions within the Balkans, by themselves they would have been insufficient to cause the Kosovo war. What ignited the conflict was the simultaneous demand by Serbs and Kosovars to press for political autonomy and sole political control of the same land. By imposing Serbian control over Kosovo, Serbs fueled Albanian nationalism and the quest for Kosovar self-rule. The Albanian response was first framed by the Democratic League of Kosovo (LDK), which sought to advance Kosovar interests through nonviolent resistance and noncooperation. When this strategy failed to restore partial autonomy, Kosovar radicals turned to violence through the Kosovo Liberation Army (KLA). Whereas the LDK pursued increased autonomy through passive resistance, the KLA sought political self-determination through force, beginning in 1995 with small-scale operations but expanding its covert operations in the late 1990s.

When Albania imploded in 1997,[38] the disintegration of the Albanian police and army created a ready supply of weapons for the KLA. As KLA violence became more pervasive and lethal, Serb leader Slobodan Milosevic responded by increasing the Serb military and police forces and imposing greater political repression, including widespread deportation and ethnic cleansing.[39] As Stanley Hoffmann has noted, however, Milosevic's goal was not to carry out police actions but to eliminate the KLA threat altogether: "What the Serbs are doing is not a police operation against political dissenters or ordinary criminals. It is the destruction of a movement of national liberation from extremely repressive rule, the crushing of a drive for self-determination."[40]

As a result of Serb repression, tens of thousands of Kosovars were forced from their homes and villages, and many began fleeing the country. It is estimated that by late 1998 some 250,000 Kosovars had been displaced and were facing inhumane living conditions. To seek to ease the humanitarian crisis, the United States dispatched Richard Holbrooke, the U.S. negotiator who had brokered the 1995 Dayton Accords that ended the Bosnian war, to help restore peace. In his October 1998 negotiations, Holbrooke succeeded in arranging a Serb cease-fire and a promise from Milosevic to reduce Serb military forces in Kosovo to prewar levels. To ensure compliance with the negotiated settlement, a monitoring force (the Kosovo Verification Mission) of some fifteen hundred international observers was established to report on human rights violations. Once the cease-fire was in place, however, the KLA, which had not been a part of the October negotiations, used the peace to resupply their fighters and to prepare for the resumption of guerrilla operations and terror attacks. As a result, sporadic fighting resumed in early 1999, bringing to an end the cease-fire.

Led by the United States, a consortium of leading powers (known as the Contact Group)[41] agreed to impose a settlement on the Serbs and Albanians in Kosovo. Meeting in a chateau in Rambouillet, France, in February, Western leaders presented the terms of a cease-fire to both Serbian and Kosovar delegates. Fundamentally, the Rambouillet accord promised to maintain Serb sovereignty over Kosovo, to restore the autonomous status of Kosovo, and to demand a cease-fire between KLA and Serb forces.[42] To facilitate compliance with the cease-fire, Serbia had to withdraw their army, reduce its police force to prewar levels (about twenty-five hundred police), and allow a large (thirty thousand) NATO peacekeeping force to ensure domestic order, while the KLA had to accept demilitarization. As expected, Serb leaders refused the Rambouillet settlement, believing that the introduction of NATO troops in Kosovo was inconsistent with their claim of sovereignty. But to the surprise and chagrin of Western leaders, the Kosovar delegate also refused to accept the Rambouillet accord. Since Albanians were fighting not only to end Serb repression but, more important, to assert the right of political independence, Rambouillet was regarded as a second-best alternative. Only after repeated negotiations with other Kosovar leaders, coupled with the growing awareness that NATO would not protect Kosovars from further ethnic cleansing if they refused the Rambouillet settlement, did the Kosovars finally accept the terms of accord.

THE ETHICS OF SELF-DETERMINATION

In confronting group demands for political self-determination, one of the difficult ethical challenges is to determine which peoples have the right to claim political autonomy in the international community. For example, do the Kosovars have the right to secede from Serbia and establish their own political community? What about the Kurds in Iran, Iraq, and Turkey? If the Palestinians are entitled to statehood, can the Chechens demand this right as well? Fundamentally, the collective right of self-determination, as I will argue in chapter 9, depends largely upon political power—on the ability to make and sustain a claim to self-rule in the face of political actors who oppose such a development. Since no ethical framework exists by which a people's right to self-rule can be defined, the claim of self-determination depends less on morality than on the ability to defend the claim. As a result, the collective right of self-determination has been considered legitimate historically if a people can demonstrate the collective will and military capacity to claim and sustain political independence by exerting sole and ultimate control over a specified territory. In short, the claim of political self-determination ultimately depends on the capacity to control political life within a territory (internal sovereignty) and the public recognition of this fact by other states (external sovereignty).

Typically, when a people demand political autonomy and press this claim with violence, the result is often war. Rarely have states peacefully accepted the demands for self-rule by minority groups. And when groups have sought to secede from an existing state, the ruling regime has generally opposed such action with force. For example, when Confederate states sought to secede from the United States, Abraham Lincoln resorted to war to maintain the union. And when Chechens sought to secede from Russia in the early 1990s, the Russian government used brutal force to keep Chechnya within the Russian state. Even President Clinton expressed sympathy toward the Russian government as it faced increasing terrorist threats from Chechens, comparing Yeltsin's policies toward the Chechen war to those of President Lincoln during the Civil War.[43] Thus, when Albanian Muslims began demanding the right of political self-determination in the mid-1990s, Serbian authorities responded with violence. Like other governments that have faced similar demands for political autonomy from ethnic groups, the Serbs were so committed to keeping control of Kosovo that they were prepared to use political oppression, human rights violations, and war itself to counter the violence

from the KLA. As Zimmerman notes, Milosevic saw the KLA as a "mortal threat. He could live with Rugova's non-cooperation but not with the KLA's armed confrontation."[44]

Historically, Serbs have regarded Kosovo as the symbolic center of the Serb nation. Because this small territory holds many of Serbia's holiest Orthodox monasteries and churches and is the site of an epic medieval battle with Muslims, Serb nationalism is deeply associated with the region. Indeed, Serb political leaders view the territory as their nation's Jerusalem. Although the borders of Balkan political communities had been contested, since the end of World War II the Serb claim to Kosovo had been internationally accepted, in great part because the 1974 Federal Constitution of Yugoslavia had given Kosovo a high degree of autonomy. The status quo was broken when Serbia imposed direct control on the province, precipitating Kosovar–Serb violence.

Fundamentally, the conflict between Albanians and Serbs in Kosovo was over political control of land, not over human rights abuses, political repression, or unjust, discriminatory policies. To be sure, the conflict had aggravated human rights violations. But the fundamental tensions derived from a quest by two peoples to govern the region of Kosovo. Kosovars, to their credit, had managed to define the conflict largely in humanitarian terms. But while the KLA–Serb conflict had resulted in gross violations of human rights, secret killings, and ethnic cleansing, Serb violence was the result of a political contest, not simply the by-product of ethnic hatred of Albanians. As Judah notes, the Kosovo conflict was fundamentally a "struggle between two people for control of the same piece of land."[45] Thus, while the Rambouillet initiative was designed to halt the military conflict, the accord failed to address the future status of Kosovo. Thus, the Western initiative was not designed to resolve the political dispute but only to halt the humanitarian suffering that had resulted from the political conflict.

THE ETHICS OF WAR

In March 1999, Secretary of State Madeleine Albright sent U.S. emissary Richard Holbrooke to

Belgrade to warn President Milosevic that if he did not accept the Rambouillet accord NATO would initiate war. Since China and Russia, veto-wielding members of the Security Council, were staunchly opposed to using force against Serbia, the Western Alliance had resolved to threaten military action outside of the normal United Nations peacekeeping framework. For China and Russia, foreign intervention was inappropriate because the conflict in Kosovo was fundamentally a domestic political issue. While foreign states might assist in resolving the conflict, the fundamental challenge was for the Serbs and Kosovars to resolve the dispute. Western states, however, regarded the widespread abuse of human rights in Kosovo as a threat to the peace and security of the Balkans. For them, the time had come to defend the primacy of human rights in the face of political oppression and ethnic cleansing by Serb military and paramilitary forces.

There can be little doubt that NATO's goal of halting gross human rights abuses, including ethnic cleansing, was morally legitimate. For President Clinton, ending the humanitarian crisis in Kosovo was "a moral imperative,"[46] while for Secretary of State Madeleine Albright, "Kosovo was not going to be this administration's Munich"[47]—that is, the United States was not going to accept appeasement as the British government had done in 1939 toward Germany. Czech president Vaclav Havel claimed that the Kosovo war was probably the first one ever waged for moral values rather than the pursuit of national interests. "If one can say of any war that it is ethical, or that it is being waged for ethical reasons," he wrote, "then it is true of this war."[48] For Havel, as for other Western leaders, the decision to use force against Milosevic was morally correct because "no decent person can stand by and watch the systematic, state-directed murder of other people."[49]

But if NATO's goals in Kosovo were morally legitimate, the means—an intense air war against Serbia and Kosovo—raised serious ethical concerns. Since foreign policy must be concerned not only with goals but also with the means and anticipated results, the challenge in devising an effective yet moral foreign policy must necessarily reconcile means and ends. The fact that widespread ethnic cleansing was morally repugnant did not obviate the need to devise a morally prudent strategy that achieved the desired goals. But for many foreign policy observers, including former secretary of state Henry Kissinger, the decision to rely solely on bombing to halt Serb oppression and ethnic cleansing was not the most appropriate means.[50]

In particular, NATO's war strategy was challenged morally for a number of reasons. First, since NATO was seeking to halt ethnic cleansing in Kosovo, a credible military strategy should have involved the use, or at a minimum the threat of use, of both ground and air operations. Not only did the bombing campaign prove ineffective in achieving the desired humanitarian objectives, but it also had the paradoxical effect of compounding human suffering for Serb victims. As soon as NATO bombers began attacking Kosovo and Serbia, Serbian military and paramilitary soldiers in Kosovo embarked on a systematic campaign of ethnic cleansing (known as Operation Horseshoe), forcing tens of thousands of Kosovars to flee west toward Montenegro and Albania and south toward Macedonia.[51] Indeed, within a week the ethnic cleansing campaign had forced more than 300,000 Kosovars to leave the country. And by the end of the war, the United Nations High Commissioner for Refugees (UNHCR) estimated that 848,100 Kosovars had fled Kosovo—444,600 to Albania, 244,500 to Macedonia, and 69,900 to Montenegro, while 91,057 were airlifted to other countries.[52] Rather than alleviating human suffering, the immediate effect of the war was to greatly aggravate the humanitarian crisis. This is why Leon Wieseltier argues that the Kosovo war was "a good fight badly fought."[53]

A second shortcoming of NATO's strategy was that the pursuit of a risk-free war compromised the moral objectives of the war. Because NATO sought to minimize military casualties, it carried out its air war from an altitude of fifteen thousand feet or higher—that is, high enough to avoid ground fire and missiles yet too high to carry out precision bombing and thereby minimize civilian casualties. The problem with such a riskless strategy was that it effectively undermined the norm of human equality, the core humanitarian principle for which the war was being waged. Since a risk-free air war communicated the message that NATO personnel were of greater value than the lives of those for whom the war was being waged, the risk-averse strategy was morally problematic. As Paul Kahn notes, risk-averse humanitarian warfare is contradictory because the morality of ends, which are universal, is incompatible with the morality of means, which privilege a particular group of people.[54] Noting the inconsistency between NATO's goals and means, Kissinger observed, "A strategy that vindicates its moral convictions only from altitudes above 15,000 feet deserves to be questioned on both political and moral grounds."[55]

A third limitation of the war strategy was the failure to devise a plan to force an early Serb capitulation. Western leaders had no doubt assumed that systematic bombing would result in the withdrawal of Serb military and paramilitary forces from Kosovo. But rather than undermining ethnic nationalism, the bombing had the paradoxical effect of reinforcing Serb nationalism and increasing their determination to maintain control over Kosovo. While NATO's ineffectiveness in achieving political objectives was no doubt due to its failure to accurately anticipate Serbian resolve, it was also due to the complex political nature of a multilateral war campaign—war by committee, as some critics termed it. Since the major decisions of the war required the consent of the NATO member states, the collective approach to decision making led to a cautious and limited air campaign. But the failure to escalate rapidly the scope and intensity of the bombing no doubt contributed to the belief that Serbia could survive an air campaign. Had the scope and lethality of the bombing increased in the early phase of the war, the suffering within Kosovo and civilian casualties within Serbia may have been greatly reduced. Even after dropping more than twenty thousand bombs that resulted in more than $60 billion in economic destruction in Serbia and Kosovo, Milosevic was still unwilling to give up control of Kosovo. Indeed, only when NATO began targeting the principal communications, electrical, and power infrastructure of Serbia did the air campaign begin to severely undermine Serb resolve. In fact, only when NATO began making preparations for a ground invasion

and Russian president Boris Yeltsin signaled his unwillingness to support Serb intransigence did Milosevic finally capitulate to NATO.

In the final analysis, NATO achieved its goal of the withdrawal of all Serb military, paramilitary, and police forces from Kosovo. Even though a large NATO peacekeeping force was immediately introduced after Serbia gave up control of Kosovo, the transfer of authority to a multinational force led to the return of most of the 850,000 Kosovar refugees. But the return of the Kosovars to their destroyed villages was accompanied by widespread acts of revenge against Serbs. Despite the efforts of the 42,500-member NATO peacekeeping force (known as Kosovo Force or KFOR) to maintain political order, the return of Kosovars resulted in widespread ethnic cleansing of Kosovo Serbs. It is estimated that in the aftermath of the Kosovo war, more than 150,000 Serbs fled the province, leaving Pristina, Kosovo's capital, with only about 200 Serbs out of a population of 500,000. Additionally, some 150 Orthodox churches were totally destroyed. But the most daunting challenge that the UN interim governing authority (UNMIK) continued to confront was the maintenance of law and order. Not surprisingly, as of mid-2012, KFOR maintained a force of more than 5,500 soldiers to ensure peace and stability in the territory.

KOSOVO'S INDEPENDENCE

Once the United Nations assumed administrative oversight of Kosovo, the next challenge was to determine who would have responsibility for this territory. Should the province be returned to Serbia, provided it allowed a high degree of political autonomy? Or should Kosovo be integrated into a greater Albania? Or should the UN encourage the development of a new sovereign state? Beginning in 2005, the UN Special Envoy Martti Ahtisaari, the former president of Finland, began negotiations between Kosovar Albanians and Serbs over the future status of Kosovo. After more than a year of talks, the parties were unable to reconcile their deep differences. Because Serbs viewed Kosovo as part of their country, they were willing to give Kosovars significant self-rule but not sovereignty. For the Kosovars, nothing short of full political independence would satisfy them. Since bilateral negotiations failed, the UN envoy decided to make public his own proposed solution.

According to Ahtisaari's plan, Kosovo would become independent, but only after institutions had been developed that would protect minority rights and be capable of fulfilling international responsibilities. When the plan was presented to the Security Council in early 2007, the response of the major powers was mixed: Britain, France, and the United States strongly supported the move toward independence, while Russia and China opposed it. As a result, on February 17, 2008, Kosovo unilaterally declared its political independence, with the United States, Britain, France, and Germany immediately recognizing that act. Since then, more than eighty-five additional countries have recognized Kosovo's independence. Believing that Kosovo's unilateral declaration was inconsistent with international law, the UN General Assembly, at Serbia's request, asked the International Court of Justice to issue an advisory opinion on the matter. In 2010, the court declared in a nonbinding decision that Kosovo's independence was not contrary to international law. Since Russia, a permanent member of the Security Council, remains opposed to Kosovo's political independence, the new state is unlikely to become a United Nations member in the near future.

Although NATO intervened in Kosovo ostensibly to protect human rights, the immediate effect of the war was to exacerbate ethnic cleansing and inflict widespread destruction on Serbia. And while Western involvement in the conflict was inspired primarily by humanitarian concerns, the ultimate effect of NATO's military intervention was to support Kosovar claims of political autonomy. It may well be that in the long term Kosovo will become a humane and prosperous community. But the international process of advancing human rights and regional peace in Kosovo has been morally ambiguous at best.

MORAL REFLECTIONS

This case study illuminates the complexity and ambiguity of pursuing moral objectives in foreign affairs. Contrary to the widespread realist assumption that foreign policy involves solely the pursuit of national interests, the Kosovo war illuminates the significant role of moral values in defining foreign policy goals as well as the ethical challenge of devising appropriate strategies in the pursuit of moral objectives. The following questions illustrate some of the important moral issues raised by this case:

- When the quest for self-determination involves violence leading to widespread human rights abuses, how should foreign governments respond? How much human suffering must occur before foreign states should consider military intervention to protect the innocent?
- Humanitarian intervention involves violence in the service of human rights. When confronting competing obligations of state sovereignty and human rights, which norm should take precedence? Vaclav Havel has observed that the Kosovo war gave precedence to human rights over the rights of the state.[56] Did the defense of human rights in Kosovo justify foreign military action?
- According to widely accepted moral principles of warfare, the use of force should be proportionate to the political ends being pursued. It has been estimated that NATO bombing killed around five thousand Serb military and paramilitary members, while the economic destruction in Yugoslavia was estimated at $60 billion to $100 billion. Moreover, the Serb campaign against Albanians was thought to have killed ten thousand civilians. Given the high human and material cost of the NATO war, was the violence justified by the outcomes? In other words, were the material and human losses of the war justified by the goal of ending a humanitarian crisis?
- The immediate effect of the NATO war was the forced deportation of nearly nine hundred thousand Kosovars to neighboring countries and the internal displacement of nearly five hundred thousand others. After Serbia capitulated, most Kosovar refugees returned to their destroyed villages and

towns. In view of the significant humanitarian crisis in the immediate aftermath of
the war, was the short-term suffering justified by the long-term promise of greater
stability in Kosovo?

- Assuming the Kosovo war was justified by
the egregious human rights abuses carried out by the Serbs, was NATO's risk-free

air strategy morally appropriate? Why or
why not?

- NATO's intervention in Kosovo was carried
out without the approval of the UN Security Council. Must multilateral peacekeeping missions be approved by the
international community in order for them
to be morally legitimate?

SUMMARY

In this chapter I have argued that moral values and ethical reasoning are essential
dimensions of foreign policy decision making. While the political challenges in the
international community may differ from those commonly found in domestic society,
the quest by states for territorial security, economic well-being, and the preservation of
a stable, humane global order are rooted in moral values. As Arnold Wolfers's statement
at the outset of this chapter suggests, foreign policy decision making is not beyond
moral judgment but rests on moral choices. To be sure, personal morality cannot be
applied directly to public policies, nor can widely shared moral norms be simplistically
used in the conduct of foreign affairs. As I will argue in later chapters, the challenge in
designing a prudent foreign policy is to identify interests and relevant moral norms and
then to integrate them through ethical reasoning in specifying the ends, means, and
likely outcomes of political action. Frequently, moralists give priority to intentions, but
focusing solely on goals is insufficient. Indeed, the great moral challenge in political
life is to define just ends and then to devise morally appropriate strategies to achieve
them. Thus, in developing a moral foreign policy, ethical reasoning must identify and
prioritize goals in light of shared moral norms and assess the moral legitimacy of alternative strategies in light of anticipated outcomes. As the Kosovo case illustrates, foreign
policy is often a daunting task involving competing and conflicting values and resulting
in morally ambiguous outcomes. NATO's action to halt Serb ethnic cleansing was
undoubtedly just, yet the use of coercive force in the pursuit of humanitarianism proved
to be a challenging and morally ambiguous enterprise.

Chapter Two

Ethics and Global Society

[I]f we want individuals to face less oppression, violence, and fear in this world, we should wish for stronger sovereigns, not weaker ones. By stronger I mean more capable, more responsible, and more legitimate. If we want human rights to be anchored in the world, we cannot want their enforcement to depend on international institutions and NGOs. We want them anchored in the actual practice of sovereign states.[1]
—MICHAEL IGNATIEFF

[T]he international legal order is by nature an accommodation among peoples who persistently disagree about justice.[2]
—BRAD ROTH

A global ethic should not stop at, or give great significance to, national boundaries. National sovereignty has no intrinsic moral weight. What weight national sovereignty does have comes from the role that an international principle requiring respect for national sovereignty plays, in normal circumstances, in promoting peaceful relationships between states.[3]

—PETER SINGER

C HAPTER 1 EXAMINED the role of moral values in the conduct of foreign relations. In this chapter we explore how moral values structure our ideas about the international community and, more particularly, how conceptions of justice apply to global society. Given the decentralized character of the international community, interstate relations do not automatically promote the common good. Indeed, collective action in addressing global problems like deforestation, global warming, genocide, and protection of endangered species is difficult not only because the problems are intractable, but also because of the absence of authoritative institutions to make and implement decisions for global society.

The structure of the international community poses major ethical questions. For example, how should the world system be conceived—as a single global community or as a society of states? Does the moral legitimacy of states depend on their willingness and ability to protect human rights? Who should be responsible for the well-being of migrants and refugees? When genocide occurs, who should seek to halt the killing? Are the rules and institutions of the international economic order fair? Additionally, in view of the significant international economic inequalities, do high-income states have a moral responsibility to provide economic assistance to low-income states? Should the aid be given to governments, to relief NGOs, or directly to poor people? Finally, who is responsible for protecting the global commons, such as the atmosphere, oceans, and land shared by all member states? How questions such as these are addressed will depend in great part on how one conceives of world order. Thus, the purpose of this chapter is to examine the nature and role of political morality in global society.

This chapter begins by contrasting three major conceptions of the international community—as a system of independent nation-states, as an international society of states, and as a morally coherent global community. It then examines different ways that political theorists have applied the idea of justice to the international community, focusing on two major ethical perspectives—*communitarianism* and *cosmopolitanism*. The first applies political morality to the international community as it currently exists—that is, to the existing United Nations political system rooted in the legal primacy of states. The cosmopolitan perspective, by contrast, views the world as an integrated moral society where the rights and welfare of individuals is primary. Communitarianism, the most influential approach to global ethics among international relations (IR) scholars, is given its most powerful defense by John Rawls, the leading American political theorist of the late twentieth century. In the next section, I highlight key elements of Rawls's theory of international justice. I also examine elements of Peter Singer's cosmopolitan approach to global society to illustrate the alternative world justice perspective. The chapter concludes with a case study on global poverty to highlight how different conceptions of international political morality influence public responses to global human needs.

ALTERNATIVE CONCEPTIONS OF GLOBAL SOCIETY

Following the analysis of Hedley Bull, a leading international relations scholar, the international community can be conceived in three ways: as a system of states, as a society of states, and as a world community.[4] The first approach assumes that the world is composed of distinct political communities. Since the international community is merely an ideal, there are no moral values that guide the behavior of states in pursuing peace and justice in the world. The only force that structures the international community is the power of member states. According to Bull, the logic of this approach was best illuminated by Thomas Hobbes, the sixteenth-century political theorist, in his *Leviathan*. In that classic study, Hobbes argues that the fundamental task of political society is the creation of social order. Since humans are selfish and egotistical, people's rights are not secure in prepolitical society (the state of nature). As a result, people accept the creation of political society where government has a monopoly of force. State sovereignty means that the government has the power and authority to make binding decisions and ensure social peace within its territorial boundaries. In effect, government creates order through its coercive power. Additionally, since sovereign states are the ultimate source of political authority in the world, international peace can only be realized through the management of power among member states. Power, not morality, determines international relations.

At the opposite extreme is the "universalist" conception of global society as a coherent moral community. According to this view, the primary political community is global society itself, rooted in the well-being and human rights of persons. States are important only insofar as they contribute to the individual rights of people and to the peace and stability of the world. Bull thinks that philosopher Immanuel Kant best represents this conception of world order. In his essay "Perpetual Peace," Kant called for the creation of a federation of states based on republican states—that is, regimes ruled in accordance with law. Although such an alliance among constitutional regimes would not necessarily assure peace, it would best advance global order and human rights. Ironically, Kant did not call for world government. Rather, he believed that global peace and justice could best be advanced through beneficent constitutional regimes that acknowledged moral obligations based on universal reason (what Kant termed "the categorical imperative"). The idealistic conception of global society advanced by Kant highlights the role of universal reason as the basis for pursuing peace and justice in the world. This approach contrasts starkly with the Hobbesian conception of the world as a system of states governed by the distribution of power.

Between the Hobbesian and Kantian conceptions of global order is a hybrid approach that emphasizes the moral significance both of member states and of the global community. According to this perspective, states are the primary political communities to ensure the well-being of persons, but the world is also morally significant as it seeks to advance justice within and among states. Bull calls this hybrid perspective Grotian after Hugo Grotius, the seventeenth-century Dutch jurist who is considered the father of international law. According to Grotius, although sovereign states were the primary political actors in the international community, state sovereignty was qualified by transcendent moral norms. These norms, which were based on natural law and divine revelation, placed constraints on states—during peacetime, but especially in war. International justice was therefore possible when the behavior of states was guided by such moral norms.

These alternative approaches to world order give rise to three distinct ways of looking at the international community. The first conception, called *realism*, views global society as a system of states where power governs international relations. According to this perspective, the world is a community where national power determines the welfare and prosperity of citizens. The second conception, called *cosmopolitanism*, views global society as an ethical community based on universal moral obligations. This idealistic conception of the world assumes that universal reason provides the basis for individual as well as collective moral obligations. Although states are a part of global society, cosmopolitanism gives moral primacy to global welfare and views state sovereignty as unimportant. What matters is global welfare and in particular the welfare of persons. The third conception, called *communitarianism*, views global society as a society of nation-states. According to this perspective, moral obligations apply both to individuals and to states. Unlike cosmopolitanism, which emphasizes global society at the expense of states, this perspective assumes that states are the primary communities by which human welfare is promoted and protected. As the quotation by Ignatieff at the outset of this chapter suggests, the communitarian approach assumes that protecting human rights requires sovereign states. In short, to advance human well-being, you need strong, beneficent states.

Since this chapter seeks to illuminate how political morality influences not only the idea of global society but also the conceptualization of global justice, our analysis focuses only on the two approaches that explicitly integrate moral reasoning—cosmopolitanism and communitarianism. The realist perspective is not assessed here because it deemphasizes the role of moral values and disregards altogether the quest for global justice. In the following chapter, however, the tradition of realism is analyzed as one of the common methods used in foreign policy decision making.

JUSTICE IN GLOBAL SOCIETY

In order to assess the justice or moral legitimacy of global society it is necessary to have a transcendent standard for judgment. Although theorists define political morality in a variety of ways, the dominant ethical paradigm for judging political legitimacy is political liberalism—a tradition that grounds morality in the inherent claims of individual rights. This tradition emerged in the seventeenth and eighteenth centuries with the political writings of theorists such as John Locke, Jean-Jacques Rousseau, James Mill, Jeremy Bentham, and John Stuart Mill. Fundamentally, liberalism espouses two basic principles. First, because human beings possess rights, the primary task of government is to secure and protect those rights. Second, the most effective way to inhibit tyranny and promote the common good is through limited government based on consent.

Because liberalism first developed as a domestic political theory, its application to international society was, as Hoffmann has noted, "little more than the projection of domestic liberalism on a world scale."[5] Indeed, liberals have argued on the basis of the "domestic analogy" that states possess rights and duties comparable to those of individuals in political society.[6] The application of liberalism to global society has resulted in the development of *liberal internationalism*—a doctrine that emphasizes the peacefulness of democratic regimes, a belief in the fundamental harmony of interests among different peoples, and the universality of human rights. In addition, this doctrine, following the claims of early-twentieth-century American liberals such as Woodrow Wilson, asserts that peoples (nationalities) have an inherent right to political self-determination and that this political right is not only consistent with but also conducive to global order.

Liberal internationalism has contributed to the development of two metaethical perspectives on international justice: communitarianism and cosmopolitanism. *Communitarianism* accepts the existing community of states as normative, believing that the quest for human dignity is best secured within and through each of the distinct political societies of the international system.[7] Although the state can impede justice, it also serves as the primary political agency to ensure human rights domestically and peace internationally. However, the communitarian approach recognizes that because domestic order is not sufficient to ensure human dignity, pursuing international peace and justice among states is also necessary. Thus, a central concern of the communitarian perspective is to define the obligations that contribute to a humane and just global order.

Cosmopolitanism, by contrast, seeks to promote human dignity by giving priority to global or cosmopolitan bonds.[8] The origins of cosmopolitanism date from the fourth century BC, when Cynics coined the term, meaning "citizen of the world." Stoics subsequently developed the idea by emphasizing the fundamental equality of persons by virtue of human reason. Although some cosmopolitan thinkers view local, national, and regional affinities as legitimate, they claim that the primary bonds are to global society. Indeed, when conflict arises between a commitment to a state and to the world, the latter allegiance must take precedence. Moreover, since state sovereignty is not morally significant in the cosmopolitan paradigm, international morality requires the subordination of state boundaries to human dignity. Thus, whereas communitarianism accepts the legitimacy of the existing international order, the cosmopolitan approach denies the moral significance of the existing neo-Westphalian order. Because of its idealistic orientation, cosmopolitanism is sometimes referred to as global utopianism.

In his recent book *Cosmopolitanism: Ethics in a World of Strangers*, philosopher Kwame Appiah argues that the cosmopolitan ethic has two distinguishing features: first, people have obligations to others, including strangers, and second, people hold different values and cultural traditions, and legitimate differences must be respected. As Appiah put it, "We take seriously the value not just of human life but of particular lives, which means taking an interest in the practices and beliefs that lend them significance. People are different . . . and there is much to learn from our differences."[9] In effect, cosmopolitanism has two strands—universalism and respect for legitimate differences. How these two elements are reconciled is the great task of political society.

In comparing communitarianism and cosmopolitanism, it is significant that both perspectives assert the primacy of human dignity but differ in how best to secure and protect human rights.[10] Whereas the former assigns primary responsibility to the state in securing and protecting individual rights, the latter assigns primary obligation to global society. In addition, it is significant that both approaches assume the primacy of morality. Indeed, both perspectives are rooted in the tradition of "common morality," which regards ethical norms as rationally accessible and universally binding. Despite cultural pluralism in global society, common morality assumes that the quest for peace and human dignity must be based on moral norms that are transculturally authoritative.

Communitarianism and cosmopolitanism give rise to two distinct emphases on political justice. For the communitarian, states are the primary actors in global society and thus are presumptively legitimate and entitled to sovereignty, that is, political independence and self-rule. Because communitarianism is concerned mainly with the promotion of a just peace among states, global political ethics is approached as a quest for *international justice*, involving equity and peace among member states. Because states vary considerably in their size, power, and economic resources, the quest for interstate justice is a daunting task. Moreover, because there is no common power within international society to resolve conflicts, the establishment and maintenance of order is similarly difficult. Thus, when a state commits aggression, communitarians believe that force can and should be used to defend the legitimate rights of states.

Communitarians recognize that the quest for interstate justice will not ensure justice within states. Indeed, some regimes might deliberately pursue policies that inflict great harm on their people. When gross injustices occur, communitarians and cosmopolitans differ in their readiness to use external force to correct the alleged injustices. Because communitarians believe that the protection of existing rules of global society is foundational to domestic and international order, they are reluctant to override the sovereignty norm in the name of human rights. As a result, communitarians are willing to intervene only as a last resort. At the risk of oversimplification, it can be said that liberal communitarians are eager to affirm individual rights but are reluctant to protect or advance such rights through foreign intervention.[11]

Cosmopolitanism, by contrast, is concerned mainly with the well-being of persons. Cosmopolitan thinkers argue that states have a moral obligation to defend and protect basic rights; when they fail to do so, they lose their moral standing within international society. Because cosmopolitans view nation-states as legitimate political actors only to the extent that they protect and secure human rights, state boundaries are not morally significant.[12] While affirming the legal principle of nonintervention, *cosmopolitan justice* assumes that the existing structures and rules of international society should not be used to protect injustice within states. Thus, when gross human rights abuses occur, foreign intervention, whether individual or collective, is not only permissible but also, in exceptional circumstances, morally obligatory. Accordingly, when states are unable or unwilling to secure citizens' rights and, more importantly, when they intentionally violate universally accepted human rights norms, they lose their moral standing in the international society of states. In short, sovereignty is subordinate to human rights.

These two conceptions of political justice provide alternative approaches to the pursuit of world order and the protection of human rights. Because the communitarian approach emphasizes the role and legitimacy of states, it is more likely to foster international stability. The cosmopolitan approach, by contrast, focuses on individual welfare and thus is more likely to encourage the protection of human rights. Because the quest for global order and the protection of human rights are not complementary processes, the pursuit of order will often come at the expense of human rights and vice versa. If the pursuit of world order is primary, honoring state autonomy may require tolerating domestic injustices. However, if human rights claims are primary, sovereignty might have to be compromised through humanitarian intervention to halt the gross violation of human rights. Thus, because the pursuit of international justice frequently involves a trade-off between sovereignty and human rights, between autonomy and suffering, the quest for a just international order can be realized only imperfectly, most often by giving precedence to either a cosmopolitan or a communitarian perspective.

Finally, some IR scholars have advanced a third approach to global justice. This emerging school, known as *transgovernmentalism*, emphasizes the role of global civil society in fostering functional transnational ties to address specific issues and challenges confronting the international community. Although this approach is concerned more with transnational cooperation than with the pursuit of justice per se, it is an alternative perspective on international political morality because it seeks to advance the global common good through nongovernmental cooperation across national boundaries. Unlike the two other approaches, which emphasize the moral obligations of persons and states, this approach is chiefly concerned with facilitating problem solving of global issues. But unlike traditional foreign policy making that focuses on intergovernmental relations, the new approach emphasizes the role of nongovernmental actors in fostering transnational webs of shared concerns. Anne-Marie Slaughter writes, "The frontier of foreign policy in the 21st century is social, developmental, digital, and global. Along this frontier, different groups of actors in society—corporations, foundations, NGOs, universities, think tanks, churches, civic groups, political activists, Facebook groups, and others—are mobilizing to address issues that begin as domestic social problems but that have now gone global."[13]

MORAL THEORIES OF GLOBAL SOCIETY

To further illuminate the distinctive features of the communitarian and cosmopolitan perspectives, I first examine John Rawls's theory of international justice, as developed in his *The Law of Peoples*. Rawls's theory is important because it offers a rigorous defense of the communitarian approach by showing how global justice can be advanced in the existing international order. I also describe key elements of philosopher Peter Singer's cosmopolitan approach to global society, as set forth in his book *One World: The Ethics of Globalization*.

Rawls's Theory of International Justice

Rawls's most important work is *A Theory of Justice*, which sets forth a moral framework for pursuing social and political justice in domestic societies.[14] The theory, however, neglects international relations altogether. To address this omission, Rawls wrote *The Law of Peoples*.[15] In this book, Rawls seeks to uncover the principles that are most likely to advance a just international order based on "the political world as we see it," using what he terms a perspective of "realistic utopia."[16] His theory builds on the following premises: First, peoples, not states, are the key actors. Unlike the traditional IR game, which focuses on the rights, duties, and interests of states, Rawls focuses on the institutions and moral character of societies. He does so in order to identify those political communities that are most effective in securing human rights. Second, a just international order is possible only among well-ordered societies. Such societies comprise two types of regimes: (1) "liberal peoples"—constitutional, democratic regimes that protect human rights domestically and fulfill international responsibilities; and (2) "decent hierarchical peoples"—nondemocratic regimes that respect human rights and are nonaggressive in global society. Third, the world has societies that are not well ordered and are therefore incapable of contributing to international peace and justice.

These nonliberal societies are of three types: (1) "outlaw states"—societies that do not respect human rights; (2) "burdened societies"—those that are incapable of protecting human rights because they lack the institutions, cultural values, resources, and human capital necessary for maintaining a decent, well-ordered society; and (3) "benevolent absolutisms"—societies that protect many human rights but do not allow their people to participate in political decision making.

Since liberal societies are thought to be reasonable and rational, Rawls claims that they will tend to work with other liberal societies in establishing "fair terms of political and social cooperation."[17] Such cooperative action is important because it illuminates the core moral principles governing the international community and thereby sets forth the structure of international justice. According to Rawls, the following eight principles characterize liberal societies:

1. Peoples are free and independent, and their freedom and independence are to be respected by other peoples.
2. Peoples are to observe treaties and undertakings.
3. Peoples are equal and are parties to the agreements that bind them.
4. Peoples are to observe a duty of nonintervention.
5. Peoples have the right of self-defense but no right to instigate war for reasons other than self-defense.
6. Peoples are to honor human rights.
7. Peoples are to observe certain specified restrictions in the conduct of war.
8. Peoples have a duty to assist other peoples living under unfavorable conditions that prevent their having a just or decent political and social regime.[18]

Rawls acknowledges that these norms are incomplete and that some of the rights—such as nonintervention and independence—may have to be circumscribed when dealing with autocratic, corrupt, and unstable societies. Although these norms are appropriate for decent, well-ordered communities, they may not apply fully to societies that are incapable or unwilling to protect human rights or to live peacefully with neighboring societies. While acknowledging the incompleteness of this list, as well as the possibility of exceptions to implementing some of its provision, Rawls claims that these principles constitute the basic framework of just international relations—or what he terms "the basic charter of the Law of Peoples."

Rawls's theory illuminates the quest for justice among distinct nations. Admittedly, Rawls focuses on peoples, not states, but he does so only to highlight that international peace and justice are dependent upon the nature of the societies themselves. For Rawls, international justice can be secured only if two conditions are fulfilled: first, states are well-ordered and protect human rights, and second, states respect the autonomy of other states and cooperate to ensure a peaceful, stable, and prosperous international community. In short, international justice can be advanced only through just societies that behave peacefully with other nations.

In sum, the communitarian perspective assumes that a peaceful and just world is best advanced through the right actions of member states. In particular, a just global peace is most likely to be promoted when states, especially major powers, behave in accordance with the principles and rules of international political morality. Since state officials and political realists tend to identify with the communitarian perspective, the emphasis on state behavior is the dominant perspective in IR and among some political philosophers.

Singer's Theory of World Justice

Peter Singer, a leading cosmopolitan philosopher, argues in *One World* that globalization is resulting in a more interdependent global society—a world with one atmosphere, one economy, one law, and one community. Since globalization is making state boundaries more porous and undermining the sovereign authority of governments, the time is ripe to call for a new political morality that emphasizes universal obligations over narrow nationalistic preferences. In view of the rise of the "global village," Singer says that the world needs a "new ethic" that can serve the interests of all persons. As a leading utilitarian philosopher, he wants to advance the greatest good for the greatest number of persons in the world. Thus, he emphasizes global bonds over the particular bonds that have been artificially created by the establishment of nation-states. "Our newly interdependent global society, with its remarkable possibilities for linking people around the planet," Singer writes, "gives us the material basis for a new ethic."[19]

The foundation of this new political morality is that all people matter; state sovereignty is an outmoded concept that unnecessarily confines people's interests and obligations. In his view, "there is no sound reason the citizens of a state should be concerned solely with the interests of their fellow citizens." Building on the foundational premise that human beings are the "basic unit of concern for our ethical thinking," Singer calls for an ethic of impartiality where political and national identity cease to be morally important. Whereas Rawls pursues justice through the existing global order of states, Singer seeks to promote an alternative global system where sovereignty is no longer ethically significant. He writes, "Rawls's model is that of an international order, not a global order. This assumption needs reconsidering."[20]

Singer's cosmopolitan project does not seek to eliminate all cultural and political differences. Rather, it highlights the universal bonds among all persons, regardless of where they live. If legitimate social and cultural differences are to be respected and protected, however, pluralism must become a widely and deeply accepted worldview. But until the world becomes one culture and one society, political institutions will be required to secure human rights in global society. Devising a new ethic will not be sufficient to ensure a just and peaceful world. Global institutions will also be necessary to balance the demands of universalism and particularism. Singer writes, "I have argued that as more and more issues increasingly demand global solutions, the extent to which any state can independently determine its future diminishes. We therefore need to strengthen institutions for global decision-making and make them more responsible to the people they affect."[21]

In his recent book *The Life You Can Save*, Singer applies his cosmopolitan perspective, or what he terms a "planetary focus," to the issue of global poverty. He begins the book with a hypothetical case of a child who is in danger of drowning in a shallow pond. All that is required to save the child is to wade into the pond and rescue him. In his view, most people would walk into the pond and rescue the child, even if they ended up wet and dirty or damaged their clothes and shoes. From this hypothetical account, Singer explores how rich people should respond to those suffering from extreme poverty. He claims that based on UNICEF statistics, close to ten million children under the age of five years die each year from poverty-related causes. Why don't rich people do more to prevent such deaths? Singer writes,

> Most of us are absolutely certain that we wouldn't hesitate to save a drowning child, and that we would do it at considerable cost to ourselves. Yet while thousands of

children die each day, we spend money on things we take for granted and would hardly notice if they were not there. Is that wrong? If so, how far does our obligation to the poor go?[22]

Since all persons are members of one global society, Singer argues that people who are rich should help the one billion who are extremely poor. In his view, rich people should give at least 5 percent of their annual income to help alleviate global poverty. Such a level of giving would not only help reduce child mortality and improve the lot of many but also mark "the first step toward restoring the ethical importance of giving as an essential component of a well-lived life."[23]

Traditionally, economists have emphasized economic development as the most effective means of reducing poverty. Perhaps the most powerful illustration of economic growth's effect on poverty is the dramatic reduction in the proportion of the Chinese people who are poor. According to some estimates, China's annual economic growth rate of nearly 9 percent over the past thirty years has helped to bring more than six hundred million people out of poverty.[24] This development is surely one of the most significant humanitarian achievements of the modern world. The recent rapid economic growth in India has similarly uplifted tens of millions out of poverty. What is significant, then, about Singer's cosmopolitan approach to poverty reduction is his conviction that transnational financial transfers can reduce extreme poverty. His world justice perspective totally discounts the importance of the state in providing order and the rule of law, without which job creation is impossible. Paul Collier, a noted economist, has argued that domestic political conflict and instability along with bad government are two major "traps" that keep poor countries from meeting human needs.[25]

Economic transfers from the rich to the poor can of course help meet short-term humanitarian needs caused by environmental disasters, civil war, or famine. But Singer's distributional model is unlikely to meet the long-term needs of those living in extreme poverty. Indeed, Singer's moral analysis points to the fundamental shortcoming of the cosmopolitan perspective that disregards states and focuses solely on human welfare.

Having examined two alternative conceptions of global society, we close this chapter with a case study on global poverty to illustrate the challenges of pursuing global justice.

CASE 2-1: GLOBAL POVERTY

THE NATURE OF THE PROBLEM: POVERTY OR INEQUALITY?

From an economic perspective, poverty can be defined as absolute deprivation or relative deprivation. The first approach views poverty as a failure to achieve specific social and economic standards of living; the second approach, by contrast, regards poverty as the maldistribution of economic resources. If poverty is defined in relation to the living conditions of others, then poverty can be addressed through the redistribution of economic resources—either within a community, a society, or the world as a whole. When poverty is defined in terms of inequality, poverty will always exist where significant inequalities abound. Moreover, when justice is conceived as a distributive concept and poverty is regarded as the highly unequal distribution of resources, the moral pursuit of justice will necessarily involve redistribution.

By contrast, if poverty is defined in absolute terms—namely, as the failure to provide essential services to meet basic human needs—then improving the standard of living becomes the primary moral concern. In this case, poverty reduction need not focus on redistribution. Indeed, the welfare of the poor can improve while inequalities persist, or even if they increase. What matters is whether the standard of living improves for those at the bottom of the economic ladder. When he was president of the World Bank, Robert McNamara approached the problem of poverty from this perspective. In the late 1960s he coined the term "absolute poverty" to describe the condition of life characterized by illiteracy, malnutrition, and disease as beneath any reasonable definition of decency.[26] The challenge for modern societies, he believed, was to eliminate this condition, which existed in many nations in Asia, Africa, and Latin America.

In 2000, the United Nations General Assembly adopted a series of goals—the so-called Millennium Development Goals (MDGs)—to help eradicate extreme poverty. These include ending malnutrition and hunger, reducing infant mortality, advancing universal education, and eliminating gender inequality in schools. According to the UN Millennium Campaign, contemporary human suffering is manifested by such conditions as one billion people living in extreme poverty, eight hundred million people suffering from chronic hunger, and the annual death of nearly eight million children before their fifth birthday.

What explains Third World poverty? Two popular theories are that (1) the rich exploit the poor and (2) modern economic development exacerbates inequalities, which in turn increase global poverty. Both explanations are false. The first view—often captured by the saying, "The rich get richer and the poor get poorer"—is that the poverty of the Third World is a direct result of the economic growth of the rich countries. According to this perspective, economic life is static. Total wealth is fixed, and increases in income for some can only occur through a fall in income for others. Although powerful states undoubtedly pursued economic exploitation in past centuries, modern economic growth is not necessarily exploitative. According to modern economic theory, wealth creation is a positive-sum process, where all members of society can benefit from growth. Economic development is not a zero-sum process, where the gain of one country must involve a loss to another. The best evidence for the unfounded nature of this claim is that, despite the alleged unfairness of the world economy, many poor countries have achieved significant economic growth in the past three decades. Indeed, low- and medium-income countries have been growing at a faster overall rate than the rich nations. China and India—the two most populous countries—have achieved record economic growth rates of 7 to 9 percent per year in the new millennium. Recent experience indicates that when countries—regardless of their level of development—adopt policies favorable to job creation, most citizens will benefit.

This conclusion is supported by the economic history of most developing nations. For example, fifty years ago almost 20 million children under the age of five died every year. By 2010, however, that number had fallen to 7.6 million—a 60 percent reduction in childhood deaths. Additionally, life expectancy in developing nations rose from an average of forty-six years in 1960 to an average of sixty-two years in 1987—an increase of sixteen years in less than three decades.[27] Perhaps the best measure of poverty reduction is the rise in the Human Development Index (HDI)—a United Nations index based on longevity, education, and per capita income based on purchasing power.[28] Mali and Nepal, for example, increased their coefficients between 1980 and 2011 from .174 to .359 and .242 to .458—reflecting an average annual HDI growth of 2.28 percent and 2.08 percent, respectively. When the world's countries are divided in terms of development levels, the average annual HDI growth rates range from .48 percent for the very high human development countries to 1.31 percent growth for the medium human development countries. Significantly, the countries in the low human development category had an average growth rate of 1.19.[29] Thus, contrary to the exploitation thesis, the poor have not been getting poorer. Indeed, the physical quality of life in low- and medium-income countries, based on HDI data, has improved more than in high-income countries.

The second theory—that economic modernization fosters income inequality and that such inequality is harmful to those living in poor countries—is also untenable. Although income inequality among nations has increased in the past century,[30] such inequality rose not because the poor became poorer but because some societies became more productive. Global inequality would be morally significant only if increased income in the rich countries came at the expense of the poor nations. This, of course, is not the case. Since economic growth is potentially beneficial to all members of society, it does not cause poverty. Indeed, without economic modernization, the living conditions of the poor would be even worse.

Poverty is not caused by modernization's inequalities. Indeed, the problem of the poor is that they are not benefiting from integration into the modern global economy. Wolf argues convincingly that modernization does not foster global poverty. Rather, poverty persists because societies are unable to take advantage of economic modernization. Wolf writes,

> The proportion of humanity living in desperate misery is declining. The problem of the poorest is not that they are exploited, but that they are almost entirely unexploited: they live outside the world economy. The soaring growth of the rapidly integrating developing economies has transformed the world for the better. The challenge is to bring those who have failed so far into the new web of productive and profitable global economic relations.[31]

The core moral challenge posed by the contemporary global economic system is how to reduce poverty, how to uplift people living in degrading, inhumane conditions. Despite significant improvements in living conditions among most of the world's people, a large portion of the world's population continues to suffer from absolute poverty. While more than five billion people benefit from globalization and the miracle of economic growth, more than one billion people live in societies plagued by violence, disease, ignorance, and hunger. In his compelling book *The Bottom Billion*, economist Paul Collier argues that roughly one billion persons live in countries that are "stuck at the bottom."[32] They are stuck not because they are poor but because they are unable to generate economic growth because of fundamental "traps," such as bad government, excessive reliance on natural resources, and civil war.

STRATEGIES TO REDUCE POVERTY

Throughout the Cold War, two approaches dominated the analysis of Third World poverty: redistribution and job creation. The first approach is based on the ideology of socialism and favors strict regulation of economic and social life. This perspective regards the just distribution of economic resources as the fundamental challenge of national economic life, a task best realized through government. The job-creation approach, by contrast, is based on the ideology of market capitalism and regards wealth creation as the fundamental challenge of national economic life. According to this perspective, economic development, not redistribution of existing resources, best alleviates poverty.

The redistributive approach is based on a number of core assumptions. First, it assumes that the basic condition of humankind is sufficiency, not poverty. Second, it assumes that extreme poverty is a human creation, the direct result of the global expansion of capitalism. As one radical economist put it, traditional societies were originally primitive, "undeveloped" communities, but after modern capitalism was introduced, some countries developed while others remained "underdeveloped."[33] Underdevelopment is therefore a direct by-product of the economic dislocations and disparities arising within and among capitalist countries. Third, the redistributionist perspective assumes that economic life is a zero-sum game where the economic benefits of one group or nation result in losses for another. Net wealth creation is difficult, if not impossible. Thus, gains in business and commercial life must inexorably result in economic losses for other firms, groups, or nations, and the economic development of some nations necessarily leads to the decline of others. In short, wealth and poverty are direct by-products of economic modernization.

The redistributive approach has significant moral appeal stemming from its concern with world justice, defined as a fair distribution of economic benefits. Cosmopolitan philosophers like Peter Singer and Thomas Pogge identify with this approach.[34] For them and other cosmopolitan thinkers, the primary moral task in global society is to meet the needs of people suffering from abject poverty. According to this perspective, more than enough resources exist in the world to meet essential needs for all human beings; all that is required is a more just distribution of existing resources.

The job-creation approach, by contrast, is based on radically different assumptions about the nature and causes of poverty. First, it assumes that the basic condition of life is scarcity and poverty. In the beginning, poverty and a short life expectancy are the norm. The rise in living standards is a human creation. The major economic challenge is to generate wealth through increased productivity, which is the only effective way to reduce poverty and improve physical quality of life. Second, it assumes that wealth creation is a positive-sum process where an increase in the welfare of one nation or group does not necessarily come at the expense of another. Since the rewards from production and trade go to the individuals, enterprises, and nations that are most economically efficient in providing goods and services that people want, income is not distributed equally. Rather, distribution is based on different productive capacities, not exploitation. A third underlying belief is that the most effective system of job creation is

a market economy that maximizes human freedom. This does not mean that "the best government is the one that governs least." Rather, a market economy requires a strong state that protects economic competition, maintains the rule of law through limited government, protects property rights, and maintains a stable monetary system.

To a significant degree, the conflict between these two approaches to economic life is over. While the dispute between socialism and capitalism was intense during the Cold War, by the time the Soviet Union collapsed in 1990, its state socialism system had been totally discredited. Free enterprise became the dominant model simply because it proved more effective in generating wealth than the alternative system of structuralism. In 1989, as the Cold War was ending, economist Robert Heilbroner wrote of the victory of capitalism over socialism as follows:

> Less than seventy-five years after it officially began, the contest between capitalism and socialism is over: capitalism has won. The Soviet Union, China and Eastern Europe have given us the clearest possible proof that capitalism organizes the material affairs of human kind more satisfactorily than socialism: that however inequitably or irresponsibly the marketplace may distribute goods, it does so better than the queues of a planned economy; however mindless the culture of commercialism, it is more attractive than state moralism; and however deceptive the ideology of a business civilization, it is more believable than that of a socialist one.[35]

In the two decades since the collapse of the Soviet Union, most developing nations have shifted from a government-controlled economy toward a freer, private-enterprise approach. Rather than seeking to reform global structures and demanding greater foreign aid, many developing nations—led by such emerging countries as Brazil, Chile, China, India, and Indonesia—adopted market-friendly policies that resulted in significant economic growth. Indeed, from 1990 to 2005, the world's low- and medium-income nations grew faster than high-income nations. According to the UN Human Development Report, developing nations had an annual per capita growth rate of 3.1 percent during the 1990–2005 period, whereas developed nations had a growth rate of 1.8 percent. The high rate of average growth in the developing nations was due to the exceptional performance of East Asian and Pacific economies, which grew at an annual rate of 5.8 percent annually, while sub-Saharan African states grew at only 0.5 percent. Indeed, from 1975 to 2005 sub-Saharan Africa experienced an average annual economic decline of 0.5 percent.[36]

Notwithstanding these improvements in living conditions in the developing nations, a large segment of the world's population continues to live in abject poverty. While the percentage of the world's population living in extreme poverty has declined markedly in the past thirty years, the total number of people suffering from absolute poverty has not declined significantly. The reason for this is that the population growth rate of the poorest countries is nearly double that of the developed nations. As a result, of the world's seven billion people in 2011, nearly a billion continue to suffer hunger, deprivation, and abject poverty.

THE ETHICS OF GLOBAL POVERTY

From an ethical perspective, the problem of global poverty poses two fundamental issues—first, the nature and scope of moral responsibility toward the poor, and second, the agents and beneficiaries of poverty assistance. The first issue concerns whether or not rich people and developed societies have a moral responsibility to eliminate poverty. The second issue concerns identifying the peoples or nations that should provide aid as well as identifying those peoples or nations that should receive that aid.

Since political philosophers distinguish human actions that are morally obligatory from those that are praiseworthy, poverty eradication can be similarly justified as a moral duty or as a morally desirable act. From the latter perspective, foreign aid is offered as an act of charity or benevolence to meet human needs. Since acts of charity are voluntary, they do not impose moral

obligations on aid-granting nations. When poverty reduction is conceived as charity, societies that do not transfer resources to those in need are not morally blameworthy, since such assistance is a "supererogatory" act that is expected only of moral exemplars, not of average human beings.

Using the alternative perspective, some theorists approach poverty eradication as a moral obligation. This claim is typically justified from the perspective of distributive justice. Henry Shue, for example, argues that although food and shelter are essential sustenance rights, providing assistance to the poor is a moral duty rooted in claims of distributive justice.[37] Thomas Pogge, using a cosmopolitan worldview, similarly regards poverty eradication as a moral imperative, based on claims of global distributive justice.[38]

An even more compelling argument for aiding the poor is the belief that absolute poverty impedes human flourishing. According to this perspective, since people are moral agents, they are entitled to fundamental human dignity regardless of their ethnicity, nationality, or citizenship. When people suffer from hunger, disease, malnutrition, and other calamities, their fundamental worth as moral agents is compromised. In his recent book on global poverty titled *A Life You Can Save*, Singer follows this approach. His basic thesis is that if people can relieve suffering and prevent death without sacrificing anything of comparable moral importance, they have a moral obligation to aid those in need.[39] The biblical parable of "the Good Samaritan," the story of a stranger who assists an injured traveler, illustrates the moral obligation to others.[40] When applied to international affairs, the logic of the parable can be expressed in the following propositions: (1) X nation has experienced a human disaster and its people are suffering; (2) the citizens of Y have knowledge of X's human needs as well as the resources to relieve X's suffering; (3) even though the people of X and Y are strangers, they share a common humanity; and (4) the people of Y have a moral obligation to help the citizens of X.

The second ethical issue—the agents and beneficiaries of aid—can be approached from the two theories of justice examined earlier in the chapter. According to Peter Singer, peoples and societies that have abundant resources have a moral obligation to assist those peoples and societies that are suffering from poverty. As a cosmopolitan, Singer is not concerned with justice among nation-states. What matters is world justice, an ideal that is advanced by meeting the fundamental needs of the maximum number of people in the world. In order to advance global justice, leading nations need to make substantial transfers to those nations suffering from poverty. Singer, like other cosmopolitans, is not concerned with the development of self-sustaining growth to enhance human dignity. Rather, his focus is on meeting the current needs of those in absolute poverty.

John Rawls's communitarian conception of global society leads him to emphasize international justice. For him, reducing global poverty and improving the well-being of people are best addressed through nation-states ("peoples") rather than by focusing on redistribution among member states. Since the basic social and economic needs of people are best satisfied within the communities in which they live, promoting democratic, developed nations ("liberal peoples") is a necessary precondition for securing basic human needs. Poverty assistance can help meet current needs but will not foster self-sustaining development. Only by establishing sound governance can human rights be secured. Rawls supports foreign aid for "burdened states"—societies that suffer not because they are poor but because they have weak governance. "A society with few natural resources and little wealth," he writes, "can be well-ordered if its political traditions, law, and property and class structure with their underlying religious and moral beliefs and culture are such as to sustain a liberal or decent society."[41] For Rawls, therefore, justice demands that developed liberal communities assist other societies in establishing political, economic, and social conditions that will make them more humane and productive.

In the final analysis, the only long-term approach to poverty reduction is job creation. This is so for two reasons. First, since the population of many poor nations continues to grow at 2 to 3 percent per year (largely because of better nutrition, hygiene, and medical care), improved living conditions can only be realized when economic growth exceeds the population growth rate. It is not enough to give poor people bread and fish; they must be taught to fish to reduce their economic dependency.

And second, job creation offers much more than material needs. It provides an opportunity for people to become creators—to use their abilities and imagination to be productive workers. According to economist Amartya Sen, poverty is much more than material deprivation. In his compelling book *Development as Freedom*, he argues that what impairs human flourishing is not simply low income or insufficient resources, but rather barriers to the development of human capabilities. For Sen, freedom to develop and use human capabilities is both the means and the end of development.[42] As Don Eberly notes, government foreign aid programs have generally approached the problem of Third World poverty as an issue of limited financial resources.[43] Approaching poverty as a lack of financial resources is of course appealing because it provides an easy way to measure generosity. But if poverty is not simply a lack of money but a sign of insufficient human capabilities, then poverty reduction will demand much more than financial transfers.

MORAL REFLECTIONS

The problem of global poverty raises a number of fundamental ethical issues:

- From an ethical perspective, which approach is preferable to address the problem of global poverty—cosmopolitanism or communitarianism, redistribution of income or economic development?
- Since nearly one billion people continue to suffer from extreme poverty, who is morally responsible for meeting their basic needs? Ethicist Peter Singer writes, "When subjected to the test of impartial assessment, there are few strong grounds

for giving preference to the interests of one's fellow citizens, and none that can override the obligation that arises whenever we can, at little cost to ourselves, make an absolutely crucial difference to the well-being of another person in real need."[44] Do you agree with Singer that the location of poverty is not morally important?

- Should donors be concerned primarily with meeting immediate needs or with developing institutions and transforming values and traditions in order to achieve self-sustaining economic growth?

SUMMARY

The world can be conceived either as a unitary moral community or as a society of independent member states. The first approach gives rise to a cosmopolitan ethic that views the boundaries of nation-states as morally insignificant. The second approach gives rise to a communitarian ethic that considers the sovereign independence of states as morally significant.

Cosmopolitanism and communitarianism provide polar opposite approaches to political justice in the international community. The cosmopolitan approach gives precedence to the welfare and dignity of persons and focuses on the fair distribution of economic resources among all of the world's people. Since states are morally unimportant, the role of government in the process of job creation is neglected altogether. The communitarian approach, by contrast, assumes that states are not only morally significant but are the institutions through which wealth is created. From this perspective, the reduction of poverty will necessarily depend upon stable, just government.

Chapter Three

The Role of Ethical Traditions

There is a truth in realism that ought not to be lost sight of: In the hands of public officials, moral principle is too easily transformed into crusading doctrine, which invites misperception, rhetorical manipulation, and public hypocrisy.[1]
—CHARLES BEITZ

A democratic definition of the national interest does not accept the distinction between a morality-based and an interest-based foreign policy. Moral values are simply intangible interests.[2]
—JOSEPH S. NYE JR.

It is the easiest thing in the world to proclaim a good. The hard part is to think through ways by which this good can be realized without exorbitant costs and without consequences that negate the good. That is why an ethic of responsibility must be cautious, calculating a perennially uncertain mass of means, costs and consequences.[3]
—PETER BERGER

MOST HUMAN ACTIONS are based on moral presupposi-
tions. Whether or not persons recognize such moral pre-
suppositions explicitly, human decision making will be
based, of necessity, on moral assumptions. The moral assumptions that structure
human choices are not random but tend to be a part of general ethical paradigms or
traditions. Although these ethical perspectives vary greatly in terms of their nature and
relevance in global politics, they play an important role in the conduct of foreign relations, providing ethical road maps to decision makers. Thus, when statesmen develop
and implement foreign policies, they utilize particular ethical frameworks that establish
the parameters within which issues are debated and decided.

For example, Otto von Bismarck, Germany's chancellor from 1870 to 1890, pursued
domestic and international policies that were profoundly influenced by his realist
Christian worldview—a dualistic Lutheran perspective emphasizing a radical distinction between the temporal and spiritual realms. As a devout believer, Bismarck pursued
a life of personal piety, but as a statesman he believed that he was responsible for using
political power to bring about political order, even if it entailed power politics and
war. By contrast, William E. Gladstone, a British prime minister in the late nineteenth

century, sought to carry out his political responsibilities as a Christian idealist—a believer who, unlike Bismarck, assumed that there was no radical discontinuity between personal and political morality, between individual obligations and government duties. In examining the leadership styles of these two prominent European statesmen, it is clear that different religious and ethical perspectives influenced the nature and style of their leadership.[4]

As noted earlier, when political leaders and government officials apply moral values to public policy decisions, they use ethical strategies that guide the process of ethical reasoning and moral judgment. In this chapter, I explore the nature and role of ethical traditions in the making, implementation, and interpretation of foreign policy. In the following chapter, I describe ethical methodologies that link good and bad, right and wrong, to substantive moral rules (rule-based action) and to consequences (ends-based action). Whereas ethical strategies provide procedures and methodologies for applying moral norms to political decisions, ethical traditions provide the framework for structuring the process of moral decision making. Thus, whereas ethical strategies influence how moral values are applied in public life, ethical traditions provide the substantive norms and principles for judging political decisions and public policies.

This chapter begins by sketching the nature and role of ethical traditions in foreign affairs. It then examines three traditions—realism, idealism, and principled realism. The first two are the most influential traditions representing the polar opposites of power and morality, responsibility and justice. Because idealism and realism represent extreme ideal-type perspectives, most political action will necessarily involve some elements of each. We therefore sketch a third perspective—principled realism or realistic idealism—which represents an intermediary perspective along the idealistic-realistic continuum. I illuminate each of the traditions with case studies: a military intervention (the 1983 U.S. intervention in Granada) to illustrate realism and two modern U.S. foreign policy initiatives (President Jimmy Carter's human rights policy and President George W. Bush's campaign for human dignity) to illustrate idealism and principled realism.

THE NATURE AND ROLE OF ETHICAL TRADITIONS

Terry Nardin defines a tradition as "the thing handed down, the belief or custom transmitted from one generation to another."[5] As utilized here, an ethical tradition refers to a system of substantive moral rules and normative principles that have been passed along from generation to generation and that have been recognized as imposing binding obligations, achieving, as one scholar notes, authority that is something equivalent to "the force of law."[6] Although traditions are based on a variety of sources, including religion, political consent, law, and culture, widespread customary practice is essential in the development of a tradition. Indeed, a tradition's authority is a direct by-product of the extent to which its values, practices, and customs have been institutionalized.

A number of different ethical traditions influence the conduct of contemporary international relations. Indeed, in their study *Traditions of International Ethics*, Terry

Nardin and David Mapel identify twelve major ethical traditions, including international law, realism, natural law, Judeo-Christianity, Marxism, Kantianism, utilitarianism, liberalism, and human rights.[7] Some of these traditions utilize ends-based analysis (e.g., realism, utilitarianism, and Marxism), whereas others rely on rule-based analysis (e.g., natural law, Kantianism, liberalism, and human rights). Although all these traditions have guided modern international politics, the analysis here focuses on only three of these: *realism*, *idealism*, and *principled realism*. These three traditions are important because they have played an important role in structuring American foreign policy.

Before analyzing these alternative paradigms, it is important to call attention to one problem posed by competing ethical traditions. Although traditions provide the moral architecture to identify and apply morality to the conduct of foreign relations, the existence of competing and conflicting moral traditions poses a serious challenge to the universal demands of moral obligation. Because statesmen and political officials from a given country often rely on different traditions, the ethical deliberations that they undertake are likely to result in different emphases, if not different policy conclusions. Moreover, because statesmen from different countries are even more likely to apply different ethical traditions, the challenge in reconciling conflicting moral claims is even greater in international diplomacy. For example, Dutch political leaders applying Kantian, realist, and legal traditions are likely to draw different policy conclusions about genocide in Rwanda or about peacemaking within Bosnia. However, French, Indian, Russian, and Japanese diplomats, representing not only divergent ethical traditions but also divergent political cultures, are likely to draw policy conclusions even more disparate than officials from a single country.

David Welch observes that, because policy conclusions drawn from a particular tradition are likely to be accepted only by adherents to that tradition, the existence of a plurality of traditions poses a major challenge—namely, how to select the most desirable one.[8] However, if a tradition is to be adopted on moral grounds, ethical criteria extrinsic to any particular tradition will be required to select the most desirable one. Because such criteria do not exist, Welch concludes that there is no authoritative ethical method of selecting a preferable tradition. Thus, Welch suggests that, rather than relying on an ethical tradition, one should apply ethics based on moral consensus, or what he terms "conventionalism." According to such a system, right and wrong, justice and injustice are defined by consent among the relevant parties. Whatever they agree to regard as just or legitimate is just or legitimate.[9]

Although an ethical system rooted in agreement might be more palatable in confronting the problem of cultural pluralism noted in chapter 1, consensus does not provide a satisfactory basis for morality. As English philosopher David Hume observed long ago, consent provides no adequate basis for morality because it is impossible to develop a theory of moral obligation from existing facts, that is, to derive "ought" from "is."[10] To be sure, identifying shared moral norms among different societies can contribute to the development of authoritative moral regimes. For example, postwar efforts by the United Nations and its related agencies to define human rights have resulted in a more robust doctrine of rights. Notwithstanding significant differences in human rights conceptions, transnational discussion and deliberation have contributed to the internationalization of rights. However, the proliferation of global human rights discourse has not necessarily strengthened the ethical foundation of international rights claims. Indeed, as contemporary history has demonstrated, regimes not only have frequently pursued policies involving gross human rights violations but also have sought to justify such actions.

Despite the challenges posed by competing ethical traditions, there is no need to jettison them. Although a plurality of traditions can make authoritative ethical judgments more difficult, it need not paralyze ethical reasoning. Indeed, the existence of multiple traditions can provide alternative systems for judging moral action, thereby strengthening moral analysis.

REALISM

Realism, arguably the oldest ethical tradition relevant to international relations, dates from the origins of political thought in the ancient Greek civilization. The historian Thucydides, author of the classic *History of the Peloponnesian War*, is often regarded as the father of realism. Other ancient and modern political thinkers who contributed decisively to the development of this tradition include St. Augustine, Niccolò Machiavelli, and Thomas Hobbes. In the twentieth century, scholars such as Herbert Butterfield, E. H. Carr, Robert Gilpin, Hans Morgenthau, George Kennan, and Reinhold Niebuhr have contributed to the further development and application of realism in modern international relations. Like most traditions, political realism is not easily defined, in part because it is a living, dynamic tradition that is continuously evolving and also because it is a pluralistic movement comprised of distinct strands. For example, the Christian realist strand emphasizes the role of human nature in the development and maintenance of political order, whereas classical realism emphasizes the nature, role, and distribution of power in the development of political order, whether domestic or international. Moreover, *structural realism*, sometimes called *neorealism*, focuses on the nature and implications of political structures of global society. Such an approach differs from classical realism in that it disregards human nature and political morality and focuses exclusively on structural patterns and behavioral norms that explain the political behavior of states in the anarchic international environment.

Despite significant disparities among its different schools, the ethical tradition of realism is a coherent and powerful political worldview, deeply influencing the nature of decision making in the international community. Some of the tradition's most important elements include a pessimistic view of human nature, the priority of power in developing and maintaining political order, the primacy of the state in global politics, the anarchic character of international society, and the priority of consequences in making ethical judgments. I now briefly examine each of these norms.

First, realists assume that human nature is motivated mainly by self-interest. Because individuals and groups tend to seek their own interests first, often in disregard for or at the expense of the interests of others, the establishment of a peaceful and just order is a difficult and never-ending task. In developing political order, realists believe that political action should always be guided by how human beings are likely to behave rather than on how they ought to behave. Although realists hold a pessimistic view of human nature, they believe that the development of order and justice in the anarchic global community can be advanced through policies based on power. Because realists assume that peace is a by-product of an international balance of power, they believe that the management of power is a central requirement in pursuing a moral foreign policy. Only by balancing and counterbalancing the power of other states can a state contribute to global order and establish the preconditions for international justice.

Second, realism emphasizes power. Hans Morgenthau, arguably the most influential postwar international relations realist, views politics, whether domestic or international, as essentially a struggle for power.[11] This struggle is more pronounced in global society because there is no central authority to moderate and resolve interstate disputes. Not surprisingly, Morgenthau views statesmen as officials who "think and act in terms of interest defined as power."[12] Moreover, because there is no central authority to ensure the existence of nation-states and the promotion of their national interests, Morgenthau argues that if statesmen disregard power, they will become the victims of those who have learned to acquire and use it.

Third, realism is characterized by its state-centric approach. It assumes that, although many actors participate in global politics (e.g., international organizations, nongovernmental organizations, multinational corporations, religious movements, and individuals), the main actor is the nation-state. The dominance of nation-states is rooted in the fact that they are sovereign, that is, independent, self-governing political communities not subject to any higher authority. Because power is the principal determinant of a state's capacity to act independently in the world community, the degree of a state's self-government will depend greatly on its own political, military, and economic resources. However, a state's capabilities will also be due in great measure to the capabilities of other states, which can challenge other states' power. Nation-states are a relatively recent development, dating from the mid-seventeenth century, and although they might someday be replaced by other structures, such as a global federal government or regional political unions, realists assume that nation-states will remain the principal actors in global politics in the foreseeable future.

Fourth, realism assumes that the international community is a decentralized, anarchic environment—a self-help system. According to Kenneth Waltz, such a system is one "in which those who do not help themselves, or who do so less effectively than others, will fail to prosper, will lay themselves open to dangers, will suffer."[13] Because there is no common authority in the world, each state's survival and well-being ultimately depends on its own capabilities and resources. Moreover, because the survival of states is not ensured, the most fundamental national interest is assumed to be survival. Although there are a variety of means by which states can promote their interests in the international community, realists assume that military force is the most important. Because the protection of vital interests ultimately depends on the capacity to punish aggression, states continuously seek to deter aggression by expanding their military resources and establishing alliances.

Finally, realism is characterized by its reliance on consequential ethics. Realism is often critiqued as being an amoral approach to international politics because power is regarded as the main instrument of foreign policy and national security as its principal end. One scholar, for example, argues that realism's excessive concern with national security "dissolves moral duties";[14] another suggests that the realist tradition simply excludes morality altogether from foreign policy.[15] Perhaps the most extreme version of realism is advanced by traditional theorists such as Machiavelli and Hobbes and modern scholars such as George F. Kennan, who argue that politics is essentially an amoral activity. Kennan writes, "Government is an agent, not a principal. Its primary obligation is to the interests of the national society it represents . . . its military security, the integrity of its political life and the well-being of its people. These needs have no moral quality. They are the unavoidable necessities of national existence and therefore are subject to classification neither as 'good' or 'bad.'"[16]

However, most realists do not deny morality. Indeed, they assume with Aristotle that politics is rooted in ethics. As Morgenthau has noted, "Realism is aware of the moral significance of political action."[17] Thus, realism is distinguished not by its amorality or immorality but by a morality of a different sort, one that differentiates political ethics from personal ethics and judges action in terms of consequences. Because of the radically different nature of individual and political obligations, realists assume that individual morality, such as the Sermon on the Mount, is not directly applicable to political action. Moreover, they believe that basing policy decisions on abstract moral principles is harmful to the conduct of foreign relations because it undermines the national interest and makes compromise more difficult. Rather than relying on isolated, detached moral norms, realists believe that decision making should be guided by *prudence*—pursuing the greatest good from among morally acceptable alternatives. The aim is not to ensure compliance with particular moral rules and norms but to ensure the most effective realization of goals. Fundamentally, then, realism is a consequentialist tradition.

To illuminate how the realist tradition structures foreign policy decision making, I next examine the American intervention in Grenada in 1983.

CASE 3-1: U.S. INTERVENTION IN GRENADA

Grenada, a microstate about twice the size of the District of Columbia, is an island in the southeastern Caribbean Sea with a population of about 110,000 persons. After receiving political independence from Britain in 1974, Grenada established a parliamentary government headed by Eric Gairy, an eccentric, populist leader. Gairy sought to consolidate his power by creating paramilitary squads designed to intimidate opposition groups. However, the shift toward more repression backfired and led to even greater opposition from left-wing groups, especially a radical nationalist group known as the New Jewel Movement (NJM). Headed by Maurice Bishop, the NJM emphasized nationalism, mass participation, a Marxist ideology, and closer ties with Cuba.

In March 1979, while Gairy was out of the country, Bishop led a bloodless coup, overthrowing Grenada's weak but increasingly corrupt government and establishing his own People's Revolutionary Government (PRG). Bishop immediately began espousing Marxist ideas and aligned his country with Cuba and other communist regimes. As a result of Grenada's ideological shift, the Carter administration distanced itself from the PRG and even considered blockading the island. After Ronald Reagan became president in 1981, the United States became even more aggressive in its opposition to Grenada's PRG, halting virtually all multilateral economic assistance to the island. When Grenada began building a nine-thousand-foot runway with Cuban assistance, Reagan administration officials regarded this development as part of a strategy to radicalize the Caribbean basin and to directly challenge U.S. efforts to extend democratic capitalism in the region.

Moreover, as a result of growing ideological tensions within the PRG, Bishop was forced to share political power with a hard-line Leninist faction headed by Bernard Coard, the deputy prime minister. When tensions between radical Marxists and hard-line Leninists proved insurmountable, Coard, with the support of Army Commander General Hudson Austin, carried out a coup in October 1983, placing Bishop under house arrest. The arrest precipitated public demonstrations, riots, and a breakdown in public authority. A mass demonstration in St. George's, Grenada's capital, resulted in the freeing of Bishop, but in the ensuing power struggle Austin's revolutionary guards recaptured and executed Bishop and killed several government and union officials. The guards then turned their guns on the demonstrators, killing up to one hundred of them. In the immediate aftermath of Bishop's execution, the new military and political leaders, headed by Coard and Austin, announced the creation of a new government headed by a revolutionary military council.

After the massacre, Sir Paul Scoon, the island's governor-general, concluded that foreign assistance was needed to restore order. At the same time, the elected leaders of five neighboring states (Barbados, Dominica, Jamaica, St. Kitts-Nevis, and St. Lucia), comprising the Organization of Eastern Caribbean States (OECS), concluded that the revolutionary conditions in Grenada threatened the region's stability. As a result, two days after the October 19 massacre, the OECS, along with Scoon, requested help from the United States to restore order in Grenada.

THE U.S. INTERVENTION

On October 25, four days after receiving the request for assistance, U.S. military forces invaded Grenada. The military intervention began with the night landing of Navy commandos near St. George's (to protect the island's governor-general). At daybreak, Marines attacked and captured Grenada's sole functioning airport on the eastern side of the island and then proceeded to take control of the southern, more populated area. Some five thousand U.S. Army Rangers parachuted into Point Salines on the southern tip of the island, where the new airport was being constructed. Although U.S. forces encountered heavy resistance at first, especially from some several hundred armed Cubans, they rapidly consolidated control over the southern region, capturing the island's rebel leaders and securing all key military objectives within three days. Because the U.S. forces had destroyed all military opposition and consolidated power throughout the island by early November, the U.S. government began withdrawing troops so that by early December only token, noncombatant forces remained to assist Grenada in transitioning to democratic rule.

U.S. government officials offered three justifications for taking military action against Grenada.[18] First, the intervention was undertaken to protect the lives of U.S. citizens in Grenada. Second, the U.S. action was justified as a response to a joint request from eastern Caribbean nations.[19] And third, the U.S. action was taken in response to a request from Grenada's governor-general.[20] Although these three elements were the precipitating factors for the American intervention, the more basic reason for U.S. military action was geopolitical, not humanitarian. Fundamentally, the Reagan administration ordered the military intervention in order to halt the spread of Marxism in the Caribbean basin. In particular, the United States sought to contain the threat posed by Grenada's radicalization that was being supported by economic, political, and military resources from Cuba and other communist regimes.[21] During his first two years in office, President Reagan had repeatedly called attention to Grenada's increasingly radical politics and the threat that its Marxist alignment posed to democratic countries in the region. He believed that Grenada's radicalization threatened not only the Caribbean region but, by extension, U.S. regional interests as well. As he noted in a speech in March 1983, "It isn't nutmeg that's at stake in the Caribbean and Central America, it's the United States' national security."[22] Thus, after U.S. forces found a large cache of weapons, sufficient to equip a ten-thousand-person army, and discovered an extensive network of secret bilateral agreements with Soviet-bloc states, Reagan administration officials felt vindicated in their judgment that Grenada's Soviet alignment and increasing militarization had threatened the region's security and the consolidation of democracy in the Caribbean basin.[23]

From a strictly juridical perspective, the invasion was contrary to international law, notwithstanding the Reagan administration's claim to the contrary.[24] It was illegal because it involved the violation of a country's sovereignty without the authorization of a legitimate international organization. This was the widespread view of a majority of UN members, who expressed their opposition by adopting a General Assembly resolution (108 votes for, 9 against, and 27 abstentions) that deplored the intervention as "a flagrant violation of international law." Even close U.S. allies failed to support the Grenada action, abstaining on the UN vote. Clearly, the preferable approach would have been to secure authorization from the UN Security Council. Reagan administration officials, however, believed not only that the quest for multilateral support would have failed but also that it would have alerted opposition forces to imminent military action.[25]

Although the UN Charter prohibits foreign military intervention, it does not prohibit the use of force for self-defense. When destabilizing events in Grenada followed Bishop's execution, the governor-general, along with OECS leaders, regarded the domestic events as deeply unsettling and a threat to regional order. As a result, they sought help from the major regional power, the United States. Although intervention critics were correct to point out that legally, the OECS lacked a clear mandate to address collective defense, they also failed to appreciate the potential dangers from the growing threat of radical revolutionaries. Michael Doyle notes that critics of U.S. action seemed to have had more confidence in the views of distant states in Asia and Africa than in the views of Grenada's close neighbors, who called for the intervention. "Those are neighbors," writes Doyle, "whose democratic practices reflected Grenadian hopes, whose security was proximately involved, whose economies were closely linked to that of Grenada, whose Afro-Caribbean citizens have friends and relatives in Grenada."[26]

However legally ambiguous the intervention might have been, it is significant that citizens in Grenada staunchly supported the U.S. action. In one poll taken soon after the invasion, 91 percent supported the intervention and the toppling of the Coard-Austin revolutionary regime. In a later, more sophisticated poll, 86 percent of the respondents indicated their approval of the intervention.[27] Although the United States undertook the intervention to support its strategic geopolitical objective of containing the spread of Marxist influence in the Caribbean basin, it was also evident to Grenadians that the U.S. action was designed to assist them in restoring representative government. To pursue this end, it was necessary to depose a revolutionary regime that had not only betrayed the people's trust but also was threatening the order and stability of the Caribbean basin. Ultimately, the goal of the intervention was to restore domestic order and create the preconditions under which Grenadians could resume democratic self-government. The U.S. commitment to Grenadian self-determination was confirmed with the withdrawal of American military forces three months after they had arrived.

A REALIST PERSPECTIVE ON THE U.S. INTERVENTION

The American intervention in Grenada highlights a number of realist values and principles. First, the Grenada coup and subsequent U.S. intervention illuminates a pessimistic account of social and political life. Unlike political idealism, which assumes that human relationships are funda- mentally harmonious, realism regards human nature as self-centered and communal relation- ships as fundamentally conflictual. The turbulent political conditions that emerged in 1983 as a result of ideological conflicts between moderate and radical elements in the NJM were evidence of the intense quest for power. The domestic events also illuminated the growing communist influ- ence in the region. When radical Marxist forces led by Coard and Austin replaced the moderate government of Bishop, they not only threatened domestic order in Grenada but they also threat- ened to destabilize the Caribbean region as well.

Second, the Grenada case highlights the state-centric nature of international politics. Since there is no central governing authority in the world, the security and well-being of coun- tries is ultimately in the hands of each state and its allies. When revolutionary conditions emerged in the sovereign country of Grenada, it was Grenadians themselves who had to resolve their governance problem. In the absence of a demand for collective self-defense, international organizations like the United Nations and the Or- ganization of American States could not inter- vene to restore a legitimate government. Since Grenada's democratic institutions no longer reg- ulated public life, only a foreign power would help restore legitimate authority. Thus, when the island's governor-general, along with the leaders of the OECS, requested American assistance, the U.S. government responded by taking control of the island for two months.

A third realist value illustrated in the Grenada intervention is the importance of power in deter- mining international affairs. As noted earlier, re- alism assumes that the dominant currency in international relations is power—the ability to apply tangible and intangible resources to deter- mine outcomes. Idealists, by contrast, tend to emphasize the role of international law and inter- national organizations as a means of fostering global cooperation and facilitating conflict reso- lution. Although international organizations and nongovernmental organizations can influence in- ternational affairs, ultimately power—expressed individually or collectively through alliances—

settles disputes and determines the nature and direction of international relations. When Ameri- can citizens' lives were threatened by the coup, the Reagan administration, without consulting allies or the United Nations, ordered a military intervention. It did so not only to save the lives of Americans but also to oust the radical procom- munist regime that had taken control of the country in a coup. American power determined the historical evolution of Grenada. After Ameri- can forces withdrew from Grenada, its people were able to restore democratic institutions and the rule of law.

Fourth, the Grenada intervention was under- taken because of a shift in the balance of power in the Caribbean basin. Although the Reagan ad- ministration justified military action using human- itarian (protecting American lives) and political (a request for assistance from OECS countries and Grenada's governor-general) arguments, the fun- damental goal was to challenge the rising in- fluence of revolutionary Marxist politics in the Caribbean. For Reagan, it was now time to roll back some of the Soviet Union's strategic gains from the late 1970s by supporting anticommunist movements. This effort, subsequently termed the Reagan Doctrine, had two major dimensions: con- taining Soviet expansionism and defending and promoting democracy.[28] Although the U.S. con- tainment strategy focused chiefly on Afghanistan and Central America, the action taken in Grenada was part of the rollback strategy.

MORAL REFLECTIONS

This case study raises a number of important ethical issues about the nature and role of the realist account of international affairs.

- Is realism a moral tradition, and does it provide an adequate account of interna- tional political morality?
- Is realism's pessimistic account of human nature and political life valid, and does it offer a satisfactory approach to the con- flicts and competition among nation- states?
- Was the U.S. strategy to contain the spread of Marxism in the Caribbean a

morally legitimate foreign policy goal? Can the pursuit of strategic geopolitical goals, such as the containment of Marxism, be morally justified?

- Did the growing instability and repression in Grenada justify U.S. military action? Moreover, did the foreign intervention facilitate or impede political self-determination?

- Were requests for help from the island's governor-general and the leaders of the OECS sufficient to justify U.S. action legally and morally?

- Grenada established a peaceful, democratic political system in the aftermath of the invasion. Did this outcome justify the morally ambiguous intervention in 1983?

IDEALISM

Like realism, political idealism is a tradition rooted in ancient thought, although its application to politics, especially international relations, is comparatively recent. Two early thinkers who contributed to its early development were Thomas Aquinas, a thirteenth-century Catholic theologian, and Dante Alighieri, a fourteenth-century Italian scholar. Aquinas believed that reason could help define and establish a just political order. Despite human sinfulness, natural law could be apprehended by reason, thereby providing a basis for political justice. Dante, too, contributed to the development of the idealist tradition by emphasizing the vital role of international governmental institutions in promoting world order. In *Of Monarchy*, he argued that centralized political authority was essential for resolving interstate disputes. More particularly, he suggested that a world government ruled by a monarch was the most effective way of promoting global peace.

The most important elements of political idealism emerged in the eighteenth and nineteenth centuries with the contractarian theories of John Locke and Jean-Jacques Rousseau and the liberal philosophies of thinkers such as Adam Smith, Jeremy Bentham, and John Stuart Mill. These thinkers gave rise to an idealist strand known as *political liberalism*. Liberalism emphasized consent as a basis of legitimate political authority and limited, constitutional government as a foundation for human rights. Because liberal thought has dominated modern political and economic theory, international relations scholars often define the idealist tradition simply as *liberalism*.[29]

Another important strand of idealism is *internationalism*, a perspective that emerged with the writings of the nineteenth-century German philosopher Immanuel Kant and was further developed by President Woodrow Wilson in the early twentieth century. Kant's analysis is important because it calls attention to the major role of domestic and international structures in promoting global order. In *On Perpetual Peace*, Kant argued that peace among nation-states is best maintained through an informal federation of republican regimes. Although Kant thought that some centralization of global power was necessary in global society, international structures alone were insufficient to ensure international peace. If a just global order was to be secured in the world, states themselves had to be governed responsibly, and this could occur only if regimes were based on limited, constitutional authority.[30]

President Woodrow Wilson, the father of the League of Nations, further refined internationalism by calling for the creation of global institutions to replace realist power politics. Wilson was so confident in the human capacity to establish peaceful and just communities that he espoused political self-determination as a basic principle of world order. According to this notion, peoples sharing a common nationality and culture had a right to political self-rule. Although this claim contributed to the decolonization movement of the mid-twentieth century, it has also contributed to significant political turmoil in the post–Cold War era, as ethnic and religious minorities have demanded increased political autonomy from existing states.

Although idealism is expressed in various strands, several core features characterize this tradition.[31] First, political idealism is optimistic about political life, including the establishment and maintenance of a just international order. For most idealists, this optimistic view of international affairs is rooted in a benign view of human nature. Idealists have faith in the long-term benevolence of human nature, believing, as Michael Smith has noted, that human nature "will eventually express its true interests in peace and a thoroughly reformed international system."[32] Because human beings are fundamentally good, the evil and injustice in the world is due largely to the unjust and imperfect political and economic structures of global society. Idealists also base their optimistic political assessment on the effectiveness of human reason in developing norms and facilitating international coordination and cooperation. For them, the ability to promote international peace and tranquility is rooted in human enlightenment and rational communication and negotiation. Still other liberals view international peace and tranquility as an automatic by-product of the utopian conviction that the vital interests of states are fundamentally complementary. This notion, which historian E. H. Carr defines as the "doctrine of harmony of interests," was expressed in a variety of ways in nineteenth-century international relations but especially in the belief that free trade encouraged international peace.[33]

Although some idealists deemphasize human nature and political morality, it is clear that idealists share an optimistic view of international political life. They believe that global harmony is possible and that states, although motivated to maximize national gains, can work cooperatively toward the common good. Although idealists might not attribute their optimistic assessment of global relations to political morality, it is clear that their assumptions about international relations are rooted in an optimistic view of individual and collective behavior.

A second distinctive feature of idealism is the important role assigned to moral values in defining foreign policy interests and strategies. Whereas realism's struggle for power leaves little room for moral judgment in foreign affairs, idealism emphasizes moral norms in developing and implementing foreign policy. Moreover, to the extent that realists make room for ethical judgment in international relations, they do so through a consequentialist strategy. Idealists, by contrast, emphasize rule-based ethics, seeking to ensure that the goals, intentions, and outcomes are consistent with common morality. However, it is important to emphasize that modern international relations scholarship has disregarded the impact of human nature on global politics while deemphasizing the role of political morality. As noted previously, liberal internationalism stresses structures and institutions, paying little attention to the role of ethics and moral values in structuring analysis of foreign policy and international politics. For example, for contemporary neoliberal scholars, global social and economic cooperation is to be explained largely by structural conditions, rather than moral values. Despite the modern predilection to emphasize empirical analysis, the tradition of idealism is nonetheless grounded in political ethics.

The third distinctive feature of idealism is the priority given to human rights and to the constitutional structures essential to protecting these rights. This dimension of the idealist tradition is rooted in the doctrine of political liberalism, which developed during the seventeenth, eighteenth, and nineteenth centuries. Liberal political thinkers, such as Locke, Rousseau, Bentham, and Mill, developed theories that asserted the priority of individual rights and the responsibility of government in securing and protecting such rights. Because government oppression was thought to have been a major barrier historically to individual rights, liberal theorists argued that a primary task of government was to secure and protect such rights by establishing limited constitutional regimes. While liberal theorists devised a variety of procedures and institutions to this end, an essential feature of liberal thought was the need for periodic elections and shared government authority to ensure limited government and to inhibit tyranny.

Because the idealist tradition is rooted in liberalism, individual rights, human dignity, and political freedom are primary. Since the tradition is confident that procedures and institutions can be established to foster and protect basic rights, idealists are fundamentally optimistic about the expansion of human dignity and the promotion of communal justice. Moreover, the idealist tradition assumes that because interstate conflicts and wars are often the result of autocratic, illegitimate regimes, the spread of constitutional, democratic governments can help foster peace and global order. For example, President Wilson, who helped establish the League of Nations, believed that making governments and international diplomacy more responsive to public opinion would lead to a more stable, just international order. In fact, Wilson, along with other idealists of his era, had so much faith in the general public that he believed that secret diplomacy was counterproductive to global order. Indeed, this conviction became a rallying cry of the League of Nations' principle of "open covenants openly arrived at."

A final distinctive feature of idealism is the priority of international law and transnational organizations. Whereas realism emphasizes the balance of power in promoting international order, idealists believe that law and international structures—especially regimes and international governmental and nongovernmental organizations—contribute decisively to the development of global cooperation and world order. As noted earlier, the modern idealism expressed in the early part of the twentieth century gave special emphasis to international law and organization, whereas liberal institutionalism, the more recent expression of idealism, has emphasized state and nonstate actors that contribute to transnational cooperation and to the development of international regimes.

To illustrate the role and impact of the idealist tradition on foreign policy, I next explore President Jimmy Carter's human rights policy.

BACKGROUND

During the 1977 presidential campaign, Democratic Party candidate Jimmy Carter emphasized repeatedly that if elected he would make the promotion of human rights a foreign policy priority. According to Zbigniew Brzezinski, his national security advisor, Carter's commitment to human rights reflected his own religious convictions as well as his political acumen. Brzezinski writes, "He deeply believed in human rights and that commitment remained constant during his Administration. At the same time, he sensed, I think, that the issue was an appealing one, for it drew a sharp contrast between himself and the policies of Nixon and Kissinger."[34]

The idea that human rights should be an integral element of U.S. foreign policy did not originate with Carter. Indeed, throughout the twentieth century, statesmen and leaders, beginning with Wilson, had periodically sought to promote human rights abroad. For Wilson and other idealists, the myth of American exceptionalism had convinced them that the world would be a better place if other countries were to adopt America's traditions of individual rights and to implement its institutions of representative government. Moreover, other recent administrations had emphasized human rights, albeit through quiet diplomacy. However, as R. J. Vincent has observed, what was different about Carter's human rights policy was the adoption of human rights both "as a standard by which to judge the conduct of others and as a set of principles that was to guide its own foreign policy."[35]

It needs to be emphasized, too, that before Carter assumed the presidency, a number of developments were under way within Congress that greatly reinforced Carter's human rights initiatives. Two of the most significant of these legislative actions were the hearings and legislative proposals of the House of Representatives Subcommittee on International Organizations and the passage of the 1975 Jackson-Vanik amendment, which linked most-favored-nation (MFN) status to compliance with human rights norms.

Beginning in 1973, Congressman Donald Fraser, chairman of the House Subcommittee on International Organizations (later renamed Human Rights and International Organizations), began holding hearings on human rights. After initial hearings, in 1974 the subcommittee issued a report calling on the U.S. government to more effectively defend human rights around the world. By the time the Fraser subcommittee ended its work in 1978, it had held some 150 hearings and was responsible for several important changes in U.S. foreign policy statutes. One of the most significant of these—the amending of Section 502B of the 1961 Foreign Assistance Act—required "that, except in extraordinary circumstances, the President shall substantially reduce or terminate security assistance to any government which engages in a consistent pattern of gross violations of internationally recognized human rights." Thus, when Carter began his presidency in 1977, Congress had already established a number of major human rights initiatives making foreign security assistance and MFN status conditional on human rights.[36]

It is important to emphasize that the principal inspiration for the development and implementation of human rights initiatives was the president himself. His idealistic worldview not only provided an optimistic outlook on international affairs but also contributed to the importance of human rights. In his inaugural address, Carter called attention to the priority of human rights and especially individual liberty. "Because we are free," Carter said, "we can never be indifferent to the fate of freedom elsewhere." Several months later, the president set forth his conception of human rights and political democracy in an important speech at the University of Notre Dame. In that address, Carter described his idealistic political worldview as follows:

> Because we know that democracy works, we can reject the arguments of those rulers who deny human rights to their people. We are confident that democracy's example will be compelling. . . .

We are confident that democratic methods are the most effective, and so we are not tempted to employ improper tactics here at home or abroad. . . . Being confident of our own future, we are now free of the inordinate fear of Communism which once led us to embrace any dictator who joined us in that fear. I am glad that that is being changed. . . . We can no longer separate the traditional issues of war and peace from the new global questions of justice, equity and human rights.[37]

After describing major elements of his worldview, Carter outlined several foreign policy initiatives that expressed his core convictions. Not surprisingly, his first policy initiative was human rights, not international peacekeeping, U.S.-Soviet relations, or nuclear arms control, as might have been the case under the previous Republican Party administrations.

CARTER'S HUMAN RIGHTS POLICY

After assuming office, President Carter faced the challenge of translating the human rights vision that he had articulated in the campaign into an operational policy. This was not easy, as his human rights ideas were deeply rooted in moral convictions but were not integrated into a public philosophy about international affairs. One former aide has noted that because Carter had a moral ideology but no political ideology, his human rights policy reflected "strong moral impulses tethered somewhat loosely to a set of political goals."[38] However, if U.S. foreign policy was to advance the cause of human rights, it was essential to establish realistic policies and priorities that would effectively advance such rights.

The Carter administration sought to promote human rights abroad in a variety of ways. First, it used public diplomacy—pronouncements, policy statements, declarations, and condemnations—to draw attention to the priority of rights and to regimes in which major abuses were occurring. Second, it emphasized human rights initiatives within regional and international organizations, encouraging the further institutionalization of human rights norms. Third, it strengthened the U.S. institutional support for human rights by

transforming the Department of State's Office of Human Rights into the Bureau of Human Rights, headed by an assistant secretary of state. A major task of the new bureau was to prepare an annual report on human rights abuses and violations in foreign countries.[39] Finally, the Carter administration used sanctions to promote human rights. For example, during Carter's term, the U.S. government cut its security assistance to at least eight countries and its economic aid to an even greater number of countries because of major human rights abuses.

As Carter administration officials began to express human rights concerns publicly and privately, profound tensions began to emerge not only between the United States and other governments but within the administration itself. For example, when a reporter asked an administration official in the new administration how the U.S. government viewed continuing Soviet threats against human rights activist Andrei Sakharov, the Department of State issued a statement expressing admiration for Sakharov's role as a champion of human rights within the Soviet Union. "Any attempts by the Soviet authorities to intimidate Mr. Sakharov," the statement went on to say, "will not silence legitimate criticisms in the Soviet Union and will conflict with accepted international standards in the field of human rights."[40] However, Soviet government officials did not appreciate this shift in U.S. foreign policy. In their view, no other state had a right to tell the Soviet government how to treat its citizens. As a result, Soviet Ambassador Anatoly Dobrynin immediately protested to Secretary of State Cyrus Vance, and shortly thereafter Tass, the Soviet news agency, denounced the U.S. statement as an "unsavory ploy." Given the Soviet Union's superpower status and the need to balance human rights concerns with other legitimate interests, such as arms control, nuclear proliferation, and global order, the United States immediately backed off from its public denunciation of Soviet human rights. However, this was not the case with lesser powers, especially Latin American authoritarian regimes with whom U.S. strategic interests were minimal. As a result, the United States pursued a more vigorous human rights policy toward countries such as Argentina, Brazil, Guatemala, and Uruguay than toward Indonesia, the Philippines, and South Korea, where security interests were at stake.

However, as Carter officials discovered, pursuing human rights often necessitated trade-offs with other core interests. As one observer noted at the time, although self-determination, majority rule, minority rights, and international order are all desirable, most of the time we can enjoy only some of these good things in life, and then only at the expense of others. "Refusing to accept this fact of life is like refusing to grow up because adults lead such sordid lives."[41] To develop a more coherent human rights strategy, Carter signed a presidential directive on human rights (P.D. 30) to clarify goals and establish clear policy priorities. Among other things, the directive established priorities among major types of human rights, emphasized the role of positive sanctions, prohibited aid to regimes guilty of serious rights violations, and encouraged the use of international financial institutions in promoting human rights.[42] Despite these explicit guidelines, the tensions surrounding the administration's human rights initiatives persisted as the administration sought to balance human rights with other important foreign policy goals.

ASSESSING THE POLICY

Despite inconsistent policy implementation, some scholars and officials regard Carter's human rights policy as a major foreign policy success. Brzezinski, for example, identifies human rights among the foremost foreign policy achievements of the Carter administration. In his view, the human rights policy was important because it encouraged the identification of the United States with the ideals of justice, equity, majority rule, self-determination, and human dignity.[43] Others credit the reduction of human rights abuses in authoritarian regimes (e.g., Argentina, Indonesia, and Uruguay) to the international human rights campaign.

However, this policy was also strongly criticized by many. Some argued that it was hypocritical because of its selective and inconsistent application. Others, such as Joshua Muravchik, argued that the policy lacked balance because it focused attention on individual human rights abuses while overlooking system-wide violations by totalitarian regimes. As a result, the Carter administration emphasized the less serious human rights abuses of authoritarian regimes while neglecting the more egregious systematic suppression of freedom in totalitarian regimes.[44] In addition, Carter's human rights policy was criticized for its conceptual confusion about rights. Rather than clarifying and prioritizing rights, some critics suggested that Carter added to the conceptual muddle. For example, Jeane Kirkpatrick, who served as U.S. ambassador to the United Nations during the Reagan administration, argued that Carter increased conceptual confusion by the broadening of the definition of rights. As Kirkpatrick noted, "Human rights in the Carter version had no specific content, except a general demand that societies provide all the freedoms associated with constitutional democracy, all the economic security promised by socialism, and all of the self-fulfillment featured in Abraham Maslow's psychology."[45]

In short, the tradition of political idealism contributed decisively to the foreign policies of President Carter. The tradition not only provided a worldview by which international events and developments were assessed but also served as a source of inspiration and guidance in public affairs. As this case study suggests, the development and implementation of Carter's human rights policy were a direct by-product of the president's idealistic worldview.

MORAL REFLECTIONS

This case study raises a number of important issues about the role of moral values in the development and execution of foreign policy. Some important questions are the following:

- Is idealism necessary in developing state actions that advance global justice and international peace?
- When ideals come into conflict with political realities, which should take precedence, and why?

- What policy strengths and weaknesses can be attributed to idealism? If President Carter had relied on political realism rather than idealism in defining and implementing human rights, how might the policy have differed?

- Would a human rights policy rooted in political realism have been more effective or less effective in promoting international human rights? Why?

PRINCIPLED REALISM

Unlike realism and idealism, principled realism—also referred to as neoliberalism or realistic idealism—is less an established tradition than an intermediary perspective that combines the moral values of idealism and the power politics of realism. The noted historian E. H. Carr argued that an adequate approach to foreign affairs required a synthesis of realism and idealism. In *The Twenty Years' Crisis*, his seminal study of international relations, Carr wrote,

> Any sound political thought must be based on elements of both utopia and reality. Where utopianism has become a hollow and intolerable sham, which serves as a disguise for the interests of the privileged, the realist performs an indispensable service in unmasking it. But pure realism can offer nothing but a naked struggle for power which makes any kind of international society impossible. Having demolished the current utopia with the weapons of realism, we still need to build a new utopia of our own, which will one day fall to the same weapons. The human will continue to seek an escape from the logical consequences of realism in the vision of an international order which, as soon as it crystallizes itself into concrete political form, becomes tainted with self-interest and hypocrisy, and must once more be attacked with the instruments of realism.[46]

Fundamentally, principled realism integrates political morality with the responsible use of power. Like realism, this tradition regards the world as an anarchic community where power is necessary to secure and protect vital interests. Moreover, principled realism is skeptical of the role of global institutions in maintaining global order, promoting human rights, and protecting the global commons. Unlike realism, however, this perspective assumes that the quality of domestic politics will shape global order. More specifically, it assumes that domestic institutions like the rule of law, constitutional government, and human rights will influence not only foreign policy but also the nature of global politics. Moreover, principled realists believe that foreign policy decisions necessarily entail moral values both in defining interests and in devising strategies to pursue them. Whereas realists emphasize security above all else, principled realists recognize that other moral values, including liberty, human rights, and protection of the global commons, must also have priority in public affairs.

Since foreign policy often involves competing and conflicting interests and goals, statesmen must devise policies that have the greatest prospect of advancing the national and global welfare. Pursuing foreign policy from a principled realist perspective will thus necessitate both wisdom and courage—wisdom to choose among competing values and interests and courage to reconcile moral ideals with power. Hans Morgenthau, the father of modern international relations theory, has written,

> We have no choice between power and the common good. To act successfully, that is, according to the rules of the political art, is political wisdom. To know with despair that the political act is inevitably evil, and to act nevertheless, is moral courage. To choose among several expedient actions the least evil one is moral judgment. In the combination of political wisdom, moral courage, and moral judgment, man reconciles his political nature with moral destiny.[47]

This principled realist tradition is well illustrated in the American foreign policy of Ronald Reagan. His approach is captured by the so-called Reagan Doctrine, which sought to advance the cause of human freedom by supporting fragile democratic governments while undermining expansionistic communist regimes. This foreign policy is appropriately labeled principled realism because it entailed, on the one hand, an international moral crusade for liberty and, on the other hand, a robust use of military and economic power to pursue that goal. To combat the Marxist revolutionary insurgency in El Salvador, for example, the Reagan administration provided significant political and economic resources to support the country's fragile democratic government. At the same time, the U.S. government provided significant covert military aid to undermine the revolutionary influence of the Sandinista regime in Nicaragua.

Contemporary scholars, journalists, and public officials have also advanced the tradition of principled realism. Two strands have been especially noteworthy—one emphasizing the global expansion of democracy and human rights and the other emphasizing a more constrained, prudential use of power in advancing moral ideals. Advocates of the first strand argue that since human rights and democratic governance contribute to peace and global order, foreign policy should be used to advance the cause of freedom. Some of the most ardent defenders of this principled realist tradition include political analysts like Robert Kagan, Charles Krauthammer, William Kristol, Norman Podhoretz, and Francis Fukuyama. Although thinkers associated with the first strand express different views about the expansion of human rights and democracy, they all share the conviction that power should be used, where possible, to advance human dignity and a peaceful, democratic international order. Krauthammer, for example, argues that the United States should pursue a strategy of "democratic realism"—one in which the United Sates provides universal support for democracy but commits tangible resources only where it is "strategically necessary."[48] He thinks that the George W. Bush administration strategy of "democratic globalism" is too idealistic because its commitment to democratic expansion is too universal and open ended. Democratic realism, by contrast, commits resources to democratic development only "where it counts"—that is, only where American strategic interests are at stake.

Although the constrained strand of principled realism shares with democratic realists the goal of advancing moral ideals through the responsible use of power, the second strand is more skeptical of the capacity to advance human rights and democracy. To begin with, the constrained perspective of principled realism views the world as a very complex environment where simple moral verdicts are impossible. As a result, it demands a far more tentative and prudential use of power to advance moral ideals. Moreover, such ideals are not abstract, universal values but tangible values rooted in a country's fundamental values and interests. In their book *Ethical Realism*, Anatol Lieven and John Hulsman articulate this modest, constrained version of principled realism. They argue that the thoughts of Reinhold Niebuhr and Hans Morgenthau provide the foundation for the constrained strand through their emphasis on prudential, responsible political action coupled with an awareness of the dangers of moralism. Lieven and Hulsman claim that this constrained version of principled realism is characterized by five virtues: prudence, humility, knowledge of other countries, responsibility, and patriotism.[49]

Although scholars and public officials are likely to differ significantly over the appropriate balance between power and morality, the distinctive feature of principled realism is the effort to integrate the moral claims with power. To further explore and illuminate this moral tradition, I next examine the Bush Doctrine developed in the wake of the 9/11 terrorist attack.

CASE 3-3: ETHICS AND THE BUSH DOCTRINE

There is a broad consensus that a new national security paradigm emerged in the aftermath of the September 11, 2001, attacks. The core ideas of this new paradigm, known as the Bush Doctrine (BD), were first expressed in the president's declarations and speeches and then in the September 2002 *National Security Strategy of the United States* (NSS).[50] While the new NSS repeated a number of themes emphasized in previous NSS reports (e.g., the importance of cooperation with allies, the need for a robust military power to deter and prevail, and the need for a liberal international economic order), the 2002 statement was noteworthy for its emphasis on promoting human dignity and democracy, maintaining military supremacy, responding to unconventional threats with preemptive force, and the willingness to act unilaterally, when necessary. As with President Ronald Reagan's national security strategy (known as the Reagan Doctrine), the Bush Doctrine integrates moral ideals and political power, a commitment to democracy and human dignity and American might. The NSS declares that the United States

should seek to advance liberty and human rights in the world. To do this, it calls for policies that, among other things, strengthen world order, prevent rogue states from acquiring weapons of mass destruction (WMD), inhibit international terrorism, promote the development of democratic states, foster a liberal international economic order, and encourage market strategies that facilitate job creation.

Following the issuance of the 2002 NSS, President Bush continued emphasizing the BD's core themes by highlighting the need to pursue security with an integrated strategy rooted in power and morality that contributed to "a balance of power favoring freedom." Two of the most important subsequent expressions of the doctrine were the second inaugural address on January 20, 2005, and the revised NSS, released in March 2006.

THE BUSH DOCTRINE

Scholars differ on which elements constitute the BD. Some thinkers view the doctrine chiefly in terms of power and security, while others regard it as an exercise in Wilsonian idealism.[51] Still others emphasize the unique relationship of the United States to Israel.[52] For the purposes of this analysis, I regard the doctrine as an expression of principled realism in which security threats are addressed by both power and morality. The doctrine, as defined here, has four distinct elements:

- belief that unipolarity is conducive to peace and that a preponderance of American power can contribute to a peaceful and prosperous world order;
- belief that multilateralism is necessary to advance peace, freedom, and security, but a willingness to act unilaterally when necessary;
- belief that the United States must be willing to use preemptive and preventive force to confront terrorist groups and rogue states, especially those seeking to acquire weapons of mass destruction; and
- belief that the United States must champion human rights and help foster political democracy.

Of the doctrine's four features, the first three are based on power and are concerned with security, world order, and the international management of power. The fourth element, by contrast, is based on political morality and is chiefly concerned with fostering human dignity through the expansion of free societies. The doctrine's dimensions of power and morality, realism and idealism, are thus integrated in the conviction that democracies are inherently pacific and "have common interests in building a benign international environment that is congenial to American interests and ideals."[53]

Most of the criticism of the BD has focused on the shortcomings of unilateralism and the dangers in shifting strategy from deterrence toward preemption.[54] But most of these criticisms have exaggerated the alleged changes. Both the 2002 and 2006 NSS, for example, emphasize the need for coalition building and call for unilateral action only as a last resort. Moreover, the idea that preemption is a new doctrine is without foundation, for states have always possessed an inherent right of anticipatory self-defense. What is clear is that the emergence of international terrorism, especially when coupled with access to WMD, poses an unprecedented security threat. Given the widespread criticism precipitated by the claim of preemption, the NSS 2006 introduced the following qualification: "The United States will not resort to force in all cases to preempt emerging threats. Our preference is that nonmilitary actions succeed. And no country should ever use preemption as a pretext for aggression."

Although most of the opposition to the BD has focused on its military dimensions, the most noteworthy feature of the BD is its emphasis on moral values. Indeed, Norman Podhoretz claims that the power of the BD is its "incandescent moral clarity."[55] Political morality is used not only to champion human dignity and self-government but also to justify the cause of freedom. In the 2002 NSS, for example, the term *freedom* is used at least forty-six times, while the notions of democracy and liberty appear, respectively, thirteen and eleven times. Nowhere is the role of political morality more evident than in the president's second inaugural address. In that noteworthy speech, Bush stated the moral basis of American foreign policy as follows:

> From the day of our founding, we have proclaimed that every man and woman on this earth has rights, and dignity, and matchless value, because they bear the image of the maker of heaven and earth. Across the generations, we have proclaimed the imperative of self-government because no one is fit to be a master and no one deserves to be a slave. Advancing these ideals is the mission that created our nation. It is the honorable achievement of our fathers. Now it is the urgent requirement of our nation's security and the calling of our time. So it is the policy of the United States to seek and support the growth of democratic movements and institutions in every nation and culture, with the ultimate goal of ending tyranny in the world.

Historically, foreign policy has been regarded as the pursuit of vital interests, with moral values playing a subsidiary role, if any. Challenging this traditional conception of foreign policy, the president boldly announced, "America's vital interests and our deepest beliefs are now one."

Historian John Lewis Gaddis regards this conflation of ideals and interests as a major shift in the Bush strategy. No longer is freedom simply the aim and aspiration of American foreign policy, but it is now the strategy itself.[56]

Of course, the emphasis on right and wrong, good and evil, can be deeply disturbing not only to those who do not share a belief in transcendent morality but also to those who differ with the claimed normative judgments. Since reliance on moral norms presents a direct challenge to the prevailing moral relativism common in contemporary discourse, Podhoretz argues that the emergence of a strategic vision rooted in morality was not a "happy circumstance" for some foreign policy pundits. He writes,

> Given its dangers, who but an ignoramus and a simpleton—or a religious fanatic of the very type with whom Bush was going to war—would resort to archaic moral absolutes like "good" and "evil"? And then, who but a fool could bring himself to believe, as Bush (like Reagan before him) evidently had done in complete and ingenuous sincerity, that the United States represented the "good"? Surely only a virtual illiterate could be oblivious of all the innumerable crimes committed by America both at home and abroad—crimes that the country's own leading intellectuals had so richly documented in the by-now standard academic view of its history?[57]

Philip Zelikow similarly suggests that Bush's political ethics were likely to be troubling to left-ist moralists, who, like their American predecessors in the 1920s and 1930s, preferred isolation to passing judgment on foreign injustice.[58] For such thinkers and leaders, some of them religious officials of mainline Protestant denominations, it was often preferable to focus on the imperfections of the United States than to confront oppression, injustice, and egregious human rights abuses in other countries.

MORAL REFLECTIONS

- Since global society is anarchic, each state is responsible for the political and economic affairs within its territorial boundaries. Although many governments are well governed, some are not. When regimes abuse human rights and threaten regional order, which states or international organizations should confront unjust regimes?
- Regime change can be highly destabilizing to world order. Which value should take precedence in global society—order or liberty?
- Since democracy is conducive to human dignity, should foreign powers help to institutionalize democracy in other countries? More specifically, should the United States, the world's most powerful country, use its influence to advance democracy and human rights in other countries?
- Assuming it is morally appropriate to champion human dignity and democracy in the world, how should major powers promote democratic values and institutions without succumbing to self-righteousness and political arrogance?

SUMMARY

Ethical traditions play an indispensable role in international relations. In a world in which moral values are being increasingly neglected, undermined, or misused, traditions provide a structure for identifying and applying moral norms to international relations. By illuminating widely shared moral values, ethical traditions help guide individual and collective political action, thereby contributing to the development of humane foreign policies and just international structures. Ethical traditions also provide the moral architecture necessary to critique and assess the foreign policy behavior of states and the international structures of global society. Ethical traditions are not self-validating. As a result, the plurality of traditions requires that the competing and conflicting claims of different traditions be examined with care and reconciled when possible.

Chapter Four

Strategies of Ethical Decision Making

When it comes to politics, we get no moral Brownie points for good
intentions; we will be judged by the results.[1]
> —PETER BERGER

What is wrong is not the impulse to give foreign policy a moral content,
but the presumption that doing so is an uncomplicated business, one not
requiring calculation and compromise but merely purity of intention.
Cheap moralists are as dangerous as cheap hawks—indeed they are often
the same people.[2]
> —OWEN HARRIES

Moral Politics is an art of execution: principles unaccompanied by
practical means or by an awareness of possible tradeoffs remind one of
Peguy's famous comment about Kant—his hands were pure, but he had
no hands.[3]

> —STANLEY HOFFMAN

I N CHAPTER 1, ETHICS was defined as the identification,
interpretation, and application of moral principles to specific
issues or problems. In carrying out this task in the political
sphere, statesmen and political thinkers rely on distinct traditions and strategies. As I
noted in the previous chapter, ethical traditions provide substantive frameworks that
structure moral reasoning and action. In this chapter I examine the nature and role of
ethical strategies that offer alternative methodologies to decision making based on different emphases being given to goals, means, and consequences. Unlike ethical traditions, which provide a normative structure of rules and principles that are regarded as
authoritative, ethical strategies are mainly methodological tools for guiding decision
making. Both ethical traditions and ethical strategies are important in international
relations because they provide perspectives, approaches, and tools by which political
morality is applied to thought and action in global society.

In this chapter, I examine the nature and role of two dominant strategies of ethical
decision making: ends-based action and rule-based action. These two strategies are
illustrated with case studies on nuclear deterrence and famine relief. In addition, I

describe and assess a third approach, a tridimensional ethical model, that judges international political ethics by its comprehensive emphasis on goals, means, and results. This approach is illustrated with a case study on the Reagan administration's Strategic Defense Initiative (SDI), a program that explored the feasibility of developing a protective shield against strategic nuclear attack. In the chapter's concluding section I explore the complex issue of how moral decision making is developed.

ENDS-BASED ACTION

This approach, generally defined by philosophers as *consequentialism* or *teleological ethics* (from the Greek *teleos*, meaning "end" or "issue"), assumes that the morality of an action must be ultimately judged by the good results that are realized. In contrast to rule-based action, which assumes that the morality of a decision should be judged by the faithfulness with which moral rules are applied, consequentialism believes that the most important moral criterion is the overall outcome. Political actions typically involve three distinct elements: goals or intentions, means, and results. Although all three elements are incorporated into ends-based thinking, the consequences of human choices are given priority.

As noted by Peter Berger at the outset of this chapter, the moral legitimacy of an action ultimately depends on its consequences. Policies involving questionable means, or even morally ambiguous goals, may be morally permissible if outcomes are beneficial. To illustrate, in October 1983 U.S. military forces intervened in Grenada, toppling its Marxist revolutionary government. Although the intervention was legally dubious (because it violated the island's sovereignty) and morally questionable (because it involved armed violence), the action was ultimately deemed just because it restored public order on the island, reestablishing the basis for electoral democracy. Most significantly, an overwhelming majority of the Grenadians expressed their approval of U.S. military action. Thus, from an ends-based perspective, the U.S. military intervention was morally justified by its beneficial outcomes—the protection of human life, the establishment of civic order, and the restoration of democracy.

One of the major philosophical expressions of ends-based thinking is *utilitarianism*, a doctrine that assumes that individual and collective actions should be judged mainly by their "utility" or results. As Jeremy Bentham (1748–1832), the founder of this movement, argued, "Nature has placed mankind under the governance of two sovereign masters, pain and pleasure."[4] The task of government is thus to establish policies that maximize collective pleasure and minimize collective pain. He proposed that policy making should be judged by the principle of *utility*, which he defined as the "greatest good for the greatest number." Because Bentham was concerned with increasing the scientific basis of policy making, he developed a number of quantitative norms for measuring societal pleasure and pain. Subsequently, his disciple and friend, John Stuart Mill (1806–1873), sought to further refine utilitarianism by distinguishing between desirable and less desirable pleasures.

More recently, political philosophers have distinguished between two types of utilitarianism: *rule utilitarianism* and *act utilitarianism*. The former applies the principle of utility to rules and procedures, holding that such norms derive their ethical legitimacy from their "procedural utility," that is, their perceived fairness and expected contribution to the common good. In global politics, such utilitarianism applies to the norms and structures of the international community's political, economic, and legal systems, and the validity of such norms and structures depends on their overall effect on individual and global welfare. The moral legitimacy of a basic rule, such as nonintervention, is thus judged in terms of its contribution to global order and international peace as well as its impact on the welfare and security of individual countries. Rule utilitarianism, in short, judges the inherent "usefulness" of policies and structures in terms of their consequences.

Act utilitarianism, by contrast, applies the utility criterion to particular actions, holding that the moral legitimacy of decisions must be based on the extent to which overall good (i.e., utility) is maximized in each particular circumstance. Political actions based on act utilitarianism are thus judged in terms of their anticipated results. For example, the decision of whether the United States should assist a country or region facing a major financial crisis (as was the case with Mexico in December 1994 and with East Asia in 1997–1998) would be determined by the anticipated short-term and long-term consequences of such aid.

Ends-based thinking is an influential ethical strategy in domestic and international politics in great part because government decisions are judged in terms of results, not motives. As a result, political ethics, whether domestic or international, tend to be consequentialist. However, the widespread support for ends-based action in public life should not obscure the strategy's limitations. One of these is decision makers' inability to fully determine or predict policy outcomes. Because policy making is at best a probabilistic science in which outcomes depend on many factors, including some over which decision makers have little or no control, government initiatives frequently fail to promote desired goals. For example, although economic sanctions are often imposed to foster behavioral reforms, economic penalties seldom lead to desired behavioral outcomes. Similarly, foreign aid is often given to promote democracy and economic prosperity even though such aid sometimes fails to advance desirable outcomes and can even undermine the goals being pursued. Given the indeterminacy of public policies, the moral assessment of political action from an ends-based strategy is likely to involve uncertainties and ambiguities.

A second and more important limitation is the inability of ends-based thinking to provide an authoritative ethical standard by which to evaluate action. Bentham, who defined the principle of utility as the greatest good for the greatest number, provided a number of general norms by which to judge this principle. However, his conceptualization of outcomes, like that of other consequentialist political thinkers, provides no clear, unambiguous standard by which to establish and judge results. Whether the end is defined as stability, pleasure, happiness, fairness, human rights, or economic and social well-being, there is no widely accepted framework by which to assess political outcomes. In short, although an ends-based perspective needs to be incorporated in political ethics, consequentialism alone does not provide a fully satisfactory ethical methodology for applying morality in international affairs.

Because politics is fundamentally about the art of the possible, political action is generally judged primarily by its results. As noted previously, ends-based analysis is the dominant ethical methodology in politics. The following case study illustrates the nature and role of this methodology in terms of the ethics of nuclear deterrence.

CASE 4-1: THE ETHICS OF NUCLEAR DETERRENCE

BACKGROUND

Historically, military force has been viewed as a morally legitimate means to protect and defend vital interests and to deter aggression. Theologians and strategists have developed an elaborate moral theory of military force, known as "just war," that specifies when a state may resort to war and how such a war should be conducted. After nuclear weapons were invented in 1945, it was clear that the new weapons could not easily be encompassed by existing conceptions of military force. In particular, traditional just war norms designed to help determine whether, when, and how force should be used in settling global conflicts no longer applied to nuclear weapons because of their extraordinary destructive power. Typically, atomic (nuclear) bombs were many thousand times more powerful than conventional arms, and hydrogen (thermonuclear) bombs were many million times more powerful than conventional weapons. As a result, a war between two nuclear powers could threaten not only the mutual destruction of the two combatants but also, in the words of Jonathan Schell, "the extinction of the species." "To say that we and all future generations are threatened with extinction by the nuclear peril," Schell wrote in 1982 in *The Fate of the Earth*, his influential and popular account of the nuclear dilemma, "is to describe only half of our situation. The other half is that we are the authors of that extinction."[5]

The development of nuclear arms thus posed profound moral issues. Was it morally permissible to possess such weapons? If so, could a state threaten their use? In addition, if the threat failed to deter action, could nuclear arms be used?

After atomic bombs were used in Hiroshima and Nagasaki, it became evident that nuclear arms could not be encompassed by conventional strategic thought. The power of these new weapons was so overwhelming that they could no longer be regarded as instruments of warfare. Nuclear and thermonuclear weapons provided a nation with military power but not with usable force to compel a foreign state to alter its behavior. One of the first thinkers to recognize the moral and strategic problem posed by the nuclear invention was Bernard Brodie, who in 1946 observed, "Thus far the chief purpose of our military establishment has been to win wars. From now on its chief purpose must be to avert them."[6] Subsequently, strategists continued to emphasize the strategic significance of nuclear arms while calling into question the military utility of such weapons. Henry Kissinger, for example, describes the radical challenge posed by nuclear arms to traditional strategic thought: "In the past the military establishment was asked to prepare for war. Its test was combat; its vindication, victory. In the nuclear age, however, victory has lost its traditional significance. The outbreak of war is increasingly considered the worst catastrophe. Henceforth, the adequacy of the military establishment will be tested by its ability to preserve peace."[7]

Fundamentally, nuclear weapons pose two major moral problems. First, because their destructive power is based not only on blast but also on heat and radiation, nuclear weapons can inflict greater and longer-term destruction, involving both immediate human suffering from severe burns and long-term genetic deformities. Second, because of their extraordinary power, nuclear weapons are indiscriminate instruments of mass destruction. As a result, they cannot be regarded as war-fighting instruments that give states another means of implementing policy. Because of the qualitative differences between nuclear and conventional arms, the former, unlike the latter, do not provide usable force to compel an enemy. "A weapon," writes George Kennan, "is something that is supposed to serve some rational end—a hideous end, as a rule, but one related to some serious objective of governmental policy, one supposed to promote the interests of society which employs it. The nuclear device seems to me not to respond to that description."[8] Although nuclear arms are not useful war-fighting instruments, they are a vital element of the national security of some states. Their usefulness, however, does not lie in their ability to compel but to deter.

Given the significant qualitative differences between conventional and nuclear arms, the traditional prudential and moral analysis of war is not immediately applicable to nuclear power. Michael Walzer, for example, argues that nuclear weapons "are the first of mankind's technological innovations that are simply not encompassable within the familiar moral world."[9] Indeed, he suggests that they "explode" the theory of just war.

Because nuclear weapons are the most powerful weapons ever devised by human beings, a nuclear military capability can provide a state with a dramatic expansion in perceived national power. At the same time, because nuclear weapons are instruments of indiscriminate destruction, they do not provide a state with usable military force, especially if an enemy state also has such weapons. This is the situation that developed between the United States and the Soviet Union in the late 1940s after the latter became a nuclear power. Moreover, as both states expanded their nuclear arsenals in the 1950s, they became mutually vulnerable to each other's nuclear power. By the early 1960s, both superpowers had achieved arsenals sufficiently large and invulnerable that a condition of mutual assured destruction (MAD) emerged, a condition by which neither state could win a major war but both could lose. MAD was not a policy; rather, it

was a condition reflecting a nuclear "balance of terror" by which each rival could destroy the other, even after being subjected to a nuclear surprise attack.

Because nuclear arms imposed mutual vulnerability on the superpowers, the American challenge in devising a moral strategic policy was to reconcile the demands for national security with the demands for global order without increasing the risks of nuclear war. Not surprisingly, nuclear deterrence, that is, prevention by threat, emerged as the principal American strategic doctrine. As articulated by U.S. strategists, nuclear deterrence would help keep peace by inhibiting aggression through the implicit threat of unacceptable nuclear retaliation. According to deterrence theory, as long as U.S. nuclear forces could carry out unacceptable punishment, no rational state would risk major aggression. Moreover, the credibility and stability of deterrence were assumed to rest on two essential conditions. First, societies needed to be vulnerable (there could be no effective strategic defense). Second, nuclear forces needed to be sufficiently invulnerable to carry out nuclear retaliation involving unacceptable damage. As a result, deterrence did not rest so much on the number, quality, or size of strategic weapons as on their invulnerability to attack. As long as a significant part of a state's nuclear arsenal could be used to retaliate following a major nuclear attack, deterrence would remain credible.

THE MORAL JUSTIFICATION OF DETERRENCE

War is evil. It is evil because it results in death and destruction. Despite its evil effects, war can be morally justified when certain moral conditions are fulfilled.[10] However, from an ends-based, or consequentialist, approach, which is the perspective I am seeking to illuminate here, war can be morally justified when the good outcomes of war outweigh the evil undertaken in war. Thus, when the anticipated results justify the means—when a war results, for example, in the restoration of a just peace without excessive destruction—a war can be morally justified by a consequentialist ethic.

However, if conventional war can be morally justified under some circumstances, this is not the case for nuclear war. Michael Mandelbaum, for example, writes, "In the sense that the term 'war' connotes some proportion between damage done and political goals sought, an all-out nuclear conflict would not be a war at all."[11] Similarly, the U.S. Catholic bishops, in their influential 1983 pastoral letter on nuclear strategy, argue that a nuclear war is morally unacceptable and that every effort must be taken to ensure that nuclear arms are never used in resolving international disputes. As a result, the bishops argue that the church should emphasize not the morality of war fighting but the avoidance of nuclear war altogether. The letter observes, "Traditionally, the church's moral teaching sought first to prevent war and then to limit its consequences if it occurred. Today the possibilities for placing political and moral limits on nuclear war are so minimal that the moral task . . . is prevention."[12] In sum, strategic thinkers and ethicists have generally agreed that nuclear war is morally wrong because the political goals could not legitimize the society-wide destruction resulting from a major nuclear conflict.

Like nuclear war, nuclear deterrence is evil. It is evil because it threatens to do what is morally impermissible, namely, to carry out mass destruction. Although threats and actions are not morally identical, nuclear deterrence bears some of the evil of nuclear war because the credibility of deterrence rests partly on the fact that nuclear weapons might be used. In assessing the morality of nuclear deterrence from an ends-based perspective, the issue comes to this: Can the implicit or explicit threat of nuclear retaliation be morally justified by the policy's alleged contributions to peace and security? Because the answer will depend on the good that is achieved in light of the evil involved in the threat, I briefly examine various costs and benefits, evils and goods, involved in nuclear deterrence.

In assessing the evil involved in nuclear deterrence, numerous factors need to be considered. First, the aim of deterrence is not to inflict destruction but to prevent unwanted behavior through the promise of unacceptable punishment. Thus, deterrence does not intend evil; rather, it seeks to do good (e.g., prevent aggression or foster peace) by threatening evil (retaliation). Second, the extent of evil involved in explicit or implicit nuclear threats is difficult to ascertain, in great part because of the infinite number of degrees of intention involved, varying from a bluff (a threat without a commitment to fulfill it) to assured retaliation (certain punishment in response to aggression). Third, although scholars hold different views on the moral effect of intentions and actions, ethicists generally concur that intentions do not bear the same moral consequences as actions. As a result, because the threat of force is normally considered to involve less evil than the use of force itself, nuclear deterrence is likewise not considered to be morally commensurate with nuclear war. Finally, not all strategic policies are morally equivalent. Because a major aim of deterrence is to achieve political goals without resorting to nuclear war, strategies that maintain a robust "firebreak," or gap, between conventional and nuclear arms (thereby maintaining a low risk of nuclear conflict) will be judged more acceptable morally than those strategies that undermine the firebreak.[13] Thus, nuclear strategies that inhibit resort to war (e.g., countervalue strategies based on massive nuclear retaliation) will be deemed morally preferable to those that encourage limited nuclear war-fighting strategies (e.g., counterforce strategies based on small, accurate, flexible threats).[14]

Despite the evil involved in relying on nuclear arms, such weapons contribute to the well-being of global society in a number of ways. First, nuclear deterrence can inhibit aggression. Because of the enormous power of nuclear arms, nuclear or conventional attack is virtually unthinkable. John Mearsheimer writes, "The more horrible the prospect of war, the less likely war is. Deterrence is more robust when conquest is more difficult. Potential aggressor states are given pause by the patent futility of attempts at expansion."[15] Second, nuclear deterrence can promote international stability and foster world peace. It does so because deterrence helps preserve the status quo. In international politics, nuclear deterrence fosters global stability because it prevents aggression and forcible changes in global cartography. A number of scholars have argued that despite significant conflict between the United States and the Soviet Union during the Cold War, the existence of a nuclear balance between them and their respective allies resulted in a "long peace," unprecedented in modern history. In writing about the postwar peace, strategist Thomas Schelling observes, "Those 40 years of living with nuclear weapons without warfare are not only evidence that war can be avoided but are themselves part of the reason why it can be."[16] Finally, nuclear weapons can provide security at a comparatively low cost, thereby conserving scarce national resources. For example, in extending the nuclear shield to Western Europe during the Cold War, the United States was able to deter potential aggression from the much larger conventional Warsaw Pact forces by maintaining a defense strategy of "flexible response" based in part on nuclear arms.

From a consequentialist, or ends-based, perspective, nuclear deterrence is considered morally legitimate when the strategy's beneficial outcomes (e.g., the prevention of aggression, the fostering of regional peace, and the maintenance of global order) outweigh its evils (e.g., the threat to carry out massive nuclear retaliation). This is the conclusion of many strategists and ethicists who have examined this extraordinarily complex moral problem. Walzer, for example, argues that in conditions of supreme emergency—when the existence of a state is threatened by potential aggression—nuclear deterrence can provide a morally defensible strategy. In defending nuclear deterrence, he writes that "we threaten evil in order not to do it, and the doing of it would be so terrible that the threat seems in comparison to be morally defensible."[17] Following a similar consequentialist logic, the U.S. Catholic bishops conclude their pastoral letter on nuclear strategy by conditionally endorsing deterrence. Deterrence, they suggest, can be justified only temporarily while states seek to reduce political tensions and carry out arms control and disarmament. They conditionally defend such a strategy

in light of geopolitical realities because they believe that it contributes to "peace of a sort."[18]

From an ends-based perspective, nuclear deterrence is morally permissible only if deterrence succeeds in keeping peace and nuclear retaliation is unnecessary. However, how is strategic success to be ascertained? For example, numerous scholars have argued that the general global peace achieved during the Cold War was a result of the existence of nuclear weapons and the implicit strategy of nuclear deterrence. Historian John Lewis Gaddis has argued that the "long peace" of the second half of the twentieth century was due in part to the superpowers' nuclear arsenals, which made major war between them unthinkable.[19] Schelling also attributed the unprecedented Cold War order to nuclear weapons.[20] Others, however, have argued that nuclear weapons and the threats they pose have been largely irrelevant to global order.[21] Because the efficacy of deterrence can be proved ultimately only by its failure, it is impossible to either confirm or disprove the claim that nuclear weapons contributed to the Cold War's long peace. Still, there can be little doubt that the existence of major nuclear stockpiles contributed to fear of nuclear war, which in turn inhibited major military conflict between superpowers.

MORAL REFLECTIONS

This case study raises several important issues about the strategy of nuclear deterrence as well as the ends-based ethical reasoning used to justify it.

- Given the extraordinary destructiveness of nuclear armaments, are such weapons fundamentally immoral? Because nuclear arms "explode" the just war doctrine, is it moral for states to possess and threaten to use them?
- Although it is evident that war and the threat of war are both evil, is the threat of war less evil than war itself? As suggested previously, is nuclear deterrence more moral than nuclear war?

- Because deterrence might fail, does the possibility of carrying out nuclear retaliation undermine the moral justification of deterrence? More particularly, is it immoral to declare a policy of deterrence if there is no intention of ever fulfilling the threat? In effect, is a policy of deceit morally permissible if it contributes to global order and inhibits aggression?
- Is the resort to nuclear war, however limited, ever morally permissible? If deterrence fails, is it morally permissible to carry out the promised nuclear punishment?
- Is the proliferation of nuclear weapons contrary to the order and well-being of the international system? In mid-1998, both India and Pakistan, sworn mutual enemies that have fought three wars in the postwar era, each carried out five nuclear tests. Western nations, especially the United States, strongly condemned these nuclear tests, implying that the attempt to acquire nuclear weapons was contrary not only to the nonproliferation norms but also to international morality. Is the development of nuclear capabilities by India and Pakistan contrary to international ethics?
- Is an ends-based ethic an adequate methodology for judging nuclear deterrence? Is it an adequate ethical strategy for assessing and implementing a moral foreign policy?

RULE-BASED ACTION

Rule-based analysis, known as *deontological thinking* (from the Greek word *deon*, meaning "duty" or "obligation"), denies what consequentialist analysis asserts, namely, that an action is good or bad depending on the goodness or badness of its consequences. Deontologists assert that actions should be judged by their inherent rightness and validity, not by the goodness or badness of policy outcomes. Because deontological thinking places a premium on duty and right intention, rule-based analysis is agent centered, emphasizing the duties and obligations of actors, not the results of decisions. Thus, this approach or methodology appeals to the goodness of policies themselves, not to their effects. As a result, ethical decision making is determined mainly by the morality of goals and intentions. Decisions that disregard moral obligations or utilize morally questionable means are themselves immoral, even if desirable outcomes are achieved. For example, from a deontological perspective, the firebombing of Dresden and Tokyo, carried out by the allies to defeat Germany and Japan, is regarded as immoral because civilians were part of the intended targets of those raids. Because reliance on evil means can never be condoned, even if it results in good outcomes, the use of evil means (intentionally killing civilians) cannot be justified by good intentions (defeating the Axis powers).

However, how can a statesman or political decision maker know what his or her ethical duties are? How are goals and methods to be determined to ensure ethical action? Immanuel Kant, the eighteenth-century German philosopher and father of rule-based analysis, argues that the rightness of a rule or action should be based on the *categorical imperative*. This principle has two key dimensions: First, persons should be treated as having value themselves (i.e., persons are always ends, never a means to an end). Second, individuals should act in accordance with principles or maxims that can be universalized.[22] Kant defines the universalization norm as follows: "Act only on the maxim through which you can at the same time will that it should become a universal law." In other words, ethical decision making should be judged on the basis of the extent to which a principle should be applied to others. It is important to emphasize that in Kantian ethics moral obligations should be fulfilled not because they are more effective in creating a better, more just world but because they are what moral action requires. "An action done from duty has its moral worth," Kant observed, "not in the purpose to be attained by it, but in the maxim in accordance with which it is to be decided upon." Finally, how can persons discover which moral principles should guide their behavior? According to Kant, reason is the faculty by which norms can be discovered and applied.

A deontological approach contributes important perspectives about the development of ethical behavior, especially its emphasis on good intentions and the inherent value of persons. A Kantian perspective is important because it guards against the relativism of consequentialism. However, critics of rule-based analysis have suggested that deontological ethics is overly rigid in requiring universal or absolutist morality. In view of the vagaries and contingencies of life, some critics argue that principles need to be adapted to the specific cultural environment and particular circumstances in which actions are carried out. Lying is wrong, but under some circumstances, so goes the argument, it might be morally permissible, such as to protect a child from a madman or to threaten massive destruction to prevent aggression. Moreover, critics argue that Kantianism is unduly optimistic in at least two respects. First, it assumes that human beings have the capacity to rationally identify appropriate moral rules. Second, it assumes that human beings will behave in accordance with known moral obligations.

Although political actions based solely on moral obligations are rare, rule-based action is nonetheless undertaken periodically in global society by states and other international nonstate actors in fulfillment of perceived moral duties. For example, throughout the Cold War era, Western democratic countries provided significant economic assistance to developing nations, in great part because of the conviction that economically prosperous states had a moral obligation to assist poor peoples. In his study of postwar foreign aid, David Lumsdaine found that the strongest source of support for assisting poor countries was "the sense of justice and compassion."[23] This sense of global compassion for the poor was evident at the G-8 Economic Summit, an annual gathering of heads of state of the leading Western economies and Russia, held in Germany in June 2007. At the summit, the leading economies promised to give Africa $60 billion in economic assistance. The international responsibility of responding to human need was most vividly evident when the United States gave food aid to North Korea, a communist enemy state. When famine broke out in this oppressive and reclusive state, the U.S. government nevertheless responded to human need by giving substantial foodstuffs to relieve starvation.

To illustrate rule-based action, I next examine the humanitarian assistance that the United States provided Soviet Russia in 1921–1923.

BACKGROUND

In 1921, a massive famine developed in Soviet Russia, threatening the lives of some thirty million persons. Seven years of civil and international wars had devastated agricultural production, and when drought hit the Volga valley in the southwestern region of the Soviet Union, it resulted in a disastrous crop failure, leading to unprecedented mass starvation. Hundreds of thousands of Russian peasants fled their rural communities in search of food, flooding major cities and further aggravating famine-related epidemics, especially typhus and smallpox. The Bolshevik revolutionary rulers recognized that the famine threatened not only the lives of tens of millions of Russians but also the new Marxist regime itself. In light of Soviet Russia's famine, the Russian author Maxim Gorky was authorized to make a public appeal for humanitarian assistance.

At the time of the famine, U.S. foreign relations with the Soviet Union were bitterly strained. After communists had forcefully taken control of the Russian regime in 1918, President Woodrow Wilson refused to recognize the new regime or to establish diplomatic relations with it, preferring instead to isolate the Soviet government in the hope that it would be overthrown. In the aftermath of the Bolshevik Revolution, U.S.-Soviet trade came to a virtual halt, with the Wilson administration refusing to accept Russian gold for U.S. imports because it regarded such gold as "stolen." Three issues in particular had contributed to poor relations between the West and the new Soviet government. First, the revolutionary regime had resorted to propaganda to destabilize Western governments. Second, the Soviet government had repudiated prerevolutionary foreign debts. Third, the Soviet government had expropriated foreign holdings without providing compensation, as required by international law.[24] Although U.S. investment in Russia was comparatively small, the U.S. government regarded the Soviet communist policies as contrary to international law and a threat to peaceful global political relations. Not surprisingly, when Warren Harding became president in 1921, he reaffirmed the policies that his predecessor had instituted. The United States would not attempt to overthrow the Soviet regime but would seek to weaken it politically and commercially through isolation.

The Soviet appeal for famine relief presented U.S. policy makers with a moral dilemma. On the one hand, the famine offered an opportunity to further undermine the communist government. For some, the Russian famine of 1921 appeared to be "divine retribution for Bolshevist crimes,"[25] whereas others regarded the human suffering as another instrument by which to undermine the power of the new Soviet state. At the Tenth Party Congress in March 1921, V. I. Lenin, the Bolshevik head of government, had warned his communist comrades that a major crop failure would weaken his regime and could possibly lead to the toppling of the government and the end of Soviet communism. Thus, when the crop failure became even more severe than first anticipated, the famine appeared to provide a means to advance the very goals being officially pursued by the U.S. government.

On the other hand, the severe famine offered people of goodwill an opportunity to respond to human needs—to fulfill the "Good Samaritan" principle of caring for human beings in need, regardless of their race, gender, or nationality. During the nineteenth century, international humanitarian relief had been increasingly accepted as a legitimate moral obligation of peoples and states, so that by the early twentieth century, famine relief was a widely accepted moral norm within the international community. For example, in the aftermath of World War I, the American people had established the American Relief Association (ARA), a nongovernment humanitarian relief organization, to coordinate famine relief in war-torn Europe. Internationally, the League of Nations, the international government system established in the aftermath of World War I, had explicitly recognized humanitarianism. According to the League's charter (Article 25), member states were expected to provide humanitarian relief in times of crisis. Other evidence of the further acceptance of global society's commitment to humanitarian relief was the establishment of the International Red Cross in 1921 to strengthen coordination of international humanitarian aid.

AMERICAN HUMANITARIAN ASSISTANCE

The American response to Gorky's appeal was initiated, developed, and implemented largely by Herbert Hoover, President Harding's secretary of commerce.[26] Hoover had played a key leadership role in developing and guiding the U.S. humanitarian relief effort in Central Europe in the aftermath of World War I; and, although he was a cabinet officer, Hoover continued as head of the ARA, the principal nongovernmental relief organization in the United States. Hoover's background and moral sensibilities made him especially well equipped to address the Russian appeal for famine relief.

Fundamentally, there were two alternative policies that Hoover and other leading U.S. officials could pursue: provide assistance and thereby help alleviate human suffering or disregard the appeal and thereby reinforce the isolationist strategy of U.S. diplomacy. Hoover, along with other government leaders, decided immediately that the first moral obligation of the American people was to alleviate human suffering. Hoover recommended to Secretary of State Charles Evans Hughes that the United States provide famine relief through the ARA, but only if four preconditions were met. First, the Soviet government had to release all Americans confined in Russian prisons. Second, the Soviet government needed to officially declare a need for relief. Third, relief workers needed to have complete freedom of movement without Soviet interference. Fourth, the Soviet government was responsible for providing free transportation and housing for American personnel. The ARA, for its part, would provide relief impartially to all persons in need and would carry out its work in a nonpolitical manner.[27] After brief consultations, the Soviet government agreed to these terms.

Although the ARA served as the major organization for collecting and distributing relief supplies, the U.S. government provided substantial assistance in supporting and funding the effort. At President Harding's request, in December 1921 Congress approved a humanitarian relief request of $24 million ($20 million for grain purchases and $4 million for medical supplies), a sum that was about 1 percent of the total 1921 U.S. government budget. By early 1922, the ARA had established some thirty-five thousand distribution centers in Russia and was regularly feeding more than ten million persons at the height of the famine in mid-1922. By mid-1923, most regions in Soviet Russia had regained agricultural self-sufficiency, resulting in the termination of the American relief effort by the end of the year. It has been estimated that the American relief effort, which involved the transfer of some 540,000 tons of food, or about 90 percent of the total, was responsible for saving at least 10.5 million lives. As Benjamin Weissman notes, the major effect of the American relief mission was "the defeat" of the worst famine in the history of modern Europe.[28]

THE ETHICS OF FAMINE RELIEF

The U.S. government's decision to permit and then directly support humanitarian relief illustrates rule-based ethical analysis, as the dominant motive in undertaking the relief mission was to respond to humanitarian needs regardless of how such aid might impact the political system. Although the U.S. government was embarked on a campaign to isolate and weaken the communist government, and although famine provided a natural means by which to undermine the regime, American leaders and citizens believed that it was their moral duty to relieve starvation. American officials made the commitment to humanitarian relief rather than to realpolitik because they recognized that international morality "obliges nations with food surpluses to aid famine-stricken countries regardless of their political regime."[29]

From an ethical perspective, the American policy was moral in its goals and methods but morally problematic in its overall consequences. Famine relief saved the lives of millions of peasants, but it also unwittingly helped keep in power a despotic, revolutionary regime. Although scholars differ on the impact of the humanitarian relief program on the stability of the Soviet regime, some argue that the assistance helped stabilize and strengthen the communist regime. George Kennan, for example, argues that the Soviet government was "importantly aided, not just in its economic undertakings, but in its political prestige and capacity for survival" by the American humanitarian assistance.[30] Regardless of how much ARA's relief program contributed to the stabilization of the Soviet communist regime, it is evident that American benevolence directly contradicted its official policy of undermining the Bolshevik regime.

MORAL REFLECTIONS

This case study suggests a number of important moral issues about both famine relief and the ethical methodology employed in developing the aid policy.

- Since the U.S. decision to offer famine relief to Russia was influenced in part by the reliance on a rule-based ethical methodology, did U.S. policy succeed in fulfilling the humanitarian norm?
- If U.S. leaders had applied a consequentialist methodology, what might have been the response to Gorky's appeal for food?
- In view of the great human suffering and political oppression imposed domestically by the totalitarian communist regime in the decades following the famine—suffering that led to more than thirty million deaths and untold human rights abuses—would the denial of food aid have been a morally appropriate response? In other words, would efforts to undermine the existing communist regime through the denial of food aid have been a moral response?
- In view of the differences between rule-based and ends-based analysis, how should policy makers determine which ethical methodology is appropriate in making foreign policy? Is a rule-based strategy morally superior to an ends-based strategy, as most ethicists contend?

TRIDIMENSIONAL ETHICS

The two ethical strategies sketched previously emphasize different ways of applying moral norms to international relations. Moreover, the alternative methodologies apply moral values and judgments to different elements of ethical decision making. Ends-based analysis judges the morality of acts mainly on the basis of their consequences, whereas rule-based analysis judges the morality of acts mainly on the basis of goals and intentions. Philosophers typically identify with the latter approach, whereas decision makers typically rely on the former. Although both the consequentialist and the deontological viewpoints offer important perspectives in developing ethical decision making, neither approach is sufficient. Indeed, both are essential in developing morally prudent foreign policies and just global political relations. Stanley Hoffmann has written, "I repeat that morality is not merely a matter of ends or intentions, and that the likely consequences of acts must be taken into account. . . . [A] morality that relies exclusively on expected, calculated outcomes is not acceptable either: no statesman can be sure of

Table 4-1.   Three Dimensions of Moral Judgment

	Motives	Means	Consequences
Scenario 1	good	good	good
Scenario 2	good	good	bad
Scenario 3	good	bad	good
Scenario 4	good	bad	bad
Scenario 5	bad	bad	good
Scenario 6	bad	good	bad
Scenario 7	bad	good	good
Scenario 8	bad	bad	bad

SOURCE: Adapted from Joseph S. Nye Jr., *Nuclear Ethics* (New York: Free Press, 1986), 22.

all effects, and confident that he will be able to avoid perverse ones altogether. Neither pure conviction nor unbridled 'consequentialism' will do."[31]

As noted previously, ethical actions typically involve three distinct elements: motives, means, and results. Whereas political actions are commonly judged in terms of one or possibly two of these dimensions, a sound ethical strategy must assess action in terms of each of these dimensions. Political ethics, in effect, should be tridimensional. Table 4-1 identifies eight different decision-making scenarios based on this tridimensional framework. From the eight possible options, the most desirable policy is clearly scenario 1 and the least desirable is scenario 8. To the extent that good intentions are important in decision making, scenarios 5, 6, and 7 are morally problematic, although scenarios 5 and 7 have some legitimacy since good ends are realized despite the evil intentions. Moreover, it is clear that scenarios 5 and 7 are morally preferable to scenarios 2 and 4, both of which have bad outcomes.

Because few public policy issues are totally evil (scenario 8) or totally good (scenario 1), most issues and problems in global politics are likely to involve a mixture of justice and injustice. When confronted with choices among different decision-making issues, such as between scenarios 2 and 3, how should the statesman decide? One possible approach is to rely on a particular ethical strategy, choosing actions that are consistent with either an ends-based or a rule-based methodology. All that is required is to select a consequentialist or deontological methodology and apply it as consistently as possible.

Another preferable approach is to make the necessary trade-offs between means and results, translating ethical intentions and purposes into actions that will maximize morally desirable outcomes. This approach is essentially the practice of *prudence*, which Aristotle defined as "right reason applied to practice." Christians have generally regarded prudence as a personal virtue that makes possible the moral life. But prudence is also used to define the practice or craft by which people weigh alternatives and then choose the one most likely to advance the common good. According to Alberto Coll, the prudence tradition, as exemplified by Aristotle, Thomas Aquinas, and Edmund Burke, has two distinctive features. First, while acknowledging the evil of human affairs, prudence insists on the ultimate authority of morality over circumstances, of "ought" over "is." Second, prudence regards human virtue and personal character, rather than religion, ideology, or worldview, as the major determinants of moral statecraft.[32] Thus, while a well-developed moral philosophy can help to structure ethical analysis and guide in the development of sound public policies, it does not guarantee moral political action. Ultimately, ethical leadership will depend upon courage and wisdom rather than knowledge and technical skills.

However, because prudential decision making provides no fixed norms to guide the process of trade-offs among relevant norms, decision making in foreign affairs can quickly succumb to consequentialism. To protect the tridimensional system from becoming simply a tool of ends-based thinking, decision makers need to follow norms that contribute to moral accountability. One useful set of rules has been developed by Nye, who argues that ethical decision making is encouraged when it is guided by the following norms: (1) clear, logical, and consistent standards; (2) impartiality (i.e., respect for others' interests); (3) a presumption in favor of rules; (4) procedures that protect impartiality; and (5) prudence in calculating results.[33] In short, a tridimensional ethical framework can contribute to moral action provided that decision makers rely on norms that protect the moral reasoning process from consequentialism.

To explore the nature and role of the tridimensional strategy, I next explore the morality of President Reagan's Strategic Defense Initiative (SDI).

CASE 4-3: THE ETHICS OF STRATEGIC DEFENSE

BACKGROUND

In the early 1980s, President Ronald Reagan called on the U.S. scientific community to investigate the possibility of developing a defensive system against ballistic nuclear missiles. In his famous "star wars" speech, delivered on March 23, 1983, the president suggested that because it was better "to save lives than to avenge them," the United States should explore the feasibility of shifting its nuclear strategy from offense to defense. Thus, he proposed that the U.S. scientific community explore the technological feasibility of developing a comprehensive defense system against ballistic missiles. As perceived by President Reagan and some of his advisors, the short-term aim of the initiative was to provide limited protection from deliberate or accidental attack; the long-term aim would be to render strategic nuclear arms "impotent and obsolete."[34]

As envisioned by some scientists, the idea of SDI involved a multilayered defensive system.

Because the trajectory of a ballistic missile typically involves several stages, strategic defense would attempt to destroy enemy missiles and warheads in each of them, but especially in the first (boost) and last (terminal) phases. Scientists acknowledged that the most important phase in which to destroy a missile was in its first phase, when the missile was flying more slowly and all its warheads were still together. Once the missile entered space and launched its warheads, tracking and destroying the nuclear warheads would be much more difficult. The other critical phase for SDI was the terminal stage, when warheads were reentering the atmosphere. According to SDI reasoning, if it were possible to destroy 50 percent of all enemy missiles and warheads in each of the four major missile phases, then only six or seven warheads out of one hundred launched would reach their targets. Although a success rate of 93 or 94 percent would still allow for mass destruction, SDI advocates argued that an increased defensive capability would greatly contribute to national security from deliberate or accidental attack.

From 1984 until 1990, the U.S. government devoted more than $20 billion to SDI research. When the program was launched, some defense analysts estimated that a modest strategic defense system would cost as much as $150 billion and that a comprehensive system might cost more than $1 trillion.[35] However, the most damaging criticism of SDI came from the scientific community, which argued that a comprehensive shield was technologically unfeasible in the near future. In an important article in 1985, four influential thinkers argued that there was no prospect that science and technology could in the near future "make nuclear weapons 'impotent and obsolete.'"[36]

The SDI also raised profound issues about shifting the national security paradigm from strategic offense to strategic defense. Would a shift from mutual assured destruction (MAD) toward mutual assured security (MAS) foster peace and world order? If military conflict among superpowers were to occur, would the existence of SDI reduce wartime destruction? In the final analysis, was SDI morally desirable? In exploring the morality of SDI here, I assess the proposed initiative using a tridimensional framework that emphasizes moral judgment based on intentions, means, and outcomes.

TRIDIMENSIONAL ASSESSMENT

The fundamental aim of SDI was to defend a country from ballistic missile attack. Because the initiative's basic goal was to develop and deploy a ballistic missile defense system that would protect society from nuclear aggression, the intentions of SDI were morally unassailable. Thus, at the level of *intentions*, SDI was wholly ethical.

At the level of *means*, SDI sought to develop a system of satellites, missiles, laser beams, and other instruments that would protect society from deliberate or accidental nuclear attack. Whereas the existing offensive nuclear policy also sought to protect society, SDI's method was radically different. Whereas MAD inhibited

nuclear aggression by threatening unacceptable nuclear retaliation (deterrence), SDI aimed to protect society by destroying nuclear missiles. In promoting SDI, Reagan administration officials emphasized the moral superiority of SDI over MAD by noting that the former would destroy weapons only, whereas MAD would destroy cities. Of course, Reagan's comparison was disingenuous, as SDI was not an unambiguous defense system. As Leon Wieseltier observed at the time, "The notion that SDI is a purely defensive system is an insult to intelligence. If a laser beam can hit a missile that has been launched, it can hit a missile that has not been launched, too. Between offense and defense, these systems are essentially ambiguous."[37] Although SDI proponents viewed the space-based defense initiative as purely defensive, SDI critics argued that such a system could also be offensive, increasing a state's overall strategic nuclear capabilities. Thus, given SDI's uncertain role involving both defensive and offensive capabilities, the means of SDI were necessarily morally ambiguous.

At the level of *likely consequences*, SDI presented even greater challenges. Using three widely accepted arms control goals (war avoidance, the minimization of destruction in war, and the reduction in weapons expenditures), strategic defense could be considered moral to the extent that it reduced the risk of war, decreased the potential for wartime destruction, and reduced the cost of military defense. In terms of the war avoidance standard, however, SDI was unlikely to be as effective as MAD because the latter policy sought to keep the peace through the threat of nuclear retaliation, whereas SDI sought to protect society by destroying nuclear missiles and warheads. As noted earlier in this chapter (see case 4-1), it is widely assumed that nuclear deterrence contributed to global order and stability during the Cold War. Given the record attributed to nuclear deterrence, most strategists doubted that a shift in strategy from nuclear offense to nuclear defense would strengthen international peace. Of course, if nuclear war were to commence, SDI was likely to be more effective in minimizing wartime destruction than in strategic offense. Because SDI sought to protect society from missile attack, SDI was clearly a more effective alternative in minimizing wartime damage. Thus, SDI was morally superior to MAD in fulfilling this arms control norm.

Finally, although policy advocates differed greatly on the anticipated cost of developing and deploying a comprehensive strategic defense system, it was clear that deploying even a modest strategic defense system would be exceptionally expensive, costing as much as $500 billion. Although the replacement of MAD with a MAS system could potentially reduce long-term national security expenditures, the transition from strategic offense to strategic defense was expected to be difficult, unpredictable, and very costly. Clearly, from a short- and medium-term budgetary perspective, maintaining the existing strategic nuclear system was preferable to undertaking the expensive and uncertain transition to a MAS security.

Thus, although SDI was morally impeccable at the level of intentions, the program's means and likely outcomes raised profound moral questions. To be sure, SDI was morally troubling because of its inordinate costs. However, SDI's more serious shortcomings were doctrinal. Because SDI tended to undermine deterrence, some SDI critics argued that the shift from MAD, a predictable and stable global order based on

strategic offense, to MAS, an uncertain and elusive global order based on an unpredictable strategic defense, might lead to greater global instability.

MORAL REFLECTIONS

When President Reagan was seeking support for his initiative, he claimed that SDI was a more moral system than nuclear deterrence because the former was defensive, whereas the latter was offensive.

- Assuming that a comprehensive strategic defense system could have been developed, was President Reagan's judgment about the moral superiority of MAS over MAD justified? Was the evil involved in nuclear deterrence reduced by the adoption of an SDI strategy?
- It was suggested above that from a tridimensional perspective SDI was morally ambiguous. Do you agree with this assessment? Why or why not?
- If decision makers had assessed SDI on the basis of an ends-based strategy, how would the initiative have been assessed morally? What would have been the moral judgment of SDI from a rule-based strategy?

ETHICAL DECISION MAKING

How do government officials make good decisions that contribute to peace and justice in the world? How do they incorporate moral principles in decision making? More generally, how is ethical decision making undertaken?

It is commonly assumed that governmental decision making involves, at a minimum, the following steps: (1) developing knowledge of and competence about an issue or problem, (2) devising alternative strategies to address the particular concern, (3) selecting the strategy that most likely will advance the desired goals, and (4) implementing the chosen policy. Rational decision making does not necessarily lead to moral outcomes, since reason alone does not assure the pursuit of justice, of the common good. As a result, moral values must be integrated into the policy-making process if it is to be ethical. Additionally, leaders must have the courage to carry out the moral action. Dietrich Bonhoeffer, the German theologian who was executed for participating in a plot to kill Hitler, once observed, "Action springs not from thought, but from a readiness for responsibility." Since politics is the art of the possible, not the quest for the ideal, a rational, detached approach to decision making is necessary to advance moral goods. But competence alone is not sufficient. In the end moral knowledge must be translated into action.

Below I first describe each of the four steps of a rational decision-making process and then outline how moral values and ethical perspectives can be incorporated at each of these four steps. I conclude with a brief discussion of the courage required to pursue the action considered right or moral.

Making Political Decisions

Some global issues are relatively simple to understand, such as the need to protect endangered species, the responsibility of nonintervention, and the need to regulate weapons of mass destruction. Most global issues and foreign policy problems, however, are complex, multidimensional concerns. As a result, developing an accurate and complete account of an issue or problem is a daunting challenge. For example, developing knowledge about the nature and causes of the ongoing Syrian rebellion in 2012 is difficult because it presumes significant knowledge of the country, including its political system, history, religion, international relations, and social and cultural life. Similarly, developing a sophisticated understanding of the nature, causes, and effects of greenhouse gases requires a high level of technical and scientific knowledge.

Once an international problem has been accurately defined, leaders can proceed to identify different approaches and alternative strategies to address the issue. The aim of policy making is to devise actions that help resolve problems or promote desired results. Devising alternative strategies is desirable because they offer different ways, involving different costs and benefits, to advance desired goals. Although policy outcomes are never assured, rational assessment of policy alternatives can help identify actions that are most likely to succeed with the fewest unintended or harmful by-products. Such assessment can also help identify the risks and costs involved in each of the policies.

The third stage—selecting the action that is most likely to advance desired outcomes—is also challenging since knowledge alone does not assure sound decision making. This is because information about issues and problems, as well as about the alternative policies being considered, is always incomplete. Additionally, decision making does not flow inexorably from factual knowledge. To be sure, information is indispensable to a sound understanding of problems and a competent analysis of policies, but data, technical skills, and logical analysis alone are insufficient to ensure wise decision making. If reason alone were sufficient, then leaders' intellectual abilities would ensure foreign policy success. But as one journalist has noted, it was "the best and the brightest" leaders who made the most serious foreign policy mistakes and misjudgments in the Vietnam War.[38]

In the final stage—policy implementation and assessment—leaders must ensure that government officials and bureaucrats execute the policy decisions. And once an action is undertaken, leaders should assess a policy by ascertaining whether the desired goals were achieved. It is important to stress that what counts in politics is not theory but action, not intentions but results. As Peter Berger's quotation at the beginning of this chapter suggests, in public life what really matters are the results of political decisions. Motives are of course important, but leaders are ultimately judged by outcomes—by the consequences of decisions taken by governmental officials.

Integrating Political Morality

Moral decision making involves the incorporation of moral values into the development and implementation of public policies. This means that political morality must be integrated in each of the four decision-making steps outlined above.

In the first stage, decision makers identify and apply moral values and integrate ethical perspectives into the analysis and assessment of issues—a process that some ethicists call "moral imagination." This task is challenging since it requires distinguishing between the moral and nonmoral dimensions of issues and then identifying fundamental moral values that apply to the particular issue or problem. For example, in confronting the looming global climate change precipitated by greenhouse emissions, leaders must determine which moral values are threatened by climate change. More generally, they need to ascertain what are the most important short-term and long-term ethical concerns arising from the global warming. And in addressing a more specific challenge, such as the 2011–2012 Syrian revolt against the Bashar al-Assad regime that had killed more than twenty-five thousand persons as of this writing, leaders must identify which moral values are most relevant to the crisis.

Although identifying relevant moral values can be difficult, reconciling the demands of competing and conflicting moral norms is especially challenging. Since most international issues involve multiple moral norms, the pursuit of moral international politics will necessarily require ethics—weighing and assessing the relative merits of competing moral values. In carrying out ethical analysis, decision makers begin by prioritizing moral norms and then seek to reconcile competing moral demands. In the Syrian political crisis, the primary ethical dilemma facing Western statesmen concerned the tension between two fundamental moral values—human rights and nonintervention, state sovereignty and the protection of human life. How leaders reconcile the demands of these two competing moral norms will determine not only how they define issues and problems but also how they respond to them.

In international affairs, some issues—such as genocide, sex trafficking, foreign aggression, and ethnic cleansing—may permit simple moral judgments. In such cases, decision making can follow a "good versus bad" approach to decision making. Although some international problems may be subject to simple moral verdicts, most issues in international affairs cannot be addressed through this process. Indeed, one of the great dangers in this first stage is the temptation to oversimplify political morality in the quest for unambiguous moral solutions. Such oversimplification is often expressed in a Manichean dualism that defines issues as good or bad, just or unjust. Although such a process can simplify policy making by offering simple solutions to complex global concerns, it also impedes ethical reflection and action. Since most international problems involve competing fundamental moral values, leaders must pursue problem solving from a "good versus good" or "right versus right" approach that facilitates the weighing of the merits of moral norms.[39]

Years ago I participated in a debate on nuclear deterrence. I was asked to defend the policy, my opponent to oppose it. Although I sought to offer conditional support for the policy based on the claim that peace and human rights were both important, my opponent, a pacifist, argued against deterrence by claiming that peace was the only relevant goal. Since nuclear weapons could destroy the earth, what was at stake, my opponent claimed, was the possible extinction of the world. Whereas my opponent approached the challenge of nuclear arms in dichotomous terms of survival versus destruction, peace versus war, I approached the task as a quest for three moral goods: peace, freedom, and security. Given our contrasting political moralities, the debate provided little discussion on the announced topic of nuclear deterrence. Instead, it illuminated how different policy prescriptions arise from alternative conceptions of the world.

In the second and third stages of moral decision making, leaders incorporate moral values into alternative policies and then judge their relative merits using moral criteria. Since such assessment is anticipatory—based on intended goals and likely outcomes—it provides at best a preliminary evaluation of a government's action. Such preliminary assessment is important but not decisive since public policies are ultimately judged by their outcomes. The decision to go to war provides an appropriate illustration of the value of a policy's preliminary assessment. In deciding whether or not to go to war, moral leaders can apply the just war doctrine (examined in chapter 7), which provides criteria on the justice of going to war. These criteria (known as the *jus ad bellum*), which differ from those governing war conduct (*jus in bello*), provide moral principles for determining whether or not a state should resort to war. The morality of going to war is therefore distinct from the morality of the war itself. And it is of course distinct from the overall moral assessment of a war once peace has returned.

In the final decision-making stage, leaders are called to judge the overall moral effect of governmental decisions. Such assessment must of course emphasize the overall outcomes of a policy. But it should also take into consideration other dimensions. As noted earlier, the tridimensional framework provides a useful benchmark to assess public policies by focusing on its goals, means, and outcomes. Although an ethical policy should seek to maximize justice at each of the three levels of decision making, achieving this ideal standard is unlikely in public life. This is because, as noted in the earlier analysis of the tridimensional framework, conflicts and compromises inevitably arise among the different elements of policy making, especially between a policy's means and its ends. Consequently, a moral politics that pursues perfection is likely to impede action rather than advance public justice. As a result, political justice requires responsible decision making, not perfect action.

The idealized decision-making model described above presumes that statesmen pursue decision making from a rational and logical perspective. I have used the rational model not only because it provides a simple and logical explanation of decision making but also because it provides an easy way to illuminate the different steps involved in moral decision making. It is important to stress, however, that rationality does not fully explain how governmental decisions are made. In his landmark study on the Cuban missile crisis of 1962, Graham Allison showed how two additional models also explained decision making.[40] He called these two alternative approaches to decision making the "bureaucratic politics" model and the "organizational process" model. The first of these showed that decisions were the product of political competition among different bureaucratic offices and governmental institutions. The second model emphasized decision making as a by-product of the established routines or standard operating procedures (SOPs) of relevant governmental organizations. Although moral values and ethical perspectives could be integrated in each of these decision-making models, the rational actor model provides the most compelling approach to ethical decision making.

Moral Courage

In May 2011 President Barack Obama authorized a commando raid on a large compound in Abbotabad, Pakistan, located some 120 miles inland from the country's border. The compound had been under surveillance for some time, and there was circumstantial evidence that Osama bin Laden, the leader of Al Qaeda, the terrorist group that had attacked the United States on 9/11, was living in the compound. Although enormous resources had been devoted to finding bin Laden, he had proved an elusive target. Eventually, agents were able to identify and locate one of his personal couriers in Peshawar, Pakistan, which in turn led them to the Abbotabad compound.

From a decision-making perspective, the president was faced with three policy options: first, he could continue surveillance, with the risk of breaching secrecy; second, he could order the bombing of the compound, risking collateral death to all those in the compound; and third, he could authorize a military raid by special forces. This third option had the advantage of limiting collateral destruction, determining whether or not bin Laden was in the compound, and if he was there, either capturing him or killing him. But the raid also had significant risks, including harming bilateral relations with Pakistan for violating its sovereignty, fighting with Pakistan's armed forces if the raid were uncovered, and pursuing a futile raid if bin Laden was not in the compound.

The president's senior advisors were deeply divided on how best to proceed. After weighing the options, the president ordered the Pentagon to carry out the third option. Proceeding with great stealth, a team of Navy Seals carried out a nighttime raid in which their helicopters were able to enter and leave Pakistani airspace without being identified. Most significantly, the special forces found and killed bin Laden and gathered significant intelligence before returning to their base in Afghanistan. The decision to carry out the raid illustrates the importance of moral courage—the willingness to act for moral ends in the face of significant risks. The decision was moral because the goal—capturing or killing the leader of the terrorist organization responsible for the deadly attacks on 9/11—was just and it was courageous because of the potential adverse consequences that could have resulted.

Based on this example, we define moral courage as the courage to carry out morally inspired actions in spite of potential dangers, harmful results, or other negative consequences. Courage is important in ethical decision making because political and moral reflection does not automatically lead to moral action. Since a gap exists between thoughts and deeds, between knowledge and fulfillment of one's moral responsibilities, ethical action can only occur when moral ideas are transformed into action. But people do not always do what is right—either because they are indifferent to morality or because they lack courage to fulfill its demands because of fear. Martin Luther King Jr. once observed that people "must repent, not so much for the sins of the wicked, but for the indifference of the good."

The leadership of Nelson Mandela, the longtime South African leader of the African National Congress (ANC) who spent twenty-seven years in prison, provides a further illustration of moral courage. Guided by the ideal of ending the racist apartheid state and building a nonracial democratic regime, Mandela became a militant political activist as a young adult and was sentenced to life in prison for committing sabotage. After the ANC was unbanned in 1990, he was released from prison and subsequently was elected president. Although his moral courage in confronting the apartheid regime made him a leader of the antiapartheid movement, what made his leadership extraordinary was what he did after he was elected president in 1994: he forgave his former enemies and pursued national unity and political reconciliation. Since many of his followers were eager for retribution for the injustices they had suffered under apartheid, political activists opposed Mandela's call for political reconciliation. While fighting the evils of racial discrimination was of course difficult, challenging his ANC followers to pursue national unity and reconciliation with the enemy demanded even greater moral courage. More than twenty years after Mandela was released from prison, South Africa today is a largely peaceful society because of his moral leadership in pursuing the ideal of nonracial democracy.

A further example of moral courage is the action taken by Todd Beamer on September 11, 2001. Todd, a graduate of the college where I teach, boarded United Airlines Flight 93 early that morning, and soon after the plane's departure, it was hijacked. When Todd and other passengers learned through in-flight phones that other passenger planes had been flown into the World Trade Center, they became deeply concerned. Todd attempted to make a credit card call but was routed to Lisa Jefferson, a telephone operator. Todd told the operator that one person had been killed and that the pilot and copilot had been forced from the cockpit. He also told the operator that some of the passengers were planning to "jump on" the hijackers. According to the operator, Todd's last words were "Are you guys ready? Let's roll"—a phrase that would become the rallying cry for the battle against Al Qaeda. The passengers then headed into the cockpit where they fought the hijackers over the plane's controls. Soon after, the jumbo jet crashed in a rural area of Pennsylvania, killing everyone on board. Although Todd did not know the hijackers' intentions, he and other passengers assumed that their plane might also be used against an important governmental center. Since Flight 93 had turned toward Washington, D.C., some observers surmise that, in the absence of the passengers' actions, the plane would have probably been used to attack the U.S. Capitol, the White House, or some other important governmental building. Todd Beamer is today regarded as a hero because of his moral courage in confronting the hijackers.

What is the source of moral courage? Why are some people more willing and able to confront wrongdoing than others? Philosophers suggest three possible answers: Kantian rule-based ethics, utilitarian ends-based ethics, and virtue ethics. According to the first school, people's behavior is guided, especially when confronted with complex moral challenges, by moral duties and obligations. The second school suggests that people's actions are guided by the quest to bring about good consequences. And the third school, virtue ethics, suggests that behavior is a result of personal character—of the inward traits and habits that have been developed through reason and practice.

Although morally courageous action may appear to emerge spontaneously in response to a crisis, virtue ethicists claim that behavior emanates from character traits. According to the virtue ethics perspective, moral action does not derive simply from rational reflection about moral duties and behavioral consequences. Rather, it emerges from the moral dispositions of persons. The virtue ethics perspective thus provides an important supplement to our account of moral decision making described earlier. In sum, ethical decision making presupposes knowledge, dispassionate analysis, moral imagination, and the courage to act.

SUMMARY

International political action can be undertaken using a variety of ethical strategies. Three major types of decision-making approaches are ends-based analysis, rule-based analysis, and tridimensional analysis. Each of these methodologies is distinguished by different emphases given to intentions, goals, and outcomes. Although each of these strategies can help illuminate the relationship of moral values to political action, the most demanding and effective approach to ethical decision making is tridimensional analysis. But integrating political morality into the definition and resolution of global issues is not enough. In the end, decision makers must have the moral courage to do what is right—to act in accordance with fundamental moral norms. Only when people's actions are consistent with global political morality can the world become more humane, just, and peaceful.

PART TWO

Global Issues

Chapter Five

The Ethics of International Human Rights

[Human rights] have become a kind of *lingua franca* of ethics talk so that much of the discussion about ethics in international relations takes place making use of the vocabulary of rights.[1]
— R. J. VINCENT

Considerations of "justice"—democracy, human rights, human welfare—would . . . ordinarily be of a lower priority. . . . The reasoning here is simple. Order is the most basic concern. One can have order without justice but not the other way around.[2]
— RICHARD H. HAASS

There are goods more important than order. There are wrongs worth righting even at the cost of injuring order.[3]
— CHARLES KRAUTHAMMER

THE NEWS MEDIA regularly reminds citizens in the developed nations that there is much suffering in many poor, undemocratic states of the Third World. This suffering—manifested by hunger, disease, religious persecution, ethnic conflict, displacement, and mass killing—is often a direct result of power struggles among political groups. For example, the post–Cold War disintegration of Yugoslavia led to a bitter ethnonationalistic war within Bosnia-Herzegovina among Croats, Muslims, and Serbs that resulted in an estimated three hundred thousand deaths and more than a million refugees. In Rwanda, the animosity between Hutu and Tutsi peoples led to a tribal genocide in 1994 that claimed more than eight hundred thousand lives and left more than two million refugees. And in Syria in 2012, the insurgent effort by antigovernment forces to topple the Alawite minority regime of President Bashar al-Assad resulted in more than twenty-five thousand deaths and displaced hundreds of thousands of civilians.

Besides politically based violence, human rights abuses are also perpetuated through traditions, social customs, and cultural values that foster intolerance, racial discrimination, ethnic cleansing, and religious persecution. For example, the practices of honor killing, slavery, child labor, and female genital mutilation are widespread in some poor traditional societies. Although laws may exist to protect people from such abuses, they continue nonetheless. According to one 2009 study, more states are placing increasing restrictions on religious freedom, leading to more discrimination and even persecution.[4]

This chapter examines the quest for human dignity in global society. Because the international community is a society of states, each with its own social, political, and economic institutions and cultural traditions, defining human rights is a daunting task. Although political thinkers have theorized about the nature of people's fundamental rights for many centuries, the task of specifying a comprehensive list of human rights began in 1948 with the UN General Assembly's adoption of the Universal Declaration of Human Rights. Since then, states have cooperated in developing treaties and conventions, resulting in a substantial body of international humanitarian law. Thus, even though global society is comprised of many distinct cultures, the proliferation of international human rights statutes has reinforced the belief defining and promoting the dignity, respect, and equality of persons as a universal moral task.

Individual rights can be defined and justified in either positive or normative terms. The positive, or empirical, approach describes those individual rights that are already claimed. Positive rights consist of those personal entitlements that are specified in domestic statutes or international treaties. According to the positivist perspective, persons are entitled to rights because governing bodies have established binding rules and conventions to give effect to such claims. The normative perspective, by contrast, views human rights as fundamental claims that ought to be universally protected because of the inherent dignity of all persons. According to the normative approach, the validity of human rights derives from the inherent moral legitimacy of the claims. Consequently, human rights are extralegal rights, deriving their validity not from institutionalized practices and rules but rather from the inherent dignity of all persons. Thus, whereas positive rights are rooted in fact, normative rights are based on morality.[5]

In defining human rights, it is important to recall that morality can itself be differentiated between positivist and normative conceptions.[6] A normative conception of morality consists of rules and principles that are considered binding regardless of whether they are in fact universally upheld. By contrast, a positivist conception of morality consists of the rules or directives that are in fact upheld as obligatory by what individuals say, believe, or do. However, whether the rules and directives of conventions, such as the Universal Declaration of Human Rights or the International Covenant on Civil and Political Rights, are part of a moral structure will depend on whether persons (as well as groups and states) believe that such rules *ought to be upheld*. As Alan Gewirth has noted, for customs to become morality, there must be a normative component.[7]

The distinction between international morality and international mores is significant because it highlights the important moral role of international treaties and conventions in strengthening the definition and enforcement of human rights in global society. International human rights directives are frequently considered part of international law but not part of international ethics. However, if morality includes rules that people believe should be enforced in global society, such directives are an important part of international morality. Thus, in exploring human rights as a problem of international ethics, this chapter examines the role of international human rights law in the quest for human dignity and global justice.

This chapter has three parts. First, it examines the nature and origins of the human rights doctrine in terms of alternative human rights theories and in light of the problem posed by cultural pluralism. The challenge of competing interpretations of human rights is illustrated with a case study on caning in Singapore. Second, this chapter explores the role of human rights discourse in contemporary international politics, focusing on international humanitarian law. Third, it examines the challenges of devising foreign policies that can aid in promoting and protecting human rights.

THE IDEA OF HUMAN RIGHTS

The idea that human beings have individual rights is of comparatively recent origin. Throughout antiquity and the medieval age, Western political thinkers emphasized the development of just political communities by calling attention to the duties and responsibilities of individuals. Human dignity was assumed to be a by-product of participation within and obligations toward a political community. However, with the rise of humanism, the modernization and integration of markets, and the political consolidation of nation-states in the sixteenth and seventeenth centuries, European societies became increasingly urbanized, secularized, and fragmented. In addition, with the consolidation of state power, government authority expanded its scope and reach as it made ever-increasing claims on individuals. At the same time, political thinkers began to emphasize the basic (or natural) rights of persons in political society, the conditional authority of government, and the necessity for limiting the power of rulers to minimize the possibility of tyranny and political oppression. The development of ideas such as these resulted in the theory of political liberalism, a revolutionary doctrine that was to provide the most comprehensive and compelling definition and justification of human rights in the modern world.[8] However, what is important to emphasize at this point is that human rights claims emerged within the context of political liberalism and were expressed fundamentally as claims of individuals against the state.[9]

Although the notion of human rights is a relatively modern political discovery, its development is rooted in a number of major ideas from ancient and medieval political thought. One of the most important of these ideas was the Stoic belief in the universality of moral reason, a concept that reinforced the notions of moral equality of persons and the priority of political obligations to all human beings. Because individuals were joined by reason, their political obligations were not limited to the city-state, as the Greeks had believed, but extended to the universal community.[10] These two Stoic ideas—the universality of moral reason and the priority of the universal community— are important because they contributed to the rise of natural law, from which the notion of natural rights first emerged in the seventeenth century.

Christianity also contributed to the development of human rights by emphasizing, among other things, the inherent worth and dignity of every person and the conditionality of temporal obligations.[11] Christianity affirms the dignity of persons not only by claiming that human beings were created in God's image but also by granting the ultimate divine gift—salvation through Jesus's atonement—to all persons. Most importantly, Christianity asserts that God has established a divine, transcendent moral order to which all human beings are subject. In effect, human beings are subject to two authorities: the temporal power of the state and the divine commands of God. According to the Scriptures, citizens should render to Caesar the things that belong to Caesar and to God the things that belong to God. However, when conflict develops between these two realms, citizens should obey God rather than human authorities. Although scholars differ on Christianity's contribution to human rights, it is clear that religion played an important role in developing the notion of human dignity by affirming the existence of a transcendent order that was beyond the control of the state.

Theories of Human Rights

As first articulated, human rights are natural rights rooted in the moral nature of human persons. This perspective can be defined as the *moral theory of human rights*, because the claim that persons are entitled to fundamental claims or rights is grounded in morality. According to this classical theory, persons are entitled to particular benefits or goods by virtue of their humanity, that is, their essential moral worth as human beings. Because human rights are rooted in the fundamental dignity of persons, they are timeless and universal. Moreover, because these rights are rooted in the unique moral nature of persons, they exist independently of the communities, societies, and states in which people live. Thus, human rights are extralegal, deriving their legitimacy from their inherent (or moral) validity, not from constitutional or legal provisions or particular actions by states and international organizations.[12]

In the modern world, the idea of human rights has gained increasing influence. As noted by R. J. Vincent, the idea that human beings have rights as humans "is a staple of contemporary world politics."[13] Whereas the moral theory of human rights provided a convincing argument in the seventeenth and eighteenth centuries, that theory has been increasingly challenged by alternative conceptions of rights in the modern world. The earliest major challenges to the classical doctrine of individual rights were developed in the nineteenth century by such political thinkers as Edmund Burke and Jeremy Bentham. Burke, a late-eighteenth-century British parliamentarian, argued that human rights are rooted in communal customs and traditions, not in abstract reason and universal morality. As a result, human rights are not individualistic claims justified by reason but rather benefits that persons receive through participation in political society. Bentham, a cofounder of utilitarianism, was even more critical of human rights by disavowing the idea altogether.[14] Because Bentham believed that there was no such thing as transcendent morality or natural law, human rights were entirely fictitious. To speak of individual rights was to speak nonsense. Because human rights were rooted in civil laws, the rights derived from the "imaginary" laws of nature were themselves imaginary.

Although political thinkers have continued to challenge the idea of human rights since Burke, Bentham, and others first called into question the morality of individual rights, discourse on human rights continues to dominate contemporary international relations. And notwithstanding the denial of human rights by postmodern scholarship, intellectuals have continued to develop alternative conceptions of human rights as they seek to develop a more compelling justification for them. To illustrate some of these different perspectives, five alternative human rights theories are briefly sketched here.

One alternative approach seeks to define and justify human rights in terms of basic physical needs. According to the *human needs theory*, persons are entitled to physical survival and security because without them, human life is impossible. Thus, human rights claims are rooted in the requirements of sustaining life and personal well-being.[15] Although this theory has the advantage of focusing on the tangible needs of human life, it fails to illuminate which physical requirements are essential. Moreover, it assumes that human dignity is necessarily achieved by giving priority to the physical dimensions of life.

Charles Beitz has developed a *social justice theory* of human rights that justifies rights in terms of distributive justice rather than the moral nature of persons.[16] According to this theory, human rights are entitlements, based on social justice norms, that ensure the well-being of persons. Beitz claims that because the classical doctrine of natural rights limits entitlements to personal security and fails to include socioeconomic claims, the social justice model provides a more comprehensive account of human rights. Beitz's model, however, suffers from two major shortcomings. First, because distributive justice necessarily depends on the cultures and capabilities of communities, human rights are conditioned by context. Second, by defining rights in terms of the distributive capabilities of a particular community, the social justice theory dissolves the fundamental distinction between government goals, such as providing welfare entitlements and individual rights.

A third approach is the so-called *constitutive theory* of human rights, which specifies the rudimentary rights that are necessary for the enjoyment of other human goods. According to Henry Shue, a proponent of this theory, human beings are entitled to those rights without which other desirable goods are impossible to attain. Shue argues that there are three such rights: security, subsistence, and liberty. These rights do not represent a complete list of basic rights, nor are they necessarily more desirable than other rights.[17] Rather, they specify the collective requirements that are necessary in fulfilling other desirable human goods. Although Shue argues that basic rights are collectively necessary to secure other goods, it is clear that individuals frequently enjoy basic rights to different degrees, thereby calling into question the mutual interdependence of basic rights.

Political theorist Michael Ignatieff offers a fourth way of conceiving human rights. The approach that he favors emphasizes the *free agency of persons*—that is, the rights that are necessary for people "to help themselves." Ignatieff writes, "Human rights is a language of individual empowerment, and empowerment for individuals is desirable because when individuals have agency, they can protect themselves against injustice."[18] By grounding individual rights on human agency Ignatieff bypasses the religious and metaphysical justifications for rights. He does this in order to avoid the criticism of Western approaches to human rights that have been associated with natural law and transcendent claims to human dignity.

Finally, a fifth approach to human rights, the *social-scientific theory*, seeks to ground human rights claims on the basis of cross-cultural consensus. Because of the high degree of cultural pluralism in the contemporary world and because of the continually changing role of mores and values in different societies, finding a high level of consensus on human rights is likely to prove elusive. However, even if broad international agreement were to be found, such an approach would still not offer a compelling justification for human rights, because a moral claim cannot be deduced from empirical facts.

In sum, although scholars continue to differ on how best to define and justify human rights, there is widespread political agreement that such rights claims are legitimate and provide a basis for making demands within states and the international community itself. Before examining the widely accepted international legal principles and conventions on human rights, I briefly address the problem posed by the doctrine of universal human rights in a global community characterized by cultural pluralism.

The Problem of Cultural Relativism

As noted previously, the international community is a society of multiple societies, each with its own languages, historical traditions, cultural norms, and religious and moral values. Cultural pluralism is a fact of global society. However, if moral, religious, and political values differ from society to society, and if human rights conceptions will necessarily reflect the cultural environment in which they are defined and applied, are all cultures equal? If not, whose culture is normative? When values and human rights conceptions come into conflict, who is to determine which interpretation is authoritative?

Because of the widespread relativity of values found in the world, some thinkers have concluded that there can be no international morality. The only morality that can exist is the morality of each particular society. If global society is simply the addition of shared cultures and morality, no doctrine of human rights is possible. The challenge posed by cultural pluralism is how to reconcile universal human rights claims with the fact of cultural and moral relativity.

There are two important points that need to be made about the claims of cultural relativism, one empirical and the other normative. Empirically, the claim of total moral diversity is simply untenable. As A. J. M. Milne has noted, moral diversity cannot be total because "certain moral principles are necessary for social life as such, irrespective of its particular form."[19] Milne argues that there is a common morality shared by all peoples. This morality involves such moral norms as justice, respect for human life, fellowship, freedom from arbitrary interference, and honorable treatment. However, every community also is based on a "particular" morality that is derived from each community's distinctive institutions, social order, and cultural values. As a result, the actual morality of a community involves both a common and a particular morality. Universal human rights are those rights rooted in a shared, or common, morality.

At a normative level, the claims of the doctrine of cultural relativism are similarly untenable because the fact of cultural relativity is not an ethical argument at all. To state that the world is comprised of different cultures is a descriptive statement. Its validity wholly depends on whether the empirical assertion is true. However, the doctrine of cultural relativism claims more than mere description. Because moral values are assumed to be valid only in their particular cultural contexts, cultural relativists claim not only that the values of one society are inapplicable to other societies but also that no moral hierarchy among cultural systems is possible. Cultural relativists thus seek to derive an ethical doctrine from the fact of cultural pluralism. But as Vincent has observed, the doctrine of cultural relativism cannot logically rank cultures or pass judgments about them. All the doctrine can do is assert that values are rooted in the particularities of each culture.[20] Cultural values might deserve equal respect, but whether they are worthy of such respect depends on the impact of such norms on persons' behavior and quality of life. In short, because it is impossible to derive morality from empirical conditions, cultural relativism must remain a descriptive fact, not a normative proposition.

In reconciling cultural relativism with the universality of human rights, it is important to emphasize that universalism and relativism are not mutually exclusive categories but rather different ends of a continuum. The choice is not between the extremes of *radical universalism*, which holds that culture plays no role in defining morality, and *radical cultural relativism*, which holds that culture is the only source of morality. Rather, the affirmation of human rights in global society will necessarily be based on an intermediary position that recognizes both the reality of cultural pluralism and the imperative of rights claims rooted in universal morality. This is the view taken by Jack Donnelly, who terms his approach "weak cultural relativism." According to him, such a position recognizes "a comprehensive set of *prima facie* universal human rights" while still allowing "occasional and strictly limited local variations and exceptions."[21] In defining and promoting international human rights, the challenge is to assert and defend the universality of basic rights while recognizing that the formulation and application of rights claims will depend in part on the social and cultural context in which rights claims are asserted.

A case study on flogging in Singapore in 1994 illustrates the tension between universalism and cultural pluralism.

CASE 5-1: CANING IN SINGAPORE

In 1994 Michael Fay, an eighteen-year-old American youth, was found guilty of vandalism in Singapore after he and several other adolescents spray painted about fifty automobiles in a high-income area of the city. Fay was sentenced to six lashes with a cane, four months in prison, and a $2,200 fine—a punishment that was consistent with the severe penalties imposed on lawlessness in the quasi-authoritarian city-state of Singapore but that seemed grossly excessive from an American perspective. Because the punishment involved flogging, a practice long considered inhumane in the West, the Singapore court verdict precipitated a brief public debate in the United States over the legitimacy of Fay's punishment. The media debate also spread to other related themes, including the relative effectiveness and morality of the Western and Asian approaches to law and order.

CRIMINAL JUSTICE IN SINGAPORE

Although Singapore is a modern, economically prosperous city-state, it is a tightly regulated society with limited political freedoms and strict social and cultural controls. Economically, Singapore is a relatively free, competitive market system, prospering greatly from global trade; however, politically and socially Singapore is a quasi-authoritarian state, an illiberal society with significant governmental controls over political, social, and cultural life. According to one comparative study of political and civil freedoms, in 1994–1995 Singapore ranked toward the bottom of the countries classified as "partly free."[22] For example, Singapore permits the detention of suspects for up to two years. It also requires organized groups of ten or more to register with the government, and permission from the police is required for any meeting of more than five persons. In addition, Singapore's police must approve speakers at all public functions. Socially, the regulations seem even more draconian: public acts such as chewing gum, spitting, or feeding birds carry a fine of several hundred dollars; there are even severe penalties for failing to flush a public toilet or eating in the subway.

Flogging, as practiced in Singapore, consists of tying a prisoner to a wooden trestle and striking him or her on the buttocks with a damp rattan cane. Although the effects of caning depend on the number and intensity of the strokes, the punishment involves intense physical suffering, frequently resulting in the tearing of skin tissue that leads to permanent scars. It is a generally accepted principle of international law that torture is an unacceptable form of punishment. For example, Article 7 of the International Covenant on Civil and Political Rights, which went into force in 1976, declares, "No one shall be subjected to torture or to cruel, inhuman or degrading treatment or punishment."

THE MORALITY OF CANING

When Fay was sentenced to six lashes, an intense public debate emerged in the United States over the appropriateness of such punishment and the relative effectiveness of Singapore's criminal justice system. The debate increased in intensity when President Bill Clinton condemned the punishment as "excessive" and called on Singapore's president, Ong Teng Cheong, to commute the sentence. In response to Clinton's appeal, President Cheong decreased the caning from six lashes to four, with the punishment being served on May 5, 1994. After an additional month in prison, Fay was released and then returned to the United States to live with his father.

The discourse precipitated by the caning of Fay was fundamentally a public debate of alternative theories of political society and human rights—a debate between the "Asian School" and Western liberalism. Had Singapore been a poor, backward, corrupt society, and had the United States not experienced significant social and moral decay in recent years, it is unlikely that the Fay verdict would have erupted in widespread public debate. However, Singapore is not a corrupt Third World nation, nor is the United States an example of civic virtue and social development. Indeed, Singapore has become a modern, dynamic economic society, providing ample economic and social benefits to its people in an urban environment of safety, low crime, social order, and economic prosperity. By contrast, the United States, the leading industrial democratic society in the world, has experienced a dramatic loss of social order, involving the breakdown of family life, the disintegration of neighborhoods, and a rise in crime. The cultural and social decay of the United States is dramatically illustrated by a comparison of Los Angeles and Singapore, cities of roughly the same size: in 1993 Singapore had 58 murders and 80 rapes, whereas Los Angeles had 1,058 murders and 1,781 rapes.[23]

Lee Kwan Yew, the former long-term prime minister of Singapore and the chief architect of the country's political and social system, believes that the social and cultural decline of the West is due to its excessive emphasis on individualism and freedom. The East Asian approach to political society has the advantage, he believes, in more effectively balancing the claims of social and communal goods with the demands of individuals. In his assessment of the social decline of the United States, Kishore Mahbubani, an official of Singapore's foreign ministry, writes, "This social deterioration is so drastic that it cannot possibly be the result of a mere economic downturn or fewer resources for law and order. To Asian eyes, it suggests that something fundamental has gone wrong in the United States."[24] Mahbubani goes on to suggest that the source of social ills in the United States is its ideology of excessive individualism and personal freedom, which has helped to undermine the family and other social institutions. The celebration of individual freedom, in his view, has had an ironic outcome, contributing to social decay and a cultural decline that now threatens the personal security and economic and social well-being of individuals. Mahbubani is critical of Western societies because he thinks that the rights of criminals have been given precedence over the rights of victims. He writes, "It is obvious that this enormous reduction of freedom in America is the result of a mindless ideology that maintains that freedom of a small number of individuals (criminals, terrorists, street gang members, drug dealers), who are known to pose a threat to society, should not be constrained . . . even if to do so would enhance the freedom of the majority."[25] For Mahbubani and other East Asian officials, American culture has become flawed because of its excessive emphasis on individual rights that has, in turn, weakened social institutions and impaired the criminal justice system.

In sum, the moral debate over caning was rooted partly in alternative conceptions of political society and human rights. What was considered cruel treatment in Western societies was regarded as necessary punishment to protect social and political life in Asia.

MORAL REFLECTIONS

This case raises a number of important issues about the conceptualization and implementation of human rights.

- Is caning torture, as the West asserts, or a harsh punishment, as some Third World countries claim?[26]
- When states hold different conceptions of human rights, as was the case in this dispute, which party is to decide whose political morality is correct?
- Does Western political morality emphasize individual rights and freedoms excessively?
- Is the Western emphasis on individual rights claims morally superior to the Asian approach that emphasizes communal obligations? Why or why not?
- How should the West respond to Asian claims that countries such as Singapore have a more stable and secure social order because they emphasize social and community obligations rather than individual rights?

INTERNATIONAL HUMANITARIAN LAW

Despite the divergent theories, competing ethical and philosophical justifications, and contested interpretations of human rights, there is widespread *political* acceptance of the idea of human rights in the contemporary world. This political agreement is evident in the large and growing body of international law of human rights that has developed through the codification of norms, rules, and directives in binding conventions. Although international human rights law first began to emerge in the nineteenth century with norms such as the prohibition against piracy and slavery, such laws have developed mainly since the end of World War II.

The first major modern international legal agreement to highlight human rights in contemporary global society was the UN Charter. Although the charter is essentially a constitutional document delineating the institutional structures and functions of the UN system, it is also an important human rights document because it specifies the promotion and protection of human rights as one of the major purposes of the United Nations. In its preamble, the charter reaffirms faith in "fundamental human rights" and then calls on member states to promote and encourage "respect for human rights and for fundamental freedoms" (Article 1). Later, the charter delineates some of the international human rights obligations that member states should promote (Article 55), calling on states to take individual and collective actions in support of these norms.

In 1948, the UN General Assembly adopted the Universal Declaration of Human Rights. Because of its inclusive, comprehensive nature, the declaration is generally recognized as the charter of international human rights, providing its most authoritative global definition.[27] The declaration does not distinguish or rank different types of human rights; rather, it affirms a comprehensive listing of basic civil, political, social, economic, and cultural rights. The inability to develop a listing of foundational rights and to discriminate between rights and worthy socioeconomic goals was due in great measure to the growing ideological conflict between the two major powers—the United States and the Soviet Union. As a result, the declaration is rooted in a plural conception of human rights, with the West championing civil and political rights and the East championing socioeconomic rights. It is important to emphasize also that although the declaration is not formally international law (it was adopted as a resolution, not as a binding treaty), it is nonetheless viewed as part of the international law of human rights, providing direction in the development and codification of human rights norms.[28]

The international law of human rights is expressed in a number of legally binding agreements. The two most important of these are the International Covenant on Civil and Political Rights and the International Covenant on Economic, Social, and Cultural Rights (see table 5-1), which together essentially legislate what the declaration proclaims.[29] Although the drafters of the declaration had originally intended to follow up their work with a single treaty, Cold War rivalries delayed its development and adoption by more than a decade. Moreover, rather than drafting a single convention, superpower politics resulted in two different agreements, with Western democracies identifying much more with the convention on political and civil rights and the communist states identifying much more with the convention on social and economic rights.

Although the UN has sought to proclaim the interdependence and indivisibility of human rights, political leaders, representing various types of political regimes and diverse cultural traditions, continue to espouse different and at times conflicting conceptions of human rights. International tensions over human rights doctrine are inevitable when statesmen proclaim divergent political ideologies. However, rather than assessing the legitimacy of the different human rights claims and seeking to reconcile the relative merits of competing theories, international organizations have simply expanded human rights, incorporating new claims advocated by influential transnational political groups. For example, new rights claims that have been gaining legitimacy in the international community include the "the right to development" and "reproductive rights."[30]

Table 5-1. Selected International Human Rights

According to the *International Covenant on Civil and Political Rights* (1966), states are obligated to respect and promote a wide variety of basic rights. These include:

- the right to life and physical security of the person;
- freedom of thought, religion, and expression;
- freedom of association and peaceful assembly;
- due process of law and a humane penal system;
- freedom from torture; and
- the right to legal equality and nondiscrimination.

According to the *International Covenant on Economic, Social and Cultural Rights* (1966), states are obligated to respect and promote such rights as:

- the right to work and to enjoy an adequate standard of living;
- the right to just working conditions, including fair compensation;
- a safe and healthy working environment and periodic holidays;
- the right to form trade unions and to strike;
- the right to education;
- the right to social security; and
- the right to participate in cultural life.

Both covenants emphasize that human rights must be available on the basis of equality and nondiscrimination.

The limited consensus on human rights doctrines, coupled with the ever-expanding list of rights, has had a deleterious effect on the moral foundations and priority of international human rights claims. Because of growing pluralism and confusion about human rights, it has become increasingly difficult to differentiate between basic rights claims (e.g., freedom of conscience and freedom from torture) and secondary rights claims (e.g., the right to work and the right to a jury trial).

This contemporary confusion about human rights was amply evident at the 1993 World Conference on Human Rights, the largest international meeting on human rights in twenty-five years. The aim of this UN-sponsored conference was to bring together governmental and nongovernmental representatives to develop a post–Cold War declaration on international human rights. Prior to the Vienna Conference, several preparatory meetings were held in different geographic regions. The most important of these was held in Bangkok among Asian representatives. The statement resulting from this meeting, the so-called Bangkok Declaration, is significant because it represented a blatant challenge to the idea of basic human rights rooted in limited, democratic government. According to the Asian statement, human rights must be approached from a pluralistic perspective that acknowledges the cultural, religious, and historical diversity of each region.

In view of the increasing conceptual pluralism of human rights, the development of a consensus at the Vienna conference among government representatives from 171 countries proved to be a daunting task. However, what enabled the conference to issue a collective declaration was not the development of greater agreement about the nature of human rights but rather a procedural decision that the Vienna proceedings would be carried out through a "consensus" in which the conference decisions would be based on unanimity. This meant that the final declaration had to be approved by all 171 governments or there would be no agreement at all. Because there was significant international pressure to adopt a concluding declaration, efforts to resolve competing and conflicting norms would have delayed the proceedings and possibly threatened the conference itself. As a result, the aim of the conference proceedings was to develop a comprehensive statement that partially satisfied each of the regional groups and many of the two thousand nongovernmental organizations represented at the conference.

The Final Declaration and Action Program of the World Conference on Human Rights, known as the Vienna Declaration, reaffirms widely accepted political, social, and economic rights but noticeably omits such core rights as freedom of religion, freedom of assembly and association, and freedom of speech. Indeed, the document places its greatest emphasis on social and economic rights, giving cursory coverage to civil and political rights. One critic suggested that the Vienna Declaration was "a hodgepodge collection of high principles, stolen wording and bad compromises" and was likely to be used by authoritarian rulers "to justify old and new human rights violations."[31]

Because respect for human rights depends in great measure on the underlying political and cultural values of the international community, the Vienna Declaration is noteworthy because it illuminates the contested and increasingly pluralistic political foundation of global society.[32] However, to the extent that human rights are approached from an increasingly pluralistic or multicultural worldview, the international law of human rights is likely to be regarded as less authoritative. The challenge for the international community is to delimit human rights and to emphasize only those rights considered essential to human dignity.

Although definitional challenges are a major obstacle in strengthening global human rights, designing policies that enhance human dignity is even more difficult. How should human rights be promoted and protected? When regimes perpetrate atrocities, who should halt such human rights violations? More specifically, who is responsible for halting and punishing such evil? Do citizens from one state bear moral responsibilities for the personal security and well-being of persons in other states? When governments carry out mass murder and genocide against their own people, how should foreign states respond? As noted earlier, one of the basic ethical norms of global society is that moral obligations are not limited by territorial boundaries. However, if individuals, groups, and states bear moral obligations toward human beings in foreign lands, it is much less clear what those obligations are and how they should be fulfilled.

Since states are autonomous political communities, the effort of foreign powers to try to influence domestic policies and alter political behavior is deeply problematic. When governments attempt to promote human rights in foreign societies, such initiatives need to be undertaken with diplomatic skill in order to minimize the threat to a government's sovereignty. State independence, after all, is the foundation of the world's constitution, and to the extent possible, major powers need to respect the independence and inviolability of foreign countries. But state sovereignty is not the only value in global society. When people's rights are threatened or abused in foreign societies, major powers may try to encourage domestic reforms through their own foreign policies. Of course, when egregious abuses occur, such as genocide in Rwanda in 1994 or widespread ethnic cleansing in the Bosnian war of the early 1990s, the need for international action to deter and prevent mass atrocities is all the more necessary.

In the remainder of this chapter I explore some of the limits and possibilities of states seeking to advance human rights internationally. In particular, I focus on the moral responsibility of states in deterring and halting mass murder and genocide with a case study on the Rwanda genocide of 1994. Given the rise of failed states and the rise in mass killings from civil wars, ethnic cleansing, and genocide, I examine in chapter 9 the increasing international acceptance of the "responsibility-to-protect" (R2P) norm. According to this principle, states have an obligation to care for their people's human rights, and when they are unable or unwilling to do so, sovereignty gives way to an international responsibility to protect people's rights.

HUMAN RIGHTS AND FOREIGN POLICY

Although UN membership requires that states promote human rights domestically and internationally, there is no international consensus about the role that human rights should play in foreign policy. Not only do states hold different conceptions of human rights, but they also assign a different priority to human rights goals in international affairs. The United States, which as noted earlier has been inspired periodically by moral idealism in its foreign policy, has undoubtedly been a strong proponent of human rights in world politics. However, its approach has also varied greatly, from the public expressions of humanitarianism by such presidents as Jimmy Carter and Bill Clinton to the democratization initiatives of Ronald Reagan and George W. Bush. Moreover, northern European countries, such as Denmark, Norway, Sweden, and the Netherlands, have emphasized socioeconomic rights through their foreign aid and humanitarian assistance programs. Still other major powers, such as Japan and Germany, have deemphasized human rights altogether, believing that the definition and expression of basic rights must be derived from the particular political and cultural environment of each nation-state.

Regardless of how states approach and define international human rights, it is clear that human rights norms play a decisive role in contemporary international relations. Indeed, a significant portion of bilateral and multilateral diplomacy is concerned with promoting human dignity through the establishment of treaties, conventions, and agreements that define human rights and specify how such claims should be fulfilled. Legal scholar Helen Stacy captures the centrality of human rights discourse in modern global politics in the following observation:

> Increasingly in the second half of the twentieth century, human rights have become the language with which people, groups, and even nation states, frame their requests for better treatment from others—whether those others are citizens, governments, international capital, or neighbors. Human rights have, in short, become the lingua franca of request; the language of human rights has become the language of demand

by citizens pressing their government for better treatment at the hands of the policy, for cleaner air and fairer distribution of environmental harms, or for universal health care or the special educational needs of a minority group.[33]

Mary Robinson, the first female president of Ireland (1990–1997) and the former UN high commissioner for human rights (1997–2002), echoes the view that human rights are becoming more important in international relations. She writes,

> A culture of human rights is growing throughout the world. Governments have taken many important steps to place human rights at the top of international and national agendas. Civil society . . . is expanding its vital contribution. And the United Nations family has made important progress in integrating human rights throughout the work of the entire system, thus enhancing our ability to assist all partners in our common goals of peace, development, and democracy.[34]

Despite the prevalence of human rights discourse, there is little consensus on the impact of human rights norms on the domestic and international behavior of states. Some scholars argue that human rights make little difference on governmental policies, whereas others claim that human rights ideals and legal claims contribute to a more humane, democratic world. For example, in *Bait and Switch*, a book on U.S. foreign policy and human rights, Julie Mertus argues that a significant gap exists between the American rhetoric on human rights and the actions taken by the U.S. government. Although the American regime has consistently proclaimed the importance of human rights, U.S. foreign policies have frequently betrayed human rights norms. Mertus writes, "Policy makers may talk about human rights now more than ever, but the talk does not lead to consistent human rights abiding behaviors and decisions. The manner in which human rights have been understood and applied threatens to strip human rights ideas of their central content."[35]

Journalist James Peck similarly argues in *Ideal Illusions* that the U.S. government has shaped and used the ideology of human rights to advance its national security interests rather than to promote the liberty and well-being of foreign peoples. He argues that human rights NGOs, like Amnesty International and Human Rights Watch, have themselves been co-opted by American governmental institutions. The human rights community has regularly highlighted human rights abuses but has failed to confront the fundamental structures of American power. As a result, it has thereby "unwittingly served some of Washington's deepest ideological needs."[36]

By contrast, C. William Walldorf Jr. argues that the conventional wisdom that human rights norms have little impact on the foreign policy of great powers is wrong. In *Just Politics*, he argues that humanitarian norms frequently play a decisive role in the foreign policy of great powers, especially in liberal democratic states. He supports his argument with foreign policy decisions by the British and American governments that ended political and economic programs and partnerships in order to advance humanitarian concerns. Since human rights concerns have trumped strategic considerations on numerous occasions in the foreign policy of Britain and the United States, Walldorf argues that human rights are an important foreign policy guide.[37]

Promoting Rights

There is no simple way by which states can promote international human rights in other countries. The idea of human rights is, after all, subversive to the idea of an international society of sovereign states.[38] It is subversive for at least two reasons. First, because human rights are, as George F. Kennan has observed, inextricably related to the cultural values and political, economic, and social structures of society, it is impossible to demand human rights reforms without also demanding corresponding changes in other aspects of society on which those rights depend.[39] Some regimes might tolerate human rights violations even though their laws and prevailing cultural and political norms affirm individual rights. However, most human rights abuses involve more than a failure to live up to domestic rules. Instead, they are a direct by-product of a deficient (often an antidemocratic) political culture and an inadequate institutionalization of human rights norms. Thus, when a government demands that another state carry out its human rights obligations, it typically involves a challenge not only to that society's governmental rules but also to its prevailing cultural mores.

Second, the idea of human rights is subversive because it establishes norms that if not implemented by a state can undermine its international legitimacy. Since the international legal order is based upon the sovereign independence of states, each government is responsible for the well-being of its people. When governments abuse or disregard the human rights of people, they potentially forfeit their claim to sovereignty. The notion of human rights is therefore subversive to the international legal order, especially when states fail to fulfill their legal obligations.[40] Notwithstanding the widespread popularity of human rights, there is a large gap between the rhetoric and behavior of governments on human rights. Moreover, the idea of human rights can be destabilizing in authoritarian regimes that abuse human rights. Although reforms in the legal system can enhance human rights, the most important change involved in strengthening basic rights is the development of a political culture conducive to a humane political order.

How should major powers promote human rights in global society? What norms should guide their actions? In devising an effective human rights policy, the challenge consists of improving rights without unduly threatening the decentralized nature of global society. The U.S. human rights policies of the 1970s and 1980s offer a number of lessons and insights about the international advocacy of human rights. In light of past experience, the following five principles can contribute to a prudent and effective human rights policy: (1) the priority of actions over declarations; (2) the necessity of developing preconditions for sustaining and protecting basic rights; (3) the superiority of quiet over public diplomacy; (4) giving priority to the development of strong, humane states; and (5) the imperative of humility and modesty. Each is discussed here.

1. Giving priority to actions over rhetoric is important in promoting human rights because the bilateral and multilateral initiatives on human rights have traditionally focused on declarations and conventions. However, the achievement of rights does not depend on pronouncements, constitutions, and international conventions. The emphasis on human rights pronouncements has no doubt contributed to the widespread acceptance of the human rights idea in global political discourse, but it has also had a

deleterious effect in fostering the illusion that constitutions, bills of rights, and conventions are sufficient for the implementation of rights. However, declarations and conventions are not self-activating. Robert Goldwin has observed that it is regrettable that so much time and energy has been devoted to creating the illusion that enunciating rights will necessarily lead to their enforcement. He writes that it is either "a conscious fraud, or a naive faith in the magic of words" to assert that recognizing the human right to enough food will resolve the problem of hunger.[41] Thus, some scholars argue that excessive emphasis on the rhetoric of rights can be counterproductive to the advancement of human dignity of persons because it can distract attention from the task of securing basic human rights.

2. Developing socioeconomic and political preconditions is also essential in maintaining a credible and effective human rights policy. As noted earlier, because human rights cannot be separated from the institutions and practices of government or the social and cultural mores of society, it is impossible to promote human rights in other societies without also changing other dimensions of those societies. Thus, a credible human rights policy must cultivate the essential social, political, and economic preconditions for human rights.

3. Quiet diplomacy is also important in devising a sound human rights policy. The reason that secret diplomacy is important in addressing human rights is that states are reluctant to alter their policies solely in response to foreign pressure. Soviet leader Leonid Brezhnev once remarked, "To teach others how to live cannot be accepted by a sovereign state." Although President Carter's highly public human rights policy elevated human rights to a prominent place in U.S. foreign relations, there is considerable disagreement over the extent to which such open diplomacy contributed to an improved observance of human rights. Some scholars argue that public pronouncements, condemnations, and sanctions not only fail to encourage human rights but frequently help to further consolidate oppressive regimes.[42] William Gleysteen Jr., a former U.S. ambassador, has written that condemnatory public statements about human rights are "one of the most tempting but most counterproductive [foreign policy] instruments."[43] The difficulty of linking human rights to economic interests is also illustrated by the failure of the United States to use most-favored-nation status to foster more humane treatment of dissidents. In the mid-1990s President Clinton sought to promote human rights in China by making economic trade conditional on improvements in human rights. But this practice had limited effect and forced the president to delink trade from human rights. Given the complexity and sensitivity of human rights, a prudent foreign policy should be formulated with care and implemented with sensitivity, preferably through confidential channels.

4. Another important element of an effective human rights policy is giving priority to state building. Because human rights need to be anchored in domestic institutions that are authoritative, sovereign states are essential in promoting and protecting human liberties. But this task can be carried out only if governments fulfill two conditions: they must have the power to enforce decisions, and they must also be based on the supremacy of the rule of law. In other words, governments must be strong and good, authoritative and constitutional. Michael Ignatieff writes, "If we want human rights to be anchored in the world we cannot want their enforcement to depend on international

institutions and NGOs. We want them anchored in the actual practice of sovereign states."[44] Thus, an effective human rights foreign policy must seek to both strengthen recipient governments as well as encourage the development of constitutional practices that are conducive to human liberty.

5. Finally, a prudent human rights policy should be modest in scope. This is true for at least two reasons: first, to minimize moral ethnocentrism and, second, to decrease moral self-righteousness and hypocrisy. In calling attention to the dangers of "cultural imperialism," Kennan has written that Americans who profess to know what other people want and what is good for them "would do well to ask themselves whether they are not actually attempting to impose their own values, traditions, and habits of thought on peoples for whom these things have no validity and no usefulness."[45] To be sure, avoiding moral judgments in developing and executing a human rights policy is impossible. However, a state that seeks to foster rights in foreign countries should proceed tentatively, recognizing that international society is comprised of a plurality of cultures and worldviews.

Modesty is especially important in minimizing moral self-righteousness and hypocrisy. Self-righteousness typically arises from excessive confidence in one's own rectitude and the certainty of iniquity in another. However, if a human rights policy is to be credible, the articulation and application of norms must be undertaken dispassionately, remembering that moral indignation itself can impair judgment. Herbert Butterfield wisely noted earlier in the twentieth century that "moral indignation corrupts the agent who possesses it and is not calculated to reform the man who is the object of it."[46] At the same time, human rights also can contribute to hypocrisy when they are not articulated and promoted in a wise, prudent manner. Hypocrisy—the pretentious use of moral slogans for national gain—can arise when a state clothes its national interests in moral (human rights) language, thereby seeking to gain universal approbation. Thus, when human rights are used to justify national interests, the credibility of international morality, and especially of human rights, can be jeopardized.

Preventing Mass Murder and Genocide

The international protection of human rights in the modern world is an especially difficult task not only because human rights are regarded as part of the domestic jurisdiction of governments but also because governments themselves abuse rights. Indeed, the most serious human rights violations in the past century were due not to war, intergroup conflict, or domestic disorder but to deliberate government campaigns of mass murder, or what Stanley Hoffmann terms "the institutionalization of cruelty."[47] According to R. J. Rummel, governments in the twentieth century were far more brutal to their own people than to foreigners. Whereas international and civil wars resulted in the death of 35 million persons, Rummel found that domestic killing by authoritarian and totalitarian regimes claimed the lives of 169 million persons, nearly four and a half times the rate of wartime deaths.[48] The two most destructive regimes were the Soviet Union and communist China, which murdered roughly 97 million people.[49]

In the mid-twentieth century Raphael Lemkin, a Polish Jew, coined the term *genocide* to distinguish killing in wartime from the deliberate effort to exterminate ethnic or religious groups. Limkin had become concerned with ethnic killing when the civilized world failed to hold Turkey accountable for the mass extermination of Armenians during World War I. After Germany invaded his homeland, Lemkin fled to the United States where he continued his single-minded struggle to combat the deliberate and systematic efforts to destroy national, ethnic, racial, or religious groups of people. Since this crime did not have a name, he developed the concept *genocide*, rooted in the Greek word *geno*, meaning "race" or "tribe," and the Latin suffix *-cide*, meaning "killing."

As a result of his tireless efforts, the United Nations General Assembly passed a resolution in December 1946 condemning genocide "as contrary to moral law and to the aims and spirit of the United Nations." More importantly, the measure called for drafting a treaty that would ban this crime. In 1948 the General Assembly approved unanimously the Convention on the Prevention and Punishment of the Crime of Genocide, and two years later the treaty entered into force after a sufficient number of states had ratified it.[50] Although more than one hundred states have ratified the treaty, the convention appears to have had little impact on the eradication of mass violence. As Samantha Power notes in her Pulitzer Prize–winning book *"A Problem from Hell,"* the United States, along with other major powers, has generally failed to use its power to protect civilians from society-wide killing.[51] For example, beginning in the late 1970s the United States failed to respond to the mass ethnic killings in Cambodia (two million deaths), Iraq (one hundred thousand Kurds killed), Bosnia (two hundred thousand deaths), Rwanda (eight hundred thousand Tutsi deaths), and Sudan (more than two million deaths). When rebels from Darfur, Sudan, demanded greater political autonomy in 2004–2006, the government-supported Arab militia (*janjaweed*) responded with brutal violence, killing more than two hundred thousand people and forcing many more to flee to Chad. Only in Kosovo in 1999 (see case 1-1) and in Libya in 2011 (see case 9-1) did the United States, in concert with other NATO powers, use force to halt and prevent mass atrocities.[52]

If the promotion of human rights is a legitimate end of foreign policy, surely the protection of life from genocide and mass murder must be regarded as an essential element of a comprehensive human rights policy. Regrettably, however, states have rarely used their individual and collective power to halt the most serious violations of human rights. For example, major powers did not attempt to halt either the Soviet communist government's deliberate starvation of 5 million Ukrainian peasants in the 1930s or to halt the mass murder of 6.5 million Soviet peasants (kulaks) who were resisting collectivization. Moreover, the international community did nothing to prevent the Chinese communist government from slaughtering more than 20 million of its citizens in the 1950s and 1960s.

From time to time governments have tried to prevent genocide when such mass murder threatens regional security. This was the case with Pakistan's mass murder of 1.5 million Bengalis in Bangladesh (formerly East Pakistan) in 1971, when, in response to this genocidal campaign, some 10 million persons fled to India. This influx of refugees precipitated India's military intervention that ultimately led to West Pakistan's political independence. In 1992–1995, Western powers failed to halt ethnic cleansing in Bosnia, but when the Balkan conflict threatened to expand beyond the Balkans, the United States helped to broker a NATO-enforced cease-fire. Similarly, when Serbs threatened to repeat their ethnic cleansing and killing toward Albanians in Kosovo, NATO used an intense ten-week bombing campaign to force Serb military and police forces from Kosovo.

Why have major powers failed to halt the brutality of modern authoritarian and totalitarian regimes? Why have they failed to protect innocent masses from the breakdown of domestic regimes and the spread of civil strife? To a significant degree, states have been reticent to protect human rights in foreign countries because they have been unwilling to challenge the norm of sovereignty and to risk war over interests not considered vital to the nation. Historically, states have used military force to protect core interests, such as territorial security, but have been reluctant to use force to pursue secondary interests, such as the welfare and humanitarian needs of foreign societies. According to Power, the fundamental reason for the failure of the U.S. government to respond to genocide is lack of political will, not lack of knowledge or lack of military and political resources. Power writes, "American leaders did not act because they did not want to. They believed that genocide was wrong, but they were not prepared to invest the military, financial, diplomatic or domestic political capital needed to stop it."[53] According to Power, what is most shocking about U.S. foreign policy is not its failure to directly intervene militarily. Rather, what is most disturbing is that the U.S. government did almost nothing to deter genocide. Since the country's vital national interests were not threatened by mass killing, Power claims that senior U.S. officials "did not give genocide the moral attention it warranted."[54]

In view of the rise of unprecedented atrocities in the post–Cold War world, UN secretary-general Kofi Annan called on the international community, in 1999 and again in 2000, to develop consensus on when and how foreign intervention for human rights purposes is permissible. In response to this call, world leaders developed a framework for reconciling the conflict between state sovereignty and the protection of human rights. The framework was crystallized in the "responsibility-to-protect" principle—a norm that was subsequently endorsed by both the General Assembly and the Security Council. In chapter 9, I discuss the nature, role, and limitations of this principle.

In pursuing a principled foreign policy, states must face the inevitable tension between two legitimate international norms—sovereignty and human rights. If states are to pursue their legitimate national interests as well as the global common good, then they need to reconcile the competing and conflicting claims of short-term strategic interests and long-term global values. To the extent that states have been reluctant to prevent atrocities, it may be because they have given precedence to national interests over cosmopolitan values, sovereignty over humanitarian goals.

To illuminate the tensions between sovereignty and suffering, power and human rights, I next examine the 1994 Rwanda genocide.

On April 6, 1994, as President Habyarimana was returning to Kigali, Rwanda's capital, two missiles hit his jet as it approached the airport. The plane spun out of control and crashed, killing all passengers. Within hours of Habyarimana's death, Hutu militia began a systematic massacre of Tutsis and politically moderate Hutus.[55] When ten Belgian members of the UN's peacekeeping mission (UNAMIR) were killed, Belgium decided to withdraw its four hundred other troops, thereby virtually paralyzing the UN force.[56] Encouraged by political and civic extremists, Hutu killing spread quickly throughout the land, resulting in the coordinated murder of tens of thousands of civilians. One of the largest massacres occurred in mid-April in the western city of Kibuye, when more than five thousand Tutsis were rounded up in a stadium and slaughtered. Although the government forces were well equipped with modern weapons, the genocide was carried out by tens of thousands of Hutus at close quarters with primitive weapons. "If people murdered with machetes," writes David Rieff, "it was because the Hutu leadership had conceived of a genocide that would involve the entire Hutu people."[57]

The genocide did not end until the Rwandan Patriotic Front (RPF) took control of major Rwandan centers by mid-June. By that time, however, the Hutus had killed at least eight hundred thousand Tutsis and moderate Hutus, making this genocide campaign one of the deadliest and most destructive in modern times. One observer has written that the Rwandan genocide "claimed more lives more quickly than any campaign of mass murder in recorded history."[58] Moreover, the RPF's rapid conquest of Rwanda led to one of the largest and fastest refugee movements ever, with more than two million persons fleeing to neighboring states in the immediate aftermath of the collapse of the Hutu regime.

THE FAILURE OF INTERNATIONAL HUMANITARIAN PROTECTION

In view of the disintegration of Rwandan society, the mass killing, and the displacement of some 2.2 million refugees, what actions should neighboring African states have taken to prevent or, at a minimum, limit human suffering? What actions should the major powers have carried out when the evidence of mass killing first came to light? Should an international peacekeeping force have been deployed, and if so, what should have been its short- and long-term missions? Which states should have participated in and paid for such an operation?

When the genocide began, the only foreign troops in Rwanda were some fourteen hundred troops of the UN observer force. UNAMIR, created solely to assist implementation of the Arusha Accords, was not authorized to use force to keep peace. Thus, when the genocide began, the UN force was unable to deter mass killing, and after Belgium recalled its troops in mid-April, the remaining UN troops were kept in the barracks. Subsequently, the Security Council, on the recommendation of UN secretary-general Boutros Boutros-Ghali, called for a reduction in the UN observer force to less than five hundred soldiers. Eventually, Boutros-Ghali reversed his views by calling for the creation of a five-thousand-member peacekeeping force. The Security Council, however, refused to support his request. The United States opposed the proposed peacekeeping operation partly because of cost (the U.S. share of peacekeeping operations is 30 percent) but also because of a lack of clarity about the operation's mission and organization. Speaking about the need for a Rwandan peacekeeping operation, President Bill Clinton said that it was important for the United Nations to learn "when to say no."[59] But other major powers on the Security Council, including Britain and France, also had misgivings about military intervention. As Michael Barnett has argued, senior UN leaders could have taken action to either halt or limit the scope of the genocide. In his view, "High-ranking UN staff and some council members either knew of, or had good reason to suspect, crimes against humanity. They had a moral obligation to urge UN action. They did not."[60]

Only one major power (France) temporarily deployed troops after the RPF had gained substantial control of the country. When Hutus began fleeing to surrounding states, France, a supporter of the fallen Hutu regime, carried out a temporary humanitarian intervention to prevent Tutsi military forces from retaliating against fleeing Hutus. The French force established a security zone in the southwestern part of Rwanda, thereby providing foreign protection for a two-month period (June 23 to August 21). It has been estimated that the French intervention was responsible for saving the lives of tens of thousands of fleeing Hutus.

However, states did provide significant humanitarian assistance to the large Rwandan refugee camps in Zaire, Tanzania, and Burundi.[61] Major international governmental and nongovernmental organizations played a key role in providing humanitarian supplies and medical aid. The U.S. government, in particular, gave significant financial and humanitarian assistance, and when a cholera epidemic began to spread among the 1.2 million Hutu refugees in Goma, Zaire, it authorized the deployment of four thousand soldiers to assist the relief effort and to prevent the spread of cholera. However, the introduction of U.S. forces was solely for humanitarian relief rather than peacekeeping.

The Rwandan genocide and the subsequent displacement of refugees suggest that, despite the claims and rhetoric of international human rights, foreign states are not eager to intervene to prevent mass killing. Even though international humanitarian law has become increasingly accepted as part of the legal and normative structure of global society, the promotion and protection of human rights is still regarded as an obligation mainly of states. As one scholar has observed, "Until the great powers in the Security Council are willing to act together, and to absorb comparatively small numbers of casualties to prevent the large-scale slaughter of innocent people, there will continue to be after-the-fact hand-wringing and emergency aid efforts. And once again it will have been too late for everything except the grief."[62]

MORAL REFLECTIONS

This case raises troubling moral issues about international responsibility for mass atrocities.

- Samantha Power writes that the Rwandan genocide was "the fastest, most efficient killing spree of the twentieth century."[63] In view of the widespread commitment by Western nations to the principle "Never Again," how could a genocide that killed persons at a rate faster than the Nazi Holocaust have been allowed to occur in the late twentieth century?

- When it became evident that society-wide killing was under way, should the United States and other major powers have intervened to halt the genocide, even if such intervention would have required a long-term nation-building program?

- When a genocide is under way, is unilateral military intervention by a foreign power legally and morally permissible, or must such a state secure prior approval from the Security Council?

- During his trip to Africa in 1998, President Clinton expressed regret that the international community had not acted more decisively in halting the Rwanda genocide. In light of his apology, who should bear political guilt over the failure to prevent mass killing—the United States, other major powers, the United Nations, or the international community?

SUMMARY

Despite significant pluralism on human rights, there remains widespread international agreement about the nature and role of human rights. This consensus is best affirmed and expressed through the substantial body of contemporary humanitarian international law. Because international political society is anarchic, international institutions do not have the authority to ensure compliance with human rights norms. As a result, the international enforcement of human rights ultimately depends on the foreign policies of states, especially major powers, and on the actions of international organizations. However, formulating a credible and effective human rights foreign policy is especially difficult because human rights practices are normally a reflection of the social and cultural values of countries. Because states normally interpret the international enforcement of rights as a qualification of national sovereignty, the international pursuit of human rights will necessarily require modesty of purpose and diplomatic sensitivity. Nevertheless, when egregious human rights violations occur, there is significant international agreement that the international community has a responsibility to prevent atrocities and protect human rights even when states fail to do so.

Chapter Six

The Ethics of Political Reconciliation

The extension of forgiveness, repentance, and reconciliation to whole nations is one of the great innovations in statecraft of our time.[1]

—WALTER WINK

The deadly cycle of revenge must be replaced by the newfound liberty of forgiveness.[2]

—POPE JOHN PAUL II

A duty to prosecute all human rights violations committed under a previous regime is too blunt an instrument to help successor governments which must struggle with the subtle complexities of reestablishing democracy. . . . Rather than a duty to prosecute, we should think of a duty to safeguard human rights and to prevent future violations by state officers or other parties.[3]

—CARLOS SANTIAGO NINO

IN CONFRONTING the crimes and injustices of former regimes, emerging democratic governments have pursued a variety of strategies, ranging from denial to trials. The challenge of how best to deal with regime atrocities—a process scholars have termed "transitional justice"[4]—will depend, of course, on the emerging regime's commitment to justice and human rights and on the political resources available to address the crimes and injustices of former governments. Some of the major goals pursued by transitional regimes include the restoration of the rule of law, the consolidation of democratic institutions, justice for human rights victims, and political reconciliation and national unity.

RECKONING WITH PAST REGIME OFFENSES

Fundamentally, these strategies have involved two distinct approaches—engagement or avoidance. The engagement approach is based on the assumption that before nations can be healed and reconciled, regime wrongdoing must be disclosed, acknowledged, and redressed through appropriate strategies of accountability. Although it may be desirable to emphasize the immediate restoration of communal relationships and the consolidation of constitutional norms, this approach assumes that healing can take place only when past atrocities have been confronted directly. Coming to terms with past collective wrongdoing is important because the failure to do so may result in latent, festering problems that impair normal interpersonal and civic relationships. Just as the failure to excise a cancer from the human body can lead to serious illnesses or even death, so too can the failure to explicitly address collective offenses result in severe social and political pathologies.

The foundation of any strategy of accountability is the discovery, disclosure, and acknowledgment of truth. There can be no reckoning with past regime offenses if there is no knowledge of wrongdoing. In effect, if a community is to effectively come to terms with past regime offenses, the public must have knowledge of regime atrocities and know which individuals, groups, or organizations are responsible for perpetrating them. While investigations of limited offenses may be undertaken by private organizations, major human rights violations, especially those involving state organizations, need to be carried out by government-appointed commissions, such as South Africa's Truth and Reconciliation Commission (TRC) or Chile's National Commission on Truth and Reconciliation. Although disclosure and public acknowledgment of past human rights violations does not necessarily lead to justice or reconciliation, scholars regard truth as indispensable to an engagement approach and essential in political healing. José Zala-quett, an influential human rights advocate and a leading advisor to Chilean president Patricio Aylwin, for example, argues that disclosure and acknowledgment of truth is an "inescapable imperative."[5]

The most widely used strategy of accountability in political communities is legal prosecution. In constitutional regimes, courts have the responsibility to determine criminal behavior and to punish wrongdoing. Once evidence is obtained, an offender is prosecuted and then punished, if found guilty. Although punishment of legal offenses raises a number of challenges, especially when crimes are pervasive, some scholars argue that the restoration of the rule of law and the integrity of the constitutional order requires that wrongdoing be publicly prosecuted. Quite apart from the long-term effects of trials on victims and offenders, the immediate impact of such initiatives is the reinforcement of the supremacy of the law. The punishment of offenders can take a variety of actions, ranging from monetary reparations and community service to incarceration. Courts and political authorities can, of course, mitigate sentences through compassionate acts of mercy or legal pardons. Although mercy and pardon have a similar effect in qualifying the punishment of an offender, mercy is an ethical action motivated by humanitarian considerations, whereas pardon is a legal act motivated by a political judgment about the common good for society.

Besides legal retribution, states also apply accountability through other strategies, such as official purges, restitution, reparations, public apologies, truth commissions, and even political forgiveness. Although these strategies are rooted in truth, each addresses past wrongdoing in a different manner. Purges impose accountability by demanding that leaders, agents, and supporters of the discredited regime be restricted from politics and even barred from government service. Restitution and reparations impose accountability by the transfer of tangible resources to victims and their families. Whereas restitution involves the return of stolen or confiscated property, reparations entail financial compensation as a sign of the old regime's culpability. Public apologies—the expression of remorse by government leaders for past regime offenses—can also foster political healing through truth telling followed by public acknowledgment of, and contrition for, past collective offenses. The most important innovations in the disclosure of past wrongdoing are truth commissions, which are ordinarily established to uncover and disclose the nature and magnitude of past regime atrocities. Finally, political forgiveness—the lifting of debts or penalties for collective wrongdoing—is also a form of accountability because the mitigation of the deserved punishment is granted only after truth has been acknowledged and leaders have expressed remorse for the offenses.

The second major strategy for reckoning with past collective offenses is avoidance or denial. Governments that pursue this approach frequently do so for a number of reasons. First, because responsibility for regime wrongdoing is often pervasive throughout society, focusing chiefly on the culpability of perpetrators and decision makers may be politically desirable but may impede political reconciliation. Moreover, because prosecuting leaders and agents could further polarize society, the new regime may be tempted to avoid trials altogether.

Another reason governments may try to avoid confronting past regime offenses is the belief that accountability may inhibit national reconciliation. Since the crimes, injustices, and structural evils of the past cannot be undone, some officials assume that the best approach is to allow the balm of time to heal the social and political wounds of the past. Confronting the unjust, evil deeds of the past might only increase resentment, distort priorities, and inhibit political healing.

Finally, government officials pursue avoidance and denial in the belief that a forward-looking strategy is most likely to prevent human rights crimes and atrocities from reoccurring. To this end, they give priority to the building and consolidation of a humane political order over claims of retributive justice. Rather than seeking to settle legal claims about past collective offenses, this approach emphasizes the institutionalization of constitutional norms and structures and the renewal of political morality. Constitutional norms are indispensable in fostering a humane political order that protects human rights, while political morality is essential in fostering reconciliation.

The two most common expressions of the avoidance approach are historical amnesia and amnesties. Amnesia is the deliberate effort to deny the past or to neglect memory. Amnesties, by contrast, are public acts that relieve offenders of their individual and collective responsibility. Whether through amnesia or amnesties, this approach focuses on the consolidation of a new legal and political order by concentrating on the restoration of peace and the pursuit of national reconciliation. Its goal is the institutionalization of a new constitutional political order by emphasizing the present and the future and by neglecting memory. In effect, it disregards the legacy of past offenses. Tadeusz Mazowiecki, Poland's first democratic prime minister, emphasized this approach when he called on his people to draw a "thick line" between the present and the past in order to focus exclusively on building a new democratic order.[6]

THE QUEST FOR POLITICAL RECONCILIATION

In common usage, the term *reconciliation* denotes the restoration of friendship or the reestablishment of communal solidarity. From a religious, especially biblical, perspective, reconciliation implies the renewal or restoration of broken relationships—between God and humans and among humans themselves. Historically, political thinkers and public officials have been reluctant to view reconciliation as a legitimate goal of politics. Because of the religious connotations of the term, they have generally regarded reconciliation as a spiritual process for restoring interpersonal relationships. As a result, theologians have tended to view reconciliation primarily as a spiritual concept relevant to an individual's relationship to God and secondarily as a process between persons, thereby underestimating its social and political dimensions.[7]

What does political reconciliation mean? Fundamentally, reconciliation involves the rebuilding of understanding and the restoring of harmonious relationships. To become reconciled is to overcome alienation, division, and enmity and restore peaceful, cooperative relationships based on a shared commitment to communal solidarity. In his important book *Just and Unjust Peace: An Ethic of Political Reconciliation*, Daniel Philpott defines political reconciliation as "the restoration of right relationship."[8] He identifies six practices that he associates with the implementation of this ethic: building socially just institutions and relations between states, acknowledgment, reparations, punishment, apology, and forgiveness. Whereas some scholars argue that the pursuit of political reconciliation is inconsistent with liberal democratic politics, Philpott argues that an ethic of reconciliation is an integral element of political justice, and more specifically of human rights, since the only way to effectively address the legacy of systemic evil is to confront the past through such practices as reparations and forgiveness.

Trudy Govier and Wilhelm Verwoerd suggest that political reconciliation should be conceived as the building or rebuilding of trust. They define trust as an attitude of "confident expectation," where persons anticipate that other individuals or groups will act in a decent, competent, and acceptable manner. When people place their trust in others, they of course become vulnerable to others, but the risk of vulnerability is deemed acceptable precisely because of the relative certainty that no harm will result from such trusting attitudes and behaviors.[9]

In *Trust: The Social Virtues and the Creation of Prosperity*, Francis Fukuyama argues convincingly that social trust is indispensable to the development of orderly, creative, and prosperous societies. He shows that countries with a high level of social capital—that is, a high degree of commitment to shared values and voluntary cooperation through civic associations—enjoy greater economic growth than countries with limited social and economic solidarity.[10] Clearly, without trust, societies are incapable of developing the networks of voluntary cooperation indispensable to participatory, economically productive societies. As trust presupposes truth telling, promise keeping, and social solidarity, conceiving reconciliation in terms of trust provides a tangible way of defining the ethic of political reconciliation.

Although conflict is inevitable in politics, deep, ongoing animosity is not inevitable. Peace is possible, hatred can be transformed into friendship, and distrust and enmity can evolve into harmonious, cooperative relationships. For example, the historic animosity between France and Germany, evident in both the First and the Second World Wars, has been replaced by cooperation based on shared economic interests and increasing trust among their citizens. The creation of institutions—including the European Coal and Steel Community (ECSC), the European Economic Community (EEC), and the European Union—have greatly increased social, economic, and political solidarity among European peoples. And the deep animosity that existed between Germany and the United States during the Second World War has been transformed into a peaceful and prosperous bilateral relationship rooted in respect for democratic institutions, the rule of law, and individual freedom.

Since the end of the Cold War, many African, Asian, and Latin American countries have sought to repair the distrust and social animosity resulting from war, ethnic conflict, insurgency, and civil strife by establishing truth commissions. The goal of such commissions is to discover and disclose information about past regime violence in the hope that such truth telling will foster national healing. Since the 1980s, more than thirty countries have established truth commissions.[11] The most influential of these is the South African Truth and Reconciliation Commission, which pioneered in pursuing truth in order to advance national healing and political reconciliation. Other countries that have sought healing through the discovery and disclosure of truth include Chile, El Salvador, Guatemala, Liberia, Mozambique, Peru, and Sierra Leone.

Even if reconciliation is regarded as a legitimate goal of political communities, leaders are likely to disagree over the priority of such a goal relative to other political concerns. Michael Feher distinguishes between two different approaches to national reconciliation and the restoration of political community. According to him, "purists" are those who demand full legal accountability as a precondition for political healing. They assume that criminal behavior needs to be exposed, stigmatized, and punished in order to consolidate the rule of law, without which democratic government is likely to fail. Purists, who are typically represented by human rights activists and nongovernmental organizations, thus tend to believe that justice must be secured for victims before reconciliation can occur. By contrast, "pragmatists," represented chiefly by political leaders and governmental agencies, tend to view national reconciliation as a precondition for the consolidation of democracy and the rule of law. For them, amnesty and forgiveness are morally legitimate because they provide a means for overcoming deep political cleavages and promoting political reconciliation and national unity.[12]

In light of these two distinct approaches to political reconciliation, how should deeply divided communities pursue political healing and national unity? Should a regime follow the "Nuremberg trials" model and seek to identify and punish the major offenders and then pursue communal reconciliation through the slow process of building democratic institutions? Or should a regime consolidate national unity by minimizing differences between political antagonists and focusing instead on the shared goal of developing, in the words of Abraham Lincoln, "a just and lasting peace among ourselves and with all nations"?[13] As noted earlier, scholars' and decision makers' skepticism about the pursuit of political reconciliation derives in great part from the widespread belief that the primary moral task of the state is justice. As a result, the prevailing worldview on transitional justice is that emerging democratic regimes should identify and prosecute offenders and then pursue national unity through reconciliation. Most emerging democratic societies are guided by the principle of "first justice, then peace."

Despite the importance of justice, the "first justice, then peace" strategy itself is conceptually flawed and often unworkable. It is flawed because the approach assumes that the pursuit of justice and the quest for peace are in fundamental tension, and that the former must be achieved before the latter can be undertaken. And it is an unrealistic and unworkable strategy because the conditions of strict justice—that is, the demand that punishment must be commensurate with the nature of the offenses—can never be fully realized. In effect, by making reconciliation conditional on the prior fulfillment of justice, this approach relegates community healing and the promotion of national unity to a subsidiary role.

The "first justice, then peace" approach is also problematic because reconciliation is not an automatic or even inevitable by-product of justice. It may be possible to rectify some past offenses and restore some moral equality between victims and victimizers, but justice per se does not necessarily foster the preconditions for community. While the prosecution and punishment of some offenders may help restore the credibility of criminal justice institutions and contribute to legal accountability, imposing some justice will not necessarily create community. Establishing a minimal order, defined as the absence of war, is not the same as creating a harmonious ordering of society rooted in a shared moral order.[14] The full restoration of social and political life can occur only when antagonists demonstrate empathy and compassion toward each other and carry out mutual actions that help rebuild communal bonds based on truth telling and trust.

RETRIBUTIVE JUSTICE

The prevailing method used by governments to confront criminal offenses is legal retribution. The retributive justice tradition, rooted in both deontological and utilitarian reasoning, demands that offenders be held accountable for their wrongdoing through prosecution and punishment. According to retributive justice theory, when perpetrators commit an offense against other persons, they destroy the fundamental moral and legal equality among human beings. To repair ruptured relationships between victims and victimizers and restore their moral equality, offenders must be diminished through public condemnation, and victims must regain their former moral status. Retribution is the process by which this fundamental equality is restored. The retributive justice paradigm is thus based on the belief that a humane political community can be sustained only if wrongdoing is prosecuted and punished, for only if offenders are held accountable can a community confidently pursue and advance its future collective well-being. Thus, if a state fails to prosecute criminals, it commits impunity and thereby destroys the moral basis of political society.

Diane Orentlicher, an international human rights scholar, argues that states have a legal and moral duty to prosecute egregious human rights crimes. Because the international legal order is based in part on international human rights law, states must prosecute individuals who are responsible for serious human rights violations. She argues that when states fail to fulfill this obligation, the international community should take action against them.[15] The distinguished legal scholar Carlos Nino, by contrast, argues that there is no duty to prosecute because such state action depends on the environmental constraints faced by the new regime. Indeed, Nino claims that criminal prosecution may risk provoking further violence and a return to undemocratic rule. As a result, rather than viewing prosecution as a duty, he argues (in the epigraph at the outset of the chapter) that the state's primary responsibility should be protecting human rights and preventing future abuses.

When atrocities are widespread, as was the case in the 1994 Rwandan genocide or the civil wars in Liberia and Sierra Leone in the late 1990s, prosecution can present enormous challenges. Thus in these cases perhaps the best that can be achieved is the trial of government leaders responsible for the decisions that resulted in crimes. But such a strategy poses serious obstacles because the evidence for criminal culpability of government officials and senior military leaders is likely to be difficult to obtain. Not surprisingly, Germany found it easier to prosecute soldiers who killed citizens trying to flee East Berlin than the leaders who established the evil regime of totalitarian communism. Even when states have relatively well-developed legal institutions, as in Argentina and Chile, where widespread human rights atrocities were perpetrated by military regimes in both countries in the 1970s, prosecution can present daunting challenges. In Argentina, for example, the democratic government successfully prosecuted top military leaders responsible for widespread killing and disappearances during the country's "dirty war." But after finding the top military leaders guilty, the government was forced to halt other trials and eventually pardoned the sentenced leaders because of the political instability caused by the trials. In pardoning the five senior leaders, Carlos Menem said that his action was designed to "create conditions that permit the definitive reconciliation among Argentineans."[16]

In chapter 12 I examine the role of international courts, including war crimes tribunals and the International Criminal Court, in promoting global justice. Here I explore the challenge of prosecuting offenders for mass atrocities by focusing on the 2004 Rwandan genocide.

CASE 6-1: PROSECUTING RWANDA'S GENOCIDE OFFENDERS

Rwanda is a small nation of about eight million inhabitants in central Africa that is populated by two different peoples: the Hutu and the Tutsi. Although both groups speak the same language, enjoy the same type of food, share similar religious beliefs, and have lived side by side for centuries, they differ in physical appearance and in the vocations they pursue. The Hutu, a short, Bantu people, have traditionally lived as peasants cultivating the land; the Tutsi, by contrast, are a taller people from northern Africa who have generally worked in cattle grazing. Historically, the Tutsi minority (roughly 15 percent of the population) ruled the Hutu majority (85 percent of the population). After Rwanda became politically independent in 1962, the Hutu gained control of government and used power to redress political, social, and economic inequalities. This led to reverse discrimination against the Tutsi, leading hundreds of thousands of them to flee to neighboring states. In the 1980s, the Tutsi established a guerrilla force, the Rwandan Patriotic Front (RPF), with the aim of ending Hutu oppression. To halt the cycle of violence, Hutu president Juvenal Habyarimana and Tutsi military leaders signed a power-sharing peace agreement, the Arusha Accords, in Arusha, Tanzania, in 1993. The aim of the accords was to establish a cease-fire between the ruling Hutu and the RPF, develop power sharing among competing groups, carry out internationally supervised democratic elections, facilitate the repatriation of refugees, and encourage the integration of the RPF with the government's armed forces. To ensure the accords' implementation, the UN Security Council established an observer force of twenty-five hundred troops, known as the UN Assistance Mission in Rwanda (UNAMIR).

GENOCIDE AND LEGAL ACCOUNTABILITY

From April to July 1994, Rwanda experienced one of the most destructive mass atrocities in history, resulting in the death of some eight hundred thousand persons. The genocide began on April 6 and did not stop until the Hutu regime had been toppled in mid-July.[17] During this period of about one hundred days the government and Hutu extremists carried out a planned campaign of mass extermination of Tutsi and moderate Hutu. Although the genocide was planned at the national and regional levels, it was implemented locally by political, military, and civic leaders and trained militia (*interahamwe*). As one observer has noted, the Rwandan genocide claimed more lives in less time than any other mass atrocity in recorded history.[18] The killing came to a halt only when the Tutsi rebel force—the RPF—had defeated the Hutu extremists.

Beginning in 1995 both the Rwandan state and the international community determined to prosecute persons involved in the genocide. After gaining control of the country, the Tutsi-led government began detaining, prosecuting, and sentencing those responsible for the genocide. And because the United Nations had failed to halt the killing, Western powers were strongly

committed to creating an international court, similar to the international tribunal for war crimes perpetrated in the Yugoslavian war of the early 1990s. Thus at the end of 1994, the Security Council established the International Criminal Tribunal for Rwanda (ICTR) in order to identify, detain, and try civic, military, and political leaders who planned and carried out genocide, an egregious violation of international humanitarian law.

Immediately after defeating the Hutu extremist regime, the victorious Tutsis began detaining genocide suspects, and by 1997 some 120,000 prisoners languished in overcrowded prisons. Since the genocide had decimated Rwanda's courts, prosecuting genocide-related crimes presented a daunting challenge to the new regime. Even before the genocide, Rwanda's criminal justice system had been judged woefully inadequate, and with the death or departure of most lawyers and judges, few trained lawyers remained.[19] Peter Uvin has observed, "The almost total destruction of the Rwanda justice system, the enormity of the crime being judged, and the massive popular participation in it, created giant legal and social challenges that some observers claim no country in the world has ever encountered."[20] Despite the inadequacy of prisons, legal personnel, and judicial tribunals, the Rwandan government was nonetheless committed to holding genocide offenders legally accountable. Officials of the new government believed that impunity was not only morally unacceptable but it was also unnecessary since the Tutsi RPF had defeated the Hutu extremist regime. The victorious Tutsis would restore the state's criminal justice system and hold genocide suspects accountable for their crimes.

It is estimated that by 2003 Rwandan courts had tried some seven thousand detainees. Of these, nearly 80 percent had been judged guilty, with roughly seven hundred being given the death sentence and some two thousand others being given life sentences. As of 2005, only twenty-three prisoners had been executed—in part because of the growing Western opposition to capital punishment. Besides freeing roughly fourteen hundred prisoners who were acquitted, the Rwandan government granted provisional release to some twenty-three thousand detainees in 2003. And to further ease living conditions in overcrowded prisons, public officials announced in mid-2005 that the state would grant conditional release to an additional thirty thousand prisoners.[21]

In the late 1990s scholars estimated that at the rate at which genocide detainees were being prosecuted, nearly a third would die in prison of old age. To speed up trials, the Rwandan government established *gacaca*, an informal conflict resolution system that had been used in precolonial and colonial times to resolve low-level community conflicts. According to the 2001 Gacaca Organic Law, the work of *gacaca* tribunals was limited to crimes considered less serious that had been committed from October 1, 1990, to December 1, 1994.[22]

Despite the promise of reducing the number of inmates in overcrowded prisons, *gacaca* has been opposed by numerous human rights organizations, like Amnesty International and Human Rights Watch. To begin with, critics argue that *gacaca* courts fail the fundamental test of justice because they do not ensure impartiality or adequate legal protection for suspects. Critics also claim that *gacaca* can be manipulated and result in new injustices. They claim, for example, that victims—whether inspired by economic greed, personal revenge, or political pressures—can make untrue accusations that result in the unjust detention of others. For their part, detainees may be so eager to confess to reduce their sentence or gain early release from prison that their testimony is incomplete or untruthful and their apology inauthentic. Indeed, false confessions can potentially implicate others and lead to new detentions. Most importantly, human rights groups have opposed *gacaca* because they perceive it as "victor's justice"—Tutsi war crimes are exempted from *gacaca* courts.

The ICTR has also played an important role in prosecuting top leaders who had fled the country after the Tutsis had taken control of the state. Originally, the Rwandan government had favored the ICTR, but once it began to take shape, the government opposed it.[23] Thus, from the inception of the ICTR in the late 1990s, relations between the ICTR and the Rwandan government have been distant and at times uncooperative.

Despite having a large staff (about eight hundred persons) and a large budget (expenditures in the court's first ten years exceeded $1 billion), the ICTR's achievements have been modest, if not disappointing. As of 2011, the tribunal had arrested some eighty-three genocide suspects, tried forty-nine of them, and convicted thirty-nine.[24] Those convicted involve one prime minister, four ministers, one prefect, four bourgmesters, two militia leaders, four businessmen, a doctor, a pastor, and three media personnel.[25] It has been estimated that the cost for trying each genocide detainee was about $40 million. Whereas it took the ICTR several years before it had its first conviction, the Nuremberg military tribunal, by contrast, completed its work in little more than a year.[26]

Not only has the ICTR been inefficient and costly, but the trials have had little direct impact on Rwanda. One reason for this is the location of the tribunal in neighboring Tanzania. Although Arusha is only about four hundred miles from Kigali, travel between the two cities is costly and difficult. As a result, the events at the tribunal are seldom reported and they rarely become news, except when a suspect is released or given a light sentence. Another obstacle to engaging Rwandan society is the court's failure to use the Kinyarwandan language, further impeding the dissemination of the court's proceedings. Since the ICTR's founding document specified political reconciliation as one of its major goals,[27] the failure of the tribunal to significantly impact Rwandan society has been regrettable.

Despite administrative problems, the major shortcoming of the ICTR is not inefficiency but the inadequacy of the criminal justice system itself in dealing with society-wide atrocities. As noted earlier, judicial institutions are designed to hold individuals responsible for periodic illegal behavior. But when hundreds of thousands of people participate in an orgy of mass violence, how can individual responsibility be assigned?

Helena Cobban asks, "How can one apply conventional methods of legal judgment to the great mass of the Hutu people who were caught up in a profoundly abnormal reality"?[28] Moreover, how does the quest for human rights trials advance individual healing and communal reconciliation? Some critics of trials claim that the persistent demand for legal prosecution of genocide suspects may only destabilize a fragile regime and exacerbate the quest for peace and communal healing. According to Cobban, the persistent demand by the international community for human rights trials has tended to aggravate some of Rwanda's problems and unnecessarily limit its policy options.[29]

MORAL REFLECTIONS

Despite the desirability of holding offenders legally accountable for criminal wrongdoing, the Rwandan experience with legal prosecution raises a number of important issues about the nature, purpose, and scope of trials:

- What should be the fundamental purpose of trials for mass atrocities—punishment or prevention, justice or reconciliation?
- Is Rwanda's retributive strategy a form of "victor's justice" or a way of restoring the moral foundation of Rwandan political society?
- Are *gacaca* courts beneficial even though they are based on crude, imperfect procedures? Are these traditional neighborhood courts morally warranted even though their operation might result in some injustices?
- Has the ICTR contributed to justice in Rwanda and to the rule of law in global society? In view of the high cost, the limited number of prosecutions of top genocide planners, and the tribunal's limited impact on Rwandan society, is the ICTR nonetheless morally justified?

RESTORATIVE JUSTICE

Given the limits of legal retribution, a growing number of scholars and public officials have relied on a restorative conception of justice—a perspective that emphasizes healing and restoration rather than punishment. Unlike retributive justice, which places a premium on individual rights and the prosecution and punishment of offenders, restorative justice emphasizes the restoration of communal bonds through social and political reconciliation. Its aim is not to right wrongs, but to restore a stable social and political order. Whereas retribution focuses chiefly on objective wrongdoing, restorative justice emphasizes the transformation of subjective factors that impair community, such as anger, resentment, and desire for vengeance.[30]

Some have suggested that restorative justice is simply a strategy of easy reconciliation, seeking to create a new beginning without coming to terms with the past. But restorative justice does not disregard past wrongdoing. Rather, it seeks to describe comprehensively and fully the truth about past offenses, recognizing that antagonists may have widely divergent perspectives about the nature, causes, and culpability for past offenses. To the extent that the parties can agree on the awful truth about past crimes and injustices, the restorative justice perspective encourages individuals, groups, and institutions to admit culpability, express repentance, and authenticate remorse through acts of reparation and restitution. At the same time, restorative justice deemphasizes the division of society into perpetrators and victims, preferring instead to view most or all of society as victims or survivors.

President Abraham Lincoln illustrates the restorative approach through his efforts to foster the political healing of the United States from the injustices of slavery and the bitter, destructive Civil War. Rather than seeking legal retribution against political and military leaders of the Confederacy, Lincoln's strategy called for reconciliation among all peoples.[31] Mahmood Mamdani similarly assumes that in the aftermath of deadly political violence, such as Rwanda's 1994 genocide, a restorative approach offers the most promising hope for healing and peacekeeping. He suggests that communal healing, what he terms "survivor's justice," must be based on changes in the underlying political institutions that have permitted ongoing political violence. Thus, rather than focusing on the culpability of individual perpetrators, Mamdani suggests that the fundamental blame for the genocide should be placed on the underlying rules and practices of the political regime.[32] Accordingly, he suggests that victims, but not offenders, should be identified and acknowledged because identifying perpetrators would lead to excessive focus on their culpability, thereby detracting from the needed cultural and political reforms necessary for promoting reconciliation.

It is important to stress that restorative justice is not an attempt to bypass the rule of law. Although the restorative approach does not demand adherence to strict legalism, it nevertheless demands truth telling coupled with contrition as the way to heal individual and collective injuries. Offenses have resulted in a moral inequality between perpetrators and victims, so restorative justice seeks to restore the moral equality of citizens—not through the law but through the moral reformation of persons. This is achieved when offenders acknowledge their responsibility and victims refrain from vengeance and acknowledge empathy toward their former enemies. Although morally demanding, such behaviors have the effect of liberating victims from being captive to anger and resentment. In effect, such attitudinal and behavioral changes result in moral autonomy for both offenders and victims.

If the preconditions of restorative justice are fulfilled, individuals and communities may grant individual and collective forgiveness. Such forgiveness, which is likely to occur only when offenders' contrition is viewed as authentic, would be expressed by canceling legitimate claims of restitution and retribution. Although individual forgiveness is essential to the moral rehabilitation of victims as well as the restoration of communal bonds, such forgiveness will not necessarily abrogate legal claims for punishment and reparations. Indeed, offenders should be prepared, as an expression of the authenticity of their remorse, to accept a state's legal punishment. In effect, political forgiveness may modify and reduce, but not abrogate, the claims of legal retribution. More importantly, forgiveness increases the possibility of reconciliation. But whether the renewal and restoration of relationships results in reconciliation is up to the individuals and collectivities. Restorative justice creates the environmental context in which communal bonds can be restored, but whether or not such restoration occurs depends on the voluntary actions of individuals and political groups.

In the aftermath of collective atrocities, the only effective way of confronting systemic human rights abuses and preventing their repetition is through a comprehensive strategy of moral reconstruction and political renewal. Only through a multidimensional strategy that seeks to restore legal, social, cultural, political, and spiritual life are peace and justice likely to be realized. Legal retribution can, of course, contribute to regime accountability for egregious state crimes and injustices, but legalism alone cannot achieve the moral reconstruction necessary to restore a broken and divided society. Ernesto Sábato, the distinguished head of Argentina's truth commission, observed in his prologue to the commission's report *Nunca Más* (Never Again) that the commissioners were not in search of "vindictiveness or vengeance," but "truth and justice." In his view, courts should pursue their "transcendent mission" based on a strategy of truth and justice because national reconciliation is possible only if the guilty repent and justice is based on truth.[33]

One of the most important efforts to apply the restorative justice paradigm to regime offenses is the South African Truth and Reconciliation Commission (TRC). This body was created to investigate gross human rights violations of the apartheid era in the belief that the disclosure of past offenses would contribute to political reconciliation and national unity.

CASE 6-2: SOUTH AFRICAN RECONCILIATION THROUGH TRUTH AND REPARATIONS

THE APARTHEID REGIME

In 1948, the National Party (NP), the political party of the Afrikaner (Boer) people, gained control of parliament. For the next forty-four years they would govern the Republic of South Africa. Although racial discrimination and segregation had characterized South Africa since colonization in the mid-seventeenth century,[34] the Afrikaners established a far more comprehensive and pervasive system of racial segregation. Indeed, this program—known as apartheid, or separate development—imposed the most far-reaching racial engineering ever practiced in the modern world.[35] For example, the government imposed more stringent racial segregation by forcing the relocation of more than 3.5 million persons between 1960 and 1983. These forced removals further intensified the problem of overpopulation in the already crowded all-black Bantu homelands, increasing the proportion of the total African population in the homelands from 40 percent in 1950 to 53 percent in 1980.

As a result of the growing social, economic, and political inequalities in South African society, black political opposition to the apartheid regime increased. At first, the political opposition was limited chiefly to the actions of labor groups and the two major African opposition groups—the African National Congress (ANC) and the Pan-African Congress (PAC). But in the 1970s, political opposition efforts intensified both domestically and internationally. In 1973, the United Nations General Assembly declared apartheid "a crime against humanity," and four years later the Security Council imposed trade sanctions (an arms embargo) on South Africa as a way to foment political reform. As domestic and international condemnation of apartheid increased, the South African regime began to carry out modest structural reforms in the early 1980s.[36] Rather than mollifying public opinion, reforms only intensified the opposition's political demands. In response to growing violence, the government imposed a state of emergency that gave security forces increased authority to detain political opponents and use force against those threatening public order. The intensification of the liberation campaign is demonstrated by the growth in political violence, rising from seven thousand deaths during the 1960–1989 period to more than fourteen thousand during the

1990–1994 period preceding the establishment of multiracial democracy in April 1994.[37]

ESTABLISHING MULTIRACIAL DEMOCRACY

In February 1990, President F. W. de Klerk set in motion a reform process that would culminate four years later in the election of Nelson Mandela as president of a new multiracial democratic regime. The transition began with lifting the ban on the ANC and other opposition political groups, releasing Nelson Mandela and other political prisoners, and the partial lifting of the state of emergency. Following two years of intense negotiations among the country's political elites, especially the governing NP and the ANC, delegates to the Convention for a Democratic South Africa (CODESA) signed an interim constitution in November 1993 that established the basis for a transitional government. According to the interim constitution, the transitional Government of National Unity was tasked with establishing a permanent constitution and creating the preconditions for national unity.

Fundamentally, South Africa could have pursued one of three strategies in confronting past crimes and injustices: amnesia, punishment, or truth telling. The first strategy, based on forgetting and denial, would seek to draw a line between the present and the past, and would concentrate all political and economic resources on the consolidation of constitutional democracy. The second strategy, legal retribution, would demand full legal accountability for past offenses, believing that the consolidation of democracy and the rule of law were impossible without the prosecution and punishment of offenders. The third strategy, the one adopted by South Africa, represented an intermediary approach between the extremes of impunity and comprehensive trials, between denial and retribution. Following the psychoanalytic model of mental health, it assumed that acknowledging the truth about the past was indispensable to healing society and consolidating constitutional government. As a result, it placed retributive justice at the service of truth, and to maximize its discovery and disclosure, conditional amnesty was offered to offenders who fully confessed

their culpability. Fundamentally, South Africa's "third way" strategy combined a backward-looking focus on truth telling and accountability with a forward-looking emphasis on the moral restoration of society and the promotion of national unity.[38]

South African leaders selected the third strategy in great part because it reflected a political compromise among the major political forces in the country, but also because they believed that neither historical amnesia nor trials provided options conducive to national healing. Indeed, based on the experiences of previous truth commissions, they assumed that it was most likely to foster the consolidation of a democratic order, contribute to the restoration and healing of victims, and encourage national reconciliation. As viewed by leaders, traditional legal and political strategies rooted in retributive justice were unlikely to foster unity and national reconciliation. What was needed was an alternative strategy that gave priority to the healing of victims, the public acknowledgment of past crimes and injustices, and the restoration of communal bonds. Such an approach would provide a demanding multidimensional strategy that emphasized legal accountability yet called for political accommodation, social reconciliation, and the moral reconstruction of society. The 1993 interim constitution's postamble captured the spirit of this strategy when it declared "a need for understanding but not for vengeance, a need for reparation but not for retaliation, a need for *ubuntu* but not for victimization."[39]

In his book on the TRC, Archbishop Desmond Tutu, the commission's chairman, claims that it would have been unwise, indeed impossible, to impose retribution, or what he terms "the Nuremberg trial paradigm,"[40] on South Africa. Due to South Africa's limited political and economic resources, it was imperative that it use them with care in the consolidation of new democratic structures by balancing different claims, including "justice, accountability, stability, peace, and reconciliation."[41] In Tutu's view, applying retributive justice would have placed an undue burden on the nation's courts and would have given little emphasis to the restoration of victims and the promotion of political reconciliation. Tutu instead advocated the strategy of restorative justice, believing that such an approach would best pursue political healing and justice. For him, restorative justice was the preferred strategy because it promoted communal solidarity and social harmony by seeking to restore broken relationships, heal victims, and rehabilitate perpetrators. Most importantly, for Tutu, restorative justice was consistent with the African social tradition of *ubuntu*, which placed a premium on harmony, friendliness, and community.[42]

THE TRC

In mid-1995, the South African parliament passed the Promotion of National Unity and Reconciliation Act, which called for the establishment of a truth commission. As conceived by this parliamentary act, the major purpose for creating the TRC was to uncover knowledge about past gross human rights violations in the belief that public acknowledgment of such truth would contribute to the consolidation of democratic society and promote national unity and reconciliation.[43]

The seventeen-member commission—led by Archbishop Desmond Tutu, the 1994 recipient of the Nobel Peace Prize—was divided into three committees.[44] The Human Rights Violations Committee focused on human rights violations, the Amnesty Committee was responsible for determining which applicants would receive amnesty, and the Reparation and Rehabilitation Committee was responsible for making recommendations on financial and other assistance to human rights victims as well as offering suggestions on how to foster national healing.

The Human Rights Violations Committee pursued factual truth by gathering evidence about gross human rights violations that were perpetrated during the apartheid era by state security officials as well as by members of the liberation movement. More than 22,000 victim statements were completed and some 160 victims' hearings were held throughout the country, involving more than 1,200 victims and their families. These hearings were widely publicized by the media and left an indelible impact on South African society. Based on the evidence accumulated through investigations, victim statements, and institutional hearings, the TRC published its

findings and recommendations in a five-volume report, released in October 1998.

One of the most significant, yet problematic, elements of the TRC process was the provision of conditional amnesty to offenders. The logic for the amnesty was set forth in the interim constitution's postamble, which declared that, "in order to advance such reconciliation and reconstruction [of society], amnesty should be granted in respect of acts, omissions and offences with political objectives and committed in the course of the conflicts of the past." Since truth was considered essential to individual and collective healing, political leaders believed the investigation and disclosure of past injustices and gross human rights was indispensable to the moral reconstruction of society. To encourage perpetrators' confessions, the TRC promised amnesty to those who fully confessed politically motivated crimes.[45] Of the more than seven thousand persons who applied for amnesty, however, only about twelve hundred were granted amnesty.[46]

Compared with other truth commissions, the TRC is undoubtedly the most elaborate and influential truth commission ever established. To begin with, it functioned much longer than most other commissions.[47] Second, because the commission was created by an act of parliament and not by a decision of the executive, the TRC had significant authority. For example, it could subpoena witnesses, compel disclosure of information from governmental agencies, requisition documents from organizations, and even disclose the names of alleged perpetrators.[48] Third, unlike most other commissions, which have carried out their investigation in secrecy, the TRC carried out its work openly, providing much media coverage of the human rights hearings. Finally, the TRC had the authority to grant amnesty to offenders who confessed their politically motivated crimes, provided their disclosure was complete.

THE ETHICS OF THE TRC

Scholars and activists have raised a number of concerns about the TRC model of transitional justice. For example, some TRC critics have questioned the legitimacy of the restorative justice paradigm, claiming that such a model undermines core societal norms (such as accountability, blame, and punishment) essential in building a stable, humane society. They claim that if societies fail to identify and condemn evil, the consolidation of human rights will be thwarted. Others claim that fidelity to the law requires not only prosecution of crimes of violence but also the condemnation of the immoral laws and unjust structures and the prosecution of leaders who were responsible for their enactment. John Dugard, for example, critiques the TRC for minimizing the "memory of apartheid" by failing to hold leaders accountable for the establishment of the immoral rules of apartheid.[49] Archbishop Tutu, however, claims that trials would have been expensive and would have diverted political attention from the pressing need to consolidate constitutionalism and foster job creation. In his view, the forward-looking restorative justice paradigm offered the advantage of diverting scarce resources to the consolidation of democratic institutions and the promotion of national unity by balancing the claims of justice, accountability, stability, peace, and reconciliation.[50]

Critics have also challenged the legitimacy of reconciliation as a public policy goal. As noted earlier, a number of scholars have called into question the need to deliberately promote national unity and political reconciliation. Rajeev Bhargava, for example, writes that rather than promoting reconciliation through public policies, societies should promote a limited public order—or what he terms "a minimally decent society." He claims that reconciliation is an excessively demanding political goal.[51] Crocker similarly argues that reconciliation is a potentially dangerous and undemocratic doctrine because it could threaten individual rights. For Crocker, as well as for other scholars committed to political liberalism, the only legitimate way to reckon with past atrocities is through "democratic reciprocity."[52] But democratic procedures do not necessarily or automatically foster community. Indeed, electoral democracy may, as Fareed Zakaria has noted, exacerbate political tensions and weaken community.[53] As a result,

rather than enhancing individual freedom, democratic procedures might in fact impede communal solidarity and thereby threaten human rights. Thus, since democratic decision making presupposes a stable, unified community,[54] the consolidation of democracy is likely to occur only if national unity is strengthened through the cultivation of shared values and the development of strong institutions.

TRC critics have also expressed concerns about the presumed healing properties of truth. Truth commissions are based on the premise that knowledge of the past, coupled with the acknowledgment of the truth, will contribute to the healing of victims, the promotion of peace, and the restoration of communal relationships. Building on the biblical admonition that if people know the truth, it will set them free (John 8:32), truth commissions have pursued investigations into regime wrongdoing in the hope that such knowledge would foster individual and collective healing. The TRC, for example, is based on the belief that truth and reconciliation are inextricably linked—that the disclosure of past wrongs contributes to personal healing and communal reconciliation. If truth is to foster reconciliation, both factual and interpretive knowledge will be needed. Indeed, knowledge of the past can contribute to political healing only when it is widely known and shared and, most importantly, when victims and offenders individually and collectively confront the painful past by "working through" the legacy of suffering, anger, and guilt.[55] Of course, while truth telling may not be a sufficient condition for reconciliation, it most surely is a necessary element insofar as knowledge of the past permits individuals and collectives to confront their responsibility for past injustices.

Finally, TRC critics have alleged that the model failed to distinguish between the atrocities committed by the state and those committed by the liberation movement. Although the military conflict between the state security forces and the ANC guerrillas (Umkhonto we Sizwe, or MK)[56] was a covert, unconventional war, the TRC believed that the rules of war were nonetheless applicable to such a conflict. In particular, it viewed terror, civilian killings, abductions, and torture not only as gross human rights violations but also as violations of the laws of war.[57] Accordingly, it believed that it was morally obligated to investigate all major human rights abuses, regardless of who had perpetrated the crimes. As TRC vice chairperson Alex Boraine observed, "The goal of the TRC was to hold up a mirror to reflect the complete picture. In particular, its objective was to identify all victims in the conflict and to confront all perpetrators of gross human rights violations."[58]

ANC leaders took strong exception to the TRC approach of treating all political violence alike. Instead, they claimed that it was imperative to distinguish between the crimes and injustices of an evil, discriminatory system and the military operations of a liberation movement. Not only was the idea of moral equivalence morally problematic; it was also counterproductive to the healing and restoration of South Africa. Accordingly, ANC leaders tried to influence the TRC's findings and conclusions, and when this failed, they unsuccessfully sought a court injunction to halt the publication of the TRC final report. According to deputy president Thabo Mbeki and other ANC leaders, the fundamental charge was that the TRC, by calling attention to the crimes and abuses of the MK, was attempting to criminalize the liberation struggle. According to Mbeki, the TRC's emphasis on the MK's crimes and abuses gave the impression that "the struggle for liberation was itself a gross violation of human rights."[59]

Another contentious element of the TRC theory was the offer of conditional amnesty to offenders who confessed. Since many victims' families were eager to bring to trial political leaders and security agents who were responsible for killings and abductions, the offer of conditional amnesty was deeply offensive to some human rights activists and victims. As a result, the amnesty provision (Section 20-7 of the TRC Act) was challenged before the country's Constitutional Court. The court, however, unanimously upheld the provision.[60] This meant that perpetrators who had committed politically motivated crimes during the apartheid era could be exempt from criminal or civil liability.

In sum, South Africa's truth and reconciliation experiment represents the most successful governmental initiative to promote peace and harmony through the discovery and acknowledgment of truth. Perhaps South Africa could have pursued the consolidation of multiracial democracy through amnesia and pardon or through trials of former regime leaders. Either strategy would have no doubt compromised essential goals since amnesia would have disregarded the past and retribution would have diverted scarce resources away from the quest for national unity and political reconciliation. Since the foundation for authentic reconciliation is truth telling, the TRC's focus on the disclosure and acknowledgment of truth helped nurture a moral basis for pursuing the consolidation of communal solidarity. Of course, truth telling could not ensure peace, but without it, long-term communal unity and peace would have been impossible. As one TRC official observed, "While truth may not always lead to reconciliation, there can be no genuine, lasting reconciliation without truth."[61] This point was reinforced by a *New York Times* editorial that lauded the commission's work as the most "comprehensive and unsparing examination of a nation's ugly past" that any truth commission has produced thus far. "No commission can transform a society as twisted as South Africa's was," the editorial goes on, "but the Truth Commission is the best effort the world has seen and South Africa is the better for it."[62]

The South African TRC process did not call for either individual or political forgiveness. Individuals could—and did—forgive perpetrators, but this act was entirely personal. Moreover, the TRC did not call on Afrikaner organizations to repent or on victims' groups to forgive. Rather, the TRC established a process that focused on the disclosure of individual and collective offenses in the hope that such confession would create a psychologically and politically safe environment that might foster empathy, compassion, and reconciliation among antagonists. To be sure, whether or not individual victims chose to forgive was entirely a personal decision. The TRC, however, did offer conditional amnesty (limited institutional forgiveness) to perpetrators who confessed their wrongdoing. And while this partial forgiveness depended solely on truth telling and not on repentance, it nonetheless helped foster a public dialogue where healing, restoration, and reconciliation were emphasized.

In the final analysis, the significance of the South African experiment in transitional justice is not measured solely by the extent of truth, national unity, and political reconciliation achieved within the country. Rather, it also depends on the extent to which restorative justice is accepted as an effective strategy in confronting and overcoming past regime offenses. Judged by that standard, the TRC model provides one of the most promising innovations in moral politics in modern times.

MORAL REFLECTIONS

Despite South Africa's noteworthy peaceful consolidation of multiracial democracy, the country's strategy of reckoning with past politically inspired offenses raises a number of important issues about the nature and role of moral values in pursuing reconciliation in the aftermath of systemic injustices:

- Does the quest for truth morally justify amnesty for perpetrators? Does the quest for national unity through truth telling justify overriding victims' demand for justice?
- What is the appropriate balance between backward-looking memory and forward-looking hope, between the discovery and disclosure of past offenses and the consolidation of constitutional government? How can the goal of accountability through a backward-looking quest for truth be reconciled with a forward-looking quest for political healing and reconciliation?
- Is the quest for political reconciliation a morally legitimate goal, especially when the search for communal healing is based on the disclosure and acknowledgment of truth rather than trials?
- Is restorative justice a morally legitimate strategy in confronting past regime offenses? Is this approach a valid alternative to the more widely accepted strategy of legal retribution? Does the restorative model provide adequate accountability and memory?

RECONCILIATION THROUGH POLITICAL FORGIVENESS

In the 1990s, a number of scholars began to explore the potential role of forgiveness in politics and, in particular, how such an idea might contribute to the healing of nations in the aftermath of widespread injustice and criminal wrongdoing. Hannah Arendt once observed that the only way to overcome past wrongs, or what she termed the "predicament of irreversibility," is through forgiveness, a doctrine she regarded as Jesus's greatest contribution to political thought.[63] Like justice, forgiveness entails accepting and admitting the wrongs of the past, but unlike justice, it seeks to overcome the legacy of past wrongs through repentance and reconciliation. Forgiveness does not solve the injustice of the past, but it does create the possibility for a new, more just, and more peaceful political order through the restoration of relationships. Because forgiveness offers the possibility of reconciliation among enemies, a growing number of scholars have called attention to its potential role in international affairs. Patrick Glynn, for example, writes, "Nations may cling to the angry past or embrace the hopeful future. But the path to peace and prosperity for all nations today lies through the gate of forgiveness."[64]

Because forgiveness is seldom applied in domestic politics and even more rarely in international politics, it will be helpful to explore its nature and role in interpersonal relations. In common usage, forgiveness implies the cancellation of a debt or the pardoning of a past wrong. Theologians commonly view the process of interpersonal reconciliation as involving four distinct but interrelated elements. First, the offender confesses the evil committed, openly admitting responsibility for wrongdoing. Second, after acknowledging personal guilt, the wrongdoer apologizes for the injury committed, frequently demonstrating the authenticity of contrition through acts of restitution. Third, in response to the wrongdoer's contrition, the victim declines vengeance and instead pursues restoration through forgiveness. Finally, on the basis of the mutual interactions between the wrongdoer and the victim, the parties move toward reconciliation, creating a new relationship based on a restored moral foundation.

Repentance and forgiveness are often difficult to apply in personal life. This is so because unjust human actions frequently result in animosity that fosters a desire for vengeance and restitution. Additionally, practicing forgiveness is challenging because the moral virtues on which it depends—such as the courage to confront the past, the humility to repent, the self-control to limit anger and oppose vengeance, and the magnanimity to pursue reconciliation—are rarely cultivated in society.

However, if forgiveness is challenging in interpersonal relations, it is much more difficult in public life.[65] This is true for two reasons: first, because political morality, as noted in chapter 1, is not identical with personal morality and, second, because responsibility for political action is frequently elusive and impossible to assign. For example, who is responsible for the Bosnian war? For South Africa's apartheid? For Rwanda's genocide? To be sure, although political leaders and government officials bear primary responsibility for devising and implementing policies that resulted in these crimes and injustices, they are not the only responsible actors. Indeed, all members of a political community bear some responsibility through their actions or inactions.

The process of political forgiveness in international relations entails four elements. First, forgiveness requires complete truth telling—a full accounting of past communal wrongs. This means that a past aggressive war or other international injustice requires that a state acknowledge its collective responsibility for wrongdoing. This truth telling must be public so that knowledge of the past evil becomes part of the collective conscience of society. Second, leaders must acknowledge past wrongs and express public contrition for the injury committed. If the apology is to be genuine, the expiation needs to be specific, concrete, and public, often expressed through monetary reparations or restitution. Third, forgiveness requires that the group or state that has been victimized acknowledge the contrition and repentance of the wrongdoers and not pursue vengeance or seek retribution. Rather than attempting to rectify past wrongs, the victims pursue the restoration of political relationships based on the renewal of trust and the cancellation of debts. Finally, the forgiveness process culminates with reconciliation—the restoration of just political relationships in which enemies learn to live and work with each other. Such a condition is possible only when trust is restored through the renewal of a society's moral order.

It is important to stress that forgiveness does not deny accountability through restitution, reparations, or even partial retribution. But whereas retributive justice demands full legal accountability through trials and punishment, forgiveness emphasizes the political healing and moral restoration of communal relationships. According to the forgiveness model, such healing is likely to occur when offenders acknowledge culpability, express remorse for their offense, and promise not to carry out the offense again, and when victims reduce or altogether cancel offenders' moral debts or deserved punishment. Although public apologies have become commonplace in domestic and international politics, the practice of authentic collective forgiveness is rare in contemporary political life. This is especially the case not because forgiveness lifts offenders' debts, but because of the demanding nature of this ethic, requiring that offenders voluntarily and openly confront their moral culpability.

As a result, the ethic of political forgiveness is rare in public life, and when applied in international affairs it is usually evident in a partial or limited manner. In the South African case just examined, for example, although leaders did not seek reconciliation through political forgiveness, the TRC did pursue moral accountability through truth telling and encouraged confession through the promise of amnesty. In effect, the TRC followed dimensions of the forgiveness ethic. In the case analyzed below—President Ronald Reagan's 1985 trip to West Germany to celebrate German–American political reconciliation—a different aspect of the forgiveness ethic is emphasized. Here the healing and restoration of collective relationships occurs through reforming German political culture and developing deep political ties between two peoples committed to constitutional democracy.

The German–American case is problematic, however, because it illuminates the challenge of overcoming the lingering pain from war and, in particular, the lasting emotional scars resulting from genocide. In particular, the Reagan visit to the cemetery in Bitburg, Germany, raises challenging issues about the extent to which past gross human rights abuses can be overcome, even after governments have admitted culpability, provided substantial reparations, and sought reconciliation through the reformation of national attitudes, values, and institutional practices.

CASE 6-3: POLITICAL FORGIVENESS AND THE BITBURG DILEMMA

In January 1985, the White House announced that President Ronald Reagan would visit West Germany to commemorate the fortieth anniversary of the defeat of the Axis powers. Subsequently, the White House announced that President Reagan would lay a wreath at the German military cemetery at Bitburg as a gesture of German–American reconciliation and at the Bergen-Belsen concentration camp as a commemoration for the many Jews who died there and in other concentration camps. Soon after the planned visit to Bitburg was announced, it was discovered that forty-nine members of the Waffen SS, the Nazi movement's elite police force, were among the two thousand German soldiers' graves.

THE BITBURG CEMETERY VISIT

The decision to visit Bitburg precipitated much criticism from American Jewish groups, war veterans, and the media. Within one week of the announced visit, fifty-three senators signed a letter urging President Reagan to call off his Bitburg visit; subsequently, the U.S. Senate decisively passed a resolution recommending that President Reagan "reassess his planned itinerary." In addition, some 257 members of the House of Representatives wrote to West German chancellor Helmut Kohl urging that he release President Reagan from his Bitburg commitment. However, the most potent moral criticism of the planned trip was from Nobel laureate Elie Wiesel, a survivor of the Holocaust. In a brief address at a White House ceremony honoring his selection for the Congressional Gold Medal of Achievement, Congress's highest award, Wiesel observed,

> I belong to a traumatized generation. And to us, as to you, symbols are important. And furthermore, following our ancient tradition—and we are speaking about Jewish heritage—our tradition commands us "to speak truth to power." . . . I am convinced, as you have told us earlier when we spoke that you were not aware of the presence of SS graves in the Bitburg cemetery. Of course, you didn't know. But now we all are aware. May I, Mr. President, if it's possible at all, implore you to do something else, to find another way, another site. That place, Mr. President, is not your place. Your place is with the victims of the SS.[66]

After the discovery of the SS troops' graves and the ensuing political opposition to the planned trip, the Reagan administration faced a foreign policy dilemma. The dilemma was fundamentally rooted in morality, including the responsibilities involved in acknowledging, accepting, and overcoming the historic evil of the Holocaust. White House officials were of course aware of the evil legacy of the Nazi Holocaust, but they also knew that West Germany had attempted to atone for this unbelievable genocide through official remorse, substantial financial reparations, and the prosecution of more than ninety-one thousand persons. Most important, West Germany had developed strong democratic institutions and had become one of the strongest postwar allies of the United States in confronting the evil of totalitarian communism. Nonetheless, West Germany continued to bear the scars from the terrible evil inflicted by Nazis on all of humanity, but especially on Jewish peoples. As one commentator observed at the time of the Bitburg conflict, the Third Reich "was the greatest failure of civilization on the planet."[67]

THE ETHICS OF BITBURG

From a narrowly defined perspective, the issue facing President Reagan was whether to participate in a ceremony of bilateral American–German reconciliation in a cemetery with symbols of evil. For Elie Wiesel and other opponents of the Bitburg visit, the issue was not politics, but "good and evil."[68] Associating even indirectly with Nazi symbols was morally unacceptable. This was a time for protecting and proclaiming the truth, or what Wiesel termed the necessity of speaking "truth to power." While recognizing the development of strong bilateral ties between West Germany and the United States, Bitburg critics argued that reconciliation had to be rooted in memory. In particular, any political reconciliation between former enemies had to honor the historical record of the Holocaust and recognize anew the great evil committed by Nazis against the Jews. In Wiesel's words,

> Mr. President, I know and I understand . . . that you seek reconciliation. So do I. So do we. And I, too, wish to attain true reconciliation with the German people. I do not believe in collective guilt, nor in collective responsibility, only the killers were guilty. Their sons and daughters are not. And I believe, Mr. President, that we can and we must work together with them and with all people. And we must work to bring peace and understanding to a tormented world that, as you know, is still awaiting redemption.[69]

In short, critics argued that because remembering is more important than reconciliation and history is more significant than forgiving, President Reagan should have altered his plans and not gone to Bitburg. Laying a wreath at the Kolmeshöhe military cemetery was wrong, in their view, because it involved an unnecessary association with evil symbols, namely, the burial sites of soldiers who had participated in the Jewish genocide.

From a broadly defined perspective, the issue for President Reagan was whether memory would always define the future or whether it was possible for nations to overcome their evil legacies. Although the Reagan administration never fully explained its moral reasoning behind its actions, it was clear that President Reagan was strongly motivated by the desire to commemorate Germany's moral rehabilitation and U.S.–German reconciliation rather than dwell on the legacies of history. Those who defended the planned trip emphasized two anticipated outcomes. First, because the Bitburg visit had been developed cooperatively by U.S. and German government officials, the cancellation of the ceremony could have undoubtedly jeopardized official relations between the two countries. Second, because the ceremony was regarded by many Germans as a symbol of reconciliation between the two former enemy states as well as an expression of Germany's increased acceptance into the international community, some analysts argued that canceling the trip would be psychologically injurious to German political leadership.

After weighing the pros and cons of the Bitburg dilemma, President Reagan decided to follow the original plan and participate in a brief ceremony at the Bitburg cemetery. "I think it is morally right to do what I'm doing," he said, "and I'm not going to change my mind about that." In justifying his decision, President Reagan relied on consequentialist logic:

> But this all came about out of a very sincere desire of Chancellor Kohl and myself to recognize this 40th anniversary of the war's end—and incidentally, it's the 30th anniversary of our relationship as allies in NATO—that shouldn't we look at this and recognize that the unusual thing that has happened, that in these 40 years since the end of that war, the end of that tragedy of the Holocaust, we have become the friends that we are, and use this occasion to make it plain that never again must we find ourselves enemies, and never again must there be anything like the Holocaust. And if that is what we can bring out

of these observances and the trip that has been planned, then I think everything we're doing is very worthwhile.[70]

One of the ironies of the presidential dilemma over the Bitburg ceremony was that it greatly increased historical awareness of the Holocaust, fostering greater human sensitivity to the psychological pain rooted in the Nazi genocide committed four decades earlier. According to columnist William Safire, Reagan's blunders in dealing with this dilemma turned out to be a blessing in disguise because it made millions of people aware of the costs of reconciliation in a way that no other process could have accomplished. "In seeking at first to sidestep the smoldering resentments," Safire writes, "the President brought on a firestorm 40 years after a Holocaust, which in turn forced a forgetful world through a most necessary grief."[71]

MORAL REFLECTIONS

The Bitburg case study raises a number of issues about the morality of political reconciliation and the nature and feasibility of overcoming past regime offenses. Some of these issues include the following:

- Can nations that have abused power and committed great evils against other peoples be restored into the family of nations? Can a regime that has committed genocide ever overcome its evil past, or must its citizens bear continuing shame and guilt?
- If the bitter, angry past can be overcome, what actions must states fulfill in order to atone for past evils? If international political rehabilitation is possible, what actions must be undertaken in order to heal and restore communal solidarity?
- Has Germany atoned sufficiently for the atrocities of World War II? Given West Germany's postwar history and more particularly the political solidarity and close ties that emerged between the United States and West Germany during the Cold War, was it wrong for President Reagan to visit

the German military cemetery at Bitburg? Why or why not?

- In view of the existence of forty-nine SS graves at the Kolmeshöhe military cemetery, will the cemetery always remain a symbol of evil?
- Although Bitburg illustrates the failure to accept collective repentance and grant political forgiveness, should regimes that have accepted culpability and atoned for their offenses be forgiven? Can the process of collective forgiveness contribute to the healing of nations and to just, peaceful international relations?

- In a major speech to the Bundestag on May 8, 1985, West German president Richard von Weizsäcker observed, "Whoever closes his eyes to the past becomes blind to the present."[72] In light of this claim, how can memory be sustained to honor past suffering while also encouraging reconciliation and the establishment of new political relationships?

SUMMARY

While accountability is important in reckoning with past regime offenses, retribution alone is unlikely to provide justice to victims, healing to offenders, or reconciliation to society. Although legal retribution is essential in the functioning of a developed political community, I have argued that restorative justice provides a preferable strategy because of its emphasis on the restoration of interpersonal and communal relations. Since social solidarity is essential to national peace and prosperity, the healing of communal bonds in the aftermath of systemic crimes and injustices is crucial to the consolidation of democracy and the rule of law. Thus, rather than focusing on the prosecution and punishment of offenders, the restorative strategy focuses on healing and renewal through truth telling, public apologies, reparations, and political forgiveness. While it is still too early to assess its effectiveness, the South African experiment in amnesty for truth telling is a bold effort to place communal healing at the heart of a transitional justice process. The Bitburg case study similarly illustrates the promise of healing through moral accountability, reparations, and the pursuit of peaceful, cooperative actions. Despite the consolidation of West German democracy and the establishment of strong bilateral ties between the United States and West Germany, the celebration of German–American reconciliation was problematic because of the symbols associated with the Bitburg cemetery. Even though the Bitburg site was morally problematic, President Reagan decided to follow the planned schedule, believing that it was more important to honor U.S.–German political reconciliation than to cancel a trip because of a tainted cemetery. To Reagan, West Germany had tangibly expressed repentance for Nazi atrocities through collective remorse, tangible reparations, and the consolidation of constitutional government. Although it is important to remember the past, it was time to move forward and honor the significant reforms and changes within Germany.

Chapter Seven

The Ethics of War

[Gen. Curtis] LeMay said, "if we'd lost the war, we'd all have been prosecuted as war criminals." . . . LeMay recognized that what he was doing [fire-bombing Japanese cities] would have been thought immoral if his side had lost. But what makes it immoral if you lose and not immoral if you win?[1]

—ROBERT MCNAMARA

The aggressor is always peace-loving; he would prefer to take over our country unopposed.[2]

—CARL VON CLAUSEWITZ

There is something heroic in the effort to inject morality in the Hobbesian situation par excellence—when states, locked in war, squirm on the floor of survival. It is good to remind statesmen that the ends do not justify all means, that restraints should be observed even in an angry war, that humanity must somehow be preserved.[3]

—STANLEY HOFFMANN

STATES SEEK to influence international affairs through various types of power, ranging from positive sanctions to coercive threats, from "soft power" co-optive strategies that induce desired outcomes to "hard power" strategies that compel through military coercion. Although states rely on different policy instruments to influence the behavior of other states, force—the application of coercive power—remains the ultimate instrument for pursuing vital national interests in global society.

Sometimes international relations are categorized in terms of mutually exclusive conditions of war and peace in which force is applied in the former but not the latter. However, such analysis oversimplifies reality because all interstate relations are in part a by-product of the distribution of power among states. As a result, it is preferable to view the relations among states on a continuum between the extremes of peace and war, with most international relations occurring between these two ideal-type conditions. Although only a small portion of international relations are determined by military force, all relations among states are based partly on coercive power, with most of this power held in reserve as political and military capital. Just as financial capital provides the foundation for economic development, such strategic capital provides the basis for the credible implementation of foreign policy.

This chapter explores the political ethics of force by addressing questions such as the following: In pursuing legitimate national interests in global society, is it morally permissible to threaten and, if necessary, to use force? If force is legitimate, what types of threats and what types of force are morally appropriate? Once war begins, what moral principles should govern the use of force? Is the just war tradition an adequate moral framework for assessing modern war? In view of the rising threat of international terrorism, how should states seek to prevent such violence? Is preemption a morally legitimate strategy for protecting innocent persons from terror?

In examining the ethics of force, this chapter is divided into three parts. First, I briefly sketch the nature and role of force in global politics by focusing on three alternative moral traditions of force: pacifism, amoral realism, and just war. I then illustrate the important role of just war analysis with a case study on the 1991 Persian Gulf War. In the second section, I examine the moral challenge facing states when they seek to deter major aggression from states and nonstate actors—a task made all the more difficult when the potential of WMD is involved. When such threats arise, states can respond in one of two ways—through preventive military action and through preemptive attacks. I illustrate the former option with a case study on the U.S. preventive war of 2003 against Iraq.

THREE MORALITIES OF FORCE

Historically, three distinct perspectives have dominated the moral analysis of force: pacifism, amoral realism, and just war. The first assumes that war and violence are never morally permissible, whereas the last is based on the conviction that military force is politically and strategically necessary to protect vital national interests. Between these two polar positions is an intermediate perspective that assumes that resorting to violence should be a last resort and that, in the event of war, destruction and human suffering should be minimized.

Pacifism

The pacifist approach prohibits the threat and use of force because, in accordance with a rule-based ethic, it assumes that violence can never be a morally legitimate means to provide national security or to secure moral goods such as human rights, international justice, and peace. In its prioritization of values, pacifism holds that peace and nonviolence are the highest norms and can never be compromised to secure other ends, however important they might be. For example, the Dutch Renaissance scholar Erasmus believed that the cost of war was so great that even if a war is won, "you will lose much more than you gain."[4] Thus, for him as well as for other pacifists, force is never a legitimate means by which to protect national interests or to pursue international justice. In sum, the pacifist perspective on global politics offers a simple and categorical rule: "Do no violence."

Although pacifism is an important moral tradition, it provides little help to the soldier or the statesman in structuring moral reasoning about the defense and protection of vital interests in global society. Because the highest priorities are life and peace, this tradition does not allow for the possibility of using force to pursue other moral objectives. Pacifism's chief end is the abolition of war and violence. As a result, it provides a potent moral critique of the security structures of the Westphalian and post-Westphalian international systems but offers little guidance to decision makers pursuing justice within and among states.

Amoral Realism

This perspective represents the direct opposite position of pacifism. Whereas pacifism prohibits war and violence, amoral realism assumes not only that war is a legitimate instrument of policy but also that morality does not constrain war. Indeed, assuming the legitimacy of war's ends, amoral realism believes that the only norm governing the conduct of war is military victory. Moreover, because morality is absent in the international community, global order is achieved not by the pursuit of "moral" foreign policies but rather as a direct by-product of the balance of power among states.

Although several variants of amoral realism have been developed, two of the most important are the "cynical" perspective and the "jihad," or religious war, perspective. Both are similar in that they believe that morality is silent in wartime, denying that moral limits exist on the conduct of war. Whereas cynics justify force on the basis of self-interest, adherents to the jihad doctrine justify unlimited violence on the basis of religious convictions. The cynical perspective is the most radical because it denies morality altogether, both in the justification and in the prosecution of war. According to this perspective, because moral values are simply subjective preferences, they have no constructive role in determining and judging political action in global society. To the extent that force is justified in international relations, it is based on prudential judgment divorced from moral values. In addition, because the aim of going to war is to prevail, there are no inherent moral limitations in defeating the enemy.

The cynical perspective of force is illustrated by Thucydides' account of the Athenian subjugation of the island of Melos in the Peloponnesian War. The Athenians, believing that their own security and well-being lay in a credible balance of power with Sparta, their archrival, sought to extend their imperial control over Melos as they had over most other islands in the Aegean Sea. The Melians, however, refused Athenian entreaties, desiring instead to remain free from foreign control. Athenian diplomats tried to persuade Melos to surrender, telling them that justice depends on the distribution of power. "The strong do what they have the power to do and the weak accept what they have to accept."[5] When the Melians refuse to surrender, the Athenians lay siege to the island, eventually forcing their unconditional surrender.

A *holy war* is one that is waged for a religious cause. Because its purpose is assumed to be in accord with the divine will, it involves unlimited use of force for a holy cause. Historically, the two most important expressions of holy wars have been the Islamic jihad and the Christian-inspired crusade. The jihad, or religious war, is rooted in Islam's conviction that the world is divided into two realms—the House of Islam, where Islamic law prevails, and the House of War, comprising the non-Islamic world.[6] Between these two realms there is a "morally necessary, legally and religiously obligatory state of war."[7]

Because Islam is assumed to be universally applicable, Muslim believers have a duty to convert or at least to subjugate unbelievers. It is important to emphasize that in Islam the struggle between good and evil is both a spiritual contest and a temporal conflict. As Bernard Lewis notes,

> Muhammad, it will be recalled, was not only a prophet and a teacher, like the founders of other religions; he was also the head of a polity and of a community, a ruler and a soldier. Hence his struggle involved a state and its armed forces. If the fighters in the war for Islam, the holy war "in the path of God," are fighting for God, it follows that their opponents are fighting against God. And since God is in principle the sovereign, the supreme head of the Islamic state—and the Prophet and, after the Prophet, the caliphs are his vice-regents—then God as sovereign commands the army. The army is God's army and the enemy is God's enemy. The duty of God's soldiers is to dispatch God's enemies as quickly as possible to the place where God will chastise them—that is to say, the afterlife.[8]

Although Islamic scholars differ on whether and to what degree morality limits violence in jihad, it is clear that there are comparatively few restrictions placed on the conduct of war, especially when compared with the just war tradition.[9] The aim in the jihad, as in the crusade, is to defeat and destroy the enemies of God. Total war is morally permissible.

The *crusade*, which shares with jihad a divine justification for war, is characterized by a conflict between good and evil in which total force is used to defeat the enemy. Roland Bainton has written that the crusading idea requires that war "be fought under God and with his help, that the crusaders shall be godly and their enemies ungodly, and that the war shall be prosecuted unsparingly."[10] The origins of the crusading idea are found in the biblical accounts of Old Testament religious wars and in particular in the efforts of ancient Israel to gain control of the "promised land." According to Deuteronomy 7, the Lord commanded Israel to expel seven nations or peoples from their territory, giving them the following mandate (v. 2): "Thou shall smite them, and utterly destroy them; thou shalt make no covenant with them nor show mercy unto them." Bainton argues that the crusade goes beyond a holy war in that it was fought "not so much with God's help as on God's behalf, not for a human goal which God might bless but for a divine cause which God might command."[11] The sincerity of the warriors, he goes on to suggest, was evidenced by the fact that war booty was consecrated to God.

The first major religious crusades occurred at the end of the eleventh century, when Pope Urban II called on Christians to recapture the Holy Land from the Turks and in particular to free Jerusalem. Throughout the twelfth and thirteenth centuries, western European military forces carried out numerous expeditions to the Middle East, seeking to reclaim Palestine from the Muslims and seeking to establish strategic centers free from the threat of Muslim forces. The crusading idea was subsequently expressed in a number of different domestic and international conflicts, culminating with the Peace of Westphalia. That treaty brought the Thirty Years' War to a close by giving secular rulers sovereign authority within their states, including the right to determine their country's religion.

Throughout the Renaissance and Reformation, the crusading spirit pervaded many European countries as Christians fought to establish societies based on the true religion, to purify their churches from heretical beliefs, and to ensure civil compliance with religious norms. For example, during the Spanish Inquisition in the fourteenth and fifteenth centuries the Roman Catholic Church used torture and violence to punish heretics and to ensure conformity with established religious beliefs. During the conquest of America in the early sixteenth century, Spanish conquerors relied on the crusading idea, modified by the just war theory, to justify the subjugation and Christianization of heathen indigenous peoples. Protestants, too, resorted to military force to ensure compliance with religious beliefs. In sixteenth-century Geneva, Reformation leader John Calvin sought to use public authority not only to enforce moral behavior but to reinforce true religion. A century later, Puritan leader Oliver Cromwell sought to institute pietistic Christian norms in one of the most thoroughgoing efforts to legislate morality since the codification of the Mosaic Law.[12] As with other religious wars beforehand, morality was applied to force through a Manichean worldview in which conflict was defined in the religious categories of believer and infidel.

Just War

This tradition—which is rooted in ancient Greek and Roman philosophy and in the teachings of the early and medieval Christian church[13]—represents an intermediary position between pacifism and amoral realism. It assumes that all interstate relations, including war, are subject to widely acknowledged moral standards. Because power and force are fundamental realities of the international community, the quest for peace and justice among states can be only imperfectly realized, and then only when power and force are incorporated into the calculus of decision making. Like pacifism, just war affirms international moral constraints on war, but whereas pacifism proscribes all war and violence, just war assumes that force can be an instrument of justice. Although violence is regarded as evil, it is not necessarily the greatest evil. As a result, some moral values—such as the protection of the innocent, the recovery of something wrongfully taken, the punishment of criminal behavior, and the defense against aggression—may justify the use of force. According to this perspective, just as an individual has the right to resist injustice, so too a state has the right to use force, individually or collectively, to repulse aggression and to resist and punish evil.

Fundamentally, the just war tradition seeks to limit the violence of war by restraining the use of force and by limiting the scope of violence itself. To constrain the possibility and practice of war, the theory provides norms for judging when war might be morally justified and, in the event that it is warranted, how such a war should be limited. The aim of the theory is not to justify war but to bring international relations under the control of political morality, thereby reducing the risk and destructiveness of war.

It is important to emphasize that the origins and development of the just war tradition were rooted not in the limitation of violence but in the quest for political justice. For early and medieval Christian thinkers, the main challenge was to define not how violence might be limited but rather to define the circumstances that might necessitate force to ensure justice. For example, Ambrose of Milan, an early Christian bishop, argued that when a Christian confronts an armed robber, he may not use force in self-defense, "lest in defending his life he should stain his love for his neighbor." However, if the armed robber attacked a neighbor, the Christian, in fulfilling his duty to love others, had a moral obligation to defend the innocent victim. Charity thus imposes on believers a duty to care for others, allowing, as a last resort, limited, proportionate force to halt injustice.[14]

The foundation of just war theory is based on the distinction between the public and private use of force, between warring (*bellum*) and dueling (*duellum*). As George Weigel has noted, *bellum* is the use of force for public purposes by legitimate political authorities that have an obligation to defend the security of persons for whom they have assumed responsibility.[15] *Duellum*, by contrast, is the use of violence by private organizations for private or personal ends. The just war tradition is thus based upon a presumption that coercive power, whether used domestically or internationally, is legitimate when it serves morally legitimate purposes. War, in other words, is not intrinsically evil but rather an instrument of statecraft. Whether armed force is morally justified will depend on the agents, purposes, and methods of those who use it.

The classical just war theory is comprised of two parts: the *jus ad bellum*, the justice of going to war, and the *jus in bello*, justice in wartime. Because the theory is rooted in natural law, one scholar has defined these two dimensions as "war-decision law" and "war-conduct law."[16] According to this theory, if war is to be considered moral, it must fulfill the norms required for the justification of violence as well as the norms for prosecuting a war. A war might be waged for unjust reasons but still be prosecuted in a just manner. Conversely, even if the reasons for going to war are completely just, the war itself could be prosecuted in an immoral manner, resorting, for example, to indiscriminate attack on civilians. In short, if a war is to be moral, it must satisfy all just war norms.

In recent years, partly in response to the insurgent wars in both Afghanistan and Iraq, some scholars have suggested that the just war tradition needs to be supplemented with a third dimension—one that addresses conditions after major foreign military operations have ended. This third element is called *jus post bellum*, or justice after war. According to this emerging dimension, once war is over, the victor or intervening power must restore order, help to rebuild the economy, reestablish political autonomy to allow self-government, and hold leaders accountable for past atrocities.[17] This dimension of just war theory has become especially important in unconventional or irregular wars that do not follow the traditional legal rules of warfare.

Although the just war theory has been historically interpreted in different ways, there is a general consensus about its essential elements. The theory's core norms are listed in table 7-1.

It is important to emphasize that the aims of the *jus ad bellum* are limited in scope. The quest for political justice within states is not a central focus of just war theory. For example, it does not seek to remedy the injustices resulting from the past arbitrary delineation of state boundaries that might have disregarded cultural, linguistic, and ethnic affinities of people, nor does it attempt to relieve the suffering of citizens living in oppressive regimes. Although the absence of political self-rule or the existence of political oppression is morally unacceptable, such injustices do not justify international

Table 7-1.   Elements of Just War Theory

I. *Jus ad bellum*

1. *Just cause*: The only legitimate justification for war is to deter aggression, to defend against unjust attack, or to right a grievous wrong. Although the theory does not specify what constitutes a just global order, the effort to alter territorial boundaries by force or to extend political and economic control in foreign lands is considered unjust. Aggression is immoral and gives rise to a just cause to resist by force.

2. *Competent authority*: The use of force is morally permissible only when it is legitimate, that is, authorized by government. Violence prosecuted by nongovernmental groups or private individuals is immoral.

3. *Right intention*: A war is just only if it seeks to restore a just peace. The goal of war must be to right the evil that justifies war in the first instance. Because war is, as von Clausewitz once remarked, the pursuit of political objectives by other means, the aim of warfare must be only to alter specific conditions or morally unacceptable actions of an enemy state.

4. *Limited objectives*: A war is just only if its goals are limited. An unconditional, unlimited war of attrition is morally unacceptable. Not only must the purposes of war be limited but the goals and means must be proportionate to the ends being pursued. This means that the good to be realized by prosecuting a war must be commensurate with the probable evil resulting from war, or, as Robert Tucker has put it, "[T]he values preserved through force must be proportionate to the values sacrificed through force."[a]

5. *Last resort*: Before a state can legitimately resort to war, it must exhaust all peaceful means. War can be morally legitimate only when a state has made every effort through measures short of war (e.g., diplomacy, multilateral negotiations, and sanctions) to seek to redress the evil. Before violence can be justified, nonviolent measures must have been exhausted. Like proportionality, this is a difficult norm to apply, requiring uncommon prudential judgment.

6. *Reasonable hope of success*: The use of force against an aggressor must have a reasonable chance of success. Good intentions are not sufficient. A war that is unlikely to achieve its limited goals is immoral.

II. *Jus in bello*

7. *Discrimination*: Military force must be applied only against the political leadership and military forces of the state. Every effort must be made to discriminate between combatants and noncombatants, soldiers and civilians, to minimize civilian casualties. Direct attacks against civilian targets, such as neighborhoods, hospitals, and schools, are morally impermissible. Indiscriminate mass destruction of cities is similarly impermissible.[b]

8. *Proportionality*: The destruction inflicted by military forces in war must be proportional to the goals they are seeking to realize. An indiscriminate war of attrition that seeks to eliminate the enemy society altogether is not morally justified. The goal should be to use the minimum level of violence to achieve the limited aims of a war.

III. *Jus post bellum*[c]

9. *Restoration of a just order*: Once war is over, the victor must restore order, help to rebuild the economy, reestablish political autonomy to allow self-government, and hold leaders accountable for past atrocities and egregious war crimes.

---

[a] Robert W. Tucker, "Justice and the War," *National Interest*, Fall 1991, 111.

[b] Because war frequently results in massive collateral destruction, scholars have developed the corollary principle of *double effect* to define the problem of civilian casualties. According to this norm, civilian casualties are morally permissible only when they are an unintentional by-product of the intentional targeting of military forces.

[c] For an excellent overview of the theory and practice of the *jus post bellum*, see Eric Patterson, ed., *Ethics beyond War's End* (Washington, D.C.: Georgetown University Press, 2012).

war. Rather, they give people a right to demand self-determination and just rule. In effect, extreme domestic injustice may justify revolution but not war. I explore exceptions to this conclusion in chapter 9 on foreign intervention.

It is also important to note the presumptive conservative character of *jus ad bellum*. Fundamentally, the just war tradition is a status quo doctrine rooted in the existing Westphalian order of sovereign states. Although the theory does not explicitly endorse the anarchic global system, it presumes its moral legitimacy, seeking to advance a just peace within the context of Westphalian norms. For example, the norm of competent authority is typically applied to existing governments, not to potentially legitimate nations seeking to secede from an existing state or to political groups seeking to topple a regime. In addition, the just cause norm is generally interpreted within the context of territorial international law, which regards aggression—the forceful violation of territorial boundaries—as the most serious justification for war. To be sure, the territorial boundaries of many states have little to do with global justice. In Africa, especially, the boundaries among states were often established arbitrarily by imperial powers without taking into account the distribution of tribal, ethnic, and cultural affinities. Nevertheless, international law accepts the existing order as legitimate, proscribing war as a means to establish more just territorial boundaries.

Because the just war theory seeks to promote a just peace within the international system of nation-states, there is a significant correspondence between the theory and international law, especially the most fundamental norms that govern the rights and duties of states. According to international law, states are entitled to political independence and territorial integrity but also share a duty to respect the sovereignty of other states by not interfering in their internal affairs. Most important, states are obliged to settle disputes peacefully without resorting to force. However, if a state is the victim of aggression, it has the inherent right to use force in self-defense. International law thus shares with the just war doctrine a presumption against force. However, whereas the former provides a legal system for defining states' rights and duties, the latter provides the moral architecture for assessing the morality of force in interstate relations.

To illustrate the role of just war norms in conventional, interstate conflicts, I next examine the ethics of the 1991 Persian Gulf War.

CASE 7-1: THE ETHICS OF THE PERSIAN GULF WAR

THE CONFLICT

On August 2, 1990, Iraq carried out a massive surprise invasion of its tiny neighbor Kuwait. Iraq's much larger and qualitatively superior military forces smashed through Kuwait's defensive positions. Within twenty-four hours, Iraqi forces had taken control of all key Kuwaiti military and government centers and had installed a puppet regime. Within two days, Iraq's initial invasion force had grown to more than 120,000 soldiers and 850 tanks, with a significant portion of those forces stationed along Kuwait's southern border, potentially threatening Saudi Arabia. Within days of the invasion, Saddam Hussein, Iraq's dictator, announced the formal annexation of Kuwait.

Although numerous developments might have contributed to Iraq's decision to attack Kuwait, two factors were especially important. First, Iraq disputed its southern border with Kuwait, claiming that the existing territorial boundary was unjust and historically incorrect. Iraq had periodically pressed Kuwait for a readjustment of the border, seeking in particular to gain sole access to the rich Rumaila oil field along the border and control of two islands at the end of the Euphrates delta. Kuwait had refused Iraq's demands, arguing that the borders were legitimate, having been established by Britain in 1922 in the aftermath of the Ottoman Empire's collapse.

Second, Iraq faced major financial pressures because of its long and costly war with Iran in the 1980s. Although Kuwait had provided Iraq with some $10 billion during the war, when the war terminated in 1988, Iraq had a foreign debt of over $80 billion, making economic reconstruction difficult. If Iraq was to modernize its economy and replenish its military forces, it needed to reduce its oppressive debt, and the only way to do this was to increase its foreign sales of petroleum, its main export. In its effort to increase oil revenues, Iraq claimed that Kuwait was undertaking actions that impaired Iraq's economic reconstruction. In particular, it charged Kuwait with two acts of "financial aggression"—selling more than its allotted OPEC quota, thereby depressing petroleum prices, and pumping ("stealing") an excessive amount of oil from the jointly owned Rumaila field. As a result, Iraq demanded not only that Kuwait forgive Iraq's debt of $10 billion but also that it pay reparations of $13 to $15 billion. Kuwait refused these demands.

Although Saddam Hussein had no doubt expected that Western nations would oppose his actions, he had calculated that, as the most powerful state in the region, his invasion could not be challenged. However, he failed to anticipate the international condemnation of his action and especially the determination of President George H. W. Bush to redress the aggression. Immediately after the invasion, the U.S. government froze some $30 billion of Iraq's and Kuwait's assets in its jurisdiction. Moreover, with Syria and Turkey closing their Iraqi pipelines and foreign ships refusing to pick up Iraqi oil, Iraqi oil exports came to an abrupt halt.

In a virtually unprecedented action, the UN Security Council passed more than a dozen resolutions opposing Iraq and seeking the restoration of Kuwait's sovereignty. In its first action, the Security Council condemned the invasion and then declared Iraq's annexation of Kuwait null and void. It then adopted numerous actions, including comprehensive sanctions, to force Iraq to withdraw from Kuwait. However, after these actions failed to change Hussein's policies, the Security Council authorized (in Resolution 678) UN member states to "use all necessary means" to force Iraq's withdrawal from Kuwait if it did not do so by January 15, 1991. It is significant also that the Arab League, the principal alliance of twenty-one Arab states, condemned Iraq's action and called for the liberation of Kuwait.

After Iraq failed to comply with the international community's demands, a massive multilateral force, spearheaded by the United States, carried out a forty-six-day war to liberate Kuwait. The allied war began with a massive bombing campaign that eliminated Iraq's air force, destroyed its nuclear weapons development centers and chemical weapons facilities, eliminated the country's military and civilian communications networks, and severely weakened its ground forces. In addition, the bombing damaged the country's infrastructure, especially the transportation system. After six weeks of aerial bombardment, the allied forces launched a ground campaign involving the largest deployment of armored forces in the history of warfare. Within two days allied forces had liberated Kuwait, and within four days they had routed Iraq's armed forces, killing thousands of its soldiers and decimating its armored forces. The ground campaign ended within one hundred hours of its beginning as Iraq agreed to cease-fire terms imposed by the allies.

JUST WAR AND THE CONFLICT

Was the Gulf War just? Was the allied military campaign justified, and was it prosecuted in a moral manner? Prior to the allied liberation campaign and in the aftermath of the war, scholars and politicians, especially in the United States, debated these issues, carrying out a vigorous moral debate about the justice of this war. Although there was significant disagreement about which actions were morally appropriate prior to and during the war, the moral debate was framed to a significant degree by just war principles. Even President Bush took pains to use the moral language of just war to justify his decisions.

The case for resorting to force to liberate Kuwait was morally compelling because each of the six *jus ad bellum* criteria was fulfilled. First, because Iraq's invasion was clearly illegal (contrary to international law) as well as unjust (contrary to international political morality), the resort to force was in accord with the "just cause" norm. Regardless of the legitimacy of Iraq's territorial and economic claims against Kuwait, Iraq was duty bound to use peaceful methods to settle its dispute with Kuwait. Iraq's attack was thus an act of war, giving Kuwait the inherent legal and moral right to use individual and collective force to repulse the aggression. Clearly, this conflict provided evidence that the "just cause" criterion had been fulfilled. Indeed, Johnson argues that Iraq's aggression provides "as clear and unambiguous a case as one could hope to find in the real world."[18]

Second, the "competent authority" norm was also fulfilled since the resort to war was authorized by legitimate political authority. In particular, both the U.S. Congress and the UN Security Council authorized military action in the event Saddam did not withdraw from Kuwait. It is important to stress that this norm does not imply that the only legitimate authority for peacekeeping action in the international community is the United Nations. To be sure, since the Security Council is the most authoritative multilateral peacekeeping and peace-enforcing body of the international community, it is desirable for this organ to authorize international peace-enforcement actions. But while such an authorization may be legally desirable, it is not a moral requirement of the just war tradition.

Third, the "right intention" criterion was also fulfilled by the just purpose of liberating Kuwait. The aim was not to conquer Iraq or to topple its dictatorship. The goal was simply to restore Kuwait's sovereignty and to halt the unjust humanitarian and strategic consequences of Iraq's invasion.

Fourth, although it was clear that the allied objectives were consistent with the "limited objectives" norm (liberating Kuwait), determining whether the war's ends and means were proportionate presented particular challenges prior to the war. Although in retrospect it is clear that the liberation of Kuwait and the military defeat of Iraq justified the evil of war, at the time of the crisis it was difficult to be certain of the relationship between means and ends. Would the evil from the liberation campaign be commensurate with the evil already inflicted on Kuwait? What if Saddam resorted to weapons of mass destruction? Despite the potential for significant destruction, the evil inflicted by his regime—an evil involving human rights abuses, the pillaging of Kuwait's treasury, and the violation of core norms of global society—was so extensive that there seemed to be a compelling case for proportionality.[19]

Fifth, the use of force was also in accord with the principle of last resort. This norm is especially difficult to apply because, as Michael Walzer has observed, there is no moral theory to guide its application.[20] As a result, the decision to use force will ultimately be based on political and strategic considerations, areas in which moral philosophers have no special competence. Although critics and advocates of the war were deeply divided on whether this had been fulfilled, it was clear that additional time would not necessarily have resolved the dispute. Throughout the five-month intervening phase between the invasion and the liberation campaign, allies had individually and collectively sought to resolve the conflict through diplomatic negotiation and through the pressure of comprehensive economic sanctions, but Iraq remained belligerent and uncompromising.

Finally, the "probable success" norm was also fulfilled because there was complete certainty about the outcome of the allied liberation campaign. The allies had put together a multilateral force of more than half a million combatants, backed by an extraordinary arsenal of airpower and armored forces. There was little doubt that the allies, spearheaded by the United States, would prevail militarily. The only questions were how destructive the war would be and how quickly it would be won.

THE MORAL DEBATE

The most significant moral opposition to the war came from religious and political elites who believed that additional time was necessary to satisfy the "last resort" norm. For them, UN-imposed economic sanctions needed more time to work. However, in their eagerness to avoid war, they failed to appreciate that, from an international legal perspective, the condition of war had already begun when Iraq invaded its neighbor on August 2. More significantly, these elites failed to recognize that sanctions were a source of deep moral harm and were themselves inconsistent with the just war norm of discrimination because the harm fell disproportionately on civilians rather than on the political and military officials of the state. To the extent that comprehensive sanctions would have been given more time to work, they would have imposed an increasingly intolerable burden on the most vulnerable members of society, namely, women, children, and the aged. Walzer has noted that opponents of the war who supported a prolonged blockade of Iraq "seem not to have realized that what they were advocating was a radically indiscriminate act of war, with predictably harsh consequences."[21]

Some religious and political leaders also opposed the war out of fear that the war would be disproportionate. Following a much publicized National Council of Churches (NCC) "peace pilgrimage" to the Middle East in mid-December, leaders of mainline Protestant denominations declared that resorting to force to settle the conflict was "morally indefensible." They claimed that forcibly liberating Kuwait would "unleash weapons of mass destruction" and result in hundreds of thousands of casualties. "It is entirely possible," the NCC leaders noted apocalyptically, "that war in the Middle East will destroy everything."[22] On January 15, the day before the air campaign began, NCC Protestant leaders again urged President Bush not to resort to war because "it is unlikely that this battle can be contained in either scope, intensity, or time." In their view, the risk of war was "out of proportion to any conceivable gain which might be achieved through military action."[23]

The problem with the pacifistic pronouncements of the preachers and the bishops did not lie merely in the inadequacy of their view but also in their failure to morally assess their own position. By failing to seriously consider the use of force to halt oppression and aggression, religious elites were in effect condoning the occupation and annexation of Kuwait. According to Walzer, "It is very bad to make a deal with an aggressor at the expense of his victim," for then we "make ourselves complicitous in the aggression."[24]

Allied military planners also made significant efforts to apply discriminating force in the war. Indeed, some observers of modern war have suggested that the Persian Gulf War was the most discriminate war ever. Despite the significant destruction involved in both Iraq and Kuwait, allied forces limited civilian casualties and achieved an unprecedented level of compliance with the discrimination norm through the use of precision-guided munitions, such as laser-guided "smart" bombs and cruise missiles. At the same time, however, although Iraq's infrastructure was also classified as a legitimate target, the destruction of communications and transportation systems, electric power centers, water pumping stations and purification plants, and government buildings led some war critics to question the morality of such action.[25] Still, it cannot be denied that from a purely military standpoint, the destruction was almost wholly centered on military targets. By contrast, Iraq's missile attacks on Israel and Saudi Arabia were indiscriminate, intentionally targeting population centers.

The norm of proportionality, the second element of the *jus in bello*, was also fulfilled in significant measure by the allied liberation campaign, which sought to achieve the stated aims of war with the least destruction possible. The goal was to use overwhelming but discriminating force to achieve the liberation of Kuwait as quickly as possible and with the fewest casualties. However, it needs to be emphasized that estimating the proportionality of evil between means and ends is a highly subjective prudential judgment. The difficulty in ascertaining the morality of the means-ends relationship is due in great part to the difficulty in assigning a value to the goal of restoring sovereignty. How can the value of national liberation be determined? Is the restoration of sovereignty worth one thousand, five thousand, or even fifty thousand lives?

Some scholars argue that the allies failed to fulfill the proportionality norm because of the disproportionate losses among combatants (fifty thousand to seventy-five thousand Iraqi deaths versus several hundred deaths for the allies). Tucker argues that the war's disproportionality was problematic not so much because it was an unfortunate by-product of military battle but because it was directly intended. The American strategy, influenced by the failure of Vietnam, was designed to use overwhelming force to achieve clear, achievable goals in a short span of time.[26] Jean Bethke Elshtain, for example, attributes the "extraordinary lopsidedness of deaths and casualties" to the use of "excessive firepower," especially in the bombing of "the Highway of Death," on which Iraqis fled Kuwait City with some fifteen thousand vehicles. In her view, the destruction along that highway was not "a fight by *jus in bello* standards but a massacre."[27] Although Elshtain is correct in emphasizing the just war tradition's insistence on tempering justice with mercy, the proportionality norm applies not to the relationship of combatant casualties but to the relationship between the means and ends of war. As Francis Winters has observed, there is nothing in the moral logic of self-defense that can support the notion that "great powers may justly fight only when they reduce themselves to functional equality with small powers."[28]

MORAL REFLECTIONS

From the foregoing review, it is evident that just war criteria influenced the military liberation of Kuwait. Although some just war elements were fulfilled more fully than others, there is substantial evidence that the resort to force and the prosecution of the air and land wars was unusually consistent with just war principles. Still, some theorists have questioned both the timing and the prosecution of the liberation campaign.

- In light of this case study, was the allied resort to force warranted by Iraq's actions?
- Did the six-month interlude between Iraq's invasion and the commencement of the military liberation campaign provide sufficient opportunity to exhaust nonviolent conflict-resolution alternatives?
- Should more time have been allowed for comprehensive sanctions to affect Iraq's society? Was sufficient time allowed to fulfill the just war's "last resort" principle?
- When did the Iraq War begin—on August 2, 1990, when Iraqi forces invaded Kuwait, or on January 16, 1991, when the allied bombing campaign began?
- In terms of *jus in bello* (war conduct) norms, was the targeting of Iraq's economic infrastructure morally legitimate? More particularly, was the destruction of communications and power centers, transportation networks, and water stations consistent with the discrimination norm?
- Was excessive force used in defeating Iraq? In view of the allied goals (the liberation of Kuwait), were the military means proportional to the political ends of the war?

THE ETHICS OF PREEMPTIVE AND PREVENTIVE WAR

According to international law, every state enjoys the right of self-defense. This right is enshrined in the United Nations Charter, which provides (in Article 51) that states have "the inherent right of individual or collective self-defense if an armed attack occurs." But what if military developments begin to occur that shift the balance of power and thereby threaten the security of individual states or regional stability? How should a state respond to security threats from terrorist groups? Does national self-defense allow for "anticipatory self-defense"—that is, the use of force to prevent aggression before it occurs?

The September 11, 2001, terrorist attacks on the World Trade Center in New York City and on the Pentagon in Washington, D.C., mark a major turning point in the evolution of U.S. national security policy. Indeed, some observers classify the 9/11 terror attacks as the beginning of a new global conflict in which nonstate actors can now threaten the security of major states. This new global threat is a direct by-product of the confluence of three developments: the growing availability of modern technology, increasing globalization, and the proliferation of technology and materials used in making weapons of mass destruction (WMD). Whereas the Cold War represented World War III, the third phase of global conflict, World War IV is characterized by a "civilizational" war in which nonstate actors use terror to press their political demands on states.

In the aftermath of the September 11 attacks, the United States declared a "war" on international terrorism. Some have objected to this bellicose approach, believing that the more appropriate response to terror is to regard it as illegal behavior requiring accountability through a state's criminal justice system. However, the truck bombings of the Khobar Towers housing complex in Saudi Arabia in 1996 and the nearly simultaneous bombings of the U.S. embassies in Kenya and Tanzania in 1998 were not simply crimes, but large destructive attacks that left hundreds of innocent civilians dead. Moreover, the attack on 9/11 was an act of aggression against the territorial integrity of the United States that killed more persons than the Japanese attack on Pearl Harbor in 1941. Eliot Cohen, a specialist on national security, has written that "September 11 marked the climactic battle in an ill-defined war, but a war nonetheless."[29] It is a "strange" war, he notes, because the enemy is an elusive nonstate actor and the conflict itself does not permit simple, neat definitions of goals, methods, and outcomes. Indeed, the war on terror is likely to be a long-term conflict without an "end state" or "exit strategy."

The enormous impact of the 9/11 terrorist attack on American society, coupled with the potential threat from terrorists' access to WMD, precipitated widespread reflection and analysis among scholars and public officials about how the U.S. government should undertake to contain future terrorism. Thus, a year after the 9/11 attack, the U.S. government released a new version of the *National Security Strategy of the United States* (NSS). The 2002 NSS is noteworthy for two reasons: first, because it sets forth elements of the so-called Bush Doctrine, discussed earlier in chapter 3, and second, because it modifies U.S. security policy—shifting strategy from deterrence toward preventive action—to address the growing threat from terrorist groups and other nonstate actors.[30] In promoting national security, the NSS claims that the United States must be prepared to use its power, unilaterally if necessary.

The NSS's most significant strategic innovation was a call for "preemptive action" to counter major threats. The NSS justifies revision of the preemptive doctrine because of the growing dangers from terrorists armed with WMD. "The greater the threat," the NSS observes, "the greater is the risk of inaction—and the more compelling the case for taking anticipatory action to defend ourselves, even if uncertainty remains as to the time and place of the enemy's attack."[31] Of course, preemption was not a new element of American security policy, nor was it a new development in global political affairs. As the NSS correctly noted, legal scholars and international jurists have generally regarded preemption as legitimate when an imminent security threat exists. Nevertheless, the NSS claim of preemption was considered controversial for several reasons. To begin with, the NSS appeared to turn an instrument of U.S. national security policy into a strategic principle. Daalder and Steinberg suggest that the option of preemption was made explicit because of the potential threat of WMD from rogue states and terrorist groups. They also argue that the United States was eager to embrace a unilateral preventive strategy because of the failure of international collective action to confront international security threats in a timely and effective manner.[32]

A second criticism of the official declaration of a preemptive strategy was that it made explicit a military tactic that had always been part of the implicit U.S. security arsenal. While there is general agreement that a declaratory doctrine of preemption has different implications from an implicit option of preemption, there is much less consensus about the wisdom of publicly declaring a preemptive strategy. Announcing a preemptive strategy can enhance deterrence—that is, prevent unwanted action. But it can also, paradoxically, encourage adversaries to attack first or to pursue actions with greater secrecy, thereby impeding early detection of threats. Given the paradoxical nature of a declared policy of preemption, perhaps the most effective strategy is to maintain an ambiguous posture that assures adversaries that military action will be taken against threats at the time and manner of the government's choosing. This perspective was the basis of American strategic doctrine during the Cold War. It has also been recommended more recently by a report for Harvard University's National Security Program. That report concludes, "A deliberately ambiguous policy that neither rejects nor recommends preemption may be best. To our potential opponents, what we do is far more important than what we say. For the American public and the rest of the world, what we say is important."[33]

Although the NSS tended to conflate the preemptive and preventive use of force, it is important to differentiate the two. Preemption, as a corollary of the right of self-defense, allows for military attack when aggression is imminent. To preempt means to attack before an aggressor strikes. According to Walzer, preemptive attack is morally justified when three conditions are fulfilled: the existence of an intention to injure, the undertaking of military preparations that increase the level of danger, and the need to act immediately because of a higher degree of risk.[34] Walzer argues that since these conditions were met in Israel's Six-Day War, Israel's preemptive attack on Egypt on June 5, 1967, was a legitimate act of self-defense.

Preventive war, by contrast, occurs at an earlier stage in the evolution of conflict, chiefly in response to a growing imbalance of military power or the development of military capabilities that might pose future security threats. Unlike preemption, however, preventive attack responds not to an imminent threat but to an adversary's increasing military capabilities. The goal of preventive attack is to destroy the enemy's ability to carry out aggression before it can mobilize that capability.[35] This type of action was illustrated in June 1981, when Israel bombed and destroyed an Iraqi nuclear reactor that was about to become operational. It did so because it feared that if the reactor were used to generate nuclear fuel for a weapon of mass destruction, such a development would pose a grave security threat to Israel. Accordingly, Israel destroyed the Osirak nuclear reactor to prevent Iraq from acquiring a nuclear bomb. To the extent that preventive military action is consistent with the right of self-defense, this use of force was regarded as morally legitimate but contrary to international law because the attack involved a violation of Iraqi state sovereignty.

Distinguishing between preemptive and defensive force has of course become more difficult with the rise of WMD threats from nonstate actors. When the UN was established in 1945, the sole actors were nation-states and the primary threat to world order was military aggression. In the postmodern world, however, the major threat to peace is no longer state aggression. Rather, the major dangers arise from failed states, criminal gangs, ethnoreligious wars, and, most importantly, lethal threats from terrorist groups and religious fundamentalists. How should states seek to deter attacks from nonstate actors? Must states wait for aggression to occur before they can use force in self-defense, as specified in the UN Charter (Article 51)? Is it realistic to rely on Security Council–authorized peacemaking initiatives (based on Chapter VII of the UN Charter)?

In 2004, UN secretary-general Kofi Annan appointed a high-level panel of former statesmen to explore whether the foundational principles of the UN were still relevant in addressing lethal threats. The panel concluded that they were, arguing that when a state is faced with an imminent attack, it has the right to use force, but when faced with a latent threat (not imminent) it should not act without Security Council authorization.[36] Daalder and Steinberg think that this is unrealistic since the distinction between imminent and latent threats no longer holds. They write, "So long as the threats states face are unconventional, relying on the conventional distinction between imminent and latent threats makes little sense."[37] Although they do not fully endorse the preemptive, unilateral approach of the Bush Doctrine, they nevertheless argue that the rules of the game concerning international security need to be altered. "The UN's concept of the international system," they write, "no longer accords with the world as it now exists. That means that the rules regulating the use of force must be adapted to the world we do live in—a world in which sovereignty is increasingly conditional on how states behave internally, and in which the need to intervene in the internal affairs of states is growing accordingly."[38]

From a just war perspective, war is considered morally legitimate if its purpose is self-defense—to inhibit aggression, to protect innocent persons from unjust violence, and to restore conditions existing prior to aggression. Although both preemption and prevention pose moral challenges to the use of force, preemptive war is more easily reconciled with the demands of international political morality when it is based upon an imminent danger whose scope and certainty is empirically demonstrable. By contrast, preventive war is more problematic ethically because the knowledge justifying military action is likely to be more speculative. Determining an adversary's future intentions and capabilities poses major challenges even in the best of circumstances. To illustrate the moral difficulties of preventive war, I turn next to the 2003 war against Iraq.

After the U.S.-led coalition had decisively defeated Iraq in the 1991 Persian Gulf War, the victorious powers imposed a number of demands on the government of Iraq as part of the peace settlement. In particular, Iraq agreed to disarm and to accept economic liability for the destruction that it had inflicted by invading and occupying Kuwait. The cease-fire terms were more fully formulated in Security Council Resolution 687, adopted in April 1991, two months after the end of hostilities. Some of its major provisions demanded that Iraq: (1) provide an accurate and complete disclosure about its WMD programs; (2) not use, develop, or acquire WMD and, under international inspection, destroy all such weapons; and (3) dismantle and not develop ballistic missiles with a range of more than 150 kilometers. To ensure compliance with these and related provisions, the United Nations established a special commission (UNSCOM) to verify Iraq's disarmament. Although Iraq allowed UNSCOM and inspectors from the International Atomic Energy Agency (IAEA), the institution charged with verifying compliance with nuclear nonproliferation, to carry extensive on-site inspections, Iraqi officials repeatedly delayed and obstructed inspections. As a result of these impediments, both UNSCOM and IAEA ceased working in 1998. Although inspection teams returned temporarily a year later, they too found it impossible to carry out their work.

IRAQ'S NONCOMPLIANCE AND REGIME CHANGE

To ensure accountability with Security Council resolutions, comprehensive economic sanctions, instituted in the immediate aftermath of Iraq's invasion of Kuwait, were continued.[39] However, to meet the country's humanitarian needs, the UN authorized supervised petroleum sales under the Oil-for-Food Program. According to this program, Iraq could sell petroleum to purchase foodstuffs, medicine, and humanitarian equipment. During its seven years of operation (1996 to 2003), UN-supervised oil sales were about $64 billion, generating some $37 billion in humanitarian goods. Regrettably, the program was not well managed, and Hussein was able to generate significant revenues for his own personal use through a variety of illicit financial schemes.[40]

In addition to sanctions, the United States and Britain also used "no-fly" zones over northern and southern Iraq to contain Saddam.[41] These zones were initially established in response to Iraqi military repression of Kurds in the north and Shiites in the south after both groups had demanded increased political autonomy. But when Saddam refused to comply with the requirements of the cease-fire, the no-fly zones became a means of surveillance as well as an instrument to check the military power of the regime. Although the cease-fire had ended military operations after a ground war of about one hundred hours, Iraq's failure to fulfill the terms of surrender signified that a state of war continued to exist in the region.

By 2000, support for economic sanctions had begun to wane under the weight of human suffering that such measures had imposed on Iraq. Although the Oil-for-Food Program had sought to meet basic human needs, large sectors of society, especially children and the aged, continued to suffer from the lack of adequate nutrition and medical care. Believing that Western economic sanctions would be lifted in the near future, a number of industrial states began investing in Iraq with the anticipation of reaping significant economic advantages when the embargo was lifted. But Saddam Hussein's disregard of the UN disarmament demands would not be allowed to continue indefinitely.

After the 9/11 attacks, the United States began to view Iraq as a far greater menace to global order. Since Iraq had built up stockpiles of chemical and biological weapons, had made substantial progress in developing a nuclear bomb, and had acquired ballistic missiles, Bush administration officials began to regard Iraq's noncompliance with disarmament as a threat to regional stability. And because the Saddam regime had sponsored and harbored terrorists in the past and potentially might help terrorists acquire WMD, senior U.S. government officials began to regard it as a growing threat to U.S. security. Accordingly, President Bush identified Iraq as a part of the "axis of evil" (with the other two states being North Korea and Iran) in his 2002 State of the Union address. Soon after, senior government officials, including Secretary of State Colin Powell, began calling for regime change in Baghdad.[42]

In September 2002, President Bush addressed the United Nations and demanded that the Security Council resolutions be enforced. In his speech Bush claimed that Iraq's conduct was a threat to the authority of the United Nations and to international peace. In the weeks following the president's UN speech, the United States carried out extensive diplomatic negotiations with major powers, especially the permanent members of the Security Council, to secure one final resolution that would force Iraq to disclose its WMD programs and fully disarm in accordance with Resolution 687. Negotiations were especially difficult with Russia and France, which were opposed to an Iraqi regime change. But in the end the U.S. diplomatic initiative prevailed, with the Security Council unanimously endorsing Resolution 1441 on November 8, 2002. That resolution charged that Iraq had been "in material breach" of its UN obligations, especially Resolution 687, and that the current resolution represented "a final opportunity to fully comply with disarmament demands." To ensure that Iraq was fulfilling its obligations, Resolution 1441 demanded that Iraq report to the UN on its WMD programs. Specifically, it called on Iraq to provide "a currently accurate, full, and complete declaration of all aspects of its programs to develop chemical, biological, and nuclear weapons, ballistic missiles, and other delivery

systems" within thirty days. The resolution also noted that false declarations or omissions would themselves constitute a material breach of Iraq's international obligations.

Some have claimed that the adoption of Resolution 1441 was a victory for the UN and a triumph for international law. Michael Glennon has argued that this is simply an incorrect reading of Iraqi–UN relations. Glennon writes, "Had the United States not threatened Iraq with the use of force, the Iraqis almost surely would have rejected the new inspections regime. Yet such threats of force violate the charter . . . the council's 'victory,' such as it was, was a victory of diplomacy backed by force—or more accurately, of diplomacy backed by the threat of unilateral force in violation of the charter. The unlawful threat of unilateralism enabled the 'legitimate' exercise of multilateralism. The Security Council reaped the benefit of the charter's violation."[43]

In early December, Iraq issued its report on the state of its weapons programs, as called for by Resolution 1441. The twelve thousand pages of documents that were released were a disparate collection of files that purported to account for Iraq's WMD programs. But within days of receiving the report it was clear to U.S. intelligence agencies that the bundles of papers failed to account for past weapons programs. As a result, Secretary Powell declared that Iraq had failed to disclose the required information about its arms programs and was therefore again in "material breach" of Security Council resolutions.[44]

To help enforce the demands of Resolution 1441, UN and IAEA inspectors had resumed on-site inspections for the first time in four years. In late January, Hans Blix, the head of the UN inspection team, and Mohamed El-Baradei, the director of the IAEA, provided a preliminary report to the Security Council on the early phase of the inspectors' work. Neither report, however, provided any conclusive evidence that Saddam was carrying out a disarmament program.

In the meantime, the United States increased its pressure not only on Iraq but also on the international community. While military forces were being deployed to the Middle East, President Bush and his senior advisors were repeatedly making the case to Congress, the media, the UN and other international organizations that if the Saddam Hussein regime did not account for WMD it should be replaced. In his January 2003 State of the Union message, the president set forth the demands bluntly and starkly: "If Saddam Hussein does not fully disarm, for the safety of our people and for the peace of the world, we will lead a coalition to disarm him." Early in February, Secretary Powell addressed the Security Council, giving the most thorough and detailed presentation of any administration official on the dangers posed by Iraq's WMD programs. Speaking in a detailed and impassioned manner, Powell used intelligence to make the case that Iraq was not complying with the UN's demands for disclosure about and destruction of its WMD programs. Powell, however, failed to convince China, France, and Russia that the time had come for military action. France in particular continued to call for more time for further arms inspections. But by the middle of March, Britain, Spain, and the United States had concluded that the time for diplomacy had ended. It was now time to act. Accordingly, the president announced an ultimatum: "Saddam Hussein and his sons," said Bush in a brief televised speech, "must leave Iraq within forty-eight hours. Their refusal to do so will result in military conflict, commenced at a time of our choosing."[45]

On Wednesday morning, March 19, the president met with his National Security Council and after reviewing final preparations issued the order to commence war, dubbed "Operation Iraqi Freedom." Unlike the 1991 Persian Gulf War, which involved nearly a month of aerial bombing, the Iraq War began with combined ground and air operations. The aim was to capture Baghdad and other major urban centers with the least possible destruction. Despite significant obstacles, including an overextended supply line, sporadic battles with regular forces, guerrilla-type attacks by irregular forces, dust storms, and hot weather, the campaign proceeded much more rapidly than military planners had expected. Within three weeks U.S. forces had captured the Baghdad airport and controlled all major roads into the city, and on April 9 U.S. forces entered the city and

began taking control of key military and government centers, including most of Saddam's former palaces. Soon thereafter the occupying forces began focusing on the task of state building and nation building in order to provide a new, more legitimate basis of political authority. Given the deep political fragmentation among the Kurds, Shi'a Muslims, and Sunni Muslims, these tasks have proved far more difficult than first anticipated. Moreover, because of the low level of communal trust and social solidarity, and the depleted condition of the economy, national reconstruction has remained a daunting challenge.

THE ETHICS OF REGIME CHANGE

U.S. government officials justified the decision to topple the regime of Saddam Hussein with three major claims. First they argued that Iraq had failed to comply with the peace terms of the 1991 Persian Gulf War and more particularly with the disarmament obligations demanded by the Security Council. Second, they claimed that the Saddam government was tyrannical and abusive of human rights, having systematically tortured or killed hundreds of thousands of its own citizens. Third and most important, U.S. officials believed that Iraq's unwillingness to disarm, coupled with its past support of terrorists, made the Hussein regime a threat to world order and a potential future threat to the United States. Because of Iraq's past offensive military behavior, its development and acquisition of chemical and biological weapons, its acquisition of ballistic missiles, and its failure to account for its past WMD programs, there was widespread concern among Western states that Iraq posed a threat to world order. American government leaders assumed that in the post-9/11 global environment, the conjunction of a tyrannical regime, weapons of mass destruction, and the threat of terrorism created conditions that were a threat not only to the Middle East but also to the world itself. While the threat from Iraq was not considered imminent, it was nevertheless a growing threat, one that was "grave and gathering."

Since the international community is based upon the norm of state sovereignty, the use of force to replace a government is considered an extraordinary step in international politics—one that should be taken only when egregious offenses have been committed and all peaceful alternatives have been exhausted. Moreover, although states are legally entitled to use unilateral force to ensure their own territorial security (Article 51 of the UN Charter), the enforcement and maintenance of global order is a collective responsibility entrusted to the UN Security Council. In other words, regime change is an exceptional development that should be undertaken only when the Security Council authorizes such action or when legitimate claims of national security are at stake. Of course, the norm of sovereignty is not intended to shield rogue regimes that threaten global order or abuse the human rights of their people. Indeed, the international community can function only if member states fulfill their basic international obligations toward states and their own citizens. As a result, preventive or preemptive war may be morally justified when an outlaw state has acquired WMD and poses a significant threat to other states.

Historically, the "just cause" norm of the just war tradition has been interpreted as defense against aggression. But when rogue states like Iraq, Iran, and North Korea acquire highly destructive armaments, how should the notion of "defense against aggression" be interpreted? Must the United States wait until a rogue state launches a ballistic missile tipped with a WMD before it can legitimately attack such a state? "Can we not say that, in the hands of certain kinds of states," asks Weigel, "the mere possession of weapons of mass destruction constitutes an aggression—or, at the very least, an aggression waiting to happen?"[46] For Weigel, if the decentralized, anarchic world system is to pursue a just international order, the distinction between *bellum* and *duellum* must be preserved by limiting the use of armed force to legitimate, law-abiding states—that is, to those communities that are properly constituted and are fulfilling their international obligations. Outlaw states that condone terrorism or that disregard the demands of the international community should not be entitled to sovereign immunity.

The decision to go to war against Iraq was criticized vociferously by some. Some scholars opposed the war because they believed that the best strategy to inhibit Iraqi aggression was deterrence—that is, maintaining a credible threat of unacceptable punishment. Given the preponderance of American military power, these critics assumed that even if Iraq were to acquire nuclear weapons, the regional and global balance of power would deter Iraqi aggression. According to John Mearsheimer and Stephen Walt, a strategy of "vigilant containment" would ensure that Iraq would not resort to reckless aggression. They explained their confidence in deterrence as follows: "It only takes a leader who wants to stay alive and who wants to remain in power. Throughout his lengthy and brutal career, Saddam Hussein has repeatedly shown that these two goals are absolutely paramount. That is why deterrence and containment would work."[47]

Other critics were opposed to war because they believed that more time was necessary to allow for Iraqi compliance with Security Council resolutions. This was essentially the position of the French and Russian governments, which pleaded for more time for UN inspectors to do their work.[48] It was also the position of numerous scholars and media commentators. Michael Walzer, for example, argued that other alternatives needed to be pursued before going to war. For him the "last resort" norm of the just war theory had not been fulfilled. While recognizing that "last resort" was a metaphysical condition that could never be fully fulfilled in real life, he believed, nevertheless, that the present system of sanctions, overflights, and UN inspections was working and could be made to work better.[49] But the existing strategy, especially the reliance on economic sanctions, was not without significant moral costs. As I note in chapter 10, economic sanctions are indiscriminate tools, often imposing hardship on those most vulnerable and least responsible for a government's actions. They are morally problematic because the hardship that they inflict is indiscriminate. Thus, those who supported the continuation of sanctions were thus unwittingly encouraging further suffering on children and the elderly.

Finally, some critics of the war argued that unilateral military action against Iraq, even to enforce the disarmament provisions demanded by the Security Council, was legally offensive because only the United Nations could authorize peace-enforcement action. For them, the pursuit of a stable and peaceful international community required multilateral participation, preferably guided by the Security Council. Since the UN Charter demands that the Security Council authorize the use of force in any cause other than self-defense, the unilateral threat of military action against a member state is normally contrary to the UN Charter and therefore against international law. But while unilateral force on behalf of world order may be inconsistent with international law, such action may nevertheless be morally justified. Indeed, when legal duties confront moral obligations, the cause of justice demands that its moral claims take precedence over structural or legal responsibilities.

Prior to the war, former president Jimmy Carter argued that invading Iraq would be contrary to the just war tradition. He claimed, among other things, that the United States did not have international authority to pursue regime change.[50] But contrary to Carter, the "legitimate authority" criterion of the just war theory does not require international sanction. Rather, it demands that armed force be used by appropriate political authorities in a proportionate and discriminating manner for the public good. The moral appropriateness of force without UN sanction was illustrated in the Kosovo war of 1999. In that conflict NATO carried out an intensive two-month bombing campaign, even though the Security Council had not authorized the armed action because Russia, Serbia's ally, would have vetoed such a measure. Thus, even though the war was technically illegal, it was subsequently justified as morally legitimate because of the goals and means that were used in the defense of human rights.[51] The problem with using this logic, however, is that WMD were not found after Iraq had been conquered. Consequently, many observers have come to regard the invasion not only as illegal but also as illegitimate.

MORAL REFLECTIONS

The U.S-.led war against Iraq is challenging to assess morally because knowledge about the Saddam regime and its military capabilities and intentions remains ambiguous and incomplete. Since no WMD were found, some observers have claimed that there was no legitimate reason for going to war against Iraq. Others, however, have claimed that Iraq, having failed to comply with Security Council resolutions, remained a threat to the region's peace and stability. Some defense and foreign policy officials have argued that even if Saddam had destroyed all of his WMD stockpiles, regime change was nevertheless justified because of the past egregious abuse of human rights and the promise of establishing a more humane, democratic regime.

Regardless of how the WMD debate is settled, the preventive war against Iraq raises several important ethical issues:

- Has modern terrorism made preemptive military action or preventive war more acceptable legally and morally?
- Is the unilateral enforcement of the UN Security Council resolutions a morally valid strategy? Although multilateralism might be a prudent approach to international security concerns, is approval by the Security Council a necessary prerequisite for legitimate international peacekeeping or peacemaking initiatives?
- When legal and moral obligations come in conflict, as they did in Iraq and Kosovo, which claims should take precedence? Why?
- Does the failure to find WMD invalidate the moral justification for going to war against Iraq?

SUMMARY

Since war is evil because it leads to killing and destruction, political theorists, theologians, and decision makers have historically held widely different views about the moral legitimacy of this form of conflict resolution. Of the three important approaches to the problem of war, I argued that just war provides a useful framework by which to judge both the morality of going to war and the morality of war itself. This tradition is not intended to serve as a checklist for government leaders, but rather as a way of thinking about moral statecraft—about bringing moral reasoning to bear on the difficult issues of intractable international conflict.

When states commit aggression against other states, the just war tradition provides principles by which to devise appropriate public policies to defend the legitimate interests of political communities. But when nonstate actors commit terrorist acts, applying just war principles presents a more difficult challenge. Terrorism is of course inconsistent with political morality because the violence it inflicts is perpetrated illegitimately (by nongovernmental organizations) in blatant disregard for the principle of discrimination (intentionally harming innocent civilians). But how should a state respond to the threat of terror? Must a government wait for major aggression to occur before it can resort to lethal force? While the just war tradition has historically justified war in response to unjust aggression, preemptive or even preventive war may be morally justified in exceptional circumstances, such as to confront the dangers of terrorist groups with WMD.

Regardless of the nature and scope of threats to national security, moral statecraft demands that leaders devise public policies that involve war only as a last resort and that the violence be limited, proportional, and discriminating.

Chapter Eight

The Ethics of Irregular War

The prohibition against torture expresses one of the West's most powerful taboos—and some taboos are worth preserving even at heavy cost. . . . [T]here is a line which democracies cross at their peril: threatening or inflicting actual bodily harm. On one side of that line stand societies sure of their civilized values. That is the side America and its allies must choose.[1]

—THE ECONOMIST

In conventional wars, enemy soldiers are disabled by death or injury; in asymmetric war, they are captured, incarcerated, and interrogated. Information, not a body count, is the key to defeating many terrorist and guerrilla organizations.[2]

—MICHAEL L. GROSS

The more endangered public safety is thought to be, the more the balance swings against civil liberties. . . . Terrorists are more dangerous than ordinary criminals, and so . . . the dogma that it is better for ten guilty people to go free than for one innocent person to be convicted may not hold when the guilty ten are international terrorists seeking to obtain weapons of mass destruction.[3]

—JUDGE RICHARD POSNER

IN THE PREVIOUS CHAPTER, I examined the ethics of force in conventional interstate wars. I now turn to the role of coercive power involving unconventional military operations by nonstate actors. Unlike conventional wars between the armed forces of two states, irregular wars generally involve insurgent, revolutionary movements or radical religious groups that seek to undermine the authority of a state through terrorism and small-scale, clandestine violence. Some of the Cold War's most significant and persistent military disputes involved domestic revolutionary wars fought over the nature of the regime. Such wars frequently involved subnational armed forces using covert, guerrilla tactics. In many of these domestic revolutionary conflicts, the United States and the Soviet Union sought to advance their ideological goals—and influence the outcome of these wars—through a variety of coercive instruments. These unconventional strategies ranged from covert operations (e.g., clandestine raids) to overt political, economic, and military support to occasional small-scale military operations.

In the post–Cold War era, the major cause of domestic political strife has shifted from ideology to ethnonationalism. Whereas previous wars were fought over the nature of political regimes, current disputes are rooted in ethnic, religious, and nationalistic sources as groups compete for political control of government or demand increased political autonomy from the state. To a significant degree, the growth of intranational disputes over political self-determination has greatly weakened domestic authority and in some cases has led to "quasi" or "failed" states. Beginning in the late 1990s, Muslim fundamentalist groups declared war on Western secular society, resulting in a rising number of terrorist attacks throughout the world. Since the 9/11 terrorist attacks, Muslim radical groups have pursued violent insurgencies in Afghanistan and Iraq and carried out terrorist attacks in numerous countries, including Indonesia, Kenya, Tanzania, India, and Pakistan.

The increase in domestic political violence is significant because most irregular wars are carried out by nonstate actors using clandestine violence against civilian populations. As a result, they differ considerably from conventional wars. Whereas classical international wars involve a direct contest between the military forces of two or more states, the revolutionary wars of the Cold War era and the current terror campaigns by radical Islamists (e.g., Al Qaeda) involve violence that is not easily encompassed by traditional laws of war or the established moral principles of just war theory. Irregular wars are legally problematic because nonstate actors are not considered legitimate, competent political authorities. And irregular wars are morally problematic because violence is carried out indiscriminately and directed by illegitimate authorities.

Irregular wars typically involve two major types of operations—insurgency and counterinsurgency. *Insurgency*, also known as guerrilla warfare, involves a protracted political and military effort by irregular forces and illegal political organizations seeking to topple an existing regime. The aim of such a war is to force the collapse of the government through unconventional military tactics, including guerrilla warfare and even periodic terrorist attacks. The goal of insurgency is not to directly engage a regime's regular forces in battle, but to exhaust them through hit-and-run tactics, low-level military actions, and popular action programs and propaganda campaigns designed to gain the people's political support. *Counterinsurgency*, the second strategy, involves a government's effort to counter guerrilla activity both by maintaining the political support of the people and by overtly and covertly challenging the coercive operations of the insurgent forces. In Afghanistan, NATO forces are using this strategy to deter insurgent attacks and to consolidate the political authority of governmental leaders.

Since counterinsurgency often involves clandestine operations using unconventional force, such strategies pose ethical challenges insofar as they blur the distinction between combatants and noncombatants. Insurgencies, as previously discussed, seek to defeat the enemy not through direct military engagements, but rather through wars of attrition based on hit-and-run tactics and attacks on society's infrastructure and on key civilian institutions. A major aim of insurgents' military operations is to foster fear, demoralize citizens, weaken society, and undermine the economy. To effectively carry out military operations, insurgent forces rely on secrecy, surprise, and small-scale operations, frequently involving civilian support. Indeed, insurgencies and counterinsurgencies are morally problematic because, by engaging civilians as active participants in the war, they subvert the just war norm of discrimination that differentiates combatants from noncombatants.

Despite the moral challenges posed by unconventional operations, some scholars defend the right to fight tyranny with unconventional force. Walzer, for example, argues that, notwithstanding the moral problems of guerrilla war, insurgency can be a morally legitimate means of fighting oppression.[4] Whether or not fighting against a tyrannical regime is moral will depend on both the conditions that justify violence against a regime and the range of legitimate methods available to rebels. Charles Krauthammer similarly provides a qualified defense of guerrilla tactics when the existing oppression is the greater evil.[5] According to him, while domestic political order is essential for a peaceful, humane society, order is not the only public good by which we judge political communities. As the U.S. Declaration of Independence suggests, when a regime becomes tyrannical, people have a right to rebel and constitute a new, legitimate government authority. In short, internal, unconventional wars, like interstate wars, can be morally permissible, provided that their ends and means are just. However, unlike traditional wars, irregular wars present greater challenges in ensuring that the means of violence are morally acceptable.

TERRORISM

Terrorism is random violence carried out to communicate a political message. International terrorism, to paraphrase Carl von Clausewitz, is the continuation of politics by other means.[6] Although terrorism, like war, is a form of violence used for political ends, it differs from the armed violence of the state. First, whereas conventional war involves destruction aimed at soldiers and military and political installations, the terrorist makes no distinction between combatants and noncombatants. Second, while war is carried out by the armed forces of a state, terrorism is violence perpetrated primarily by nongovernmental agents. A third difference is that terrorism is essentially "psychological warfare"[7]—that is, violence designed to undermine communal solidarity by fostering fear. As terrorists seek to weaken existing structures and institutions by spreading fear throughout society, they rely on random violence aimed at innocent civilians. Political theorist Michael Walzer writes, "Randomness is the crucial feature of terrorist activity. If one wishes fear to spread and intensify over time, it is not desirable to kill specific people identified in some particular way with a regime, a party, or a policy. Death must come by chance."[8]

Terrorism is illegal and immoral. It is illegal because it does not conform to the codified rules of war, which require soldiers to be responsible for violence and solely target combatants. Terrorism is inconsistent with the laws of war because it refuses to make distinctions between soldiers and civilians, combatants and noncombatants. Indeed, terrorists not only refuse to distinguish between the two groups, but they intentionally target innocent civilians in order to spread fear. And terrorism is immoral because it condemns unarmed citizens to death "not for what they do, but for who they are and what they believe."[9] According to the just war tradition, political violence is morally legitimate only when its aims and methods are consistent with political morality. As Camus writes in his play *The Just Assassins*, "Even in destruction, there's a right way and a wrong way—and there are limits."[10] Additionally, terrorism is immoral because it seeks to replace political life with coercion. Michael Ignatieff writes, "Terrorism is a form of politics that aims at the death of politics itself. For this reason, it must be combated by all societies that wish to remain political: otherwise both we and the people terrorists purport to represent are condemned to live, not in a political world of deliberation, but in a prepolitical state of combat, a state of war."[11]

Although scholars and public officials generally agree that terrorism is evil because it perpetrates random violence on civilians, there is much less consensus about which individuals and groups are terrorists.[12] One reason for the lack of agreement is the propensity to treat all nongovernmental violence as morally equivalent. As the relativist cliché suggests, "One person's 'terrorist' is another person's 'freedom fighter.'" Another reason lies with the groups' political goals. As people are likely to differ in their perceptions of the moral merits of terrorists' goals, some groups are likely to be regarded as far more evil and offensive than others. An ardent advocate of Palestinian statehood, for example, is likely to view Islamic Jihad or Hamas not as terrorist organizations, but as liberation movements that rely on urban violence to dramatize the injustice of Israel's continuing occupation of the West Bank. By contrast, Israeli citizens are likely to view such organizations as evil not only in their methods but also in their goals and tactics. Finally, observers are likely to disagree about terrorism because of different interpretations about motivations. If terrorism is viewed as a by-product of economic deprivation, despair, and powerlessness, such violence will be regarded with more understanding and sympathy than if it is seen as simply a tool of power politics. Regardless of the moral merits of terrorists' goals, however, reliance on terror is inconsistent with international humanitarian law, the laws of war, and international political morality. Terrorism is evil not because of the illegitimacy of its goals but because it uses indiscriminate violence against innocent civilians.

Although terror has existed for a long time, the terrorism of the post–Cold War era differs from the "old" terrorism of the Cold War in several respects.[13] First, the "new" terrorism is more violent because it seeks not only to gain attention but also to inflict mass casualties. Second, whereas the older terrorism was undertaken primarily by revolutionary groups in their quest to transform a domestic political order, new terrorist groups tend to be transnational in scope and purpose. Their goal is not simply to undermine Western societies but to extend and institutionalize a new political order throughout the world. Third, the new terrorist groups are better organized and better financed than the older groups, which relied primarily on one or more states to provide funding and support. New groups like Al Qaeda derive their income not from states but from their own investments and business operations. Indeed, the resources of Al Qaeda are so extensive that it was able to provide Afghanistan, its primary host state, significant financial resources and to serve as a major source of military security and policy planning to the ruling Taliban. Finally, the new terrorist groups have greater access to lethal force, including weapons of mass destruction (WMD), with the result that dangers from terrorism have increased dramatically. While the 9/11 terrorist attack, the most destructive terrorist act in history, was achieved without modern weapons, the danger from chemical, biological, and nuclear weapons has greatly increased with the proliferation of scientific and technological knowledge about WMD. If trained terrorists can commandeer passenger airplanes to deploy them as large incendiary weapons, presumably they can also threaten nuclear power plants, contaminate the water supply of urban centers, spray toxic agents from airplanes, and place a "dirty bomb"[14] in a major business center.

COMBATING TERRORISM

How should a state seek to deter terrorism? How can a government minimize the threat of terrorism, especially when agents, inspired by fundamentalist religion, are prepared to sacrifice their own lives? Is it possible to inhibit or even prevent suicide bombings? Since terrorists carry out violence covertly, identifying and locating them is a daunting task. Moreover, since terrorists carry out violence randomly, making no distinction between combatants and noncombatants, devising a counterterror strategy that is consistent with widely accepted principles of humanitarianism and the international law of war presents major moral challenges. This is especially the case in applying the just war tradition to the problem of terror by nongovernmental agents. Historically, just war norms have been applied almost exclusively to states, presumably the only legitimate institutions of coercive power. To be sure, the tradition can be extended and applied to the problem of terror, but this application faces daunting challenges.[15]

When facing security threats from other states, governments have historically relied on coercive diplomacy, deterrence, and defensive power to prevent and, if necessary, repulse aggression. But these conventional strategies are unlikely to protect society from fanatical fighters committed to terror. Since terrorists are disciplined, well organized, and deeply committed to their goals, and because they undertake violence with secrecy and stealth, combating terrorism presents enormous challenges. To begin with, conventional strategies that rely on military power to deter, defend, or punish aggression are unlikely to protect society from the random, indiscriminate violence of terrorists. Because terrorists are members of an elusive revolutionary movement or small covert organization, identifying and locating members is exceptionally difficult. More importantly, because terrorists are fanatical in their devotion to the political cause they serve, the threat of retaliatory military punishment is unlikely to dissuade action. The contemporary phenomenon of suicide bombings, where terrorists willingly kill themselves in bombing missions, illustrates this high level of fanaticism.

Since deterrence is unlikely to protect society, combating terrorism will involve a two-pronged strategy, one defensive and the other offensive. The defensive strategy, known as *antiterrorism*, seeks to protect society by establishing policies, regulations, structures, and other initiatives that help to reduce a society's vulnerability to terror. Its aim is to protect people and, in the event of an attack, to minimize the effects of terror. Antiterrorism is illustrated in the initiatives and reforms instituted by the U.S. government in the aftermath of the 9/11 terrorist attack. These include the centralization of security and intelligence responsibilities in a new department (Homeland Security), increased surveillance of major transportation centers, improved border controls, more stringent security regulations at airports, and increased authority for law enforcement officials. Since protective measures alone are unlikely to save society from terror, a second strategy seeks to undermine terrorist networks and organizations before they are able to carry out their missions. This strategy, known as *counterterrorism*, uses the state's military and economic power to attack, weaken, and destroy terrorist organizations and movements. While such a strategy is appealing, it is extraordinarily difficult to implement because terrorist networks, by definition, carry out their operations with stealth and secrecy.

Given the elusive character of terrorism, an effective counterterrorism strategy will require accurate and timely intelligence and specialized military operations. From an ethical perspective, the major challenge in implementing a counterterrorism campaign is to defeat the enemy without resorting to the tactics and strategies of terrorists. When radical political groups in Argentina resorted to kidnapping and bombings in the mid-1970s, the state used abductions, torture, and secret killings to defeat the opposition. It is estimated than Argentina's war on terror resulted in more than ten thousand deaths or disappearances.[16] Although Argentina's military and state security forces won the battle against terrorists, their use of illegal, morally illegitimate tactics, especially the systematic abuse of human rights, ultimately undermined their institutional credibility and authority.

Given the secret, decentralized nature of terrorist organizations, electronic and photographic surveillance are unlikely to provide adequate information to prevent future terror. Ultimately, what is necessary is human intelligence—information gathered directly either by spies or by interrogators. Interrogation is of course difficult because agents must seek to get information that detainees do not wish to disclose. Given the immorality and illegality of torture, does this mean that all manipulative techniques of interrogation are prohibited? How must detainees be interrogated? When a community faces extreme emergencies—that is, when a community's safety and well-being are threatened—is limited coercive interrogation (what some observers call "torture lite") morally permissible?

In ancient and medieval times, torture was widely used to extract information from prisoners. Continental European states even developed legal procedures governing the use of torture to obtain evidence from suspects. After relying on torture for half a millennium, the Europeans ended the practice in the eighteenth century, not only because it was inconsistent with human dignity, but also because torture did not necessarily yield the desired information. According to John Langbein, the fundamental lesson of the European experience with torture is that "it has not been possible to make coercion compatible with truth."[17]

In the nineteenth century, as ideas of limited government, the rule of law, and human rights became more widespread in Europe and North America, states increasingly recognized that torture was inconsistent with humane governance. Although a taboo against torture began to develop in the nineteenth century, the international community did not adopt a formal prohibition of torture until 1987, when the Convention against Torture (formally known as the Convention against Torture and Other Cruel, Inhuman, or Degrading Treatment or Punishment) took effect. The statute, which has been ratified by more than 130 states, prohibits any act by which severe pain or suffering, whether physical or mental, is intention-ally inflicted on a person for such purposes as obtaining from him or a third person information or a confession, punishing him for an act he or a third person has com-mitted or is suspect of having committed, or intimidating or coercing him or a third person, or for any reason based on discrimination of any kind, when such pain or suffering is inflicted by or at the instigation of or with the consent or acquiescence of a public official or other person acting in an official capacity.

In 1994 the United States ratified the torture convention, although the Senate speci-fied a more restrictive definition of torture.[18]

Torture is contrary to the widely accepted norms of international political morality and international law. Sanford Levinson writes, "Torture is unequivocally and abso-lutely forbidden by the law of civilized nations."[19] Henry Shue similarly notes that tor-ture is "contrary to every relevant international law. . . . No other practice except slavery is so universally and unanimously condemned in law and human convention."[20] Despite the widespread condemnation of torture, the inhumane treatment of prisoners persists. Indeed, Amnesty International claims that some 130 countries continue to practice coercive interrogation, with 70 countries relying on inhumane treatment on a consis-tent basis.[21] While international law prohibits torture, some governments, especially dictatorships and authoritarian regimes, have used and continue to use torture in the belief that such a practice is necessary to counter security threats. Even democratic regimes have periodically resorted to torture when facing intractable political violence. Israel, for example, used modest torture—or what was termed "moderate physical pres-sure"—until its Supreme Court declared such action illegal in September 1999.

Perhaps the most notorious example of a democracy using torture was the French war against the Algerian FLN in the late 1950s. When the Algerian liberation move-ment—Front de Libération Nationale (FLN)—resorted to terrorism to end French colonial rule, the French government responded with a brutal war of attrition involving secret killings, torture, and disappearances.[22] The French security forces justified the use of torture through utilitarian, consequentialist logic: torture was a necessary evil in order to prevent a much more significant injustice—the deliberate killing of innocent civilians through terrorism. General Jacques Massu, a French commander in Algeria, articulated the cost-benefit logic of this view by claiming that "the innocent [the next victims of terrorist attacks] deserve more protection than the guilty."[23] When the Chil-ean military sought to eliminate Marxist opposition groups after the 1973 coup, it did so by following the French practice of targeted killings, abductions, and torture. Subse-quently, both Argentina and Uruguay used kidnappings and torture to gain intelligence about the opposition in their war against terrorist groups.

In seeking to defeat terrorism, democratic states face enormous challenges. Since an effective counterterrorism strategy will require patience, stealth, and intelligence, state security forces may be tempted to counter terror with means used by terrorists themselves. But if a democratic state is to maintain its legitimacy and credibility, it must rely on morally legitimate strategies. In seeking to protect society from terrorism, states must refrain from using illegal and immoral tactics, particularly those that under-mine human rights and question the moral authority of the state. Irregular operations must remain a last resort against legitimate targets. In devising and carrying out counterterrorism, constitutional governments are likely to face a variety of difficult moral challenges.

Below I address two contemporary military issues relating to the American counterterrorism campaign: the nature and role of coercive interrogation and the killing of individual terrorists (targeted killing). The first of these tactics was used in the early phase of the U.S. war on terror and was subject to much public debate, especially after military authorities disclosed significant abuses against detainees. Ironically, targeted killing—the far more consequential tactic—has received much less media attention.[24]

CASE 8-1: THE ETHICS OF COERCIVE INTERROGATION

THE U.S. WAR ON TERRORISM

In the aftermath of the terror attacks of September 11, 2001, that resulted in the death of close to three thousand innocent civilians in New York City and Washington, D.C., the Bush administration embarked on a war against Al Qaeda, the Taliban, and other radical Islamic groups. President Bush declared that in prosecuting the war against terrorist groups, the United States would make no distinction between terrorists and those who harbor and support them. Unlike interstate wars, a military campaign against nonstate actors is an irregular or unconventional war. Since terrorists carry out their operations covertly and seek to inflict fear in society by targeting innocent civilians, the effort to defeat such irregular forces is especially difficult. In conventional wars the aim is to defeat the enemy's armed forces. In unconventional or asymmetric conflicts, however, the primary goal is not simply to punish terrorists but to prevent them from carrying out destruction. Since preventing attack is only possible with timely, accurate information, intelligence is essential in prosecuting an irregular war.

In prosecuting the U.S. war on terror, the Bush administration decided early on that terrorists were to be regarded as "unlawful enemy combatants"—to be treated humanely but not entitled to the protections afforded under the international law of war.[25] Keith Pavlischek, a national security ethicist, has argued that the decision to distinguish between legitimate and illegitimate warriors was morally correct. He writes,

> International terrorists deserve to be treated justly. They do not deserve to be treated either as lawful combatants with the full rights due to honorable prisoners of war, or as ordinary criminals, with all the attendant due process rights. They are not ordinary criminals; rather, they are part of a global political-religious-ideological insurgency that employs terror as one means toward a well-articulated political end. However much we may quibble over the precise distinctions between what we do owe unlawful combatants by way of treatment or due process after capture, in distinction from that which we owe lawful combatants after capture, justice requires us to treat them precisely as the [Bush] administration treats them, as unlawful enemy combatants.[26]

Under the laws of war, prisoners are not required to provide information. But since captured insurgents were not considered lawful combatants, the U.S. government authorized the selective use of coercive interrogation techniques to secure intelligence from captured Al Qaeda combatants. Additionally, the U.S. government increased the use of "extraordinary rendition"—that is, sending prisoners to foreign countries where they could be interrogated with fewer legal constraints. As a result of the relaxation of the norms against coercive interrogation, numerous abuses occurred in detention centers and prisons. These abuses precipitated, in turn, an intense public debate about the manner in which military and intelligence agencies were pursuing the war on terror.

These abuses first began to surface after hundreds of prisoners were transferred to the U.S. naval base in Guantánamo, Cuba. After Amnesty International protested U.S. treatment of detained captives, President Bush reaffirmed American opposition to torture. He said, "I call on all governments to join with the United States and the community of law-abiding nations in prohibiting, investigating, and prosecuting all acts of torture . . . and we are leading this fight by example."[27] But this claim ceased to be credible when graphic photographs of U.S. prisoner abuse at Baghdad's Abu Ghraib prison became widely available in May 2004, resulting in widespread media coverage.[28]

The digital photographs, taken by military police, showed prisoners being sexually humiliated and threatened with dogs. Some soldiers charged that these actions were taken to "soften up" prisoners for subsequent interrogation. Others argued that the mistreatment was due to a lack of professionalism and a failure of military leadership, while still others claimed that the sadistic actions had been orchestrated for the guards' entertainment. Whatever the reasons, it was evident that the human depravity depicted in the widely circulated images was contrary to humanitarian law and the common morality of civilized people and was a deep embarrassment to the American people and its government. President Bush vigorously denounced the Abu Ghraib abuses, saying that such actions did not represent the values of the United States, while Senator John Warner (R-VA), the chairman of the Senate Armed Services Committee, declared that the photographs represented the worst "military misconduct" that he had seen in sixty years. Some political leaders demanded the resignation or firing of the secretary of defense, Donald Rumsfeld. However the scandal is defined and explained, the prison abuses undermined the U.S. initiative to promote a more humane and democratic Iraq along with the values necessary to sustain such a political order. As one commentator noted, "The Abu Ghraib photographs and the terrible story they tell have done great damage to what was left of America's moral power in the world, and thus its power to inspire hope rather than hatred among Muslims."[29]

Based on investigations by several government commissions, it is clear that American soldiers and security agents mistreated captives in both Afghanistan and Iraq.[30] While overcrowded prison conditions, inadequate resources and personnel, poor training, and tensions between interrogators and military police may have contributed to the mistreatment of detainees, two factors appear to have been especially important in the breakdown of military discipline. First, the U.S. government decision to treat Al Qaeda operatives as "unlawful combatants" meant that such detainees would not be accorded the legal protection normally given soldiers. Even though detainees were to be treated humanely, the removal of international legal protection may have introduced unnecessary uncertainty and flexibility in the rules governing nonstate insurgents. Second, in response to the growing Iraqi insurgency in 2003 that had resulted in hundreds of American casualties, U.S. military leaders relaxed the rules of interrogation in order to increase "actionable intelligence" from captured insurgents.[31] Although these adjustments in interrogation tactics focused on psychological techniques and excluded physical torture, they undoubtedly contributed to prisoner mistreatment.

THE ETHICS OF COERCIVE INTERROGATION

There is little doubt that torture—defined as inflicting severe physical harm on prisoners—is immoral and illegal. As James Turner Johnson notes, torture is inconsistent with the just war tradition—first, because harm may not be inflicted on those not directly involved in using force, and second, because intentionally harming or abusing a person is contrary "to what it means to be a good human person."[32] But are threats and psychological pain equivalent to severe physical harm? Are deception and isolation torture? What about sleep deprivation and loud music? In view of the lack of conceptual agreement, Judge Richard Posner has observed that torture "lacks a stable definition."[33] Given the definitional challenges posed by the idea of torture, political ethicist Jean Bethke Elshtain has observed that "[i]f we include all forms of coercion or manipulation within 'torture,' we move in the direction of indiscriminate moralism and legalism—a kind of deontology run amok."[34]

Stephen Carter, a professor of legal ethics, describes the challenge of interrogation as follows: "If those who possess the information would rather not part with it, the government will always be tempted . . . to require it out of them. The greater the sense of threat, the greater the temptation."[35] Legal philosopher Paul Kahn has observed that it is impossible to conceive of antiterrorism without torture. Terror and torture, he writes, are "reciprocal rituals of pain" that are beyond the law.[36] Thus, when the state cannot protect society from terrorism, the state will be tempted by necessity to go beyond the law in protecting itself.

The noted criminal lawyer Alan Dershowitz argues that "the tragic reality is that torture sometimes works."[37] But the belief that torture works is a dubious claim because the efficacy of such action is likely to be a short-term success at best. Indeed, the use of illegal and immoral means is likely to have deleterious effects not only on terrorists, but also on torturers and on society itself. Torture might help win a particular conflict, but it is unlikely to contribute to the defeat of a terrorist movement. For example, while the French were able to destroy the FLN terrorist network through their brutal antiterrorist campaign, the harsh strategy of repression and torture turned out to be counterproductive, eventually undermining French moral and political authority not only in Algeria but also in France. Bruce Hoffman, a leading scholar of terrorism, writes that the French army's counterinsurgency campaign alienated the Muslim masses, transformed their passive and apathetic response into political activism, swelled the popularity of and support for the FLN, and increasingly undermined French public support for continued colonial control. "The army's achievement in the city," writes Hoffman, "was therefore bought at the cost of eventual political defeat."[38] The deleterious effects of torture are also evident in Argentina and Chile, where military governments resorted to torture and secret killings in order to defeat antistate revolutionary groups.

Even if Dershowitz is correct in saying that torture sometimes "works," constitutional regimes face the challenge of defining under what exceptional national security threats such violence might be justified. Since the law is the basis of a constitutional order, torture will necessarily represent a violation of both domestic and international law. But torture is also morally unacceptable because it uses human beings as a means to an end, allowing violence to be inflicted on prisoners in order to gather information—that is, using evil (physical torture) for moral ends (preventing terror). Since Dershowitz wants to offer societal protection from terrorism without undermining the rule of law, he argues that when open, democratic nations face extreme security threats, such as prospective destruction from a "ticking bomb," nonlethal torture may be morally justified, provided it is authorized by judicial authority. For Dershowitz, nonlethal torture can be justified in exceptional circumstances if the agents seeking the desired information secure a "torture warrant."[39] The problem with courts authorizing torture, however, is that such action will undoubtedly encourage and regularize a behavior that is considered immoral and illegal. According to Judge Richard Posner, a better way to address extenuating security challenges is to allow "executive discretion"—that is, to leave in place existing legal prohibitions against torture with the understanding that they will not be enforced in extreme circumstances. Posner fears that if courts are allowed to legitimate nonlethal torture in extraordinary circumstances, such a practice will become institutionalized and in time will become commonplace.[40]

Since intelligence is essential in combating terrorist groups, international relations scholar Michael Gross argues that some forms of "interrogational torture" are not only morally permissible but also necessary in prosecuting unconventional armed conflict—or what he calls "asymmetric war."[41] For Gross, legitimate "enhanced" interrogation techniques include moderate physical pressure (e.g., stress positions, loud music, and sleep deprivation) but may never involve physical abuse. Since "torture lite" is normally illegal, Gross argues that the military and law enforcement agencies must never use such techniques. Only intelligence agencies seeking information are permitted such action in gathering intelligence to prosecute asymmetric war. In his words, "No democratic nation permits law enforcement agencies or its military to use enhanced interrogation. Enhanced techniques are restricted to intelligence agencies and only when questioning those suspected of terrorism."[42]

Zachary Calo, a law professor, argues that in conditions of "supreme emergency"—that is, when the fundamental values and security of a political community are threatened—some forms of torture may be morally warranted. He justifies his argument by attempting to find an intermediary position between the absolutist prohibition against torture and the conditional perspective based on necessity. Following the thought of political theorist Michael Walzer, Calo writes,

> [T]he only adequate response to necessity involves wrestling with the complexities that define the relationship between tragedy and democratic liberalism. It is into that dark space, neither transcendent nor pedestrian, to which the debate must move, so that we might more ably confront what Reinhold Niebuhr describes as the confusion which always exists in the area of life where politics and ethics meet.[43]

In Nazi Germany, Dietrich Bonhoeffer, a leading Lutheran theologian and pastor, had to confront the challenging ethical task of reconciling his temporal duties to obey the German state with his spiritual obligations to follow God. In the end, Bonhoeffer became not only a staunch dissident of the government but also an active participant in seeking to kill Hitler. In addressing the complex challenges of a disobedient and unfaithful Lutheran Church and an evil political regime, Bonhoeffer found that moral principles

themselves were inadequate to deal with the challenges he faced. Eric Metaxas writes of Bonhoeffer's struggle as follows: "Principles could carry one only so far. At some point every person must hear from God, must know what God was calling him to do, apart from others."[44] After he was imprisoned for undermining the Nazi regime, Bonhoeffer wrote about the moral challenges posed by the existential conditions that he confronted:

> In the course of historical life there comes a point where the exact observance of the formal law of a state . . . suddenly finds itself in violent conflict with the ineluctable necessities of the lives of men; at this point responsible and pertinent action leaves behind it the domain of principle and convention, the domain of normal and regular, and is confronted by the extraordinary situation of ultimate necessities, a situation which no law can control.[45]

In sum, if we apply the tridimensional framework developed in chapter 4 to the problem of coercive interrogation, this practice is likely to be judged morally unacceptable in most instances and morally problematic in exceptional circumstances, such as a "ticking bomb" scenario. The goal of preventing future violence, especially a major bombing attack, is wholly legitimate. By contrast, the method or means—inflicting pain and degrading treatment on persons—is morally unacceptable. To be sure, a rule-based perspective will regard coercive interrogation as completely unacceptable because imposing inhumane and degrading treatment to elicit intelligence is evil. But even an ends-based perspective is likely to regard many types of coercive interrogation as morally problematic because of the unreliability of intelligence gained through coercive methods. Finally, the results of coercive interrogation are likely to be indeterminate at best and morally unacceptable at worst. If coercive interrogation discloses vital information that prevents catastrophic harm, the protection of society might be justified as a lesser evil in exceptional circumstances. But even if torture contributed to security, reliance on degrading human treatment as a means to a more secure environment would undermine the moral values and practices on which a free society is based. As the quotation from the *Economist* at the outset of this chapter suggests, democracies using torture do so "at their peril." In short, civilized nations must fight terrorism without using terrorists' tactics.

MORAL REFLECTIONS

This case study raises challenging moral questions about the nature and role of coercive force in confronting violence from nonstate actors. Following are some key moral issues relevant to this case:

- The U.S. government regards terrorists like Al Qaeda as unlawful enemy combatants.

Should they be accorded the same rights and privileges as soldiers? Why or why not?

- If democratic states are permitted to kill in war, why is it not permissible to use some coercion to interrogate an alleged terrorist in order to secure valuable intelligence? "How can one object to torture of persons to secure valuable information for reasons of state," asks Ignatieff, "and not object to killing them?"[46]

- Do all types of coercive interrogation techniques bear the same moral consequences?

- If "torture lite" is considered morally permissible in conditions of "supreme emergency," which coercive techniques would be morally legitimate? Which ones would be immoral?

TARGETED KILLING

A second strategy used in fighting irregular, nonstate terrorist groups is the assassination of leaders of insurgent movements or terrorist groups. This practice—known as targeted killing (TK)—is carried out directly by military teams or clandestine operatives and indirectly through drones (unmanned aerial vehicles, UAVs). In ancient and medieval times, killing unjust political and military leaders was considered morally legitimate. Numerous ancient, medieval, and Renaissance thinkers, including Aristotle, Cicero, John of Salisbury, and John Milton, claimed that tyrannicide (the killing of a tyrant) was a legitimate means of ending oppression. Sir Thomas More defended assassination as a legitimate means of warfare, since it spared ordinary citizens from the suffering of political leaders' wars.[47] During the fifteenth and sixteenth centuries, as religious and political rivalries intensified in Europe, targeted assassination became even more commonplace.[48] Indeed, targeted killing was so widespread that the emerging international law of war tended to accept assassination as a legitimate instrument, making no distinction between killing the enemy on the battlefield or elsewhere.[49]

The norm against TK began to emerge in the seventeenth and eighteenth centuries as European political and intellectual leaders sought to limit the widespread practice of assassination. By the mid-nineteenth century, the murder of enemy leaders was widely regarded as an unacceptable way to resolve political disputes. The U.S. Army's Lieber Code of 1863, one of the earliest American documents setting forth norms governing war, condemned the assassination of enemies, viewing such killing as a relapse into barbarism.[50] Additionally, the code prohibited the arbitrary classification of prisoners as "outlaws," so that they could be killed without trial. Some four decades later, representatives from most states gathered in The Hague for a series of conferences that led to two major conventions. In the 1907 Hague Convention, signatories agreed to attack only combatants, spare civilians, refrain from inflicting unnecessary suffering, and treat prisoners humanely and the wounded with compassion. Killing prisoners and the wounded was prohibited, while killing combatants or civilians through "treachery" was similarly forbidden. The 1956 U.S. Army Field Manual (27–10) on land warfare incorporates this later prohibition and links it with assassination. In sum, as the laws of war greatly expanded throughout the twentieth century, the norm prohibiting assassination remained intact.

In 1975, the Senate Foreign Relations Committee held hearings that led to the shocking disclosure that the Central Intelligence Agency (CIA) had tried to kill a number of political leaders, including Congo's Patrice Lumumba and Cuba's Fidel Castro. As a result of this disclosure, President Gerald Ford promulgated an order banning assassination attempts. Executive Order 12333, which has been reaffirmed by every subsequent president, reads, "No person employed by or acting on behalf of the United States Government shall engage in, or conspire to engage in, assassination." Domestic U.S. law thus reinforces the international legal ban on assassination.

Although international law prohibits TK in peacetime, in wartime it is conditionally permissible. In times of peace, states are obligated to respect the territorial integrity of other states and not interfere in their political affairs. Article 2 (4) of the United Nations Charter provides that all member states "shall refrain in their international relations from the threat or use of force against the territorial integrity or political independence of any state, or in any manner inconsistent with the Purpose of the United Nations." Accordingly, states must never seek to assassinate foreign civilians or public officials in times of relative peace. Killing in peacetime is murder—a criminal act.

In wartime, however, the prohibition against targeted killing is more elusive because the law of war stipulates that combatants, regardless of their rank or official role, are potential targets. Since international war is waged by states, not persons, killing in war is not murder. The goal is not to target individual persons but to attack and destroy what are euphemistically termed "military targets." Such terminology sanitizes the killing, making it general and abstract. Indeed, killing in war is made palatable by the fiction that international war is waged by states, not persons. So long as the killing is not personalized, the discriminating and proportionate use of force against state security structures is deemed lawful.[51] For example, when the United States carried out retaliatory military raids against Libya in April 1986 in response to Libyan sponsorship of terror, it bombed various military and political installations, including Colonel Muammar Qaddafi's house. Although the U.S. government denied that it had intended to kill the Libyan dictator, the bombing sites suggest that the U.S. government would have been pleased had he been killed.[52] Similarly, in March 2003 the United States commenced war against Iraq by bombing a Baghdad residential site in which Saddam Hussein, Iraq's dictator, was thought to be spending the night. Although nobody admitted that the bombing aimed to assassinate Hussein, the fact that the attack involved laser-guided bombs would suggest this.[53]

The rise of unconventional war has significantly enhanced the case for TK. Since combatants can be legally killed in war, applying a criminal justice model to terrorists has the ironic effect of giving more rights to irregular fighters than to ordinary soldiers. This is why a war paradigm, rather than a law enforcement paradigm, is appropriate in confronting threats from terrorist groups. This means that irregular combatants—fighters that refuse to be identified with uniforms and insignias—are not due the legal processes of a criminal justice system. Moreover, since they are unlawful combatants, they are not entitled to all the protections of the laws of war. Consequently, since irregular fighters are not openly identified as combatants, Gross argues that TK is "an essential tool for combating nonstate actors."[54]

CASE 8-2: TARGETED KILLING WITH DRONES

DRONE WARFARE

In recent decades, dramatic changes in information and weapons technologies have changed the nature of warfare for the United States and, to a lesser extent, other modern states. These changes—collectively known as the Revolution in Military Affairs (RMA)—involve such developments as precision-guided munitions, robotics, and drones or UAVs. During the Kosovo war, covered in chapter 1, U.S. and NATO forces carried out a "virtual war" by remote control instead of sending soldiers to the battlefield. In this largely asymmetric contest, NATO combatants sat in offices behind computer screens and in jet aircraft, bombing from the air while Kosovars and Serbs did the dying on the ground.

In the past decade, significant further technological developments have been applied to military armaments, particularly in the development of drones of varying size, capacity, and purpose. Perhaps the most significant of these is the Predator, a light (1,120 pounds) UAV with a range of seven hundred miles. This drone can stay in the air for more than twenty-four hours at heights up to twenty-six thousand feet and be piloted remotely from a computer eight thousand miles away. Like fighter jets, drones can carry bombs and missiles. But what makes them remarkable weapons is their sensor and video technology, which allows them to see through clouds or at night and their ability to loiter in the sky for a full day. Most importantly, since drones do not have

pilots, they can be flown in high-risk areas, accessing invaluable intelligence and, when necessary, destroying enemy targets. Since drones carry precision-guided munitions, they are especially suited for TK missions.

When the United States invaded Afghanistan in 2001 and Iraq in 2003, the U.S. Department of Defense had only a small number of drones and used them sparingly, chiefly for surveillance purposes. But in subsequent years, especially since Barack Obama became president, drones have become the weapon of choice in prosecuting the war on terror. This development is due largely to the ability of UAVs to enter high-risk areas and carry out limited and extraordinarily accurate missile attacks, thereby limiting collateral destruction. Originally, drone TK was used primarily to carry out "profile strikes" against known high-level militant leaders. In time, however, drone TK was expanded to include "signature strikes" involving suspicious compounds and training centers in areas controlled by militants. The increase in drone warfare in recent years has been of the "signature" variety. According to one estimate, from 2009 until 2011 the United States carried out 234 drone attacks in autonomous tribal areas of western Pakistan that provide sanctuary to Taliban and Al Qaeda insurgents involved in the war in Afghanistan.[55] It is estimated that the drone attacks have resulted in the deaths of close to two thousand leaders and operatives from the Taliban, Al Qaeda, and allied extremist groups.

The increased use of drone warfare raises important legal and moral concerns. Although the Obama administration has emphasized the legality of this practice, drone TK has nevertheless pushed legal limits. This is why journalist Tom Junod writes that the Obama administration has been "legally innovative in the cause of killing." He writes, "It has called for the definition of an 'imminent threat' to be broadened and for the definition of 'collateral damage' to be narrowed. An imminent threat used to be someone who represented a clear and present danger. Now it is someone who appears dangerous. Collateral damage used to be anyone killed who was not targeted. Now the term 'collateral damage' applies only to women and children."[56]

The problematic nature of the government's drone TK program was forced into the spotlight in September 2011 when Anwar al-Awlaki, a militant cleric and U.S. citizen, was killed in Yemen by a drone missile. Al-Awlaki was targeted because of his role as an unlawful enemy combatant in seeking to kill Americans.[57] Although there is little doubt that al-Awlaki was a radical Islamist committed to violence against the United States, the issue of carrying out TK against a U.S. citizen in a foreign country raised significant legal and moral issues. The fundamental question for the U.S. government was this: could U.S. forces use TK against a U.S. citizen who had not been indicted in a court of law, and could it do so with a drone missile in a country with which the United States was not at war? In 2010, a year before the Yemen attack, the Department of Justice's Office of Legal Counsel answered the question in the affirmative.[58]

Ironically, the drone warfare spearheaded by the Obama administration has received comparatively little scrutiny. Whereas enhanced interrogation allowed under the Bush administration was widely condemned, the media and general public have given little attention to TK with drones. What explains the public's indifference to TK in general and, more particularly, to the use of drones in carrying out this task? One possible reason is that any legitimate military effort to reduce the threat of terrorism from radical Islamists is likely to be supported by the American public. To be sure, citizens desire legal and moral counterterrorism programs, but their overriding concern is to prevent terrorism, not to defend the rights of Al Qaeda militants.

A further reason for the public's indifference toward drone TK is that assassinating terrorists by remote control works—and does so at little cost to America. Drones can collect intelligence and fire precision-guided munitions without placing soldiers in harm's way. Moreover, TK with drones provides limited and accurate lethal force that can reduce collateral damage. Junod describes drone warfare as follows: "It is a war not only of technological precision but moral discrimination, designed to separate the guilty from the innocent. It is, indeed, war as an alternative to war: It saves lives by ending lives; it responds to those plotting mass murder by, well, murdering them."[59]

Finally, the public is indifferent to drone warfare because the program is shrouded in secrecy. The U.S. military uses drones openly in Afghanistan and Pakistan, and this program is subject to legal and political constraints. But the CIA uses drones clandestinely in Pakistan, Yemen, Somalia, and elsewhere. Given CIA reluctance to even admit that it has a drone program, Michael Walzer asks, "Under what code does the CIA operate?" His answer: "I don't know. . . . There should be a limited, finite group of people who are targets, and that list should be publicly defensible and available. Instead, it's not being publicly defended. People are being killed, and we generally require some public justification when we go about killing people."[60] In March 2010 Harold Koh, the legal advisor at the Department of State, gave an address in which he defended the practice of TK with drones. He declared "that U.S. targeting practices, including lethal operations conducted with the use of unmanned aerial vehicles, comply with all applicable law, including the laws of war."[61] He indicated that the procedures and practices for identifying targets were "extremely robust." In particular, he emphasized that the principles of discrimination and proportionality were applied rigorously to lethal operations to ensure that such operations were carried out "in accordance with all applicable law."

But drone warfare is not simply a legal issue. It is also a moral problem. The moral aspect of TK was given front-page coverage by the *New York Times* in May 2012. In the article, Jo Becker and Scott Shane describe the process by which target selection occurs. In their words, "It is the strangest of bureaucratic rituals: Every week or so, more than 100 members of the government's sprawling national security apparatus gather, by secure video teleconference, to pore over terrorist suspects' biographies and recommend to the president who should be the next to die."[62] After the "nominations list" is prepared, the president meets with his senior national security team to make decisions about TK. Becker and Shane write that "Mr. Obama is the liberal law professor who campaigned against the Iraq War and torture, and then insisted on approving every new name on an expanding 'kill list,' poring over terrorist suspects' biographies on what one official calls the macabre 'baseball cards' of an unconventional war."[63]

THE ETHICS OF DRONE TK

The ethics of targeted killing with drones involves two distinct issues—the justice of using drones in armed conflict and the justice of TK against militant terrorists.

Modern, sophisticated UAVs are not inherently moral or immoral. As with other applications of modern technology to military armaments, drones provide a new and innovative instrument of war. Whether or not the weapon is moral will depend on how well it can be reconciled with the norms of just war theory. In particular, it will depend on the weapon's capacity to fulfill the norm of discrimination (i.e., the ability to destroy the military target while minimizing civilian damage). There can be little doubt that modern precision-guided munitions (like the Hellfire missile used in the Predator drone) deliver discriminating force. But accuracy is not sufficient. Unlike bullets, which harm individuals, missile warheads destroy entire buildings and vehicles, killing all occupants within. Thus, TK with missiles presents a significant moral challenge because militants are rarely alone or only in the company of fellow insurgents. Typically, they are in the company of family and friends and do not present unambiguous military targets. Therefore, the moral challenge in carrying out TK is to minimize collateral damage. When significant civilian casualties result from drone TK, the negative political results within the enemy's society can override any tactical benefits derived from killing leading militants.

Another important factor in assessing the ethics of drone warfare is its psychological impact. Whereas conventional war places soldiers at risk in battle, irregular wars with drones create an asymmetric battlefield. Because the warriors who carry out TK remain in high-tech information centers far removed from the battlefield, drone warfare may seem like virtual war for those with modern weaponry but real war for those on the ground. Such an asymmetric environment creates a potential moral problem to the extent that it reduces human inhibitions against killing. David Cortright, a peace studies professor, writes, "Any development that makes war appear to be easier or cheaper is deeply troubling. It reduces the political inhibitions against the use of deadly violence. It threatens to weaken the moral presumption against the use of force that is at the heart of the just war doctrine."[64] But does justice demand symmetrical military capabilities? Benjamin Wittes and Ritika Singh challenge Cortright's thesis, claiming that the modernization of weapons need not be contrary to fundamental moral values. In their view, "Cortright objects to military robotics because the field offers effective weaponry that keeps our forces safer while enhancing their lethality and targeting precision with respect to the enemy—the combination of which invites use. In other words, he objects to precisely what any operational commander would find attractive about drones."[65] In short, drones provide an opportunity to use lethal force with greater discrimination and effectiveness, but they also lower the threshold against the use of violence. As a result, decision makers need to ensure that the gains from discrimination outweigh the harmful effects resulting from remote-control warfare.

The second issue—the moral permissibility of TK—is equally challenging. As noted earlier, although killing combatants in war is legally and morally permissible, there is a presumption against TK in interstate war. Viewed from the perspective of traditional state-centric international relations, this norm has been highly beneficial, contributing to a more civilized and humane world. But how does the TK prohibition apply when there is neither peace nor interstate war? Should states regard bombings and other acts of terror as criminal acts, subject to a state's criminal justice system, or as acts of war, subject to military action? How should states confront terrorism when it is waged by a nonstate political organization? Since self-defense is an inherent right of states, and since traditional deterrence strategies are unlikely to prevent terrorism, some national security strategists have concluded that destruction of the terrorist networks is likely to be the only effective counterterror strategy. Thus, after the horrific 9/11 attacks in New York City and Washington, D.C., President Bush was confronted with a difficult decision: whether to view 9/11 as a criminal act, subject to the government's criminal justice system, or as a global war. The president chose the latter course and launched a war on terror—a war against terrorist organizations as well as against those who provide support and sanctuary for them.

The decision to define the counterterrorist campaign as a war had decisive implications. The U.S. Congress responded to the president's initiative by adopting the "Authorization for Use of Military Force" act that gave the Department of Defense the right to use military force against suspected terrorists. But how should this war against irregular forces be conducted? Since radical terrorist groups were at war with the United States, irregular, unconventional combatants could be targeted and killed in a campaign euphemistically termed "anticipatory self-defense." In effect, government officials viewed TK as an exceptional wartime act that was legally and morally permissible.

In the early phases of the war on terror, U.S. forces placed a premium on capturing and interrogating Al Qaeda and Taliban leaders in Afghanistan, Pakistan, and Iraq. When national and international concern increased over the government's detention policies, detaining militants became less important. Interestingly, although Barack Obama was highly critical of President Bush's counterterrorism policies before he was elected president, once he assumed office in 2009 he continued most of his predecessor's policies on the war on terror.[66] Indeed, rather than seeking to detain and interrogate prisoners, he relied increasingly on drone TK. According to former attorney-general Michael Mukasey, since the Obama administration did not develop a coherent detention policy governing the capture of militants, the government's "default option" has become drone warfare.[67] Not surprisingly, the number of UAV attacks under the Obama administration increased dramatically. Whereas the Bush administration authorized 35 drone strikes in Pakistan in 2008, the Obama administration authorized 117 such strikes in 2010. In one of the most dramatic episodes in the war on terror, the United States was able to target and kill a senior Al Qaeda leader by destroying his car with an air-to-ground missile from a Predator drone in the Yemen desert.

Since TK is normally illegal in conventional international wars but conditionally permissible in irregular wars, the challenge is to ensure that the practice remains constrained by established norms. To begin with, TK should be considered only if capturing militants is deemed impossible or too costly—with the harm from a covert operation outweighing its benefits. Secondly, it should be used only as a last resort—only after other less violent options have been exhausted. And third, TK should be considered only when an attack can minimize collateral damage—avoiding the death of civilians. Because terrorists typically live within dense population centers, attacking them without harming some civilians is difficult and at times nearly impossible. As a result, deciding when assassination is legal and morally prudent is a difficult enterprise. One writer calls the weighing of alternatives surrounding TK operations the "algebra of assassination."[68] In short, TK can be morally justified as a lesser evil, but only when certain preconditions are fulfilled.

The government of Israel, which reinstituted TK in 2000 to reduce suicide bombings and other acts of terror fomented by Hamas and Islamic Jihad, has carried out an open debate about assassination. This open discussion has helped to clarify norms to avoid overreliance on this practice. Some of the preconditions determined include the following: the targets must be located in non-Israeli-controlled territory, arrest of combatants is not possible, civilian casualties must be minimized, and each targeted killing must be approved by senior government leaders.[69] In December 2006 Israel's High Court of Justice ruled that TK was conditionally legitimate provided that there was no other alternative and that innocent civilians were not harmed disproportionately. The court specified four conditions that needed to be fulfilled if targeted killing was to be considered legal: first, the potential target must be a combatant (i.e., have lost its protected status as an innocent civilian); second, less destructive alternatives are not available; third, an independent and thorough investigation must be made after each targeting operation; and fourth, the state must minimize harm to innocent civilians and carry out the killing only if the gains from the operation outweigh collateral damage.[70]

If we assess TK in terms of its goals, means, and outcomes, it is clear that this practice is morally problematic. At the level of intentions, there is little doubt that the goal of protecting innocent people from terrorism is a justifiable end. At the level of means, however, assassinating a terrorist target poses a variety of concerns. To begin with, assassination is evil because it involves taking human life. Although TK is a lesser evil in that it seeks to protect innocent civilians from terror, it is an evil nonetheless. Moreover, since assassination is undertaken as anticipatory self-defense, it is based on the belief that the targeted person is a major security threat. But since intelligence is never perfect and always incomplete, TK might be based on erroneous information. Finally, at the level of outcomes, TK is likely to be morally legitimate if it prevents harm to innocent civilians. But since preventive TK operations are likely to involve collateral damage, especially when carried out by missiles and bombs, unintended harm to civilians will inevitably compromise the moral legitimacy of the operation itself.

MORAL REFLECTIONS

- Although U.S. law prohibits assassination, government officials have defended the legality and morality of TK on grounds of self-defense. In irregular war, is TK a legal and morally legitimate practice or is it assassination?
- If TK is morally justified as a lesser evil in exceptional circumstances, why can't torture be justified in the same way?
- David Cole argues that in war, killing is legally permissible but not a crime, while torture and cruel treatment of detainees are illegal and a war crime.[71] As a result, he argues that "there is no moral equivalence" between torture and killing. From an ethical perspective, which is morally preferable—the coercive interrogation of Khalid Sheikh Mohammed (KSM), the admitted mastermind of the 9/11 terrorist attacks, or the killing of Osama bin Laden, the leader of Al Qaeda?
- Is killing by remote control with drones different from battlefield killing with guns? From an ethical perspective, what are the benefits and costs of virtual warfare?

SUMMARY

The rise of international terrorism has resulted in the renewal of unconventional military strategies. Terrorism is elusive; countering terror requires accurate and timely intelligence and covert operations that can identify and destroy terrorist networks. If counterterrorism is to succeed without undermining democratic society, it will have to conform to domestic and international law as well as international political morality. In particular, states must resist the temptation to rely on torture and targeted assassination to confront major terrorist threats. In exceptional circumstances and after alternatives have been exhausted, the state may resort to unconventional tactics in fighting irregular wars. But democratic societies run great risks in breaking down taboos that have contributed to the development of free societies. Michael Ignatieff writes, "The chief ethical challenge with relation to terrorism is relatively simple—to discharge duties to those who have violated their duties to us. We have to do this because we are fighting a war whose essential prize is preserving the identity of liberal society itself and preventing it from becoming what terrorists believe it to be."[72] Thus, while the menace from radical terror groups must be confronted, free peoples must rely on tactics and strategies that are consistent with international law and uphold human dignity.

Chapter Nine

The Ethics of Foreign Intervention

Probably more lives have been lost to ethnic, religious, or ideological crusades than to simple [national] greed.[1]
—LEA BRILMAYER

Respect for sovereignty in itself is not a moral imperative. It cannot be. The sanctity of sovereignty enshrines a radical moral asymmetry. It grants legitimacy and thus protection to whoever has guns and powder enough to be in control of a government.[2]
—CHARLES KRAUTHAMMER

Humanitarian intervention [is] obligatory where the survival of populations and entire ethnic groups is seriously compromised. This is a duty for nations and the international community.[3]
—POPE JOHN PAUL II

The idea of protecting human rights is increasingly common-place, but today's leading democracies have not yet shouldered the responsibilities that previous great powers did. We are all atrocitarians now—but so far only in words, and not yet in deeds.[4]
—GARY J. BASS

FOREIGN INTERVENTION involves the direct or indirect use of power to influence the affairs of other states. Intervention can be undertaken openly or covertly, individually or collectively, and can involve relatively noncoercive actions, such as propaganda and official condemnation, or coercive measures, ranging from economic sanctions to direct military intervention. Moreover, intervention can be undertaken for a variety of purposes, including economic imperialism, countering prior intervention, promoting political objectives, protecting human rights, and fostering national security.

In this chapter, I examine the nature, legality, and morality of military intervention—the most extreme type of foreign intervention. Such intervention involves the individual or collective use of force against another state to influence its domestic affairs. This chapter has five parts. First, it examines the significance of sovereignty, explaining why nonintervention is a core norm of the existing international order. Second, it analyzes the political and moral basis for state sovereignty and its corollary, nonintervention. In the third section I briefly describe the practice of foreign intervention—a practice that states have carried out for political, strategic, and humanitarian reasons. Since the end of the Cold War, the rise of weak and failed states has resulted in numerous humanitarian crises that have called into question the sacrosanct nature of sovereignty. In response to the Rwanda genocide and other humanitarian crises, world leaders have called for a reassessment of the relationship of sovereignty to human rights. In the chapter's fourth section I describe the emergence of the responsibility-to-protect principle, which calls on the international community to protect human rights when states are unwilling or unable to do so. I illustrate this principle with a case study on NATO's military intervention in Libya in 2011. In the fifth and final section I take up humanitarian intervention—foreign intervention for the sole purpose for rescuing people threatened by starvation, genocide, war, or other calamities. I illustrate such intervention with the American military incursion into Somalia in 1992.

SOVEREIGNTY AND NONINTERVENTION

Norms

A fundamental pillar of the world's constitutional system, as enshrined in the United Nations Charter, is state sovereignty. This legal right ensures states' juridical equality, political independence, and territorial integrity. Because states have the right to determine their domestic affairs, no foreign state may unilaterally violate the territorial boundaries of another state or interfere in its internal affairs. Moreover, states have a duty to respect the political independence and territorial integrity of other states. Thus, the norm of nonintervention is a corollary of state sovereignty, for without the latter the former is impossible.

The legal norm of nonintervention is defined and proclaimed in numerous sources. The most important prohibitions against intervention are contained in the UN Charter, which states (Article 2.4) that UN members are obligated to "refrain in their international relations from the use of force against the territorial integrity or political independence of any other state." In 1965, the General Assembly passed Resolution 2131, which states in part, "No State has the right to intervene, directly or indirectly, for any reason whatever, in the internal or external affairs of any other State. Consequently, armed intervention and all other forms of interference or attempted threats against the personality of the State or against its political, economic, or cultural elements are condemned."[5] Five years later, the General Assembly passed Resolution 2625, the Declaration on Principles of International Law Concerning Friendly Relations and Cooperation among States, which reiterated the nonintervention norm.

Regional international organizations have also affirmed the priority of nonintervention. For example, the Organization of American States (OAS), the regional association of the Western Hemisphere states, defines the principle in an absolutist, restrictive manner. According to its charter, direct and indirect intervention in the internal affairs of other states is totally prohibited (Article 15). Such prohibition applies not only to armed force but also to other forms of interference or attempted threats against "the personality of the State or against its political, economic and cultural elements" (Article 18).

The norm of nonintervention is so foundational to the contemporary international system that even the United Nations is prohibited by its charter (Article 2.7) from intervening in the domestic affairs of its member states. The United Nations can take actions under Chapter VII of the charter that might involve military operations against the wishes of a state.[6] However, such actions are exceptional and are taken only in response to a serious threat to international peace. In general, international law, as expressed in numerous charters and conventions, is unambiguous about nonintervention: states and other actors have a duty to respect countries' political independence.

Although nonintervention is a fundamental constitutive norm of international society, states have historically intervened in the affairs of other states. Indeed, intervention has been so common in modern international relations, according to Michael Mandelbaum, that the history of global politics is "in no small part the history of intervention."[7] Mandelbaum attributes the prevalence of intervention to the oligarchic distribution of power, which allows strong states to intervene in the domestic affairs of the weak. Nevertheless, while powerful states may intervene periodically in weaker states, the strong are adamant defenders of their own territorial integrity. This gives rise to a defense of sovereignty and nonintervention based on politics.

Mandelbaum observes that international boundaries must be based on some principle and that support for the status quo is the simplest one available. If this norm is discarded, all borders become suspect and the potential for international conflict and disorder rises considerably. From an ethical perspective, the problem is that this status quo argument assumes that the existing cartography is morally legitimate. However, the existing international order has not been fashioned by norms of justice and human dignity but by arbitrary decisions by military and political leaders. Indeed, the map of the world has been fashioned largely on the battlefield. And the creation of nation-states has been chiefly the result of a people willing and able to use power to control territory. As Mandelbaum notes, "Historically, the prize of independence has gone to those powerful or clever or fortunate or merely numerous enough to achieve it."[8] In short, sovereignty is a dominant norm because the powerful states of the world have an interest in maintaining the existing political order of nation-states.

Finally, sovereignty and nonintervention are based on political morality. The claim that the society of nation-states is an ethically valid system is based on several core assumptions and values: (1) the existing anarchic international system is morally legitimate, (2) peoples have a moral right to political self-determination, (3) states have a juridical right to sovereignty and territorial integrity, (4) states have an obligation to resolve conflicts peacefully, and (5) force is an illegitimate instrument for altering existing territorial boundaries.

Since the end of the Cold War a growing number of scholars have challenged the conception of the world as a Westphalian regime of nation-states. They argue that because of globalization, state boundaries are becoming more porous and the authority of governments is receding. For some, the market has replaced the state, resulting in the decline of sovereignty. There can be little doubt that the increasing speed, lower cost, and greater ease of transnational flows of goods, services, and information has contributed to greater international integration. Ignatieff has written, "The conventional wisdom wants us to dismiss sovereignty as a vestigial legalism, a Westphalian hangover in a globalized world where power has shifted decisively to the world market."[9] But viewing the world through the prism of weak sovereignty is unpersuasive. As Ignatieff notes, stable, sustainable political communities depend upon fundamental services that only governments can discharge, such as maintaining order and protecting the rights of persons. Ignatieff writes, "Sovereignty has returned . . . because citizens need a principle of authority more stable than government alone. Markets in turn cannot function without the confidence that sovereigns provide, and political systems cannot reach agreement on the appropriate functions of government without a minimal consensus on what sovereigns do. The international order cannot be understood without emphasizing the role that sovereigns play in providing ultimate authority."[10]

Behavior

Although sovereignty is a basic norm of international relations, states frequently violate the nonintervention rule. This gap between the declaration of a norm and the behavior of states has resulted not only in cognitive dissonance but also in a complex system that Steven Krasner terms "organized hypocrisy."[11] Historically, states have intervened in other states for a variety of reasons, including economic expansion, strategic interests, territorial security, and humanitarianism. For example, during the nineteenth century, major European powers intervened in Asia and Africa to establish colonies that could, among other things, provide a source of raw materials, cheap labor, and a market for goods. In the early part of the twentieth century, the United States intervened in a number of Central American countries (e.g., Cuba, the Dominican Republic, Haiti, Nicaragua, and Panama) to foster domestic political order and reduce economic corruption. Although such interventions were designed to prevent European powers from interfering in the Western Hemisphere, they also served to reinforce the dominant political role of the United States in the region.

During the Cold War, when the two superpowers dominated global politics, the most important motive for intervention was strategic security. Although both the United States and the Soviet Union were more powerful militarily than any other hegemonic powers in history, they nonetheless feared each other and sought to increase their power and influence through bilateral ties and multilateral alliances. Moreover, they intervened militarily in other states to protect and promote vital national interests or to advance ideological goals. Thus, for example, when the Soviet Union intervened in Czechoslovakia in 1968 and in Afghanistan in 1979, it did so to strengthen communism in those states; when the United States intervened in the Dominican Republic in 1965 and in Grenada in 1983, it did so to challenge antidemocratic forces. According to Mandelbaum, during the Cold War, American interventionism was driven almost exclusively by the great rivalry with the Soviet Union: "Korea and Vietnam, where the United States fought the most protracted wars of the Cold War era, were spaces on the board of global geopolitics; the United States was attempting to defend those spaces for fear that, if the Soviet Union and its clients occupied them, the Soviets would be emboldened to challenge Western positions elsewhere."[12]

Territorial security has also been an important motive for military intervention, especially among lesser powers. When a state perceives that its territorial boundaries and economic well-being are threatened by the deliberate actions, political instability, or government oppression in neighboring countries, the threatened state might seek to protect its interests through foreign intervention. For example, India intervened in East Pakistan (Bangladesh) in 1971 after the Pakistani government began a war against the Bengali people, because India perceived the war and the mass human rights violations as threatening its own security. Similarly, Tanzania's 1978 intervention in Uganda was officially justified as a response not to the human rights violations of Idi Amin's dictatorial regime, but to the potential threat to regional stability and Tanzania's territorial security posed by these violations. In other words, although gross immorality occurred, the rationale used to justify foreign intervention was national security rather than the violation of human rights.

However, the gross violation of human rights has served as a justification for some foreign interventions. When the United States intervened in Cuba in 1898 and declared war on Spain, it did so in part to overthrow an oppressive dictatorial regime that was violating human rights. And in April 1979 Tanzania's forces invaded Uganda and toppled the oppressive regime of Idi Amin after human rights abuses increased. When the United States intervened in Somalia in 1992, its main concern was to reestablish political order to resume humanitarian relief to millions of people threatened with starvation. In 1995, NATO intervened in Bosnia-Herzegovina in order to halt the civil war between the Croats, Serbs, and Muslims, while in 1999 NATO waged war against Serbia in order to protect Kosovo Albanians from Serb security forces. In short, although the international system proscribes foreign intervention, states occasionally violate the sovereignty of other states when they perceive that such action would advance their national interests or the global common good.[13]

THE POLITICAL AND MORAL BASIS OF NONINTERVENTION

Since we are concerned with arguments that might justify overriding the nonintervention norm, we first turn to examine the political and moral justifications for honoring state sovereignty.

Political Justifications

Political thinkers have offered two types of justifications for sovereignty and nonintervention. One argument is based on the legitimacy of states in the international system; the other is based on the legitimacy of a regime in terms of its people. *International legitimacy* assumes that existing states, as sovereign members of the decentralized, state-centric international community, are entitled to recognition and respect and to the right of political autonomy and its corollary, the right against intervention. International legitimacy is rooted not in the character of regimes but in the existing Westphalian order, whose viability depends on the political autonomy of states. If a state is functioning as a politically independent community, it is entitled, according to this perspective, to the rights and obligations of the international society of states. This argument, based on the application of social contract theory to international relations, assumes that the relationship of persons to domestic society is analogous to the relationship of states to global society.[14] Just as individuals have inherent rights such as life and liberty, so too political communities have basic rights, including the freedom and political independence to define, preserve, and pursue communal interests.

Domestic legitimacy, by contrast, assumes that states are entitled to respect and support only when they meet their core obligations to their people. Fundamentally, this means that states have a responsibility to honor people's collective claim to self-determination and to protect the basic rights of individuals, including freedom of conscience, freedom from torture and arbitrary arrest, and freedom to own property. From this perspective, regimes are legitimate to the extent that the people support the regime and to the extent that basic rights are protected. Since human rights conceptions vary considerably, domestic legitimacy is frequently defined primarily in terms of communal self-determination and to a lesser extent in terms of adherence to human rights norms. Thus, whereas international legitimacy focuses on the rights and duties of states, domestic legitimacy focuses on the rights of persons within political communities.

It is one thing to assert that states, which are entitled to the right of nonintervention, must be legitimate internationally and domestically. It is quite another to define what these notions mean and how they should be applied to contemporary international relations. Are all states and quasi-states entitled to sovereignty and nonintervention? If not, how, and by whom, is the legitimacy of states to be determined? What role should foreign actors play in determining state legitimacy, and what should be the role of the people? In times of domestic conflict and civil wars, which political communities are entitled to recognition and thus to political autonomy?

Michael Walzer has provided a useful criterion for judging state legitimacy. For him, states are entitled to political autonomy when they fulfill two conditions—viability and communal support. According to Walzer, a legitimate community is one that can pass the "self-help" test; that is, it must be capable of existing without external aid. He claims, "A legitimate government is one that can fight its own internal wars."[15] One political community cannot give another self-determination; the requirements for authentic self-rule must be indigenous and can be acquired only when individuals and groups struggle to affirm the right of self-determination. Walzer writes, "As with individuals, so with sovereign states: there are things that we cannot do to them, even for their own ostensible good."[16] Although self-help is no doubt important in developing indigenous self-determination, the self-help argument is morally problematic because it runs the risk of equating political success with justice, and might with right.

For Walzer, communal legitimacy is based on a community's capacity for self-determination. Such capacity, he suggests, depends on the "fit" between a political community and the government, that is, whether a regime represents "the political life of its people."[17] Walzer writes, "The moral standing of any particular state depends upon the reality of the common life it protects and the extent to which the sacrifices required by that protection are willingly accepted and thought worthwhile."[18] Just as individuals have a right to defend their homes, citizens also, he suggests, have a right to protect their homeland and the values and institutions that sustain it politically and economically. However, if this communal life is to enjoy international legitimacy, it must be authentic, which means that solidarity must exist between government and subjects. Thus, a state's right to political autonomy is rooted in the right of individuals to protect their collective life from foreign domination.

Jefferson McMahan has similarly argued that the legitimacy of the state rests on the degree to which a regime protects and promotes "communal self-determination."[19] For McMahan, communal self-determination involves the right of human communities to govern themselves freely and independently. Although democratic practices and institutions would no doubt be conducive to communal self-determination, McMahan argues that democratic government is not a prerequisite. In his view, self-determination does not require self-government. Rather, a political community must be able to control its own destiny and to govern its own affairs independently of external influences while maintaining some level of domestic legitimacy.

For McMahan, two criteria are important in ensuring domestic legitimacy. First, a state must be representative of the political community or communities within its territorial boundaries. Second, it must enjoy the support and approval of a majority of its citizens.[20] According to McMahan, a state that is representative and enjoys the approval of its citizens is domestically legitimate and thus entitled to the right of nonintervention. A state that is not representative and not supported by the people is not a legitimate, self-determining community and therefore is not entitled to the right of nonintervention.

In sum, the moral validity of states depends on two types of legitimacy: international and domestic. Internationally, states are presumptively legitimate by virtue of their ability to exist as independent, viable political communities; domestically, states are legitimate to the extent that they affirm communal self-determination—a norm manifested by a regime's representative character and the extent to which citizens approve and support its government. It is important to emphasize that the right of nonintervention does not depend on a regime's democratic self-rule; rather, it depends on two conditions: international viability and representative character. Because the domestic legitimacy of states is more restrictive, it is possible for a state to be internationally legitimate, that is, regarded as legitimate by other member states, while still being considered domestically illegitimate by a large portion of its own citizens.

Moral Justifications

Political thinkers have offered moral and legal arguments for the ethical legitimacy of sovereignty and nonintervention. The most powerful of these is the utilitarian argument that sovereignty and nonintervention must be honored if order is to be maintained in global society. According to this thesis, intervention is wrong (illegal and immoral) because it fosters international chaos and instability by encouraging counterintervention, military conflict, and even large-scale war. This ends-based morality suggests that if global order is to be maintained, it will occur only by honoring the existing cartography. International order cannot be maintained when states fail to respect the territorial integrity and political autonomy of member states. Stanley Hoffmann argues that whether or not one finds particular states morally acceptable, it is important to uphold the legal rights of states lest international society collapse "into a state of war or universal tyranny."[21]

In her illuminating study on global order titled *Code of Peace*, Dorothy Jones argues that the international community has an ethical framework—a "code of peace," as she calls it—that states have accepted as normative and legally binding in their international relations.[22] These norms are not derived from states' international behavior but rather are rooted in the shared political doctrines and legal and moral principles embodied in widely accepted treaties, conventions, declarations, and other international agreements. According to Jones, the code of peace involves the following nine tenets:

1. sovereign equality of states,
2. territorial integrity and political independence of states,
3. equal rights and self-determination of peoples,
4. nonintervention in the internal affairs of states,
5. peaceful settlement of disputes between states,
6. abstention from the threat or use of force,
7. fulfillment in good faith of international obligations,
8. cooperation with other states, and
9. respect for human rights and fundamental freedoms.[23]

Because this code specifies the acceptable behavioral mores of the international community, it provides not only a regulatory structure but, more significantly, an ethical system. The code is an ethical system because it establishes binding moral obligations on states that, if fulfilled, have the potential to contribute to peace and stability in the international system.

Walzer similarly builds an ethical theory of peace on the basis of sovereignty and other widely accepted states' rights. These foundational norms collectively form a "legalist paradigm," which provides the moral and legal structure for maintaining international peace. The paradigm includes six key principles:

1. An international society of independent states exists.
2. The states comprising the international society have rights, including the rights of territorial integrity and political sovereignty.
3. The use of force or threat of force by one state against another constitutes aggression and is a criminal act.
4. Aggression justifies two types of action: a war of self-defense by the victim and a war of law enforcement by the victim and any other members of the international society.
5. Nothing but aggression justifies war.
6. After the aggressor state has been militarily repulsed, it can also be punished.[24]

Because aggression is contrary to the legalist paradigm, the use of force against a state constitutes an international criminal act, giving rise to the legitimate use of defensive force. Although this legal framework provides the foundational structure for pursuing and maintaining international peace, Walzer recognizes that global order will not necessarily ensure domestic peace and justice. The paradigm might foster international tranquility and deter aggression, but it will not necessarily ensure justice for individual people. Regimes that are internationally legitimate might be unjust domestically. As a result, Walzer provides for some exceptions to his legalist paradigm.[25] For example, states may carry out an anticipatory military attack if they have conclusive evidence of imminent attack and may intervene militarily in other states to assist viable secessionist movements or rescue peoples threatened with massacre.

For communitarians, models such as Walzer's legalist paradigm and Jones's code of peace are important in global politics because they provide a framework for sustaining international order and promoting international justice. Although some thinkers might consider structural models such as these in purely legal and political terms, Walzer's and Jones's models need to be viewed as ethical systems because they provide norms that, if fulfilled, can contribute to international justice.

But justice among states does not assure justice within states. International justice may prevail among states even when some states abuse their citizens' human rights and pursue tyrannical policies. Moreover, governments may lose their capacity to maintain order, allowing competing militias and fighting warlords to inflict great suffering on society. Based on the cosmopolitan perspective examined in chapter 2, world justice can exist only when human rights are fully protected throughout the world. As a result, the communitarian perspective of international justice and the cosmopolitan perspective of world or global justice are not necessarily complementary. Indeed, when gross abuse of human rights occur within a state, the claims of international justice need to be weighed against the claims of global justice. In the last part of this chapter the difficult challenge of reconciling sovereignty and human rights is explored. But before turning to this topic I examine principles that should guide military intervention, regardless of the purposes justifying such action or whether it is undertaken individually or collectively.

PRACTICING INTERVENTION

Historically, states have undertaken military intervention principally to advance either their long-term strategic goals or their short-term political interests. During the Cold War, the superpowers repeatedly carried out foreign interventions for strategic ends. For example, the Soviet Union intervened overtly or covertly to support revolutionary communist regimes, while the United States intervened either to support fragile regimes or to undermine Soviet-dominated countries.[26] Examples of strategic intervention include the USSR's 1979 intervention in Afghanistan and the United States' intervention in Grenada, a small Caribbean island, in 1983. To a significant degree, the Cold War was a proxy war fought indirectly in fragile, developing nations.

Major powers have also carried out foreign interventions for short-term political reasons. One of the principal ways that states seek to advance their national interests is through coercive diplomacy—that is, through negotiations backed by the threat of credible force. Frequently states can achieve their political goals without resorting to intervention. But when threats fail to alter government behavior, they may intervene militarily to compel desired regime changes. One type of political intervention occurs when a state feels threatened by domestic developments in a neighboring state. For example, when the Khmer Rouge regime inflicted gross human rights abuses on the Cambodian people, Vietnam responded in 1979 with military intervention, forcing the regime from power. States may also seek to intervene to defend global interests. For example, when Iraq invaded neighboring Kuwait in 1990, the United States led a large multinational military force to liberate the country. More recently, when Islamic radicals began carrying out violence against civilians in northern Kenya, the Kenyan military responded in late 2011 by attacking al Shabaab fighters in southern Somalia.

Since the end of the Cold War, the defense of human rights has become the primary justification for military intervention. The collapse of the bipolar, superpower Cold War order unintentionally unleashed ethnic, religious, and tribal conflicts within fragile states. With the collapse of the central government in Somalia, warlords competed for power and economic resources in different regions of the country. In Yugoslavia the collapse of the communist empire resulted in the fragmentation of the country, with each of its different republics seeking political autonomy, if not outright political independence. This fragmentation resulted in a bitter war in the early 1990s that resulted in millions of refugees and tens of thousands of deaths. In 1994, Rwandan Hutu soldiers and militia carried out the deadliest genocide since the Holocaust while the international community stood by and did nothing. And in 1999, when Kosovar guerrillas turned to violence to demand Kosovo's political autonomy, the military and police of Serbia responded with brutal force that resulted in widespread ethnic cleansing. This led NATO forces to carry out a war against Serbia. And in 2011, NATO similarly engaged state military forces in Libya when longtime dictator Muammar Qaddafi threatened atrocities against rebel forces that had taken control of Benghazi, Libya's second-largest city. Ironically, no such response followed the Syrian government's brutal suppression of rebel attempts to topple the regime of Bashar al-Assad. As of mid-2012, more than twenty-five thousand persons had been killed in the ongoing civil war in Syria.

In the face of mass atrocities, how should the international community respond? Are major powers like the United States responsible for protecting people from atrocities—whether committed by a government or as part of civil war?

Since intervention is contrary to the fundamental norms of the contemporary international legal order, the decision to intervene must be made with care, taking into account political, legal, and moral considerations. Since nonintervention is a fundamental norm of global society, what purposes or conditions justify overriding it? Should state sovereignty be violated to advance such goals as human rights or political democracy in foreign countries? Even where compelling evidence exists for overriding sovereignty, scholars have identified conditions that should be fulfilled prior to resorting to military action. Some of the most important of these norms, which are based in the just war tradition, include (1) *last resort*—no military intervention should be attempted until all nonviolent alternatives have been exhausted; (2) *proportionality*—the evil done by the military action should be proportional to the good achieved by such action; and (3) *prospect of success*—there must be a high probability of achieving the goals justifying the intervention.[27] Others have suggested that military intervention can only be justified when authorized by the UN Security Council.

Others have argued that since foreign policy is the pursuit of the national interest, the decision by a state to intervene in a foreign country should advance the intervening state's national interests. Charles Krauthammer, for example, argues that foreign intervention should not only meet the test of morality—that is, be judged right in its goals and methods, but also be politically viable domestically—that is, be in the interests of the intervening state. Because intervention uses scarce economic and military resources, states must define those international interests that are important and those that are not. According to Krauthammer, intervention should be undertaken only when key national interests are at stake. He writes, "To intervene solely for reasons of democratic morality is to confuse foreign policy with philanthropy. And a philanthropist gives out his own money. A statesman is a trustee."[28] Thus, for Krauthammer, any foreign intervention must be rooted in the national interest.

One reason for the skepticism regarding the use of national resources to rescue failed and fragile states is that governments are reluctant to use scarce military resources to serve as a world policeman. This reticence was amply demonstrated during the Rwandan genocide, when the policy of the United States and other major powers was to not intervene. The difficulty of deciding when and how to protect people from gross human rights abuses when the state in which they reside is unwilling or unable to provide protection has given rise to a significant new principle. This emerging doctrine is called the responsibility to protect.

THE RESPONSIBILITY TO PROTECT

One of the most important and innovative ideas to emerge in response to the systemic atrocities and human rights abuses of the 1990s is the notion of "responsibility to protect" (R2P). In 2001 the Canadian government-sponsored International Commission on Intervention and State Sovereignty (ICISS) published an influential report on the challenge of reconciling sovereignty with the protection of human rights. The study was prepared partly in response to calls by UN secretary-general Kofi Annan to develop international consensus on when and how foreign intervention on behalf of human rights should be undertaken. After holding extensive discussions throughout the world, the twelve-member commission issued its report, titled "The Responsibility to Protect."[29] The commission found that a "critical gap" had emerged between the Westphalian rules of global order and the massive human suffering occurring in many parts of the world.

To reconcile the tension between human rights and sovereignty, suffering and international law, the commission proposed that the idea of state sovereignty should be reconceived. Rather than viewing sovereignty as the right to independence and state control, the ICISS boldly recommended that sovereignty should be viewed as "the duty to protect." Thus when states can no longer fulfill this responsibility, the protection of human rights should fall to the international community. From the commission's perspective, the inability to protect human rights does not give rise to a "right of intervention" but rather to a "responsibility to protect."[30] Thus, when a society is suffering from genocide, ethnic cleansing, or atrocities, and a state is unable or unwilling to protect human rights, "the principle of nonintervention yields to the international responsibility to protect."[31] The commission offered several guidelines on how this responsibility should be fulfilled: first, there should be a clear, just cause—that is, evidence of mass killing or large-scale ethnic cleansing; second, in carrying out military intervention to protect rights, several precautionary principles need to be followed, including right intention, last resort, proportionality, and reasonable prospects of success; and third, if military action is warranted, it should be carried out only with the authorization of the Security Council. The ICISS declares, "There is no better or more appropriate body than the United Nations Security Council to authorize military intervention for human protection purposes. The task is not to find alternatives to the Security Council as a source of authority but to make the Security Council work better than it has."[32]

At the UN World Summit in 2005, member states endorsed the R2P principle. Based on Articles 138 and 139 of the UN World Outcome Document, states agreed that R2P rests on three pillars: (1) the responsibility of the state to protect its people from genocide, war crimes, ethnic cleansing, and crimes against humanity; (2) the commitment of the international community (through the United Nations) to assist states in meeting these obligations; and (3) the responsibility of the member states to respond in a timely and decisive manner when a state is not providing such protection. It is important to stress that the UN conception of R2P does not create any new legal obligation.[33] Rather, it provides a normative framework for addressing state failure with respect to four types of gross human rights violations—genocide, war crimes, ethnic cleansing, and crimes against humanity. Additionally, the UN doctrine is not a recipe for humanitarian intervention. Rather, Article 139 stresses the need for capacity building in order to ensure that states can effectively protect the human rights of their people. And when peaceful means are inadequate to deal with state failure, the UN document declares that the Security Council should authorize timely and decisive action.

Subsequently, the Security Council took up the R2P principle as part of a wide-ranging resolution condemning crimes committed in armed conflicts. After several months of intense debate, much of it focused on the specific "reaffirmation" of the R2P principle, the Security Council adopted Resolution 1674 by unanimous vote, with five member states abstaining (China, Russia, Brazil, Algeria, and the Philippines).

Although R2P has become part of the lexicon of international relations discourse, the concept remains deeply contested among world leaders as well as scholars.[34] On the one hand, government officials are eager to acknowledge that sovereign governments have a responsibility to protect people. On the other hand, some government officials, including those from China and Russia, are concerned that R2P may weaken sovereignty and undermine the norm of nonintervention. This concern has been especially evident among smaller and weaker states who fear that the principle could be used as a license for humanitarian intervention. This concern was amply evident in protests against a 2007 high-level mission (HLM) report on human rights violations in Darfur after the group used R2P to criticize Sudan.[35]

Although some observers emphasize the role of nonmilitary measures to fulfill the R2P principle, the most visible application of this norm since its adoption by the United Nations has been the 2011 NATO intervention in Libya. The case that follows illustrates the nature and ethics of NATO's military campaign.

CASE 9-1: PROTECTING CIVILIANS IN LIBYA

In December 2010, a revolt in a small town in Tunisia unleashed a political uprising throughout the country. Through the technological miracle of social media, the revolt spread quickly to other nations in the Middle East, including Algeria, Egypt, Jordan, Yemen, and Bahrain. In mid-February, the political awakening—known as the "Arab Spring"—reached Libya, an oil-rich country of some 6.7 million people, when rebel groups began to openly challenge the long-standing dictatorship of Colonel Muammar Qaddafi. Qaddafi, who had taken power in a military coup in 1969, had ruled the country autocratically through a network of family and tribal alliances supported by petroleum revenues and backed by the country's military and security forces. The political unrest began some six hundred miles east of Tripoli in Benghazi, Libya's second-largest city, and spread quickly to other cities. Although the rebels had few weapons, little training, and weak organization, they were nonetheless able to seize control of Benghazi within a few days. When military and security officials fled the city, rebels also gained control of the weapons that government officials left behind. As the revolt gained momentum, Qaddafi loyalists responded by consolidating their operations, hiring mercenaries, and unleashing extreme violence against the rebels. Qaddafi, who compared the rebels to rats, promised to show "no mercy" to the opposition. By mid-March rebel forces were retreating, and Qaddafi's armored columns were within one hundred miles of Benghazi. A growing number of world leaders feared that if the international community did not respond to Qaddafi's threats,

Libya's security forces would inflict mass atrocities—not unlike what had happened in Bosnia in 1995 when Serb forces killed some seven thousand Muslim men and boys in Srebrenica. Given the possibility of a massacre, the challenge for world leaders was how to respond to the Qaddafi threat.[36]

NATO INTERVENTION

In view of the threat to civilian life, French president Nicolas Sarkozy and British prime minister David Cameron began calling for military action against Qaddafi. Following intense diplomatic negotiations among the major powers, the UN Security Council adopted on March 17, 2011, Resolution 1973 authorizing military intervention to protect people in the Libyan conflict.[37] More specifically, the resolution demanded an immediate cease-fire and an end to all violence against civilians. It also (1) authorized member states "to take all necessary measures" to protect civilians, (2) established a "no-fly zone" over Libya, (3) imposed an arms embargo, and (4) authorized the freezing of all financial assets owned by Libyan authorities.[38]

NATO military operations began two days later with the United States and Britain firing 114 cruise missiles to destroy Libya's air defense systems and to incapacitate some of the major command and control centers of the Libyan armed forces. Once NATO forces had reduced the danger to aircraft from Libya's extensive surface-to-air missiles, they were able to enforce the UN no-fly zone. In subsequent months, NATO forces continued to patrol the skies and to attack Qaddafi's major weapons systems (e.g., ships, planes, tanks, personnel carriers) when targets were located that involved minimal risk to civilians. It is significant that while the military campaign was launched to protect civilians, in short order the campaign shifted its focus to destroying Qaddafi's military forces and toppling his government. Thus, what began as a humanitarian mission evolved into a political mission of regime change.

After six months of fighting, rebel forces controlled most of the country, including most of Tripoli. A significant victory occurred when rebel forces took control of Qaddafi's fortified Bab al-Aziziya compound. This resulted in an immediate public relations victory for the rebels as video of Qaddafi's former home was distributed globally. Soon thereafter the provisional government, headed by the National Transitional Council (NTC), moved its operations from Benghazi to Tripoli. However, Qaddafi's loyalist forces continued to offer stiff resistance in some cities, especially Bani Walid and Sirte, Qaddafi's hometown. By late September, however, rebel forces had eliminated nearly all opposition. On October 20, Qaddafi himself was captured and killed, and soon thereafter Sirte, a loyalist stronghold, fell to the rebels. On October 23 the interim government declared that Libya was now free.

ASSESSING THE INTERVENTION

There can be little doubt that Qaddafi was a tyrant who had used his dictatorial powers in the service of injustice. Not only had he failed to provide for the needs of his own people, but he had used his power to support terrorism in other countries. According to Freedom House, Libya had one of the lowest ratings for civil and political freedoms. To ensure total control of Libya, Qaddafi had maintained a Stalinist police state, where security officials and police had unlimited power, and fear of the state inhibited political and civic action. Given the threat posed to human rights by the regime's ruthless, undemocratic nature, many world leaders had concluded that Qaddafi needed to leave office. President

Barack Obama declared these sentiments publicly when the rebellion began and Qaddafi security forces retaliated with indiscriminate killing. "I made it clear," the president said in an address on the Libyan crisis, "that Qaddafi had lost the confidence of his people and the legitimacy to lead, and I said that he needed to step down from power."

NATO's intervention, however, was not undertaken to change the regime but to prevent the slaughter of civilians. By the time NATO initiated its military operations on March 19, only several hundred people, mostly Qaddafi security forces and rebel fighters, had been killed. But once Qaddafi's forces had regrouped and retaken some cities and towns, they were poised to attack Benghazi, the rebellion's headquarters. There was a possibility that, seeking vengeance, they would inflict mass atrocities not only on rebels but on thousands of civilians. For Obama, U.S. participation in the military campaign against Qaddafi was justified by the threat to civilians. "We have intervened to stop a massacre," declared Obama. But this was not the whole story. NATO was not simply trying to enforce a no-fly zone and an arms embargo. Rather, the goal included bringing about the downfall of a lunatic and unpredictable dictator who was threatening massive civilian casualties. And as the civil war between loyalists and rebels intensified, resulting in increasing civilian casualties, NATO devoted increasing resources to support the NTC and its rebel forces. In other words, NATO took sides in a civil war, an action similar to what occurred in 1999 when NATO legitimated the cause of Kosovar political autonomy by initiating war against Serbia. But the United Nations had only authorized humanitarian protection, not regime change.

Although many human rights activists and public officials supported the dual goals of protecting human rights and replacing the Qaddafi regime, some observers criticized the ambiguity of NATO's mission. Michael Walzer, for example, argued against intervention not only because of limited international support[39] but also because the goal was not simply to halt a mass slaughter. "The overthrow of tyrants and the establishment of democracy has to be local work, and in this case, sadly, the locals couldn't do it. Foreigners can provide all sorts of help—moral, political, diplomatic, and even material. . . . But a military attack of the sort now in progress is defensible only in the most extreme cases. Rwanda and Darfur, where we didn't intervene, would have qualified. Libya doesn't."[40] In his reply to Walzer, William Galston acknowledged that human protection and regime change were distinct objectives but claimed that the pursuit of a dual strategy was not inherently contradictory. "While it may be complicated to say that our military intervention is bounded by the requirements of civilian protection and that we will use nonmilitary means to bring about Qaddafi's fall," wrote Galston, "it is not on its face incoherent."[41] The principal difficulty with the dual strategy of protecting civilians and promoting regime change was that this was not NATO's declared purpose. The announced goal, based on the Security Council resolution, was humanitarian protection. One leading weekly argued that to reduce confusion, the president should simply declare that toppling Qaddafi was an important goal of America's participation in the Libyan intervention.[42]

After the Qaddafi regime collapsed in October and NATO ended its mission, the challenge shifted from regime change to regime reconstruction. After more than four decades of decadent dictatorial rule, the victorious forces faced the arduous task of developing a new political order—one rooted in consent and based on the rule of law. When the old order collapsed, there were few traditions and institutions available on which to base a constitutional system. To begin with, Libya was a deeply fragmented state where tribal allegiances were more influential than national affinities. To a significant degree, Libya was an artificial state created in 1951 from three territories—eastern Cyrenaica, southern Fezzan, and western Tripolitania. While power had been centralized in Tripoli under Qaddafi's dictatorship, allegiances to the Libyan nation were weak. Not surprisingly, although rebel groups united under the goal of regime change, there was little consensus as to the structure of government or the policies that should be pursued once they

had succeeded in toppling the regime. The deeply fragmented society thus provided a weak foundation for regime reconstruction.

In September 2011 the United Nations recognized the NTC as the legitimate interim government of Libya. But once the NTC had declared Libya's liberation in October, the transitional government faced the nearly impossible task of consolidating authority. This task was especially difficult since tribal groups—known as brigades—continued to wield significant power.[43] And since Libyan society had become weaponized with the wide dispersion of Qaddafi's armaments, the task of centralizing force remained an elusive goal—made all the more challenging by the refusal of groups to turn over their weapons and return to the workforce. There were of course many promising signs, including the government's monthly income of about $5 billion in oil revenues and the scheduling of the first round of elections for mid-2012. Nonetheless, regime reconstruction remained a daunting task. The NTC's inchoate governmental institutions remained fragile, and governmental authority was shared between the many rebel groups, tribal brigades, and local militia. Tripoli's airport, for example, remained under the control of one militia leader. Similarly, when fighters captured Qaddafi's son Saif al-Islam in the vicinity of Zintan, a mountain town south of Tripoli, the Zintan militia refused to turn him over to the interim ministry of justice.

THE ETHICS OF NATO'S INTERVENTION

Although it is premature to offer a moral verdict on NATO intervention in Libya, some preliminary judgments are possible using the tridimensional framework developed in chapter 4. From the perspective of goals, the fundamental aim of protecting innocent civilians from indiscriminate killing was clearly morally unassailable. But was the implicit threat of mass killing a sufficient warrant for military action? Although there was the potential for mass atrocities when NATO began its military operations, the slaughter did not occur. And perhaps NATO's military intervention succeeded in preventing the potential atrocities.

For Galston, the key moral issue is the timing of military action. He writes, "Were we required to wait until the slaughter began in order to 'stop' it, or are we allowed to intervene to prevent a humanitarian disaster that is probable but not absolutely certain?"[44]

Assuming that the goal and timing of military action were morally appropriate, the more difficult problem is that protecting civilians was never the sole motivation for NATO's military intervention. From the outset, Western leaders wanted to topple the Qaddafi regime. Defending this secondary objective, however, is morally problematic because, as noted earlier, the legitimacy of a regime needs to be established by its own people, not by outsiders. Regime change may be morally justified if the level of cruelty and injustice rise to extraordinary levels. Qaddafi's rule had been erratic, cruel, and unjust, but other regimes had been equally or more unjust. Why not topple Robert Mugabe's government in Zimbabwe or Omar Bashir's government in Sudan? And after the death of more than twenty-five thousand of its citizens in the ongoing 2011–2012 rebellion in Syria, why not intervene to bring down the Bashar al-Assad regime? In short, regime change may have been justified, but it was at best a morally ambiguous undertaking at the time.

At the level of means, the application of coercive strategies to influence Qaddafi was fully justified. The imposition of economic sanctions and the halting of petroleum exports placed immediate economic constraints on the regime. Similarly, the freezing of financial assets deprived the government and Qaddafi's family and associates of resources, thereby reducing the regime's ability to pay loyalists and mercenaries. Consistent with the principle of discrimination, the hardship targeted on Qaddafi focused chiefly on the regime itself. The use of military power was also fully moral as it applied proportional, discriminating violence against military and political targets. Early on, the chief aim was to enforce the no-fly zone and to destroy key command and control centers. Subsequently, the military campaign expanded by providing direct support for rebel forces.

Finally, at the level of outcomes, the war is also morally ambiguous. Since the primary aim of the NATO operation was to save civilians from possible death, the effect of military intervention was at best indeterminate. This is because it is impossible to know how Qaddafi's forces would have responded had NATO not intervened and had they succeeded in retaking Benghazi and other areas under rebel control. From the perspective of the destruction from the civil war, however, the consequences are morally troubling, for rather than saving lives, the NATO campaign dramatically increased the number of casualties. When the NATO mission began, an estimated three hundred persons had been killed in the fighting. By the war's end, the estimated number of deaths exceeded thirty thousand.[45] Some of the battles in Tripoli and smaller cities like Brega, Misrata, and Sirte were especially destructive. In the battle over Misrata alone, more than two thousand fighters and civilians were killed. Of course, one should not be surprised that NATO's participation in the Libyan civil war led to an increase in deaths. Wars, after all, use lethal force to achieve their political objectives, and the Libyan war was no exception. But if NATO's war is to be judged morally by its results, clearly the high death rate is a problem, especially since the aim of the intervention was to save human lives.

MORAL REFLECTIONS

The Libyan intervention raises many important issues in international ethics. These include the following:

- Is the R2P principle an important development in global society? What are the advantages and disadvantages of this norm?
- In prohibiting gross human rights abuses and war crimes, is UN authorization necessary or desirable? Anne-Marie Slaughter writes, "It is difficult to know when a state has failed in its responsibility to protect its people, particularly when secession is involved. This is why international authorization is both required and difficult to obtain."[46] Do you agree? If so, was NATO's

war with Serbia over Kosovo (see case 1-1) a mistake?

- At the time that NATO began its military campaign, comparatively few deaths had resulted from the rebellion. Was Qaddafi's threat against the city of Benghazi a sufficient warrant for commencing foreign

intervention, or should the United States have waited until systemic atrocities were committed?

- The NATO campaign sought to protect lives and to topple the Qaddafi regime. Of these two objectives, which is the more fundamental? Why?

HUMANITARIAN INTERVENTION

According to Jack Donnelly, humanitarian intervention is foreign intervention that seeks "to remedy mass and flagrant violations of the basic human rights of foreign nationals by their government."[47] Although the grossest abuses of human rights have historically occurred in oppressive, dictatorial regimes, the most serious human rights abuses since the end of the Cold War have been due to civil war and the breakdown of government authority. Thus, although Donnelly's conceptualization might have been adequate during the Cold War, it is inadequate in addressing the gross violations of human rights in the post–Cold War era. As a result, I define humanitarian intervention as foreign intervention (whether unilateral or multilateral) carried out to limit human suffering and death because of government oppression or because of a country's political disintegration.

In the contemporary era, the major threat to human rights in global society has come from "quasi" or "failed" states, that is, political communities in which government authority is weak or absent. Failed states generally result from two developments: first, the decline in the government's perceived legitimacy because of its unwillingness or inability to respond to popular demands and, second, the growing demands by ethnic, religious, and political minorities for increased political autonomy. These two developments have led to growing civil strife and the breakdown of government authority in numerous countries, including Liberia, Rwanda, Sierra Leone, Somalia, Sudan, the former Yugoslavia, and former Soviet republics such as Azerbaijan, Georgia, Russia, and Tajikistan. Each of these territories has suffered from human rights abuses involving lawlessness, starvation, genocide, and mass migration. For example, the disintegration of Somalia's political system following the overthrow of the dictatorial rule of Siad Barre resulted in bitter conflict among Somali clan leaders (known as warlords). This war destroyed much of Somalia's infrastructure and impeded humanitarian distribution of food, resulting in widespread famine. The tribal conflict between the Hutu and the Tutsi in Rwanda similarly resulted in enormous human violence and suffering, including the death of more than half a million persons and the forced migration of more than two million Hutu. Finally, the disintegration of Yugoslavia in the aftermath of the Cold War resulted in a bitter war among Serbs, Croats, and Muslims, with the most intense fighting taking place over the political future of Bosnia-Herzegovina. This war is estimated to have caused some two hundred thousand deaths and displaced more than one million refugees.

Humanitarian intervention—foreign intervention designed to prevent and minimize gross human rights violations—poses legal and moral problems. Legally, humanitarian intervention challenges the established norm of state sovereignty; morally, it challenges the right of communal self-determination. As noted previously, because nonintervention and self-determination are not the only or even the most important norms in the international system, statesmen must devise prudential policies that take into account competing principles, including the demand for order and justice, stability, and human rights. Thus, when gross human rights violations occur in a foreign country, statesmen must determine whether, when, and how their governments should respond.

As with politically motivated military intervention, humanitarian intervention is generally justified if it passes two tests: a political test and an ethical test. First, humanitarian intervention must be in the interests of the intervening state or states. This condition is satisfied when the intervening state perceives human rights abuses in a foreign country as either a general threat to the order, legitimacy, and morality of global society or, as is most often the case, a particular threat to its own economic prosperity, political influence, and territorial integrity. The intervening state might also regard the breakdown in civic order and the growing human rights abuses as a legal obligation in fulfillment of bilateral and multilateral treaty obligations. For example, the United States viewed the political unrest in Haiti in the early 1990s as a major foreign policy responsibility in part because of Haiti's proximity to the United States. Similarly, when war broke out in the former Yugoslavia, it was widely assumed that European states had a special responsibility for containing and resolving the Balkans conflict. Europe's geopolitical responsibilities were assumed to be rooted in geographical proximity, historical ties, and close ethnic and religious bonds between European and Serbo-Croatian peoples.

Second, humanitarian intervention must be in the interests of the people and communities of the intervened state; that is, the evil of military intervention must be justified by the good accomplished in the penetrated state. Because the aim is to relieve famine, genocide, and human suffering, this condition is satisfied when existing human rights violations are reduced or eliminated and preconditions are established that prevent their immediate recurrence. It is important to emphasize that right intentions are not a sufficient condition to justify humanitarian intervention. As noted in chapter 4, because an ethical policy must be judged in terms of its goals, means, and likely outcomes, a morally legitimate intervention must be just in its goals as well as its methods and results. Noble intentions are not enough. A policy designed to relieve human suffering through military intervention must, if it is to be considered moral, have a high probability of successfully achieving its goals in both the short and the medium term.

Even when these two conditions are fulfilled, the decision to intervene is never easy because it normally will involve trade-offs among relevant norms. As noted in earlier chapters, ethics is concerned with the application of multiple and sometimes conflicting moral norms to individual and collective human conduct. For Stanley Hoffmann, four norms provide the foundation of the contemporary international system: sovereignty, self-determination, self-government, and human rights.[48] Although Hoffmann does not prioritize these norms, it is possible to classify them, as shown in table 9-1, in terms of unit of analysis (the individual or the community) and level of significance (primary or secondary). Because no ethical formula exists by which potential conflict among these norms can be reconciled a priori, tensions must be resolved through arguments based on consistency, impartiality, and potential outcomes.

Table 9-1. Classification of Global Norms

		PRIORITY OF NORMS	
		Primary	Secondary
UNIT OF ANALYSIS	Individual	Human Rights	Self-Government
	Community	Sovereignty	Self-Determination

SOURCE: Developed by the author.

In the post–Cold War era the most important tension among these norms has been between sovereignty and human rights. The dilemma of how to reconcile these two norms is difficult because both global order, maintained in part by honoring the nonintervention norms, and human rights are vital to a just and human international community. Thus, when genocide or widespread crimes against humanity occur in a fragile state, how should leaders respond? By doing nothing, as was the case in Rwanda? Or as in Kosovo, which resulted in a NATO war against Serbia? In confronting gross human rights violations in foreign countries, statesman must weigh the relative merits of nonintervention versus the merits of protecting people.

Finally, it is important to stress that humanitarian intervention is an action that contravenes sovereignty, the fundamental norm of the Westphalian order. Even though the emergence of the R2P doctrine has increased global support for humanitarianism, it would be premature to suggest that the promotion and protection of human rights have eclipsed support for sovereignty. On the contrary, the world remains fundamentally Westphalian in character. As Matthew Waxman notes, "There is currently no widely accepted right or license among individual states to humanitarian intervention, as there is one to self-defense."[49] Fundamentally, the current global constitutional order prohibits the use of force except in self-defense or when authorized by the UN Security Council.

To illustrate important ethical issues in humanitarian intervention, I next examine the nature, role, and effects of the U.S. intervention in Somalia in 1992.

CASE 9-2: U.S. INTERVENTION IN SOMALIA

The U.S. military intervention in Somalia in December 1992 was precipitated by a massive famine that had led to the deaths of more than three hundred thousand persons and threatened the lives of another one to two million. The famine was a direct result of a bloody civil war among rival clans that had developed from the ouster of the military dictatorship of General Mohammed Siad Barre, who had ruled Somalia from 1969 until January 1991. Following the overthrow of the Siad Barre regime, civil authority had broken down, and much of the country, especially the Somali capital of Mogadishu, was in virtual anarchy. When lawlessness intensified in late 1991, the United Nations halted humanitarian relief efforts until a ceasefire could be arranged. In April 1992, the UN Security Council authorized a five-hundred-member peacekeeping force—known as UN Operation in Somalia (UNOSOM I)—to protect the relief convoys. When this force proved inadequate, three thousand more peacekeepers were added. However, even this larger UN force proved incapable of maintaining rudimentary order and could not even ensure the distribution of food in the face of massive starvation.

In light of a deteriorating political situation, President George Bush authorized the intervention of U.S. forces into Somalia to permit the resumption of humanitarian relief.[50] The U.S. intervention was unique in the annals of international relations because it was the first time that the United Nations had authorized a largely single-state military intervention without an invitation or the consent of the government. Such consent was impossible because no functioning government existed in Somalia. Indeed, the gross human rights violations were a direct by-product of a civil war among warlords, each vying for the right to rule Somalia. Thus, on December 3, the Security Council adopted Resolution 794, which endorsed the U.S. offer to lead a multinational peacemaking force. Unlike other UN peacekeeping operations, the goal of this interventionary force, justified under Chapter VII of the UN Charter, was not to keep contestants apart but to impose order through military force. The aim, however, was not political but humanitarian because the goal of establishing order was to allow the resumption of humanitarian relief to prevent further starvation.

U.S. INTERVENTION

Operation Restore Hope began in mid-December with the landing of three thousand U.S. Marines in Somalia. The American military forces quickly increased in size to nearly twenty-eight thousand soldiers and in time were supplemented by some ten thousand troops from other countries. Although the Unified Task Force (UNITAF) was formally a multinational operation, in actuality it was a unilateral military operation authorized by the Security Council, as the planning, organization, and execution of the peacemaking force was carried out solely by the United States. Organizationally, the intervention was similar to Desert Storm, the U.S.-led military operation that liberated Kuwait from Iraq in early 1992.

After U.S. Marines landed unopposed, they quickly consolidated control over Mogadishu and its port and airport and then extended control over the urban centers and villages in central Somalia, where the famine was most severe. Within a month, U.S. military forces had established secure transportation links to key urban centers, thereby ensuring the effective distribution of humanitarian relief. After achieving its primary mission of establishing basic political order and ensuring the distribution of famine relief, U.S. forces were gradually reduced, so that by May 1993 only about five thousand American soldiers remained from the original deployment.

On May 4, the United States ended its peacemaking task and formally transferred authority to a new, large (twenty thousand soldiers and eight thousand support staff) UN peacekeeping mission—UNOSOM II. Unlike the earlier mission, UNOSOM II had a greatly expanded mandate, authorized not only to maintain order but also to help create the conditions and institutions considered necessary for peaceful self-rule. Whereas the first peacekeeping mission was limited to ensuring famine relief, UNOSOM II, as authorized by Security Council Resolution 814, called for the "consolidation, expansion, and maintenance of a secure environment throughout Somalia" and "rehabilitation of the political institutions and economy of Somalia." In effect, the original peacekeeping mission was extended from keeping order and facilitating humanitarian relief to nation building. In addition, the new peacekeeping operation is important because it was justified, for the first time in UN history, under Chapter VII of the UN Charter. Finally, UNOSOM II is important because, unlike the first mission, the United States pledged to support this operation with four thousand soldiers, including a thirteen-hundred-member Quick Reaction Force.

In view of UNOSOM II's broader peacekeeping mandate, conflict was inevitable between UN forces and the dominant Somali warlord, General

Mohammad Farrah Aideed, and his Somali National Alliance (SNA) forces. After SNA troops ambushed UN peacekeepers, killing twenty-four Pakistani soldiers, the Security Council authorized UN forces to "take all necessary measures" against those responsible for the attack. Over the next four months, conflict between Aideed's SNA and UN peacekeepers intensified, culminating in one of the deadliest battles in UN peacekeeping history. The October 3 firefight, which was precipitated by a surprise raid by U.S. Army Rangers on an SNA center, killed eighteen U.S. soldiers and injured seventy-eight, and killed or injured between five hundred and one thousand Somalis. Shortly thereafter, President Bill Clinton, under heavy congressional pressure, announced that he was modifying the U.S. role in Somalia from what two U.S. diplomats described as "its admittedly overambitious vision of assertive multilateralism and rebuilding failed states."[51] According to Clinton, U.S. forces would no longer seek to forcefully disarm Somali clans and would withdraw all forces no later than March 31, 1994, even though additional forces were temporarily authorized to increase the security of existing troops deployed in Somalia. Subsequently, UN secretary-general Boutros Boutros-Ghali and the Security Council set March 31, 1995, as the final date for the withdrawal of all UN peacekeeping forces.

THE ETHICS OF THE SOMALIA INTERVENTION

From a legal perspective, there is little doubt that the original Somalia intervention was legitimate. Because all civil authority had broken down in Somalia as a result of war, the Security Council–sanctioned UNITAF provided the necessary legitimacy for the U.S.-led operation to restore order and thereby resume humanitarian relief. However, it is important to emphasize that this UN-sanctioned force was legally unprecedented: it was the first time that the Security Council had authorized intervention in a state without its consent.[52]

From a political perspective, scholars and public officials disagreed over the merits of UNITAF. According to Alberto Coll, these political differences were fundamentally between "interest-driven realists" and "values-driven globalists."[53] For the former, humanitarian intervention was unwise because there were no clearly defined U.S. interests in Somalia. For example, John Bolton, the assistant secretary of state for international organization affairs at the time of the U.S. operation and an opponent of the action, has suggested that the fundamental failure of U.S. decision makers was the attempt "to adapt the world and U.S. policy to idealized and untested models, rather than to define U.S. interests and then pursue them."[54] For globalists, however, humanitarian intervention was important to prevent the spread of war and suffering in the African continent, because "[i]nternational society, morality, and basic decency form one whole fabric."[55] Despite the high cost of the U.S. intervention ($2 billion for the military operations alone), globalists, such as Chester Crocker, have argued that U.S. action was well justified in protecting life and in temporarily restoring political order to Somalia. For Crocker, U.S. general interests were served by Operation Restore Hope because the United States, as the leading state in the international system, has an interest in the overall stability and well-being of the global society. Crocker writes, "As the end of the century nears, it is surely wise that we and others broaden our understanding of national interest to include consideration of interests related to global order (sanctity of borders, extension of the Nuclear Nonproliferation Treaty) and global standards (avoiding genocide, mass humanitarian catastrophe)."[56]

From an ethical perspective, there is also little doubt that Operation Restore Hope, the first phase of the military intervention, was morally legitimate. Following the tridimensional framework developed in chapter 4, it is clear that the operation's goals (the restoration of order for humanitarian reasons), means (the use of a limited, UN-sanctioned force, undertaken as a last resort), and ends (the restoration of order to resume humanitarian relief) were consistent with moral values commonly accepted in global society. However, if the humanitarian intervention under UNITAF was morally compelling, this was not necessarily the case for the expanded mission of the United Nations under UNOSOM II. Because political viability and self-help are important criteria in determining authentic self-determination, the expansion of peacemaking to include nation building, although legally justified by the United Nations, was politically and morally problematic. Politically, it was problematic because it sought to settle an indigenous war among clans by seeking to demilitarize the warring factions while remaining impartial to their claims. However, if wars are to result in a political settlement, the parties themselves must be involved in the settlement. This normally occurs after the warring parties tire of fighting and make a compromise or when the victorious party imposes a settlement on the loser. However, seeking to build a political order without a prior fundamental settlement among the parties is unlikely to foster a long-term peace. Moreover, because nation building requires significant military forces to encourage and if necessary to impose a settlement on the recalcitrant factions, it is a demanding task that is not well suited to lightly armed multilateral peacekeeping forces. In the final analysis, since communal solidarity and legitimacy can be earned only by the people themselves, the expansion of UNOSOM's mandate was morally problematic because it impaired authentic political development.

- Was U.S. intervention in Somalia morally warranted? Given the many other needs in the world, did the Somali famine present a compelling case for military intervention?
- The U.S. intervention was precipitated by a desire to meet immediate humanitarian needs. Is short-term response to human suffering an adequate moral strategy, or must humanitarian relief also address the fundamental causes of human suffering? More specifically, should U.S. forces have sought to demilitarize the warring factions after successfully establishing the resumption of humanitarian relief?
- Although the U.S. military operation (UNITAF) is generally regarded as morally unassailable and politically legitimate, this is not the case for UNOSOM II. Was the extension of the UN mission to include nation building morally and politically prudent, or should the UN operation have simply sought to keep peace among the warlords?
- This case raises issues of moral consistency, especially when compared with the U.S. inaction in the Rwanda genocide (see chapter 5). Although the human needs in Rwanda might have been more pressing than those in Somalia, by what moral calculus could the United States have intervened in Somalia but not in Rwanda?

MORAL REFLECTIONS

This case study raises a number of critical issues about the ethics of humanitarian intervention.

SUMMARY

The nonintervention norm is an important legal and moral rule in the contemporary international system. In light of the decentralized nation-state system, honoring the sovereignty and territorial integrity of states helps maintain international peace. However, nonintervention is not the only or even the most important norm in global society.

Conditions might arise that justify military intervention against another state. From a moral perspective, the easiest type of intervention to justify is that which seeks to halt genocide, ethnic cleansing, and crimes against humanity.

Since the development of peaceful, constitutional states is a task best carried out by indigenous political leaders, foreign powers should resist the temptation to intervene in other countries to develop better, more humane regimes. But when developments arise that threaten a region or result in egregious human rights abuses, leaders of the major powers should be prepared to hold regimes accountable for the abuse and misuse of governmental prerogatives. When governments threaten to slaughter some of their people (as in the case of Libya), or fighting militia impede the distribution of food to prevent mass starvation (as in the case of Somalia), foreign powers have both a right and a responsibility to help protect the rights and welfare of innocent civilians. Interventions are always complicated affairs and should be undertaken only as a last resort and with due care—preferably with the support of the Security Council. But whether acting unilaterally or multilaterally, states should regard the violation of the nonintervention norm as an exceptional action that is contrary to the long-term interests of the international community.

The emergence of the "responsibility-to-protect" principle is significant because it highlights the important role of governmental responsibility for caring for persons within its territorial boundaries. According to the R2P norm, when states are unable or unwilling to protect their people's rights, the international community should assume that task. The significance of R2P is that rather than simply stressing the autonomy of sovereign states, it highlights the government's responsibility to protect its people. Although sovereignty is a foundational legal right, this right is not an absolute norm but a rule conditioned by moral behavior. The world will become a more peaceful and humane world if states honor their responsibilities toward their people and respect the autonomy of other states. The former will assure global justice, while the latter will foster international justice.

Chapter Ten

The Ethics of International Economic Relations

We may think we live in a world whose governance has been radically transformed by globalization, but the buck still stops with domestic policy makers. The hype that surrounds the decline of the nation states is just that: hype.[1]

—DANI RODRICK

Globalization entails the closer integration of the countries of the world; this closer integration entails more interdependence, and this greater interdependence requires more collective action. Global public goods, the benefits of which accrue to all within the global community, become more important.[2]

—JOSEPH STIGLITZ

The history of the modern world economy illustrates two points. First, economies work best when they are open to the world. Second, open economies work best when their governments address the sources of dissatisfaction with global capitalism. . . . The challenge of global capitalism in the twenty-first century is to combine international integration with politically responsive, socially responsible government.[3]

—JEFFREY A. FRIEDEN

A SIGNIFICANT CHANGE in post–Cold War global society is the rising importance of international economic affairs. According to some observers, the pursuit of global economic prosperity has resulted in greater international economic integration—a development that is associated with increased cross-border flows of information, goods, services, and money. Two developments have contributed to the emergence of the global economy.[4] First, the application of modern technology, especially computers and information networks, has led to extraordinary changes in global communication and transportation. Because of the high speed and negligible costs involved in digital communications, geography no longer impedes international communication. Modern telecommunications make instant communication possible in most urban centers of the world. Additionally, modern jumbo jets have made international travel more rapid and efficient, while the use of cargo containers has dramatically decreased the cost of global shipping. The second and even more significant development is the decision by governments to reduce obstacles to the free movement of investments and commerce. After the collapse of the Soviet Union, states adopted more liberal economic systems that facilitated free enterprise domestically and free trade internationally. The steady embrace of economic globalization by governments points to a significant danger: just as governments can create policies to encourage the free movement of goods, services, and capital, they can also adopt policies that constrain that openness. It is important to note that declining trade flows and investments in the late nineteenth and early twentieth centuries interrupted globalization for nearly half a century. Economic globalization is not inevitable. To be sustained it requires the actions and support of the world's member states.

This chapter addresses two distinct issues in global economic relations. First it examines the nature of these relations, and then it analyzes the role of economics in foreign policy. The first theme is addressed in the first two parts of the chapter. In the first part, I examine the nature and scope of globalization and highlight some of its perceived benefits and costs. This is a contentious topic since people hold radically different views about increased international economic integration. In the second part, I examine global finance and the benefits and potential costs that arise from the expansion of global capital markets. To illustrate the challenges involved in sustaining a stable international financial order, I examine the euro crisis of 2010–2012. In the third section, I address the nature and role of economic sanctions in contemporary statecraft. Decision makers use sanctions in the belief that they are preferable to more coercive foreign policy tools. Although sanctions are preferable to war, they are not morally neutral instruments of statecraft. Indeed, because they fail to protect the innocent, sanctions are a morally problematic tool of foreign policy—a truth that I illustrate with a case study on South Africa.

GLOBALIZATION

Columnist Thomas Friedman defines globalization as the integration of markets and states in a way that enables "individuals, corporations, and nation-states to reach around the world farther, faster, deeper, and cheaper than ever before," and enables "the world to reach into individuals, corporations, and nation-states farther, faster, deeper, and cheaper than ever before."[5] Although modern technology has decreased the cost and increased the speed of global transportation, the principal breakthrough in accelerating global integration was the rise of the Internet in the 1980s—a development that led to cheap global information networks. These networks have accelerated global communication and facilitated rapid and efficient transnational flows of capital and goods. Although globalization has been under way for centuries, its modern expression is unprecedented in speed and scope. In the post–Cold War world, news is available instantly worldwide, and ideas and knowledge are disseminated internationally at virtually no cost.

Given the pervasive scope of transnational networks, governments are increasingly less able to regulate transnational flows of information, goods, and services. States continue to claim sovereignty, but the application of modern technology has increased the porosity of borders. And whereas governments and corporations were the primary agents of globalization in the past, the chief agents of modern globalization are individuals, groups, and small enterprises. In the new world order, egalitarian, functional relationships among people are replacing the traditional hierarchical relationships between rulers and people, leaders and workers. The decline of governmental control over transnational flows can pose significant challenges, especially when confronting harmful cross-border developments such as the illicit trade in narcotics, weapons, money, and people.[6]

Since education and training are the chief determinants of modern economic growth, Friedman argues that individuals, not corporations or states, govern the contemporary global economy. According to Friedman, what matters in the modern world is not geography or nationality but rather the competence and capabilities of individuals. Since the world economy is no longer determined by hierarchies but by competencies, Friedman says that the world is "flat,"[7] with work going to the group or region best equipped to produce goods and services most efficiently. The rise of job "outsourcing"—the transfer of work from a developed economy with high labor costs to an emerging economy with lower wages—is an example of this phenomenon.

The expansion of economic globalization has precipitated a significant debate over the relative merits of this phenomenon. Some argue that the process is undemocratic, spawned by developed economies that have a comparative advantage in producing and distributing modern goods and services. The charge is also applied to intergovernmental organizations like the IMF and the World Bank. To be sure, the major powers have decisive influence in such organizations, but the world, including the United Nations, is not a democracy that reflects the will of the people. Rather it is governed by the will of sovereign states, especially those with wealth and power.

A second critique is that economic globalization destroys cultures by replacing traditional customs and values with modern, materialistic values. There can be little doubt that modernity challenges traditional customs, but the changes occur not because of technological determinism but because people desire modern goods and services that can make their lives more fulfilling. The introduction of cell phones in poor, isolated areas of Africa, for example, has broadened communication networks, weakening local and tribal associations.

Friedman uses the metaphors of "the Lexus" and "the olive tree" to contrast the tension between modernity and the desire for strong ethnic and cultural bonds. Modernity is important because it increases standards of living and offers greater opportunities to satisfy human desires, but economic development does not ensure human dignity. People also long for a meaningful life rooted in communal relationships and shared values that define what and where home is. The "olive tree" represents this longing for a meaningful identity. The fundamental challenge posed by globalization, according to Friedman, is to learn to balance modernity and tradition, prosperity and belonging.[8]

A third criticism of economic globalization is that it hurts workers. Since market capitalism encourages economic efficiency, globalization encourages firms and enterprises to carry out their work wherever it can be undertaken at the lowest cost. This means that some businesses will shift operations from high-wage countries to those with lower wages. In the ongoing process of "creative destruction," capitalism creates jobs and destroys jobs. Thus, while some workers are hurt by globalization, others benefit from it. One weekly describes the gains and losses of globalization as follows: "It makes some workers worse off while making others (including the poorest ones of all, to begin with) better off. And in the aggregate it makes consumers (that is, people with or without a job) better off as well. Altogether, given freer trade, both rich-country and poor-country living standards rise."[9] So the charge is partly correct: globalization hurts workers in industries that are no longer economically efficient; but it also benefits others by providing new jobs and more, better, cheaper products that contribute to an overall rise in living standards.

A related critique is that globalization increases inequality. There can be little doubt that economic development has accelerated economic inequality among countries. According to one estimate, in 1820 the richest country in the world had a per capita income about four and a half times that of the poorest. By 1913, the ratio had increased to fifteen to one, and by 2000 it had risen to seventy-one to one.[10] Although some globalization critics are deeply concerned about inequalities within and among countries, the underlying and more fundamental moral concern is globalization's impact on the poor. For some, the principal moral weakness of globalization is that it helps the rich and hurts the poor. In support of this claim economist Joseph Stiglitz writes, "Globalization may have helped some countries . . . but it had not helped most of the people even in these countries. The worry was that globalization might be creating rich countries with poor people."[11] While market systems have the potential to exacerbate inequalities, it does not follow that they cannot uplift the lives of the poor. Indeed, without economic growth, poverty reduction can only be realized through the governmental redistribution of income. The influential financial columnist Martin Wolf makes a convincing case that globalization, to the extent that it has fostered economic growth, has increased living standards worldwide and reduced poverty. "Never before have so many people . . . enjoyed such large rises in their standards of living. . . . Rapid economic growth in poor countries with half of the world's population has powerful effects on the only sort of inequality which matters, that among individuals. It has similarly dramatic effects on world poverty."[12]

Regardless of how economic globalization is assessed, the process of global integration provides opportunities to increase economic efficiency and thereby improve living conditions. This is especially the case for the increased openness of international trade. Although the gains from free trade are indisputable, the benefits of global finance are less self-evident. Financial markets present inherent risks, including the potential for global contagion of crises. Since global finance poses risks that are not present in global trade, it is important to differentiate the two. The *Economist*, a weekly that staunchly defends economic liberalism, is cautious about global finance. It states its concerns as follows: "Why is trade in capital different from trade in goods? For two main reasons. First, international markets in capital are prone to error, whereas international markets in goods are not. Second, the punishment for big financial mistakes can be draconian, and tends to hurt innocent bystanders as much as borrowers and lenders."[13] In view of the special challenges posed by global finance, we turn to this dimension of globalization.

FINANCIAL GLOBALIZATION
The Rise of Global Finance

Fundamentally, finance involves the transfer of resources from those who own them but do not wish to use them to those who invest them productively but do not own them.[14] People invest surplus funds by transferring them to a savings bank or by buying stocks and bonds so that financial institutions and corporations can use them to increase economic output. Since capital is essential to promote economic growth, banks and other financial institutions play a critical role in making investment capital available to business ventures. In order for people's savings to be transformed into institutional loans, however, people must have confidence that their savings are safe in banks and that borrowers will repay their debts. Trust and promise keeping are therefore indispensable to a stable financial system. According to Michael Lewis, a popular writer on finance, "A banking system is an act of faith; it survives only for as long as people believe it will."[15]

Although financial crises can emerge from a variety of sources, the most common cause is a loss of confidence that financial commitments will be fulfilled. And when crises become systemic, they can imperil liquidity (i.e., the availability of capital), which, in turn, can lead to national economic stagnation and even economic depression. The U.S. financial crash of 2008—precipitated by a real estate "bubble" and fueled by excessive mortgages and speculative betting with complex financial securities—illustrates this phenomenon. When the housing market collapsed and major financial institutions faced insolvency, the U.S. federal government (the Treasury Department and the Federal Reserve) responded by injecting $1.5 trillion into banks and other financial institutions to avoid a collapse of the financial system.

If maintaining a stable and predictable domestic financial system is challenging, the task is all the more difficult in the global economy. This is so for at least two reasons. First, since nations are sovereign, they pursue national economic interests through their own fiscal and monetary policies, trade and financial regulations, investment policies, and other related actions. Maintaining a stable, productive international economic order therefore requires a high level of coordination and cooperation among member states. Ultimately, increased globalization demands increased global governance. Economist Joseph Stiglitz writes, "Globalization entails the closer integration of the countries of the world; this closer integration entails more interdependence, and this greater interdependence requires more collective action."[16] But developing authoritative institutions is difficult when final decision-making authority remains with nation-states. To be sure, intergovernmental organizations (IGOs) like the World Trade Organization and the World Bank play an important role in promoting global public goods, but IGOs are not world government.

A second factor that contributes to the complexity of a stable global financial system is the existence of multiple currencies. Since each nation has its own money, international trade and global finance can only occur if a stable and efficient global monetary system exists to coordinate the different currency systems. But how is the relative value of a currency established? Who decides? In the modern economy the value of most currencies is established by currency markets based on the supply and demand for a particular currency. This means that the increased availability of a currency will depress its value, while its increasing scarcity will increase its value. Although speculation about the future value of a currency can influence its short-term value, in the longer term the relative value of a currency is likely to be influenced primarily by domestic political and economic conditions. The political stability, quality of government, and nature of the country's public policies are important because they can either augment or impede national economic growth. And persistent trade imbalances caused by excessive imports over exports are likely to undermine confidence in the economy's productive capacity.

The aim of an effective international monetary system is to facilitate efficient currency convertibility and to ensure global financial stability. Following World War II, Western leaders established an international financial system (the so-called Bretton Woods monetary system) based on fixed exchange rates, the U.S. dollar as the main foreign exchange currency, and a common pool of reserves (foreign currencies) that were available to assist countries facing balance-of-payments disequilibria. The responsibility for promoting and sustaining a stable and efficient global monetary system was entrusted to the International Monetary Fund (IMF). The Bretton Woods system ended in 1971 when the U.S. government ended automatic convertibility of the dollar into gold (at $35 an ounce).

Since then, countries have pursued a variety of foreign exchange policies ranging from managed exchange rates to flexible or floating rates. The end of fixed exchange rates, along with the significant expansion in global trade since the end of the Cold War, led to a dramatic expansion of currency exchange markets. Early on, the foreign exchange markets were chiefly concerned with facilitating global trade and meeting other financial obligations. In time, however, traders developed a futures market for currency exchange that has grown rapidly with globalization in the post–Cold War era. In 2010, it was estimated that the average daily turnover in global foreign exchange markets was close to $4 trillion, with nearly half of the trading speculative in nature.[17]

The growth of cross-border capital flows in the post–Cold War era is even more significant since such flows represent investment in real financial, property, or equity assets in a foreign land. In 1980 cross-border financial flows accounted for about $1 trillion in stocks, bonds, and other loans, but by 2007 that total had increased to roughly $11 trillion, representing roughly 5.5 percent of the world's total financial assets.[18] Since 1980, global finance has grown four times faster than world trade, accounting for an increasingly large share of the world economy.

Financial Crises

Financial crises occur when investors lose confidence in the willingness or capacity of borrowers to repay loans. In such circumstances, investors seek to redeem their investments for cash or to demand a higher rate of return. In either case, the effect of a crisis is to raise the cost of borrowing. Crises are commonly attributed to two sources: first, as a result of irresponsible human behavior, and second, from incompetent governmental action.[19] In the first view, the problem is that people vacillate between an excess of greed followed by an excess of fear and panic. The second view emphasizes the role of distortions created by government, either through excessive or insufficient regulation, or counterproductive interventions. For example, unwise governmental actions can distort incentives and contribute to excessive risk taking, leading to either significant profits or losses. If the latter occurs and the losses threaten the financial system, government institutions may be forced to assume the debt in order to maintain liquidity. This is what happened in the 2008 American financial crisis.

These two perspectives help to explain this crisis. To a significant extent, the crash was precipitated both by the greed of individuals to buy homes that were beyond their financial capabilities and by the greed of lenders who provided mortgages with little accountability. At the same time, governmental institutions failed to provide proper oversight over the expansion of highly complex securities whose risk levels were not fully apparent. Even the leading securities rating agencies, who gave high ratings to these bank securities, failed to appreciate the different risks involved. Traditionally, mortgage banks held the title to home properties. With the rise of mortgage securitization, however, banks transferred ownership of mortgages to financial centers, who then repackaged the loans in a variety of instruments, including complex collateral debt obligations (CDOs). Financial innovation thus allowed investors throughout the world to buy mortgage securities and participate in the lucrative U.S. housing market. Since financial institutions make money by selling securities, the repackaging of subprime mortgages resulted in significant income to the banking industry. Investors were happy with "paper" gains until the housing bubble began to collapse in 2006. When home values began to fall, high-risk home owners began foreclosure proceedings. In 2008, some 2.2 million homes were under foreclosure, and this number increased to 2.9 million in 2009. As with all financial crises, the collapse of the subprime market quickly spread to other sectors of the economy, resulting in little investment, negligible economic growth, and a national unemployment rate above 9 percent.

Several developments contributed to the housing crisis: first, at the encouragement of federal agencies, banks increased home lending to people who had little income to offer a down payment or collateral to guarantee the mortgage; second, because of a dollar glut made possible by the inflow of capital from China and elsewhere, interest rates were low and credit could be easily secured; and third, real estate values had been rising rapidly, encouraging the belief that people could increase their wealth through home ownership. By 2008, the higher-risk (subprime) mortgage market was estimated to account for roughly 20 percent of the $10-trillion housing market.

Given the increasingly integrated nature of international finance, it was inevitable that the 2008 American banking crisis would affect global capital markets and especially European financial centers. One consequence of the crisis was that European banks and financial institutions that had invested in American subprime securities confronted significant losses. Additionally, because of the stagnating U.S. economy, domestic demand for European exports necessarily declined, depriving EU countries of much-needed foreign exchange. Finally, the crisis demonstrated the importance of governmental action in restoring economic confidence. Only when the U.S. Treasury and the Federal Reserve intervened with bailout funds did the crisis begin to recede.[20] Although governmental intervention helped to sustain banks and financial institutions that might have failed without public aid, the costs of such action wore borne by all citizens, while the resulting economic gains were assumed by the financial institutions themselves. In effect, governmental intervention tended to socialize costs and to privatize gains.

Case 10-1 on the euro crisis illustrates the complex challenges involved in reconciling national interests with common regional/global interests. Although the European Union (EU) has achieved unprecedented levels of social, economic, and political integration, the EU remains an institution of independent countries. It is not a sovereign federal state. As a result, when the euro crisis erupted in 2010, the major economic powers of the EU had to decide how much assistance should be provided, and on what terms, to countries facing financial collapse.

CASE 10-1: THE EURO CRISIS

THE NATURE OF THE PROBLEM

The role of sovereign governmental intervention became especially important in the euro crisis of 2010–2012. Unlike the United States, where the dollar is the currency of one state, however, the euro is not the currency of one sovereign government but rather a currency shared by seventeen independent states. To be sure, these countries are closely integrated through their membership in the European Union (EU). Monetary policy for the eurozone—the seventeen countries that use the euro as their sole currency[21]—is the responsibility of the European Central Bank (ECB), whose principal task is to maintain financial stability and inhibit inflation. But unlike a central government, the ECB is not a sovereign governmental institution. Although its task is similar to that of the U.S. Federal Reserve, the ECB does not have the power and authority of its American counterpart. The reason for this is that it is not an institution of one sovereign government. Rather, it is an institution that oversees monetary policy for member states, each of which makes its own fiscal policies. To be sure, states are bound to fulfill budgetary commitments, the most important being that a government's budget deficit must not exceed 3 percent of a country's economic output. There is no provision for withdrawal from the eurozone.

The root cause of the euro crisis was the loss of confidence that some states could meet their debt obligations. The crisis began in Greece in late 2009 when the newly elected government of George Papandreou announced that the government's budget deficit was much higher than what had been previously disclosed. Whereas the deficit for 2008 had been estimated at 3.7 percent, by late 2009 it had increased to 12.7 percent—or more than four times the 3 percent deficit ceiling allowed in the eurozone.[22] These disclosures immediately raised the country's borrowing costs, especially when its government bonds were downgraded to junk status. More importantly, they undermined the widespread conviction that a country could not go bankrupt. Foreclosure on sovereign debts had not been considered. Since Greece owed more than four hundred billion euros to European banks, a bank default would pass along the costs to the lending institutions and thereby undermine economic confidence throughout the eurozone and beyond.

To avoid defaulting, Greece needed additional loans as well as the restructuring of its debt. But how should this be done? One approach, the one advocated by German chancellor Angela Merkel, demanded austerity as a precondition for any additional assistance. According to this perspective, since systemic Greek corruption had caused the crisis through rampant bribery, lax tax enforcement, an excessively large public sector workforce, and fraudulent record keeping, Germany was adamantly opposed to assuming the costs of Greek profligacy. German laborers should not be asked to pay for the irresponsibility of Greek citizens. Failure to demand a balanced government budget would simply allow irresponsible governmental policies to continue. The alternative approach, the one favored by French president Nicolas Sarkozy, was to call for simultaneous austerity and public sector investment. The infusion of government funds was necessary in order to stimulate economic growth, which in turn was necessary to increase tax revenues. Austerity alone would simply result in economic contraction and lower government revenue. Indeed, rather than helping to restore a balanced government budget, austerity would simply exacerbate Greece's fiscal problems. After numerous consultations, eurozone leaders agreed to follow the German approach.

In May 2010 the Greek government announced its decision to implement austerity measures. In return, the European Financial and Stability Facility (EFSF) and the IMF agreed to a bailout loan of 110 billion euros. This, however, was insufficient to stem the ongoing collapse of Greece's economy. As a result, EU, IMF, and ECB leaders continued to negotiate over a further bailout plan that also required cuts (known as "haircuts') by private bondholders (banks, insurers, and investment funds). The structure of this additional agreement was developed in the fall of 2011 and approved by EU, ECB, IMF, and private investors in March 2012. The new accord called for a restructuring of private debt in which bondholders would take a nominal write-off of more than 50 percent of their original investment. The effect of this debt restructuring was to lower Greek debt by more than 100 billion euros. At the same time, the accord called for a new bailout loan of 130 billion euros, conditional on further austerity measures. Implementation of this accord was delayed when the Greek government called for a referendum on the bailout initiative. When the first election proved inconclusive, a second parliamentary election took

place in mid-June. In that election, pro-bailout political parties prevailed and established a coalition government that accepted the additional austerity measures.

As noted previously, financial crises spread rapidly, and this has been the case in the eurozone. Three other countries—Italy, Spain, and Portugal—have been affected deeply by the crisis unleashed by Greece, and, because of the integrated nature of European financial systems, the collapse of one major bank or economy could have dire economic consequences in other countries. The financial vulnerability of EU countries is significant because of their large cross-border financial obligations. For example, in 2011 Greece, Italy, and Spain owed French banks roughly $54 billion, $366 billion, and $118 billion, respectively. And in 2011, German banks were owed $19 billion by Greece, $162 billion by Italy, and $117 billion by Spain. For its part, Portugal owed Spanish banks a total of $88.5 billion.[23] Consequently, given the high level of interconnectivity and inherent contagion of global finance, the financial collapse of any one country could result in widespread economic havoc.

Given the comparatively small size of the Greek economy (GDP is $.3 trillion), the major threat to the eurozone financial system in 2012 was from Italy and Spain. Italy's public debt was 21 percent higher than its GDP of $2.1 trillion. Spain, with a GDP of $1.4 trillion, had a manageable public debt of 72 percent of GDP. Spain's financial problems, however, stemmed from its excessive private debt, fueled by speculative investment in real estate. In 2000, Spanish private debt was estimated at 187 percent of the country's GDP, but by 2010, private debt had ballooned to 283 percent of GDP.[24] Thus, when the real estate market collapsed, construction stopped and unemployment skyrocketed to 25 percent.

The excessive borrowing by southern EU countries (Greece, Italy, Portugal, and Spain) was facilitated by the transition to the euro in 2002 and to the generous lending practices of the ECB and northern EU countries (especially Germany). Two factors contributed to credit expansion: first, the ECB kept interest rates low, and second, the ECB treated all eurozone economies alike. Investors and governments could now borrow money at rates substantially lower than had been the case when they had their own national currencies. Thus, since Greek investors could now borrow money at 5 percent rather than 10 to 12 percent, the lower rates stimulated borrowing. The second factor—treating all economies the same—was especially harmful since it masked disparities in the overall economic competitiveness of different EU countries. Rather than reducing productive disparities, however, the increased lending to southern states reduced their productivity. More specifically, since northern eurozone countries (like Germany and the Netherlands) tended to be more economically efficient than southern countries (like Greece, Italy, and Spain), the access to easy credit fueled an artificial boom that increased wages and thereby further reduced economic competitiveness. The result of these divergent economic capacities was that some countries ran persistent balance-of-payments deficits while others generated trade surpluses. According to Wolf, the loss of confidence in some eurozone countries arose not because of excessive borrowing but because of lack of economic competitiveness.[25]

As of 2012, the financial future of Greece and other highly indebted countries remains unclear. In July 2012, the IMF concluded that the euro was not sustainable in its current form. In its report, it indicated that more financial support from the major EU powers and the ECB was needed for Italian and Spanish banks if deflation was to be avoided.[26] Clearly, the euro crisis has placed enormous challenges on the EU and, more specifically, on southern highly indebted countries. Unlike the British or American financial institutions, which are under sovereign authority of their respective governments, the EU is an intergovernmental organization that must secure agreement among its members before it can take action. Financial crises are challenging within sovereign states, but they are especially difficult when authority is dispersed among member states.

THE ETHICS OF THE EURO CRISIS

The euro crisis involves ethical issues that are at once subtle and complex. Because decision makers generally approach global finance as a technical issue, the primary focus is on increasing efficiency and maintaining stability in financial markets. Even when crises occur, the focus is on restoring confidence in financial institutions and credit markets, not on ascertaining culpability for profligate governmental spending, excessive public debts, or the issuing of inscrutable financial instruments that obscured risk. Once the public loses confidence in financial markets and people begin to withdraw their savings from banks, the issue facing government decision makers is simple: how to restore financial confidence. And the answer is always the same: the government, as the "banker of last resort," steps in and provides further credit guarantees to sustain the system. In moral analysis, the central question is, "What is the right or just action?" But when a financial system is threatened, decision makers do not ask, "Should the system be saved?" Rather, they ask, "What actions are necessary to restore financial confidence?"

The euro crisis is also ethically challenging because it raises concerns about the nature and extent of moral obligations across borders. Although the designers of the euro currency had not considered the possibility of sovereign default (the bankruptcy of a member state), the contemporary euro crisis has in fact raised it. What are the moral obligations of EU institutions and key member states to help sustain Greece? Are these obligations conditional on responsible fiscal policies, or should the EU and ECB provide additional credit to help sustain the Greek economy and thereby inhibit default? The Greek government is morally culpable for having failed to disclose the truth of its governmental finances—a betrayal that compromised EU solidarity and ruptured trust. It is also morally culpable for failing to pursue disciplined fiscal policies. But the collapse of its economy has left Greece unable to repay its loans. And if it hadn't received additional loans in 2010 and 2012, the country would have undoubtedly defaulted. Although sovereign bankruptcy has been avoided, the Greek economy is likely to remain stagnant and highly indebted for many years.

As noted above, the euro crisis also involves other countries, notably Italy and Spain. But how should the EU and ECB respond to those economies? Given the economic size of both Italy and Spain, EU authorities would be unable to generate sufficient resources to restore confidence in their banking systems. In June 2012, EU authorities and the ECB provided an additional line of credit of $130 billion for imperiled Spanish banks. But this action contributed little to restoring confidence in the country's financial markets. Ultimately, banking involves trust, and when investors lose confidence in the capacity of financial institutions and governments to fulfill their promises, it is difficult to regain that trust.

Two moral practices are necessary to sustain trust in financial systems. First, finance requires transparency. This means that investors must have access to information on public and private enterprises that is truthful and complete. If investors do not have confidence in the truthfulness and reliability of the reports, records, and public declarations of government officials or business leaders, they are unlikely to risk their savings. Investment presupposes confidence in both the soundness of a national economy and its financial system as well as the long-term viability of business ventures. Since confidence can be sustained only when truth telling is a moral imperative, cheating, lying, and incomplete or false disclosure will necessarily undermine business enterprise.

Second, an effective and efficient financial system is possible only when people and institutions are committed to fulfilling promises. Prior to the development of the modern, impersonal economy, commerce was carried out largely through direct personal relationships. To the extent that promises were involved in commercial transactions, they were based on the presumed trustworthiness of people. This traditional approach to commerce is demonstrated in a weekly cheese market in the city center of Alkmaar, Holland.[27] Modern business transactions, such as the buying of a home or a business enterprise, use legal contracts to ensure that the terms of the agreement are fulfilled. But with financial assets, far more faith in promise keeping is required. When a person buys a corporate or government bond, for example, he or she does so in

the belief that the issuing institution will make regular interest payments and ultimately return the original investment.

Financial promises differ from interpersonal promise keeping. Whereas the latter is based on personal knowledge and trust, the former generally is impersonal, carried out through financial institutions. More significantly, a financial promise entails risk. This is so because all business investment involves some degree of risk. Typically, the greater the level of risk involved, the greater the potential rate of gain or loss. In the event of a business or financial failure, an institution may be unable to fulfill its original promise. For example, because of the virtual collapse of the Greek economy, bondholders were forced to accept a loss of more than 50 percent of their investment in 2012, thereby losing over $100 billion. But financial promises are also broken when investors decide that they do not wish to fulfill their promise, either because the cost of fulfilling the promise is considered excessive or because the original investment has failed to meet expectations. In short, financial promise keeping is a moral enterprise, but it is also a probabilistic activity involving different levels of risk. Promises should be kept, but sometimes they are not. Prudent investors need to weigh such considerations before entrusting their money to others.

Is financial promise keeping among citizens different from promise keeping with foreigners? In chapter 2, I examined the cosmopolitan perspective of Peter Singer, who argues that borders have no fundamental moral significance. For Singer, therefore, cross-border promise keeping is no different from promise keeping among citizens. Indeed, geography should have no moral impact on the fulfillment of financial transactions throughout the world. Martin Wright, however, thinks that this perspective does not account for reality. He writes, "At its most fundamental, trust in promises made by foreigners is likely to be weaker than trust in promises made by fellow citizens. This is partly because people know and understand their own economy and the behavior of the people in it better than they know the economies of foreign countries—and the more foreign or 'different' are those countries, the more that will be the case."[28]

In conclusion, we assess the ethics of the euro using the tridimensional framework developed in chapter 4. From the perspective of ends, the goal of a common currency is morally legitimate because it increases the efficiency of monetary transactions and, as a by-product, the welfare of citizens. From the perspective of means, the practices and policies to ensure a stable currency were inadequate. Because of lax fiscal oversight, some member states failed to fulfill conditions to inhibit significant balance-of-payments deficits. Thus, the means were morally unsatisfactory. And from the perspective of outcomes, the euro was successful in its early phase but deeply problematic after the crisis began in 2009. In short, the creation of the euro is a morally ambiguous development.

MORAL REFLECTIONS

Although decision makers tend to avoid the moral dimensions of financial crises, the case study on the euro raises a number of important ethical issues. These include the following:

- Some decision makers view financial systems as impersonal market systems where rationality, determined by the self-interested behavior of producers and consumers, determines outcomes. Is this claim true? How should ethical considerations be incorporated into financial decision making?
- Given the fraudulent nature of Greece's past record keeping and the failure to limit its governmental budget deficit, why should other eurozone states provide additional loans to Greece? Is additional lending a solution to overborrowing?
- When governments use loans to finance current private or public consumption, who should be held responsible for such profligacy—the banks that authorized the loan or the institutions that secured the loans?
- As noted above, the adoption of the euro is a morally ambiguous development according to a tridimensional ethical perspective. Do you agree? Why or why not?

ECONOMIC SANCTIONS

Economic sanctions are a particular type of statecraft used to advance foreign policy goals. According to David Baldwin, sanctions are "influence attempts" in which states seek to exert power over other international actors, that is, to get them to do what they otherwise would not do.[29] Strictly speaking, economic sanctions can involve positive incentives ("carrots") designed to induce or reward desirable behaviors, or negative actions ("sticks") designed to punish actors for illegal or undesirable behaviors, to deter unwanted behavior, or to compel desired political change. According to the logic of positive sanctions, an effective way to influence the behavior of other states is to provide economic rewards, such as an increase in foreign aid, the expansion of foreign loans at concessionary rates, or the granting of preferential trade treatment. By contrast, the logic of negative sanctions assumes that the most effective way to deter unwanted actions or to compel behavioral change is through the imposition of economic penalties. These sanctions might range from modest actions, such as selected quotas, limited tariff increases, or the reduction of foreign aid, to more extreme measures, such as a freeze of foreign assets, a halt of foreign investment, a ban on technology transfers, or a total economic blockade. Although some scholars have suggested that positive sanctions are much more likely to induce behavioral change than are threats or punishment, negative sanctions have been used more commonly in contemporary international relations than positive inducements.[30] Because most economic sanctions are negative in character, the discussion here is limited to this type of statecraft.

Traditionally, states have used economic sanctions for a variety of reasons. James Lindsay, for example, has identified five purposes: (1) *compliance*—forcing a state to alter its behavior in conformity with the sanctioning state's preferences; (2) *subversion*—seeking to remove particular political leaders from office or attempting to overthrow a regime; (3) *deterrence*—dissuading a target state from carrying out unacceptable behavior; (4) *international symbolism*—sending a message to other governments; and (5) *domestic symbolism*—increasing domestic political support by undertaking a popular public policy initiative.[31] In addition, Kim Richard Nossal argues that states impose sanctions as punishment for harmful or evil acts in the hope that such penalties will rectify past injustices and deter future objectionable behaviors.[32]

The Effectiveness of Sanctions

Are sanctions an effective foreign policy tool? Do they achieve desired behavioral outcomes? Many scholars and foreign policy experts doubt their effectiveness. David Baldwin, for example, notes that scholars generally tend to belittle "the utility of economic techniques of statecraft."[33] M. S. Daoudi and J. S. Dajani similarly claim that the idea that sanctions are ineffective is nearly axiomatic, based on an extensive examination of public statements and scholarship.[34] In order to assess the effectiveness of sanctions, it is important to distinguish between their economic success and their political success, between the capacity to inflict economic hardship and the capacity to achieve desired ends.

Scholars have found several factors that affect the economic impact of sanctions. First, economic hardship is more likely to be achieved when sanctions are imposed multilaterally. Because most economic goods and services are highly fungible (i.e., can be replaced or substituted), broad participation, especially from the major powers, is normally a prerequisite for imposing the desired hardship on the target state. The importance of collective action was illustrated in 1990–1991 during the Persian Gulf crisis, when the United Nations imposed comprehensive economic sanctions against Iraq. Because nearly every country honored the embargo, Iraq's gross national product (GNP) declined by nearly 50 percent. By contrast, the U.S.-led economic embargo against Cuba has been ineffective because few major states have supported this fifty-year-old policy.

A second factor that affects economic success is the participation by nongovernmental actors. Given the increasing influence of global corporations and significant NGOs, nonstate actors can greatly reinforce and intensify sanctions. For example, in response to growing U.S. domestic opposition to South African apartheid, private actors encouraged private divestment and directly pressured American banks and corporations to institute disinvestment programs.[35] These private initiatives not only reinforced the policies of Western governments but also greatly intensified them. Indeed, private disinvestment by American financial institutions and corporations brought far greater harm to the South African economy in the 1980s than did U.S. government sanctions.

Finally, domestic and bilateral domestic factors can significantly affect the economic efficacy of sanctions. According to one major study, economic sanctions have achieved their greatest economic harm when the following conditions were met:

- The target state was economically weaker and politically less stable than the sender; in effect, the relationship was asymmetrical. In successful sanctions episodes, the average sender's economy was 187 times larger than that of the average target state.
- The target and sender had a high level of economic interdependence. In successful sanctions cases, the target state depended on the sender for an average of 28 percent of its total trade.
- Sanctions were imposed quickly and decisively, thereby enhancing the political credibility of the sanctions and increasing the potential for economic harm by preventing the target state from effectively adjusting to the imposed hardship.
- The cost of the sanctions to the target state was significant, generally exceeding 2 percent of its GNP.[36]

The fundamental assumption of economic sanctions is that hardship will discourage unacceptable policies and encourage behavioral reform. Although economic "sticks" can no doubt affect the behavior of foreign actors, economic coercion alone is not decisive. For one thing, foreign policy decision making is a multidimensional process that is subject to numerous domestic and international factors. More importantly, it is doubtful that economic adversity necessarily encourages behavioral reform. Indeed, sanctions may, as the record of U.S. sanctions toward Cuba suggests, increase political resolve. Additionally, inducing behavioral change is far more difficult against autocratic regimes—the governments most likely to be subjected to sanctions. Although highly punitive economic sanctions were being imposed on Iran in 2012, there was little evidence that its autocratic government was likely to alter its nuclear enrichment program.

What is the historical record on economic sanctions? According to one comprehensive study, economic sanctions during the 1914–1990 period were successful in bringing about desired reforms in about one-third of the cases.[37] However, another scholar, using the same data, argues that the success rate is less than 5 percent![38] Regardless of whether one accepts the optimistic or pessimistic measures of political success, it is clear that economic hardship does not often achieve the desired political outcomes.

But perhaps sanctions should be viewed as part of a state's overall repertoire for communicating interests and exercising international influence. If less demanding expectations are applied, sanctions are likely to be regarded as a more useful instrument of statecraft. Indeed, Baldwin argues that the common view that sanctions are ineffective is wrong because sanctions can serve as effective communications symbols in interstate bargaining.[39] Lisa Martin similarly suggests that the role of economic sanctions has been underestimated and argues that sanctions can be especially effective in demonstrating resolve and in sending signals.[40] In her view, such signaling is most effective when carried out multilaterally and when senders demonstrate resolve by their willingness to suffer economic loss. In addition, it is important to note that the effectiveness of sanctions as instruments of communication need not be based on the direct economic harm inflicted by sanctions. As William Kaempfer and Anton Lowenberg have noted, the impact of signals and threats communicated through sanctions is "unrelated to their market or income effects" because private actors can carry out actions that hasten the desired political reforms.[41]

Sanctions can also be regarded as successful when they are used as punishment. All that is required when retribution is the goal is to bring about economic hardship on a target state. When the international community imposed major economic sanctions against Haiti in 1991, the hardship was perceived as a legitimate price for the toppling of the elected government. When the United Nations imposed comprehensive sanctions against Serbia in 1992 in response to its continued military aggression against Bosnia and Croatia, the sanctions were considered effective because they inflicted harm on Serbian society. Similarly, when the government of Sudan began carrying out mass atrocities against the people of Darfur in Western Sudan, Western democracies imposed severe economic sanctions against the Muslim regime of Omar al-Bashir as punishment.

Finally, sanctions are regarded as successful when they inhibit or delay the use of force. Because war is generally far more destructive than economic sanctions, the latter are generally considered a morally preferable tool of statecraft to military force. As a result, economic sanctions can be viewed as successful when they allow the sending state to impose harm on the target state without resorting to military force.[42] However, in using this minimalist standard, virtually all sanctions episodes are likely to be viewed as successful, whether or not the target state modifies its policies.

In short, economic sanctions remain a popular tool of statecraft not because they are effective tools of deterrence and compliance but because they are cheap and powerful symbols of communication. Although the instruments of economic coercion might not lead directly to behavioral reform, they can galvanize domestic and international public opinion, thereby weakening the government's authority in the target state. To the extent that economic sanctions weaken and isolate a regime, as was the case with governmental and nongovernmental sanctions toward South Africa in the 1980s, they can encourage the target state to alter its unacceptable structures and policies. Ironically, economic sanctions are likely to be most effective against small, moderately developed democratic states in which the citizenry is informed and involved in the affairs of state but least effective in authoritarian regimes based on limited political participation. But even when sanctions are imposed by a major power on a small state, behavioral change is not assured. This conclusion is amply demonstrated in the failure of the United States to bring about desired political changes in Marxist Cuba through five decades of comprehensive sanctions.

The Morality of Sanctions

Unlike international relations issues such as human rights, intervention, and war, scholars have undertaken comparatively little moral analysis of economic statecraft. The limited moral scrutiny given economic sanctions is no doubt due to the belief that sanctions are preferable to force. However, economic sanctions are not neutral foreign policy instruments. Rather, they are indiscriminate tools of statecraft. Joy Gordon writes that sanctions are "a tool that is indeed a form of violence—no less than guns and bombs—and it is ethically imperative that we see it as precisely that."[43] During the apartheid era in South Africa, Alan Paton, an influential antiapartheid activist and author, repeatedly highlighted the morally problematic nature of economic sanctions. In his view sanctions were unjust because they imposed hardship disproportionately on the poor blacks. Throughout his life Paton remained a staunch critic of the apartheid regime, but he also opposed the imposition of comprehensive sanctions to advance the ideal of a democratic South Africa. On one occasion he expressed his moral opposition to sanctions as follows:

> I do not understand how your Christian conscience allows you [Bishop Tutu] to advocate disinvestment. I do not understand how you can put a man out of work for a high moral principle. You put a man out of a job and make his family go hungry so that some high moral principle could be upheld. I think your morality is confused just as was the morality of the church in the Inquisition, or the morality of Dr. Verwoerd in his utopian dreams. You come near to saying that the end justifies the means, which is a thing no Christian can do.[44]

One potentially useful approach in assessing the morality of sanctions is to apply principles of the just war doctrine. Although application of just war norms to economic statecraft is based on an analogy of two different decision-making environments, just war theory can nonetheless offer an invaluable ethical structure by which to assess the moral legitimacy of sanctions. Because the environments of war and peace present radically different decision-making contexts, some scholars have suggested that the just war doctrine is "an ultimately inadequate paradigm for moral analysis of comprehensive sanctions."[45] Others, by contrast, argue that the just war tradition can strengthen the ethical assessment of the role of economic sanctions.[46] The following analysis is based on the latter conviction.

The just war tradition, as noted in chapter 7, involves two dimensions: the justice of going to war (*jus ad bellum*) and justice in wartime (*jus in bello*). Although these norms were developed to inhibit war and, in the event of war, to inhibit human suffering, they nonetheless provide a useful framework for judging the morality of economic sanctions. All eight principles (see table 7-1), with the exception of the competent-authority norm, can be applied to economic statecraft. Because private actors can contribute significantly to a sanctions regime, the requirement that governments impose sanctions is unnecessary.[47]

Following the just war theory, the *just sanctions doctrine* consists of seven principles. The first five provide a moral framework for determining when economic coercion is morally permissible, while the last two specify how sanctions should be applied. The following norms comprise the just sanctions doctrine:

1. *Just cause*: The aim of economic sanctions must be just. This can involve promoting peace among states, but it can also involve promoting human dignity within states when regimes systematically abuse basic rights.

2. *Right intention*: Sanctions are legitimate only if they are imposed to promote just structures and policies. Sanctions are not justified to increase national power or extend economic influence.
3. *Limited objectives*: Sanctions must have limited goals, involving behavioral reform of only those behaviors and institutions that are unjust and evil. In addition, the objectives of sanctions must be proportional to the good that they are seeking to achieve.
4. *Last resort*: The imposition of sanctions must be preceded by other, less coercive instruments. Only when peaceful negotiations have failed is resort to comprehensive economic sanctions morally warranted.
5. *Probability of success*: Economic sanctions must have a reasonable chance of success. That is, there must be a reasonable hope that the economic hardship inflicted on the target state will result in greater justice.
6. *Discrimination*: Economic hardship must be targeted on the government and the elites that support it. Economic hardship should not be imposed directly on innocent civilians. Following the principle of double effect, economic harm on the masses can be justified only as a by-product of the intended effects of legitimately targeted sanctions.[48]
7. *Proportionality*: The good intended from sanctions must be proportional to the harm inflicted on the target state.

The application of the just sanctions doctrine will depend greatly on the particular circumstances in which economic sanctions are employed. Earlier, I noted that sanctions are imposed for a variety of reasons. If the aim of sanctions is to bring about political reforms or policy changes in the target state, the just sanctions doctrine can provide an invaluable moral structure for judging policies. However, if the aim of sanctions is simply to punish or to signal resolve, the doctrine's usefulness in moral analysis of sanctions will be limited. As a result, the analysis here focuses solely on sanctions as a tool of behavioral reform.

In chapter 4, I suggested that an ethical foreign policy must be judged in terms of its intentions, means, and outcomes. The just sanctions doctrine provides norms by which to judge sanctions at each of these three levels. The first two norms—just cause and right intention—provide the principles for judging the moral legitimacy of sanctions goals. According to these two norms, the imposition of major economic suffering is morally legitimate only if its aims are moral. The doctrine also provides three principles for judging the policy instruments themselves—proportionality, last resort, and discrimination. Sanctions are just when (1) the harm they impose is proportional to the good they are likely to achieve; (2) other, less destructive alternatives have been exhausted; and (3) economic penalties target harm on political and government officials responsible for a state's decisions and actions. If sanctions are imposed to influence the political behavior of the target state, it follows that the pain and suffering of economic statecraft should be borne mainly by those responsible for government decision making. Finally, the sanctions doctrine justifies the imposition of economic hardship only if the political goals are likely to be realized.

Undoubtedly, the most important yet most morally challenging principle of the sanctions doctrine is discrimination. According to Albert Pierce, the major moral problem posed by sanctions is their inability to fulfill the discrimination norm.[49] When comprehensive sanctions are imposed, the hardship typically falls disproportionately on low-income sectors of society. "The principal moral dilemma posed by sanctions," write Drew Christiansen and Gerard Powers, "is that the more effective they are, the more likely that they will harm those least responsible for the wrongdoing and least able to bring about change: civilians."[50] Moreover, even when efforts are made to target a regime's leadership, government elites are frequently able to divert resources to minimize the hardships brought about by sanctions.

The difficulty of minimizing civilian harm was clearly illustrated with comprehensive sanctions imposed on Iraq after it had conquered Kuwait in 1990.[51] Although the UN-imposed sanctions had exempted food and medicine, great suffering resulted nonetheless—especially on children, the sick, and the elderly. UNICEF, the UN children's agency, estimated that economic sanctions were responsible for the death of about five thousand children under the age of five per month, or about sixty thousand annually.[52] Thus, even assuming that this estimate was inflated, it is not unreasonable to conclude that economic sanctions over twelve years had caused the death of at least half a million children. In 1996, the United Nations instituted an Oil-for-Food Program to relieve Iraq's humanitarian crisis. While the program provided essential food and medicine, the Iraqi government was able to manipulate oil sales through kickbacks and other illicit tactics so that the sanctions had the ironic effect of strengthening the regime itself. Perhaps even more deleterious, the smuggling of oil to neighboring Syria and Turkey greatly compromised UN sanctions and provided an even larger income source for Hussein's Baathist regime.

Some scholars have argued that "smart" or targeted sanctions provide a way to partially satisfy the discrimination norm.[53] Rather than implement systemic sanctions that undermine a country's economy, smart sanctions attempt to target harm on public officials responsible for a government's unacceptable public policies. The goal is to make sanctions like precision-guided munitions that destroy the intended target while minimizing collateral damage. Although the United States employs targeted sanctions like asset freezes, travel bans, and arms embargoes, there is little evidence that such targeted action imposes sufficient hardship to foster behavioral change. Indeed, to the extent that sanctions appear to foster behavioral reform, as in the case of South Africa, the reason was that comprehensive sanctions imposed significant economic hardship on the entire society, not simply on the leadership.

Despite their indiscriminate nature, economic sanctions remain a popular instrument of foreign policy. In many democratic societies, especially the United States, sanctions are regarded as morally preferable to force. During the Persian Gulf crisis, for example, religious elites opposed military action, arguing repeatedly that more time was needed for sanctions to work. In making this argument, however, such elites failed to realize that, in the words of Michael Walzer, "what they were advocating was a radically indiscriminate act of war, with predictably harsh consequences."[54] Because of the morally ambiguous nature of sanctions, some scholars have suggested that economic sanctions should be imposed only when humanitarian measures are undertaken to protect innocent civilians. Such measures might include the exemption of essential goods, such as food and medicines, and the distribution of aid to vulnerable groups.[55]

Below I illustrate the morally ambiguous nature of economic sanctions with a case study on South Africa. Although comprehensive sanctions no doubt contributed to the abolition of apartheid, they also inflicted great harm on black workers—the very people that sanctions were designed to help.

CASE 10-2: ECONOMIC SANCTIONS AND SOUTH AFRICAN APARTHEID

BACKGROUND

After the Afrikaner National Party gained control of the South African government in 1948, it began to further institutionalize racial separation (apartheid). Racial segregation was well entrenched in South Africa's social, political, and economic structures when the National Party assumed power, but the effort to establish a comprehensive legal system of racial separation was unprecedented, leading to significant international condemnation.

International opposition to South Africa's apartheid policies began in the early 1960s. For example, in 1962, the UN General Assembly passed a nonbinding resolution condemning apartheid, calling on states to break diplomatic relations with South Africa and to stop trading with it. Subsequently, the Security Council authorized a ban on arms shipments to South Africa and in 1977 imposed a total arms embargo. Another important action taken against South Africa in the early 1970s was the imposition of an oil embargo by OPEC, forcing South Africa to pay much higher costs for petroleum. None of these actions, however, had much impact on South Africa's government decision making. Indeed, the oil embargo led South Africa to pioneer in the development of oil extraction from coal, whereas the arms embargo encouraged the development of a major military arms industry, providing a significant source of foreign exchange.

In response to growing American public opposition to apartheid, some municipalities and universities began demanding divestment of stock in companies involved in South Africa. The aim of the divestment campaign was not only to force institutions to sell their stock but also to ultimately force companies to withdraw from South Africa through disinvestment (i.e., selling or closing their operations). By 1982, several state legislatures and city councils had approved measures mandating divestment, and by 1984 more than forty-five colleges and universities had adopted divestment programs. The divestment campaign accelerated in the mid-1980s, culminating with California's adoption of a $12-billion divestment program, calling for the sale of South African holdings in state pension funds and in the endowment of the state's university system.[56] It has been estimated that by 1991, more than twenty-eight states, twenty-four counties, and ninety-two cities had adopted divestment measures, resulting in the sale of some $20 billion of stock.[57]

In response to growing public opposition to apartheid, congressional support for economic sanctions began to increase in the mid-1980s. To forestall more severe sanctions being considered by Congress, President Reagan instituted modest sanctions in September 1985. The following year, however, Congress, overriding a presidential veto, passed legislation instituting more drastic economic sanctions. The 1986 Comprehensive Anti-Apartheid Act, among other things, banned new investment in South Africa, prohibited new U.S. commercial loans and the export of petroleum and computers, banned selected South African imports, and terminated landing rights for South Africa's airlines. The European Community and the British Commonwealth also instituted similar, although more modest, sanctions at this time.

Although government-imposed economic sanctions were symbolically significant, the most influential economic measures were the actions of the international business community, especially the disinvestment by major corporations and the ban on new bank loans. One scholar writes, "The real actors who overturned constructive engagement [the official U.S. foreign policy toward South Africa] were not public, but private—namely, U.S. commercial banks and foreign investors responding to economic and political risks and nongovernmental anti-apartheid organizations that magnified corporate responses to those risks."[58] It has been estimated that of the almost 400 U.S. companies doing business in South Africa in 1984, only 124 remained in 1989. Moreover, the decision by international banks to call in their loans and close their operations had an especially devastating impact. When the Chase Manhattan Bank announced in 1985 that it would no longer make new loans to South Africa, other foreign banks quickly followed suit, leading to an immediate tightening of domestic credit markets. As a result of the cutoff of loans and direct foreign investment, South Africa experienced massive capital outflows and a sharp weakening of its currency. It has been estimated that from 1985 to 1989 net capital outflows were $11 billion, leading to a significant contraction of the South African economy and a loss of at least $4 billion in export earnings.[59]

THE MORAL AMBIGUITY OF SANCTIONS

The principal justification offered by public officials and interest group leaders for the imposition of economic sanctions against South Africa was the belief that apartheid was evil and needed to be abolished. Sanctions advocates argued that economic penalties should be imposed on South Africa to punish the regime and compel the government to alter its social and political structures. Some, such as Archbishop Trevor Huddleston and Archbishop Desmond

Tutu, argued that sanctions were necessary to convey a moral message, that is, to express outrage at the inhumane and discriminatory system of apartheid. Others advocated sanctions for strategic reasons, basing their argument on consequentialist logic: economic hardship and international isolation, they believed, would compel structural reforms.

Most sanctions opponents, including British prime minister Margaret Thatcher and President Reagan, also shared the conviction that apartheid was discriminatory, undemocratic, and unjust but believed that the application of comprehensive economic sanctions was an unacceptable policy. Sanctions were opposed for two major reasons: first, because they were considered ineffective in fostering domestic reforms and, second, because they imposed unnecessary economic harm on the black labor class.

Some leaders believed that externally imposed hardship was unlikely to encourage domestic structural changes. Indeed, some sanctions critics argued that economic harm and isolation would only encourage Afrikaner resistance. A far better approach, in their view, was to foster increased participation in the global political economy. Chester Crocker, the assistant secretary of state for African affairs who was responsible for developing President Reagan's African policy of constructive engagement, believed that U.S. influence toward South Africa would be realized only by maintaining strong political and economic ties. Similarly, Helen Suzman, a long-term member of the South African parliament and a leading apartheid critic, repeatedly claimed that only a strategy of economic expansion could foster humane social change. Indeed, she argued that the major improvements in the living and working conditions for South Africa's blacks had been achieved through economic growth. According to Suzman, economic expansion was responsible for increased skilled jobs for blacks, improvements in education and training, recognition of black trade unions, acceptance of black urbanization, and the abolition of "pass laws" regulating the movement of people among different racial communities.[60] If Western states wanted to help South Africa establish the preconditions for liberal democratic society, they needed to facilitate economic expansion, without which no improvement in the black majority's living standards could be achieved. Moreover, only through a strategy of engagement could foreign states help foster capitalistic and democratic norms in preparation for establishing a more just postapartheid regime.

A second major reason for opposing sanctions was the belief that they were harmful to the economic and social well-being of the nonwhite working class. Alan Paton, author of the influential book *Cry, the Beloved Country* and a leading critic of apartheid, repeatedly condemned sanctions, especially disinvestment, for causing unjust harm to black workers. He explained his moral opposition to disinvestment as follows:

> It is my belief that those who will pay most grievously for disinvestment will be Black workers of South Africa. I take very seriously the teachings of the Gospels, in particular the parables about giving drink to the thirsty and food to the hungry. It seems to me that Jesus attached supreme—indeed sacred—significance to such actions. Therefore, I will not help to cause any such suffering to any Black persons.[61]

From the perspective of the just sanctions doctrine, two major shortcomings of South African economic sanctions were the failure to target economic harm on decision makers and the failure to protect the black majority from unnecessary hardship. In seeking to weaken and isolate the apartheid regime, economic sanctions led to a major contraction of the South African economy that resulted in mass unemployment and underemployment among blacks. Even targeted sanctions, such as those imposed on the mineral and fruit industries, imposed especially harsh costs on black laborers, as the retrenchment in these labor-intensive industries significantly increased unemployment. Scholars differ significantly over the negative impact of sanctions on the South African labor market. One study predicted that from 1986 to 1990, comprehensive sanctions would lead to more than 1.1 million lost jobs;[62] another scholar estimates the number of lost jobs at one hundred thousand.[63]

Sanctions, especially divestment (the liquidation of foreign assets), also had perverse, unanticipated effects. Rather than strengthening the economic power of the black majority, the sale of foreign subsidiaries, for example, resulted in increased white ownership of major foreign corporations. For example, when Barclays Bank (London) decided to pull out of South Africa in 1987, a large South African conglomerate (the Anglo-American Corporation) acquired the bank, paying substantially less than it was worth.[64] In 1986 alone, the Johannesburg stock market increased in value by nearly $9 billion, in great part because of the purchase of foreign assets at "fire-sale" prices. Moreover, divestment resulted in increasing concentration of South African wealth. According to Merle Lipton, in 1983 four major South African conglomerates (Anglo-American, Sanlam, South African Mutual, and Rembrandt) controlled 70 percent of the Johannesburg stock exchange; four years later, in response to divestment, these groups accounted for 83 percent of all South African stock.[65] In addition, the contraction of the South African economy led to an increase in the economic power of the state. For example, the UN-imposed petroleum and arms embargoes resulted in the expansion of major industries in synthetic fuel (from coal) and armaments. It has been estimated that from 1977, when the UN arms embargo became mandatory, until 1989, the South African arms industry (Armscor) increased employment by more than one hundred thousand jobs.[66] Moreover, during the 1980s, while the South African economy was experiencing a major slowdown, South Africa's government employment actually increased by 18 percent![67]

In 1990, President F. W. de Klerk freed Nelson Mandela and other political prisoners, unbanned the African National Congress and other black opposition parties, and set in motion a process of radical change that culminated with the election of Mandela as president in 1994. In response to these developments, Western countries gradually eliminated all official sanctions. However, as of 1997, many multinational corporations that had terminated their South African operations in the 1980s either had not returned or had failed to reestablish successful enterprises.

Although many observers now believe that economic sanctions contributed (symbolically, if not substantively) to political change in South Africa, scholars continue to disagree about the role of sanctions in bringing about an end to apartheid and the moral legitimacy of such a policy. As noted previously, there is little doubt that economic sanctions—especially those nongovernmental initiatives such as divestment and disinvestment that led to massive capital outflows—were harmful to the South African economy. However, the key issue is not whether sanctions were costly to South Africa but whether they were responsible for ending apartheid. Some antiapartheid leaders, such as Tutu and Mandela, believe that economic sanctions were essential in ending white-minority rule. Others, especially National Party officials, have suggested that sanctions played a minimal role in bringing about political reform. De Klerk, for example, has observed that although sanctions disrupted the South African economy, "it was not sanctions that brought about change."[68]

MORAL REFLECTIONS

The South African case study on sanctions raises a number of important ethical issues.

- Sanctions are morally problematic because they generally impose hardship disproportionately on innocent civilians and leave political leaders and military officials largely untouched. In view of this,
can the use of this nondiscriminatory tool be morally justified?

- Can a morally dubious policy be justified to bring about a morally just goal? Can an immoral means (comprehensive economic sanctions) be used to promote justice (the ending of apartheid)?

- From an ends-based approach (consequentialism), the use of economic sanctions is a morally legitimate policy alternative, provided that the intended goals are just and that the likelihood of achieving the desired goals is high. From this perspective, the goal of ending a racially unjust regime is morally just. Moreover, economic sanctions are superior to military force because they involve much less destruction. From a rule-based perspective, however, economic sanctions are morally problematic because they fail to protect innocent persons from economic hardship. Thus, because sanctions impose hardship on civilians, should policy makers get their hands "dirty" by using sanctions to foster a more just world, or should they attempt to keep their hands "clean" by refusing to use immoral means to pursue political justice?

- Was the economic hardship brought about by sanctions proportional to the good achieved by the collapse of the apartheid regime? Was the hardship imposed on poor, unemployed blacks justified by the victory in ending a regime based upon racial discrimination?

SUMMARY

Because of increased globalization, the political economy of international relations has become more influential in the post–Cold War era. Although greater economic integration has contributed to improved standards of living for many peoples throughout the world, globalization has also exacerbated problems and increased potential dangers. The European experience with the Euro illustrates some of the benefits and potential harms that can result from economic integration. In assessing transnational economic developments, it is important to illuminate and apply relevant moral norms to the problems and challenges of global political economy.

Economic tools also continue to be important instruments of statecraft. Because force is the most extreme and least desirable foreign policy instrument, economic sanctions offer a useful instrument short of war. But sanctions are morally problematic not only because they rarely achieve desired political results but also because they impose hardship on innocent civilians. Thus, while economic sanctions are a potentially useful instrument of statecraft, their role and impact are morally ambiguous, frequently involving legitimate ends but dubious means.

Chapter Eleven

Pursuing International Justice

I believe that any discussion of international justice must take seriously the character of relations among states, and this has been a weakness in much of the normative literature to date.[1]

—PETER KAPSTEIN

The first essential is to accept that the voters' right to a say about who and how many can enter must take precedence over the rights of those unlucky enough to be born in poorer parts of the world.[2]

—THE ECONOMIST

The extent of a country's respect for personal self-determination says something very basic about how it is governed. It is an index of a state's responsiveness to its citizens and, by extension, a measure of overall social health.[3]

—ALAN DOWTY

AS NOTED EARLIER, international relations scholars have conceived of global society from two distinct perspectives. One approach, communitarianism, emphasizes the pursuit of justice through the contemporary global system of sovereign states. The second approach, cosmopolitanism, focuses on the pursuit of justice among people while disregarding the anarchic, decentralized international community. The first process was defined as international justice; the alternative approach was called world justice. This chapter explores the nature of the first perspective by analyzing how states can pursue actions that advance the global common good. In chapter 12, I examine how global justice can be advanced through nonstate actors and other emerging institutions of global governance.

This chapter has three parts. In the first part I describe the concept of international justice and the challenges involved in defining standards by which to advance and judge this ideal. The second part illustrates the pursuit of international justice by examining foreign aid. A case study on U.S. assistance to HIV/AIDS victims illustrates how foreign aid can advance the well-being of people in poor societies. The chapter's third section examines the international migration of people, focusing on the needs of migrants, especially refugees. In pursuing international justice, sovereign states regulate migration flows in order to protect national boundaries while also seeking to care for the needs of migrants, especially refugees.

INTERNATIONAL JUSTICE

To assess international society in light of political morality, it is necessary to have a normative standard by which to judge the rightness or justness of the structures and policies of that society. In effect, what is needed is a conception of international justice. However, defining the nature of international justice and its essential principles is a daunting task. Several factors contribute to this difficulty.

First, global political justice is difficult to ascertain because of the lack of agreement in defining such a norm. This is due partly to the absence of an authoritative conception of political justice. Although justice is one of the most frequently examined themes in Western political philosophy, the different normative theories and conceptualizations of political justice have not yet yielded an authoritative definition of the term. Rather, Western political scholarship has provided a multitude of theories and perspectives about different dimensions of the quest for political justice. For example, some theories emphasize the rights and obligations of individuals in developing a just political society, whereas others emphasize the character and responsibilities of government and other public institutions. Still other thinkers approach justice by seeking to identify foundational principles of political society, whereas others focus on the policy outcomes of government. It is significant that throughout most of Western civilization the quest for political justice was viewed as a by-product of the fulfillment of moral obligations. As a result, most classical political theory emphasized the role of duties and obligation in cultivating political justice. Contemporary thinkers, by contrast, have placed priority on rights. In sum, normative political thought provides insights, perspectives, and theories about the nature of political justice but no authoritative framework for determining justice.

A second reason for the elusive nature of international justice is that global society is comprised of a plurality of cultures and moralities. Whereas domestic societies typically are characterized by comparatively coherent and authoritative decision-making structures, the international community has no comparable legal or political institutions. Moreover, domestic societies are typically based on a more coherent political morality. As Stanley Hoffmann has observed, although there is generally a consensus within national communities about what constitutes justice, in the international community there is "a cacophony of standards." Because of the moral pluralism of global society, justice becomes either "a matter of sheer force—carried at the point of a sword—or, when force does not prevail, a matter of fleeting bargains and tests of fear or strength."[4] It is also important to recognize that the quest for international justice is difficult because such a quest might involve conflict with other normative goals. More specifically, as I note in the case study below, the quest for international order might not be consistent with the quest for justice either within or among states.

Finally, determining international justice is difficult because the notion of political justice can be interpreted in two very different ways. One approach associates political justice with the rightness and fairness of the rules, procedures, and institutions of political communities and the consistent and impartial application of such norms. This perspective is sometimes called *procedural justice* because it defines justice in terms of processes rather than outcomes. According to this approach, political justice involves the impartial and nondiscriminatory application of rules and procedures, not the determination of particular desirable goals or moral outcomes. In effect, justice is realized not by pursuing particular ends but by ensuring the fairness of the system. Such an approach is illustrated by the American judicial system, which pursues justice through impartial courts. To ensure impartiality, a judge maintains neutrality as he or she enforces strict compliance with norms governing the presentation of evidence and arguments by the prosecution and defense before an impartial jury.

The second approach defines political justice in terms of the rightness and fairness of outcomes. Justice is that which promotes good or right ends. Because this perspective associates morality with particular distributions or results, it is frequently referred to as *substantive* or *distributive justice*.[5] Although this approach has become increasingly influential in contemporary political ethics, it is significant that traditional international morality was defined mainly in terms of procedural norms and in particular "the laws of nations." As Terry Nardin has observed, the association of international justice with particular outcomes is a relatively recent development, dating to the current century when the notion of distributive justice began to be applied to international relations.[6]

A sound, comprehensive approach to international ethics should be rooted in both procedural and substantive norms. Procedural norms are important because they emphasize the impartial application of authoritative rules and principles of global society; substantive norms, however, are also important because their perception of justice is partly rooted in the perception of just outcomes. To be sure, the application of distributive justice among member states presents significant challenges. However, the increased moral sensitivity to egregious inequalities within and among nations has fostered a more robust moral assessment of international relations.

PROMOTING INTERNATIONAL JUSTICE THROUGH FOREIGN AID

Foreign aid involves two types of assistance: humanitarian or emergency relief and development aid. The former involves assistance to meet humanitarian needs arising from droughts, earthquakes, tribal wars, and other disasters. This type of aid was illustrated in the aftermath of the deadly December 2005 Asian tsunami that killed more than 150,000 people and left hundreds of thousands homeless and destitute. Foreign states, led by the United States, responded immediately with large quantities of food and water, financial aid, medical care, and, most importantly, logistical support to help distribute resources. Without this foreign assistance, hundreds of thousands of additional people would have perished.

Development aid, by contrast, involves long-term assistance to help reduce poverty by fostering economic growth. Although developmental aid typically focuses on the absence of economic resources, it is important to recall that the primary impediments to economic growth tend to be political (war), social (fragmentation and distrust), and cultural (corruption). The difficulty in fostering development is well illustrated in the modern history of Haiti, one of the poorest, most corrupt, and most politically fragile countries in the world. Despite receiving significant financial aid over the past three decades, Haiti has been unable to improve its people's standard of living. The economy has remained stagnant, crime and corruption are pervasive, legal and political institutions are weak, and government remains ineffective. Not surprisingly, Haiti ranks among the least developed countries in the world, ranking 154th among 177 countries on the Human Development Index (HDI).[7]

Development aid, generally referred to as official development assistance (ODA), involves loans and grants provided bilaterally and multilaterally to assist the economic development of poor countries. It is estimated that during the Cold War era the developed democratic countries gave Third World countries more than $1.1 trillion (constant 1988 dollars) in ODA. But this total greatly underestimates total financial aid because ODA neglects humanitarian relief, foreign direct investment, commercial loans, nongovernmental financial assistance, and, most importantly, individual remittances from family members working abroad. According to one scholar, ODA included only 40 percent of total U.S. international assistance in 2000. The additional aid (about $35 billion) involved private giving from individual remittances, religious organizations, foundations, corporations, universities, and private voluntary organizations (PVOs).[8]

The purpose of ODA is to improve living conditions of low-income nations and thereby foster global economic justice. Has foreign aid succeeded in promoting economic development? Moreover, has foreign economic assistance fostered international or distributive justice by reducing economic inequalities among states? There can be little doubt that substantial sums of public and private assistance have been given to poor nations in the second half of the twentieth century, but the effects of those transfers have been mixed at best. To begin with, since poverty reduction is strongly correlated with economic growth rates, economists have concluded that a major requirement for improved living conditions is economic growth. Moreover, since economic studies have shown that there is no link between aid and growth, foreign aid can assist economic development only if other economic, social, and political preconditions are present.

In an important study, two World Bank economists found that aid has a positive effect on growth when a favorable economic environment exits—that is, when inflation is low, when government budget deficits are low, and when a country is open to foreign trade. Between 1970 and 1993 developing nations with favorable economic conditions grew at an annual rate of 2.2 percent per person, while developing nations with a favorable economic environment and significant foreign aid grew nearly twice as fast (at an annual rate of 3.7 percent).[9] But the absence of a favorable domestic economic environment can impede poverty reduction even when large aid transfers are involved. For example, Zambia's real per capita income declined by one-third between the early 1960s and the early 1990s, even though the country received some $2 billion in foreign aid during this time. According to one development economist, had Zambia succeeded in using this capital for development purposes, annual per capita income would have increased dramatically (to about $20,000) rather than declining to $600.[10]

Distinguishing between humanitarian relief and development aid is often difficult. When a society is suffering from widespread starvation, as occurred in Zimbabwe in the new millennium, human suffering may be so widespread that economic aid must necessarily include both relief and developmental assistance. In response to a growing awareness that more than two billion people continue to live in abject poverty, the industrial nations have pledged to increase economic assistance to eradicate poverty and reduce disease. At the United Nations Summit in 2000, the international community adopted the Millennium Development Program, which established a framework to eradicate global poverty. Subsequently, UN member states adopted the Millennium Development Goals (MDGs), committing the rich countries to help cut world poverty, disease, and hunger in half by 2015.[11]

Jeffrey Sachs, who helped establish the UN's Millennium Development Program, is a leading apostle of increased economic transfers from rich to poor countries. In *The End of Poverty*, his manifesto for creating a more humane international community, he argues that if extreme poverty in the developing nations is to be halved by 2015, the developed nations will have to double their overall level of aid from 0.25 percent of donor GNP to 0.5 percent, increasing total ODA from $70 billion per year to $140 billion.[12] Sachs writes, "Ending poverty is the great opportunity of our time, a commitment that would not only relieve massive suffering and spread economic well-being, but would also promote the other Enlightenment objectives of democracy, global security, and the advance of science."[13]

Despite the needs of low-income countries, some scholars and public officials argue that aid can harm growth. Aid critics claim that ODA encourages waste, strengthens corrupt regimes, overpoliticizes the process of economic growth, and results in inefficient and at times counterproductive investments. Most importantly, some economists claim that ODA harms job creation, reinforcing bad governments, inefficient public policies, and economic dependency.[14] The failures of aid are well illustrated in the economic performance of sub-Saharan Africa, a region whose per capita income has remained static even after receiving tens of billions of dollars in ODA to increase economic output. Economist William Easterly explains the failure of foreign aid as follows: "Sixty years of countless reform schemes to aid agencies and dozens of different plans, and $2.3 trillion later, the aid industry is still failing to reach the beautiful goal [making poverty history]. The evidence points to an unpopular conclusion: Big Plans will always fail to reach the beautiful goal."[15]

Although numerous justifications have been given for granting foreign aid, David Lumsdaine argues convincingly that humanitarian concerns have provided the major impetus for economic assistance to the Third World. After examining Western economic assistance during the 1949–1989 period, Lumsdaine concludes that donor countries' "sense of justice and compassion" provided the major reason for giving aid. He writes, "Support for aid was a response to world poverty which arose mainly from ethical and humane concerns and, secondarily, from the belief that long-term peace and prosperity was possible only in a generous and just international order where all could prosper."[16]

From a moral perspective, prosperous, well-governed nations should assist societies facing misfortune. They should do so not to ensure greater economic equality among states but to care for people suffering from disasters, war, and absolute poverty. Although humanitarian relief and development aid are both praiseworthy, the former is more morally compelling because it seeks to meet immediate human needs.

THE HIV/AIDS PANDEMIC

One of the most destructive diseases to emerge in modern times is HIV/AIDS.[17] The effects of the virus are devastating because, in the absence of treatment, the disease can lead to death. And since the effects of the virus are not immediately apparent, persons with the illness can unknowingly spread it to others. Additionally, since the disease is principally transmitted through sexual relations, an effective program to combat the disease would necessarily demand challenging prevalent cultural mores by encouraging greater moral self-restraint.[18]

When the disease first became known in the United States, it was associated with sexual promiscuity among homosexuals. In the 1990s, however, conservative Christians began to challenge the stigma against AIDS. When it became evident that the disease was also transmitted through heterosexual sex or even innocent contact with tainted blood, the stigma against AIDS began to recede. To a significant degree the change in attitudes, especially among American Christians, was led by individuals who witnessed the human devastation resulting from the AIDS pandemic in Africa, where the explosive transmission of the HIV virus spread through promiscuous heterosexual relations. When missionaries and relief and development workers began to describe the magnitude of human suffering wrought by AIDS in sub-Saharan African countries, especially the hundreds of thousands of orphans who had lost parents to the disease, conservative Christians began to have a change of heart toward the disease. Although the general religious public was slow to respond, Evangelical leaders like Franklin Graham, head of Samaritan's Purse; Rick Warren, the pastor of Saddleback Church; and Richard Stearns, the head of World Vision, played a crucial role in developing a compassionate response to the pandemic.[19]

By the time George W. Bush assumed the presidency in January 2001, public awareness and concern for the AIDS pandemic had begun to rise. But it was the president's passionate concern to alleviate human suffering that transformed the moral concern for AIDS victims into one of the largest humanitarian initiatives in world history. When he took office, the U.S. government was spending about $500 million to halt the spread of AIDS. In his presidential memoir, *Turning Points*, Bush writes that while this financial support was far more than that of any other country, it was "paltry compared with the scope of the pandemic." "I decided," he writes, "to make confronting the scourge of AIDS in Africa a key element of my foreign policy."[20]

One of the president's first acts to address the pandemic was to support a United Nations initiative to deal with AIDS, tuberculosis, and malaria. When UN secretary-general Kofi Annan called for the creation of a Global Fund to fight these three diseases, Bush announced that the United States would make a founding contribution of $200 million and pledged to increase this amount if the program proved effective. A year later, in June 2002, he announced the creation of a program aimed to reduce the mother-to-child transmission of HIV. Scientists had discovered a new drug (Nevirapine) that could dramatically reduce the odds that a pregnant woman with HIV would transmit the virus to her baby. Since tens of thousands of children were being born with the virus, leading to their early deaths, the Bush administration called for an allocation of $500 million to make this new drug available throughout Africa.

But Bush knew that these efforts, while significant, were not sufficient to effectively confront the pandemic. In 2002, between six thousand and eight thousand persons were dying daily from AIDS in Africa, and the rate of infection was not abating, despite widespread initiatives to distribute condoms. Accordingly, on the day that he announced the mother-child initiative, Bush told Josh Bolten, his deputy chief of staff, "This is a good start, but it's not enough.

Go back to the drawing board and think even bigger."[21] Senior White House officials worked secretly over the next several months on a comprehensive initiative that involved prevention, treatment, and humanitarian care. When they met to discuss the proposed five-year, $15-billion initiative, some advisors expressed concern about the high cost of the program. President Bush, however, was convinced that the United States had a moral responsibility to help relieve the widespread suffering caused by this disease. In his presidential memoir he indicates that Michael Gerson, his chief speechwriter and senior advisor, captured the essence of his sentiments when he declared, "If we can do this and we don't, it will be a source of shame."[22]

PEPFAR

In his State of the Union address in January 2003, President Bush announced a bold initiative to address the AIDS pandemic—the President's Emergency Plan for AIDS Relief (PEPFAR). The goals of the program were to prevent seven million new AIDS infections, treat at least two million people with life-extending drugs, and provide care to children orphaned by AIDS. Although some critics have suggested that the initiative was intended to distract attention from the president's "war on terror," Bush was clearly inspired to undertake this extraordinary initiative by the belief that this was the right thing to do. In discussing this initiative soon after it was announced, Bush described the moral basis of his program as follows:

> We have a chance to achieve a more compassionate world for every citizen. America believes deeply that everybody has worth, everybody matters, everybody was created by the Almighty, and we're going to act on that belief and we'll act on that passion. . . . As I said in my State of the Union, freedom is not America's gift to the world, freedom is God's gift to humanity. . . . In the continent of Africa, freedom means freedom from fear of a deadly pandemic. That's what we think in America. And we're going to act on that belief. The founding belief in human dignity should be how we conduct ourselves around the world—and will be how we conduct ourselves around the world.[23]

At the time of the initiative, the primary approach to prevention involved the distribution of condoms. But since the rate of transmission continued to rise, leading to 13,700 new infections daily, this approach was clearly insufficient. By 2003, the total number of Africans with the HIV virus was close to twenty million, with more than one million dying annually from AIDS-related causes. Additionally, since only fifty thousand Africans were receiving antiretroviral (ARV) drugs that could prolong life, the number of AIDS deaths continued to soar, reaching a total of nearly eight thousand deaths per day. By 2003, it is estimated that Africa had close to fourteen million children orphaned by AIDS.

PEPFAR was thus a medical as well as a humanitarian initiative—aimed at halting the AIDS pandemic, caring for those with HIV, and meeting the humanitarian needs of children and adults who had been victimized by the loss of loved ones. To advance these objectives, PEPFAR called for $15 billion in medical and humanitarian aid, of which $9 billion would be for new programs focused on a select group of countries.[24] Some of the distinctive elements of PEPFAR included, first, the establishment of specific numeric targets for prevention, treatment, and care; second, the broadening of the scope of prevention programs to include an emphasis upon abstinence and fidelity; and third, a dramatic increase in funding for treating people with AIDS.[25]

The UN Global Fund and other similar AIDS initiatives addressed AIDS prevention by focusing almost exclusively on condom distribution. What made PEPFAR unique was its adoption of an initiative pioneered in Uganda—the so-called ABC program that called for abstinence, being faithful, and using condoms. The inclusion of abstinence and fidelity were important, but considered unrealistic by some, and controversial by others, who preferred to approach the problem from a purely pragmatic perspective. But moral expectations were important not only for the long-term success of containing the HIV pandemic but also for garnering political support from religious conservatives. Clearly, religious conservatives would not have supported the program without inclusion of a call for abstinence and faithfulness as part of a comprehensive anti-AIDS initiative. PEPFAR's emphasis on treating AIDS patients was also noteworthy. In the early 1990s, the annual cost for treating AIDS patients with ARV drugs was about $12,000, but by the beginning of new millennium a generic version of these medicines had become available for as little as $295 per year. The proposed program called for allocating roughly half of its spending to treating AIDS victims with these new drugs.

Enacting legislation to fund PEPFAR required significant cooperation between liberals and conservatives in both the Senate and the House of Representatives. Congressmen Henry Hyde (R-IL) and Tom Lantos (D-CA) introduced the bill—the United States Leadership against Global HIV/AIDS, Tuberculosis, and Malaria Act of 2003—into the House of Representatives. Since they were the chairman and ranking minority member, respectively, of the body's International Relations Committee, and were regarded as influential human rights legislators, they were able to successfully mobilize support for the initiative and bring the bill to the floor, adopting it by a vote of 375 to 41. In the Senate, Majority Leader Bill Frist, an Evangelical physician who took annual medical missionary trips to Africa, and Dick Lugar, the chairman of the Foreign Relations Committee, provided significant leadership in building support for the legislation. Other senior senators who played an important part in the bill's adoption were Jesse Helms of North Carolina, Joe Biden of Delaware, and John Kerry of Massachusetts. The president signed the bill into law on May 27.

In 2007, President Bush called on Congress to reauthorize PEPFAR for an additional five years, doubling its funding. Congress subsequently approved the initiative, authorizing an additional $39 billion to continue to address the AIDS pandemic as well as an additional $9 billion to cover tuberculosis and malaria.

By any measure, PEPFAR has been extraordinarily successful. As of the end of 2008, the program had prevented the death of roughly 1.2 million persons, with HIV-related mortality having decreased by 10 percent in the fourteen countries where PEPFAR was operative. Additionally, it is estimated that 2.1 million persons received life-saving antiretroviral AIDS drugs in sub-Saharan Africa, with more than 110 million others receiving HIV/AIDS-related care, including counseling, testing, and humanitarian support.[26] According to former secretary of state Condoleezza Rice, PEPFAR will be remembered "as one of the greatest acts of compassion by any country in history."[27]

From a tridimensional ethical perspective, the American foreign aid program to combat the AIDS pandemic is wholly just. At the level of intentions—to save lives and care for the medical and humanitarian needs of AIDS victims—the program is morally praiseworthy. At the level of means, the program is also morally legitimate, although the concentration of foreign aid on one disease may have resulted in a neglect of other diseases. Because of the relatively high cost of antiretroviral drugs, some critics have suggested that treating diarrheal and respiratory diseases could have saved more lives at lower cost. But this consequentialist ethical perspective fails to take into account some of the social and economic costs involved in families and communities victimized by AIDS. Finally, at the level of outcomes, PEPFAR was fully moral in view of its significant impact in saving lives and preventing the spread of the pandemic. Moreover, by caring for HIV-infected mothers, transmission of the virus to nursing babies was minimized. In short, the U.S. program had a dramatic impact in containing the pandemic, protecting lives, and meeting the humanitarian needs precipitated by the disease.

MORAL REFLECTIONS

This case study raises a number of critical issues.

- Because the international community is a global society of many different nations, are developed countries morally obligated to assist poor nations? Was the U.S. program to address the HIV/AIDS pandemic a moral obligation or an act of charity?

- One of the educational dimensions of PEPFAR was the emphasis on abstinence and fidelity. Some observers argue that the program should have emphasized solely prevention through the distribution of condoms and avoided the call for behavioral reformation. Given the transnational nature of the program, was the educational focus on abstinence and fidelity morally appropriate?

- PEPFAR provided significant resources to address one disease. Given the many medical needs in Africa, was the large allocation of funds for the AIDS pandemic morally legitimate? Or should an effort have been made to distribute funds to maximize health care for all based on the consequentialist ethic of the greatest good for the greatest number?

INDIVIDUALS AND GLOBAL SOCIETY

Historically, liberal political thought has been concerned mainly with defining the rights and duties of citizens within the boundaries of states. From the perspective of political liberalism, theorists have consistently asserted that, just as citizens have the rights of freedom of speech or freedom of assembly, they have a right to freedom of movement within territorial boundaries. However, classical thinkers did not extend this argument to international society. Although international law has provided some regulatory principles governing emigration and immigration, transnational migration was left largely to the discretion of states. As a result, the Westphalian system of states came to regard emigration as an individual right and immigration as a sovereign right of states.

It is important to emphasize that this classical worldview did not assert unbridled nationalism. It did not claim, as Garrett Hardin has, that nations are like "lifeboats," each with a limited carrying capacity that demands the imposition of strict limits on immigration.[28] The traditionalist perspective simply asserted that states should take into consideration national and international claims when establishing rules governing migration.

However, as global interdependence has increased the ease of transnational migration, the traditional view of absolute control over borders has been increasingly challenged. Some theorists, such as Joseph Carens and Peter Singer, have argued that international justice requires an open admissions policy.[29] Since birth and citizenship are entirely a matter of chance, they claim that the distribution of economic, social, and political benefits through states is morally unwarranted. Following the cosmopolitan perspective, these thinkers have argued that the rights of persons must take moral precedence over the political claims of national autonomy. More particularly, they have suggested that citizens' economic, social, political, and cultural claims must be subordinated to the basic needs of foreigners and especially to the fundamental human rights claims of migrants.

Regulating Migration

Are the territorial subdivisions of the international community morally important? More particularly, are the rights and interests of states morally significant, as communitarians suggest, or must national interests be subordinated to the claims of individuals, as cosmopolitans suggest? How should the needs of migrants be morally reconciled with the claims of national autonomy?

From the perspective of international political morality, people have an inherent right to leave their homeland. This right, which has become increasingly accepted as a fundamental human right in the contemporary international system, is defined in categorical and unqualified terms by the Universal Declaration of Human Rights (Article 13): "Everyone has the right to leave any country, including his own." The moral basis of the right of emigration is rooted in the voluntary character of democratic societies. Alan Dowty explains the priority of the right to emigrate as follows:

> The right to leave thus gets at the very essence of government by consent—a concept that has achieved near universal acceptance in principles, even amongst states that rarely abide by it. Since government by consent holds that citizenship is a voluntary act, the right to leave a country implicitly serves to ratify the contract between an individual and society. If a person who has the right to leave chooses to stay, he has signaled his voluntary acceptance of the social contract. From this follows his obligation to society. But if he does not have the option of leaving, then society's hold on him is based only on coercion.[30]

Dowty argues that the character of a regime is revealed by the respect that it accords to personal self-determination and, in particular, to the right of emigration. As Dowty's statement at the beginning of this chapter suggests, the degree of personal autonomy is a measure of a country's "overall social health."

Although individuals have the right to emigrate, they do not necessarily have the right to immigrate to a particular state. This is because governments, not international organizations or migrants themselves, determine admission into sovereign countries.[31] Although the Universal Declaration of Human Rights (Article 15.1) affirms the right to a nationality, this claim does not entitle a person to reside in a country of his or her choice. As Brian Barry notes, "It is a general characteristic of associations that people are free to leave them but not free to join them."[32] Thus, emigration and immigration are morally and legally asymmetrical. The moral asymmetry between exit and entry, departure and arrival, is illustrated in everyday social and economic life. For example, workers have a right to leave their place of employment but are not entitled to another job of their own choosing. Employers, not prospective employees, determine employment. Similarly, students may withdraw from colleges and universities at any time, but their desire to continue their studies at another academic institution depends wholly on their admittance to that institution.

Michael Walzer has set forth a powerful argument about the ethics of border regulation. He claims that regulating membership through admission and exclusion is essential in preserving "communities of character"—that is, "historically stable, ongoing associations of men and women with some special commitment to one another and some special sense of their common life."[33] Walzer explains the necessity of regulating migration as follows:

> The distinctiveness of cultures and groups depends upon closure and cannot be conceived as a stable feature of human life without it. If this distinctiveness is a

value . . . then closure must be permitted somewhere. At some level of political organization something like the sovereign state must take shape and claim the authority to make its own admissions policy, to control and sometimes restrain the flow of immigrants.[34]

Walzer illustrates the nature and importance of membership by comparing political communities with neighborhoods, clubs, and families. Just as neighborhood unity is rooted in shared values and customs, national cohesion similarly derives from common cultural and political norms and widely shared communal aspirations. States are also like clubs in that membership is entirely up to the members themselves to decide. Admissions policies, like immigration laws, are a significant feature of communal life because they contribute to the maintenance of cohesion and a sense of shared purpose. Finally, states resemble families in that they can help meet the human needs of non-members. Although family commitments are generally directed toward next of kin, families also provide periodically for the well-being of strangers; similarly, states frequently extend refuge to persons in need even when there is no religious, ethnic, or political bond between the refugees and the state's citizens.

Walzer's analysis suggests that political communities have the right to protect their distinctive cultural, social, and political features and to seek to perpetuate those distinctive qualities through immigration controls. At the same time, political communities, he suggests, have a moral obligation to strangers, especially those who suffer persecution and destitution. Walzer's arguments are significant because they provide moral justification for the contemporary immigration regime based on widely shared rules and procedures governing migration flows. Myron Weiner characterizes this emerging consensus as follows:

> that no government is obligated to admit migrants, that migration is a matter of individual national policy, that most governments need more effective control over their borders, that more forceful measures are needed to halt illegal migration and the growth of worldwide migrant smuggling, that improved procedures are needed to distinguish genuine asylum seekers and refugees suffering from persecution and violence from individuals who use these procedures to migrate, that "temporary" guestworker policies do not work.[35]

One of the challenging issues in immigration politics is determining how open borders should be. This issue involves two fundamental policy concerns—the number of immigrants to be admitted annually into states and the criteria governing the selection process. Immigration pressures, which are much greater than at any time in either the nineteenth or the twentieth century, are a result of several developments. First, as international economic inequalities have increased, people suffering from poverty have tried to escape their relative economic deprivation by seeking entry into more economically prosperous countries. The phenomenon of "boat people"—citizens seeking to escape poverty and oppression by sea travel—is a dramatic illustration of this development. Second, as globalization has increased, information and transportation networks that facilitate international human migration have similarly increased. Even though border regulation is controlled more tightly than ever before, the means by which people can bypass such controls have also expanded.

Undoubtedly the most challenging problem in migration politics is the question of responsibility for the care and protection of refugees. Fundamentally, refugees are persons who have fled their homeland because of war, ethnic strife, religious persecution, political oppression, or other significant threats to personal security and human dignity.[36] When people flee their communities because of security threats but remain within their own country they are classified as "internally displaced persons," or IDPs. Over the past two decades the persistence of ideological, religious, and ethnic conflict has resulted in many bitter wars. Since these conflicts have brought about discrimination, ethnic cleansing, political oppression, and even the collapse of state authority, they have resulted in enormous human suffering and systematic abuse of human rights. In 2007 the number of refugees who had fled their homeland because of war and persecution was about 13.9 million.[37]

Caring for Refugees

Among the many moral challenges posed by migration politics, none is more complex and morally vexing than the issue of refugees or "forced migrants."[38] Several factors make the plight of refugees legally and morally challenging. First, because refugees fall, as Louis Henkin notes, "in the interstices of state boundaries," they suffer from a lack of protection from authoritative institutions.[39] While international humanitarian organizations, such as the Office of the UN High Commissioner for Refugees (UNHCR), play a major role in caring for refugees, it is states that serve as the principal caregivers. States decide whether to admit refugees or force them to return to their homeland.

Second, determining which persons are entitled to refugee status is difficult. Although there is broad consensus that a refugee is any person outside his or her homeland because of a "well-founded fear of persecution," governments have applied widely different admission criteria for asylum seekers. According to U.S. statutes, a refugee is a person who applies for refuge before entering the country of refuge; an asylee is a person who applies for refuge after arriving in the country where he or she seeks refuge. Determining which asylum seekers have legitimate claims is frequently complicated by the large number of refugees making claims on particular states as well as by the rising number of claims regarded as unwarranted and unfounded. When the Bosnian war broke out, for example, hundreds of thousands of refugees migrated to Western Europe, especially Germany. Similarly, the 2003–2007 humanitarian crisis in Darfur, Sudan, resulted in more than two million refugees, a large portion of them in Chad.

Third, because the number of persons desiring asylum greatly exceeds the supply of authorized visas, governments establish strict criteria for selection, giving preferential treatment to some groups. During the Cold War, for example, the United States gave priority to political refugees (persons fleeing tyrannical regimes, especially communist countries) over economic refugees (persons fleeing desperately poor nations). More recently, the United States has stressed geographic diversity in its refugee admissions.

Although scholars and public officials generally concur that states bear a moral obligation to care for foreigners in need, there is little agreement on the nature and scope of humanitarian assistance that should be provided, especially to refugees.[40] Cosmopolitans, for example, argue that refugee resettlement should be greatly increased,[41] whereas nationalists would prefer to limit such practices in the belief that significant refugee flows undermine national well-being. Communitarians, holding to an intermediary position, assume that states have a moral obligation to provide humanitarian assistance but not necessarily an obligation to accept refugees. Human suffering requires that states care for strangers but not that they grant membership. Myron Weiner has described the intermediary position as follows: "If someone is in urgent need and the risks and cost of giving aid are low, we ought to help the injured stranger—not on the basis of justice but on the basis of charity."[42]

In addressing the needs of refugees, it is generally acknowledged that for communal reasons the most desirable long-term solution for refugees is repatriation back to the home country. Although the Universal Declaration of Human Rights enshrines the right of return (repatriation), the ability and willingness of people to avail themselves of this right depends largely on local political conditions. Repatriation can be impaired when the political instability, oppression, and enmity that originally forced people to flee continue. As a result, refugee protection sometimes involves long-term humanitarian assistance by the UNHCR or even requests for permanent resettlement. Third-country resettlement, however, is generally regarded as the least desirable solution, in part because of the great cultural, social, and economic challenges that refugees must overcome in becoming fully integrated into the new society.

Although many developed states face international migration pressures, they are especially acute in several Western European countries (notably France, Germany, the Netherlands, and Spain) and the United States. Two of the major immigration challenges faced by Europeans are the challenge of integrating non-European peoples more effectively into the fabric of national culture and the need for more effective control of borders, especially maritime borders. The first challenge was graphically portrayed in 2005 when civil unrest broke out in France after the accidental killing of two Muslim teenagers. The riots, which were perpetrated chiefly by French immigrant youths, caused hundreds of millions of dollars of damage. Growing tensions with immigrant groups have also been evident in the Netherlands, a country that has maintained some of the most liberal immigration policies in the world. The Dutch model of integrating non-Europeans through education has not worked well, however. Muslim immigrants in particular have sought to maintain their own cultural traditions and language rather than integrate into Dutch society. Most Dutch-born members of immigrant families import their spouses from their "home country," usually Turkey or Morocco. Given the growth in ethnic ghettos, the government has established more restrictive immigration policies, requiring that applicants for residency have not only some knowledge of the Dutch language but also some familiarity with Dutch society and culture.[43]

The control of borders has also become a more important concern for Europeans. The problem is especially pronounced for Spain and Italy, two countries that are facing increasing numbers of illegal migrants from the sea. In 2006 alone, more than twenty-five thousand undocumented Africans arrived in the Canary Islands, off the western coast of Africa. Since the islands belong to Spain, persons who are not deported after their arrival can, in theory, travel throughout borderless Europe without a passport. Moreover, because of growing social integration among EU countries, immigration practices in one country can affect other European societies. Thus, when Spain granted residence permits to more than half a million undocumented immigrants in 2005, a number of European officials criticized the amnesty, believing that it could adversely affect the welfare of other EU nations.

To illuminate some of the ethical dilemmas involved in contemporary migration politics, I next explore some of the challenges in immigration politics in the United States.

CASE 11-2: CHALLENGES TO U.S. IMMIGRATION POLICY

Historically, the United States has been a nation of immigrants, allowing more than twenty million Europeans to enter the country. Following World War I, however, the U.S. government began to restrict immigration. Beginning in 1921, Congress passed laws that established a national origins quota system to regulate the ethnic and cultural distribution of immigrants. Because these laws sought to maintain the ethnic and cultural status quo, they favored the early immigrant peoples of northern and western Europe and discriminated against newcomers, such as Italians, Spaniards, Russians, and especially Asians, Africans, and Latin Americans. In time, the national quota system was perceived as politically and morally unacceptable. As a result, Congress passed the 1965 Immigration and Nationality Act (INA), replacing nationality with family reunification and employment-based immigration criteria. As expected, the new legislation resulted in major changes in immigration patterns, including a significant rise in the number of non-Europeans. Even more significantly, the number of foreign-born residents began to rise rapidly. Indeed, between 1990 and 2000, the foreign-born population rose by 57 percent, from 19.8 million to 31.1 million.[44]

The most recent law governing U.S. immigration policy is the 1990 Immigration Act (IMMACT). This law establishes a flexible cap on the total number of immigrants along with admissions criteria (called "preferences"). In 2006, the statutory ceiling for new immigrants (known as legal permanent residents or LPRs) was 675,000. Since the processing of immigrants takes many months to several years, the total number of persons legally admitted in any year is typically higher than the statutory limit. Indeed, during the 2000–2006 period, total legal admissions averaged close to one million persons. The major immigration preferences are for families and employment. In 2006, about 70 percent of LPRs gained entry for family reunification and 20 percent for desired employment. To foster geographic diversity, the U.S. government annually holds a lottery for aliens from underrepresented nations. The lottery allows fifty thousand aliens to become legal residents.

The basic statutory guidelines for admitting refugees were first established in the Refugee Act of 1980. This legislation is significant because it greatly expanded refugee admissions and established greater order in refugee resettlement. The latter was achieved by requiring annual executive–legislative consultations to establish the maximum number and geographical distribution of refugees. In recent years the annual ceiling for refugees and asylees has been 70,000. In 2006, the United States admitted 41,150 refugees and 26,113 asylees.

Beginning in the late 1970s, illegal immigration began to rise, chiefly from the undocumented crossings of Mexicans and other Latinos along the two-thousand-mile U.S.-Mexico border. To reduce the expanding number of illegal aliens, Congress passed the 1986 Immigration Reform and Control Act (IRCA), which sought to enhance enforcement and to create new avenues to legal immigration. Employers were required to verify the legal status of workers and could face sanctions when they knowingly hired unauthorized aliens. More importantly, the law granted amnesty to some 2.7 million illegal aliens. Because IRCA failed to contain illegal immigration, the U.S. Congress passed the Illegal Immigration Reform and Immigrant Responsibility Act of 1996—a statute that sought to strengthen border control. But this law also failed to halt the influx of undocumented aliens. Indeed, during the 2001–2005 period, the U.S. Border Patrol and U.S. Immigration and Customs Service apprehended annually an average of about 1.5 million persons, nearly all of these along the country's Mexico border.[45] Nevertheless, the number of illegals continued to grow, peaking at 11.8 million persons in 2007. Following the 2008 financial crisis, however, the number of illegals declined to 11.5 million in 2011.[46] To some degree the stabilization of the undocumented population is due to increased deportations. For example, Immigration and Customs Enforcement (ICE) announced that in 2011 nearly 396,000 persons were deported, more than half of whom had been convicted of felonies or misdemeanors.[47]

The large and growing population of undocumented aliens is sustained by numerous factors, including financial and logistical support from existing migrant communities and the demand for low-wage labor from economic enterprises. Although border control is a federal governmental responsibility, welfare costs are borne chiefly by local communities, as they provide education, health, and social services to illegals. Some critics argue that current practices favor uneducated, low-wage workers over well-trained, high-income professionals. Others argue that the main cost of illegal immigration is not economic but cultural and political. For them, the growth of undocumented aliens undermines the rule of law and threatens the cohesion and stability of American society.[48]

In 2007 the Bush administration initiated comprehensive immigration reform legislation. The so-called Immigration and Reform Act of 2007 would have provided legal status and a path to citizenship for undocumented aliens while increasing border security. Congress, however, failed to adopt the measure. In 2009 Congress sought unsuccessfully to adopt a more limited measure geared only to young people. The Development, Relief and Education of Alien Minors Act—known as the DREAM Act—would have allowed children who arrived illegally the opportunity to apply for legal status.[49] Congress similarly failed to adopt this measure. In June 2012, however, President Obama announced that the Department of Homeland Security would not deport undocumented young people who had graduated from high school—in effect implementing provisions of the DREAM Act.

THE ETHICS OF U.S. IMMIGRATION POLICY

As noted above, annual legal admissions into the United States average about one million persons. By contrast, the number of refugee arrivals is about fifty thousand per year, or roughly 5 percent of LPR totals.[50] From an ethical perspective, are such admission ceilings morally appropriate? Is the preferential treatment accorded aliens with close family ties to a U.S. citizen or needed job skills morally warranted? Clearly, there are no "right" moral answers to such questions because they depend on prudential judgments rooted in a variety of competing and conflicting claims, especially between the claims of nationals and those of migrants. Moreover, admissions policies will involve moral ambiguity because of the inevitable trade-off between the moral claim of compassion and the legitimate responsibility to protect communal rights and interests.

The existing international system gives sovereign states the legal and moral right to regulate immigration. It follows that governments are entitled to establish immigration ceilings and to implement preferential treatment that they believe will contribute to the social, political, economic, and cultural development of their nations. Ethical traditions and moral values are essential in developing admissions policies because they provide the normative structure for defining and assessing the means and goals of government action. However, although morality is important in developing a prudent admissions policy, it is not sufficient. Indeed, because moral considerations are but one element of a multidimensional process, migration and refugee issues cannot be defined solely in terms of morality.[51]

From a moral perspective, the persons with the strongest claim to admission in the United States are likely to be refugees. Because such individuals have fled their homeland to avoid persecution, there is a general consensus that such persons are entitled to special protection. However, their need of refuge does not entitle them to admission into the United States (or, for that matter, any other state), because admission in the contemporary international system is normally regarded as a humanitarian act, not a binding moral obligation. This is the underlying principle of the 1980 Refugee Act, which views refugee admissions as "an exceptional *ex gratia* act provided by the United States in furthering foreign and humanitarian policies."[52]

Although the United States follows international law in defining refugees as those persons who have fled their homeland because of "a well-founded fear of persecution," the circumstances justifying refugee status have expanded in light of growing admissions pressures. During the Cold War, the United States granted refugee claims largely on the basis of political oppression, but in the post–Cold War era, other factors, such as religion, ethnicity, and cultural mores, have been accepted as legitimate justifications for persecution. For example, a young Muslim woman successfully claimed refugee status because female circumcision was required of all young women in her homeland.[53] Moreover, because refugee admissions are governed by geographical and preferential criteria, the changing application of refugee status has resulted in different admissions policies that have modified but not necessarily increased refugee admissions.

The difficulty in responding to refugee claims is illustrated by the moral challenge posed by the

tens of thousands of Haitians who have sought to enter the United States illegally since the early 1980s. Throughout the 1970s, a growing number of Haitians migrated to the United States, most of them legally. However, in the 1980s, a large number of Haitians sought to flee their homeland not only because of its abject poverty, civil unrest, and political oppression but also out of the desire to find refuge in a developed country. The number of Haitian "boat people" increased dramatically in the early 1980s, in part because of growing leniency toward Haitian asylees (Haitian refugees in the United States) and because of the success of some 125,000 Cubans fleeing their homeland in the 1980 Mariel boatlift.[54] To stem the tide of Haitian illegal immigration, the Reagan administration made an agreement in 1981 with Haiti's dictator, Jean-Claude Duvalier, permitting the U.S. Coast Guard to interdict Haitian vessels, screen refugees at sea, and then return them to their homeland.[55]

However, following the 1991 military coup that overthrew the elected government of President Jean-Bertrand Aristide, the number of Haitian refugees increased once again, especially after the international community's economic sanctions began to inflict significant hardship on the citizens of Haiti, particularly its poor. Indeed, the number of Haitians interdicted was so high by late 1991 that the United States established a temporary processing center in Guantánamo, Cuba, that was filled to capacity by mid-1992. Because of the overwhelming flow of refugees, President George Bush issued an executive order authorizing the U.S. Coast Guard to halt all Haitian boat people and return them, as well as those held in Guantánamo Bay, to Haiti.[56] Although Bill Clinton criticized the Bush administration's policy of repatriating Haitian refugees, he followed a similar policy after he assumed office, and when the flow of Haitian boat people increased again in 1994, the United States forced the removal of the military government and the reinstatement of President Aristide. This development contributed greatly to a reduction in Haitian illegal immigration.

The moral assessment of U.S. immigration policy will depend in great measure on which ethical traditions and methodologies are utilized. For example, since cosmopolitanism regards state boundaries as morally insignificant, cosmopolitan thinkers are likely to conclude that U.S. immigration statutes are of dubious moral validity because they subordinate refugee claims to the national interest. On the other hand, nationalists (amoral realists) will similarly disapprove of American immigration policies, but for opposite reasons, namely, because citizens' claims are unnecessarily subordinated to those of immigrants and refugees. Only principled realists who seek to reconcile national claims with global needs, power, and morality are likely to endorse the American approach to immigration because it seeks to protect the legitimate interests of domestic society while also providing humanitarian care.

However, because principled realists hold a wide variety of conceptions of the nature, role, and priority of political morality, their ethical perspectives on American immigration policy differ as well. For example, some principled realists, such as Walzer, have justified the American communal approach by claiming that states are entitled to regulate migrant and refugee admissions and that no person, even a refugee, is morally entitled to admission in a foreign state. Walzer suggests that although political communities, following the principle of "mutual aid," should provide humanitarian aid as the need arises and as resources permit, refugees have no right to expect admission.[57] Other principled realists, such as Weiner, have sought to defend regulatory immigration policies while deemphasizing

morality. Although Weiner recognizes that migration and refugee issues involve both moral and political considerations, he emphasizes the prudential nature of public policies, arguing that immigration policies are "not a matter of general moral principles but of politically defined national interests and values, that is, in the broadest sense, national sovereignty."[58]

MORAL REFLECTIONS

This brief examination of U.S. immigration policy raises a number of critical moral issues about migration politics.

- What are the nature and scope of a state's moral obligations toward migrants and especially refugees?
- Is U.S. immigration policy consistent with international morality? In light of the U.S. admission of about eight hundred thousand migrants and refugees annually, does U.S. policy adequately protect the communal solidarity of the American nation while also adequately caring for the needs of immigrants?
- Is the U.S. policy of granting preferential treatment to families and, to a lesser degree, to workers with particular job skills morally justified?
- What policy should the United States pursue toward illegal aliens? Should such aliens be deported? If not, should the U.S. government offer conditional amnesty and provide a path to citizenship? What policies should be adopted to reduce illegal immigration?

SUMMARY

The quest for international justice is elusive not only because governments fail to formulate and implement policies that advance the common good but also because analysts and public officials hold different and frequently conflicting conceptions of interstate justice. Because of the competing conceptions of justice as well as alternative views of international society, public officials must frequently choose between the shared interests of global society and the immediate interests of states, between the common good and the national interest. As the analyses of foreign aid and international migration suggest, claims of sovereignty frequently conflict with the interests of foreign states and the legitimate transnational claims of people. Indeed, these two case studies demonstrate that an ethical foreign policy will necessitate balancing present and future needs, national and transnational moral obligations.

Chapter Twelve

Promoting Global Justice

How well we come through the era of globalization (perhaps whether we come through it at all) will depend on how we respond ethically to the idea that we live in one world. For the rich nations not to take a global ethical viewpoint has long been seriously morally wrong. Now it is also, in the long term, a danger to their security.[1]

—PETER SINGER

International justice turns out to be as much the prisoner of international politics as national justice is of national politics. Indeed, given the stakes, international justice may be more partial, that is, more politicized, than national justice.[2]

—MICHAEL IGNATIEFF

Rhetoric that associates international legality primarily with bringing wrongdoers to justice, rather than primarily with maintaining peaceful and respectful relations among bearers of conflicting moralities—with the cross-border exercise of power rather than with restraint on power—furnishes legitimation to agendas that are, on the whole, unlikely to serve humanitarian aims.[3]

—BRAD ROTH

We should not view national boundaries as having fundamental moral significance. Since boundaries are not coextensive with the scope of social cooperation, they do not mark the limits of social obligation.[4]

—CHARLES R. BEITZ

I N THE PREVIOUS CHAPTER I examined the ethics of inter-state relations, focusing on economic and social dimensions. My concern was with the quest for international justice—that is, justice among states. In this chapter, I explore the justice of the international system itself—the metaethics of the existing global order. The international community remains a society of states in which ultimate decision-making authority rests with member states, not intergovernmental organizations (IGOs) or nongovernmental organizations (NGOs). Although public officials frequently speak of "the international community" to refer to actions by the United Nations and other IGOs, the level of solidarity among states and the degree of communal bonds among nations remain weak. Unlike strong, developed nation-states like Denmark or New Zealand, global society is held together by feeble institutions and slender affinities.

Although the underdeveloped character of global society is manifested in the low level of solidarity and trust among member states, it is especially evident in several areas of global social, economic, and political life. One example of the world's institutional limitations is the significant and growing economic inequalities among states. A further expression of institutional weakness is the world's failure to maintain global peace. When major disputes arise between states, it is states themselves who must resolve conflicts, either directly or through intermediaries. A third evidence of the underdeveloped character of global society is the inadequate protection of human rights. Although the body of international humanitarian law increased significantly in the second half of the twentieth century, the responsibility for protecting human dignity remains with states themselves. Thus when the major powers are either unwilling or incapable of mobilizing resources to halt systemic crimes against humanity, such as those committed by warring parties in Darfur, Sudan, there is no international organization that can intervene to halt the killing. Finally, the international community's institutional shortcomings are evident in the failure to promote and protect the "global commons." Although numerous multilateral efforts have been undertaken to protect the environment, the decentralized character of global society impairs collective action.

This chapter begins by exploring the nature and role of global governance in the contemporary international community. In the second part I illuminate the challenges in defining and promoting global public goods. I illustrate some of the challenges in protecting the global commons with a case study on global warming. In the third section I examine the quest to strengthen international human rights protection. I do so by examining the nature and role of universal jurisdiction and the development of international tribunals. I illustrate the challenges of transnational legal accountability with a case study on the London detention of the late Chilean president Augusto Pinochet.

THE DEVELOPMENT OF GLOBAL GOVERNANCE

The concept of government is derived from the Greek verb "to govern," which means to steer. Thus, to govern means to lead, direct, guide, and organize the affairs of a society. The responsibilities for governing a community are thus similar to those of a ship's captain, who must make decisions regarding the speed and direction of a vessel and who has ultimate responsibility for its cargo, passengers, and crew.

Although globalization has increased the level of global integration, the international community remains a society of states. Normally, each of these states is administered by a *government*—the institution that makes, interprets, and enforces binding rules within a community.[5] Because states are *sovereign*—that is, have ultimate authority over public affairs—their governments have final decision-making authority within their territorial boundaries.[6] And since no world government exists that can override a state's authority, the state remains the fundamental actor in the international community of states.

Politics is the means by which societies decide who can make decisions (the government) and what those decisions should be. Fundamentally, it is the process for making public decisions. Since conflict is a natural by-product of all social life, politics provides the means by which conflicts are contained, managed, and resolved. Since government is ultimately responsible for conflict resolution within domestic societies, a fundamental task of politics is to develop and sustain governmental decision making. In effect, politics provides the fuel (energy) for mobilizing and guiding governmental decision making, helping to enact rules that protect human rights, encourage economic prosperity, and foster peaceful cooperation.

Government and Governance

In developed, well-functioning states, government normally plays a key role in resolving conflicts and promoting a society's economic and social welfare. In the international community, however, politics plays a far more important role because there is no central authority to make binding decisions. Nevertheless, the international society of states is not an unstable, chaotic environment, but a relatively peaceful, cooperative community. The order and stability of the world derives not from chance or from the domination of one or two powerful states but from the voluntary actions of states—actions that are taken in light of widely accepted values, procedures, behavioral patterns, and rules. When ideas, norms, and rules coalesce in areas of shared international concern, they result in what scholars call *institutions*.[7]

These global institutions are significant in the international community because they structure the behavior of state and nonstate actors, providing, in effect, the foundation of the world's political architecture. Thus, even though the world lacks central government, it has *governance* nonetheless. However, unlike government, which uses force to ensure compliance with its decisions, global governance is not based upon authority to make and impose rules. Rather, states comply with the norms, rules, network initiatives, and IGO decisions of global governance on a voluntary basis.

The scope of global governance has increased greatly in the post–Cold War era. This expansion, facilitated partly by the growth of international NGOs, has resulted in a thick, multilayer web of transnational information and action networks. Despite the increasing number of NGOs and other transnational actors, global governance has not increased its organizational capacity. Indeed, the growth of frail and failed states has created a vacuum of authority in the international community. Since the UN and its sister institutions remain wedded to the state-centric Westphalian order, their institutional capacity depends on the ability and willingness of its member states, especially the major powers, to cooperate in advancing shared concerns. Even where common interests are strongly shared—such as protecting human rights, deterring genocide, reducing absolute poverty, and protecting the global environment—collective action is often difficult. Indeed, the role of the UN is often nonexistent (failing to halt atrocities in Darfur in 2004–2006), ineffective (failing to restore a just peace in Bosnia and Kosovo), or too late (failing to expand the UN peacekeeping mission to halt the 1994 Rwanda genocide).

With the exception of the twenty-seven-member European Union, general-purpose regional organizations continue to play a modest role in promoting international conflict resolution and prosperity and managing shared social and economic concerns. In great part this is due to the limited independent authority of such organizations. The Organization of American States, like the UN, can act only where a substantial consensus exists among its member states. In contrast to the relative weakness of general-purpose international organizations, specialized international organizations tend to play a much more important role in addressing shared global concerns. Organizations like the International Monetary Fund, the World Bank, the World Trade Organization, and the World Health Organization are effective not only because their tasks and responsibilities are specific but also because their decision-making procedures are well institutionalized. Thus, in view of the limited authority of existing state-based international organizations, the challenge in building a more stable and just world is how to strengthen global governance.

Impediments to Global Governance

Several factors impair the institutionalization of global governance. One impediment is the lack of democratic legitimacy. Since global institutions are not constituted through democratic elections and do not follow democratic decision making, they suffer from a democratic deficit. Ordinarily, IGOs represent states and more particularly the policies and wants of governments. The Security Council, WTO, and IMF, for example, all make decisions based on the will of states—often weighted in favor of those with wealth and power. NGOs similarly suffer from limited democratic legitimacy, since they arise not from democratic contestation but from pursuit of specific global concerns and ideals by groups of like-minded citizens.

Another barrier to global governance lies in the fragile ties between decision makers and citizens. Robust governance presupposes a high level of *social capital*—that is, a high level of voluntary cooperation based on shared values, interests, and trust.[8] Typically, as the size of a community expands and as ethnic, cultural, linguistic, and religious differences increase, the bonds of trust and cooperation become more tenuous. Not only do the bonds among people become more fragile as communal authority is extended from the locality to the state and onto the world, but the bond between people and political institutions is similarly compromised. Thus, whereas a vigorous civic engagement is possible at the local and state level, it becomes much more difficult at the regional and global levels.[9]

A third obstacle to global governance is the limitation of centralized decision making. Central authority is of course indispensable for effective conflict resolution and the maintenance of global order. But if government is to be a positive, creative force in the international community, it must empower citizens, foster "creative destruction" in economic life, encourage group initiatives in public life, and facilitate institutional change to respond to new global challenges. And it can only do so if global institutions are effective, yet not intrusive. In his analysis of state building, Francis Fukuyama distinguishes between the strength and the scope of governance. He argues that while strong government is essential in facilitating a humane and productive society, a government that limits its scope of responsibilities is also important.[10] Historically, however, the strengthening of the state has often been associated with centralized decision making. Social scientists now recognize that excessive centralization can impair effective decision making. Nobel laureate Amartya Sen has argued that freedom is not only a necessary goal, but also an indispensable means for constituting an effective state and for creative problem solving. He illustrates the priority of freedom by showing that free societies are better able to prevent and respond to famines than are authoritarian or totalitarian regimes. This is so not because free societies can produce more food but because they disseminate information more efficiently and effectively.[11] Thus, the challenge in strengthening global institutions is to make such institutions more effective without necessarily expanding the scope of responsibility—in other words, to foster strong institutions that facilitate decentralized decision making.

Finally, global governance remains weak because of the low level of shared values and interests. The authority of law depends not only on the coercive power of institutions but also on a moral-cultural consensus. Legitimate governmental authority can exist only where a strong, consensual political culture exists. Given the absence of shared political ideals and values among different countries, developing and sustaining cooperation and trust (social capital) is likely to be difficult. And because of the wide cultural diversity, strengthening global governance is likely to remain a daunting challenge.

IR scholars tend to agree that the international community is undergoing important changes, but there is wide disagreement about the likely future role of global institutions. Although the state may be shrinking and governmental authority may be declining in many countries, the loss of sovereignty has not necessarily led to stronger international institutions. Global governance has extended its reach, taking on a wide range of transnational issues and concerns. However, this has not necessarily led to stronger, more authoritative institutions. For example, although more than one hundred states have created the International Criminal Court to prosecute leaders who commit gross human rights crimes, the new court faces a difficult future because the political and legal preconditions for a global criminal justice system are absent. The world is not a coherent, unitary global society based on one law but a decentralized society of sovereign states, each with its own legal order.

Given the frailty of many states and the institutional weakness of IGOs, strengthening global governance will most likely continue to depend upon the collective decisions of states themselves, especially the major powers of the international community. Since the United States remains the most powerful country in the world, it will necessarily play a critical role in either supporting or impeding global governance. IR scholar Michael Mandelbaum has gone so far as to claim that the United States has been serving as the "world's government" by providing global goods to the international community.[12]

Since American dominance is unlikely to be sustained in the future, global governance will likely emerge from a collective effort between the United States and other major powers. In the short term these states will include the other members of the Security Council (Britain, China, France, and Russia) along with Germany and Japan.

In the longer term, a number of emerging economies are likely to play a much more important role in global politics. China and India—the two most populous states in the world, whose economies have been growing at an annual rate of 6 to 9 percent since the end of the Cold War—will likely become the most influential countries in the international system after the United States. One study has estimated that by 2040 five emerging countries (Brazil, China, India, Mexico, and Russia) will rank among the top ten economic powers.[13] If this projection is fulfilled, Brazil and Mexico will also become major players in global governance.

PROTECTING GLOBAL PUBLIC GOODS

Public (collective) goods are ideas, values, practices, resources, and conditions that benefit everyone in a society or community. *Global public goods* are those collective goods that extend across borders. Examples of such goods include peace, financial stability, poverty reduction, clean air, environmental protection, and conservation of species; examples of collective "bads"—harmful and detrimental conditions and practices in the international community—include war, international financial instability, air pollution, global warming, and deforestation.

Public goods have two characteristics: First, their enjoyment is not diluted or compromised as the goods' usage is extended to others. This means that goods like clean air, knowledge, or highways can be enjoyed by all persons in society without adverse consequences to the good itself. Second, no person can be excluded from enjoying a public good. If global warming is halted through dramatic reductions in carbon emissions, for example, every country benefits, regardless of whether it contributed to the reduction of global warming gases. Just as domestic communities are sustained through the provision of public goods for all of its members, so the international community similarly depends upon the availability of global public goods to help sustain order, peace, and economic prosperity among states. Without collective goods, global welfare would decline with the rise of public "bads"—war and instability, increased terrorism from weak states, ocean pollution, environmental degradation, and a rise in infectious diseases.

Who provides for public goods? Although some collective goods arise spontaneously within domestic society through the self-interested behaviors of individuals,[14] the government plays an important function in directly providing some public goods (e.g., national security, airline safety) and by indirectly fostering public goods by regulating human behavior to minimize harm (e.g., promoting automobile safety to prevent accidents and protecting consumers from harmful substances). The role of government in providing institutional "safety nets" is important because of the so-called *free-rider problem*. The problem arises from the temptation to use freely available public goods without paying for them or helping to maintain them. Thus, the development and maintenance of collective goods is generally easier in smaller, close-knit communities where strong group loyalty exists among members. As the size of a community increases, it becomes easier for individuals and groups to rely on others for the provision of collective goods.

Given the temptation to "free ride," securing dependable behavioral commitments to develop and maintain global public goods is important. One way of achieving compliance is through treaties and conventions, as was demonstrated by the banning of ozone-depleting gases with the signing of the Montreal Protocol in 1987. After scientists conclusively demonstrated that chlorofluorocarbons (CFCs) were reducing the earth's atmospheric ozone (a type of oxygen that helps to protect the earth from the sun's harmful ultraviolet rays), the developed industrial states agreed to eliminate the use of CFCs. One of the reasons for the success in the elimination of CFCs, which were used in aerosol sprays and refrigeration, was that the industries were able to develop safe and economical alternatives. This has not been the case with fossil fuels, which provide most of the world's energy and are also chiefly responsible for global warming gases. Thus, while states desire to reduce the atmospheric effects of carbon emissions, they are even more concerned with short-term economic growth, which can only be sustained by increasing the availability of energy. In short, while global collective goods are important to the international community, the provision of such goods will continue to present major challenges.

Because no central authority exists in global society to make and enforce rules that manage and preserve the earth's shared resources, protecting the atmosphere, oceans, and soil is ultimately a cooperative enterprise among state and nonstate actors. As expected, states maintain widely varied policies and practices on domestic environmental protection. Some modern industrial states have developed a significant body of rules to reduce pollution, regulate waste disposal, and protect biodiversity. By contrast, other states, mostly poor, developing nations, have neglected pollution control, focusing instead on promoting economic growth. The extent to which states implement sustainable development strategies domestically is vitally important because domestic practices will profoundly affect transboundary air and water pollution and thus impact the quality of the earth's atmosphere and oceans as well as the prospect for long-term economic growth.

Global Environmental Protection

In the early nineteenth century, English political economist William Foster Lloyd developed the "tragedy of the commons" metaphor to explain the dangers of parochial, short-term practices.[15] According to the metaphor, village farmers allow livestock to graze on private and public pastures. Whereas each farmer carefully regulates grazing on private land, the commons is unregulated. As a result, the pasture on private plots is well maintained, whereas the village green suffers from overgrazing.

The commons metaphor is helpful in assessing collective-agency issues because it illuminates the dilemma of protecting resources owned or used in common. Because the village commons can sustain only a limited number of animals (this is defined as the commons' "carrying capacity"), the challenge for village farmers is to maximize their individual well-being without destroying the shared land. If each villager defines his interests in terms of the common good, he will allow only limited grazing by his animals. However, if farmers pursue their immediate self-interest and disregard the interests of others, the communal property will deteriorate and eventually be destroyed through overuse.

If the earth is viewed as a global commons, where the soil, atmosphere and water are collective goods, developing long-term, cooperative strategies might help prevent the misuse or overuse of the earth's shared resources.[16] As with the village green, the challenge for states is to manage the earth's bountiful resources by wisely protecting global goods and devising rules and cooperative strategies that foster sustainable economic development. Additionally, states have regional and international accords to help prevent transboundary pollution and to protect natural resources.[17]

Perhaps the most significant international initiative to promote global environmental protection was the 1992 UN Conference on Environment and Development in Rio de Janeiro. Billed as the "last chance to save the planet," the conference, generally referred to as the Earth Summit, was the largest international conference ever held, bringing together 172 official government delegations along with some fifteen thousand representatives from two thousand environmental NGOs. It is important to emphasize that, although government officials played a decisive role in negotiating various declarations and conventions, NGOs carried out most of the preparatory work on global environmental protection. Two major treaties were signed at the summit: the UN Framework Convention on Climate Change (also known as the Climate Treaty) and the Convention on Biological Diversity (also known as the Biodiversity Treaty). In addition, officials adopted three nonbinding agreements: a declaration of principles for establishing national environmental conservation programs, a statement of how to sustain forests, and a blueprint for promoting environmentally sustainable economic development.

Protecting the earth's biodiversity, environment, and resources presents political, technical, and moral challenges. Politically, environmental protection requires a mature collective will. Because protecting species, reducing pollution, and conserving resources involve long-term, elusive payoffs, the development and implementation of transnational environmental strategies is difficult, especially when the political decision-making process is focused on short-term goals. However, if the protection of global resources is important, all members of the international community must implement environmentally safe policies. As with the protection of the village green, countries must avoid the overuse or misuse of shared resources.

Technically, sustainable development requires the development of new technologies that reduce pollution, conserve energy, and foster the development of alternative energy sources. Most Western European and North American governments have greatly reduced the proportion of pollution in generating energy through the application of new technologies. Although the environmental safety of industrial production has increased in these countries, much more remains to be done to strengthen the environmental protection and conservation regime. Developed countries need to continue to devise new technologies and encourage more efficient use of energy. Third World nations, for their part, need to become more aware of the effects of industrialization on the environment and to apply energy conservation policies and environmentally safe technologies as a means of encouraging sustainable economic development.

Finally, environmental protection presents a moral challenge by requiring states to balance national interests with shared global concerns, current economic needs with those of future generations. If development is to be sustainable—that is, available to future generations—economic growth must involve careful use of renewable and non-renewable resources, ensuring that present demands are balanced against the potential needs and wants of future generations. In addition, a moral approach to environmental protection must ensure that access to the global commons is fair and that the distribution of the commons' resources is similarly perceived as just. This is a most difficult challenge not only because decision makers perceive political and economic reality differently but also because they hold different conceptions of justice. But regardless of how justice is defined (whether as a fair distribution of benefits or fair application of procedural rules), egregious inequalities in the use or misuse of global resources is morally problematic.

To illustrate some of the ethical challenges in promoting environmental protection in the contemporary international system, I next examine and assess the politics and ethics of global warming.

CASE 12-1: MANAGING GLOBAL CLIMATE CHANGE

GLOBAL WARMING

The earth's climate is determined principally by the balance between energy received from the sun, largely as visible light, and the energy radiated back to space as invisible infrared light. Water vapors and human-made gases (mainly carbon dioxide), however, can impair this balance by trapping solar radiation, much like the glass of a plant-breeder's greenhouse. The "greenhouse effect" thus occurs because vapors and gases allow more of the sun's heat to be absorbed by the earth than is released back into space. Although human-made gas emissions are responsible for only a small part of the greenhouse effect, they nonetheless play an important role in influencing the earth's climate because carbon dioxide and other gases linger for long periods of time in the atmosphere before dissipating.

As noted above, the 1992 Climate Treaty established a framework for reducing the growth of greenhouse gas emissions. When the agreement was signed, there was some scientific uncertainty about the role of human-made gases in climate change. Subsequently, however, the UN Intergovernmental Panel on Climate Change

(IPCC), a group of about twenty-five hundred distinguished scientists, issued a report on climate change that, although tentative and cautious in its conclusions, made a compelling case that greenhouse gases are a major source of global warming. According to its Second Assessment Report (1996), the IPCC claimed that continued reliance on fossil fuels (coal and petroleum) would increase the earth's temperature. Whereas the earth's temperature had increased by one degree (F) in the twentieth century, scientists estimated that the continued rise in greenhouse gas emission would possibly lead to a three- to eight-degree (F) rise in the earth's temperature in the twenty-first century.[18] According to IPCC's latest (2007) climate assessment, human activity is believed to be the main cause of global warming, "very likely" causing most of the rise in the earth's temperature since 1950.[19] Although global warming could cause some beneficial developments, such as an increase in agricultural land in the Northern Hemisphere, environmentalists have warned that climate change could also bring about significant harm, including a rise in the sea level due to thermal expansion. Such a development would lead to the flooding of coastal lowlands and the destruction of numerous tropical islands.

Because the 1992 Climate Treaty did not establish binding targets for states, signatory states implemented few policy reforms to reduce greenhouse gases. As a result, after numerous preparatory meetings, some five thousand officials gathered in Kyoto, Japan, in December 1997 to establish a more authoritative climate change regime. The result was the creation of a framework accord that delineated specific cuts in greenhouse gas emissions. The Kyoto Protocol—essentially an addendum to the 1992 Climate Treaty—required that industrialized countries reduce their greenhouse emissions by about 5 percent below their 1990 level no later than the year 2012. To achieve this goal, the protocol established significant cuts in pollution—8 percent for the European Union, 7 percent for the United States, and 6 percent for Japan. Significantly, no binding targets were established for China and India or other developing nations. Because the accord called for a reduction of roughly 30 percent in the projected carbon emissions of industrialized countries, the Kyoto framework represented a significant challenge to the energy consumption patterns of developed nations, especially the United States, a country that accounts for nearly one-fourth of the world's greenhouse emissions.

Since the Kyoto accord established only a general framework for action, the specific compliance mechanisms had to be worked out in subsequent meetings. This proved to be far more difficult than was anticipated, in great part because the contemplated pollution reductions imposed significant economic burdens on the major industrial states. This was especially the case for countries like Canada, Norway, and the United States, which, unlike most European Union member states, had fewer energy conservation measures in place. To facilitate compliance with Kyoto's stringent emissions targets, some industrial states demanded flexibility. Two innovations that developed were the trading of "emissions rights" (Article 17)—allowing countries with below-average pollution to sell their emissions rights to countries with excessive pollution—and the generation of "emission credits" (Article 3). Credits are generated through reforestation and other major vegetation projects, known as carbon "sinks" because they reduce carbon dioxide in the atmosphere and thereby decrease greenhouse gases. While the European Union established an emissions trading system (ETS) in 2003, little progress has been achieved in creating a global emissions trading system.

Although the United States signed the Kyoto Protocol, the Bush administration withdrew from the accord in March 2001.[20] The Kyoto accord, nevertheless, went into effect in February 2005 after Russia, a major emissions producer, ratified the treaty.[21] But by this time it was increasingly evident that the Kyoto framework was woefully inadequate and that much more needed to be done to reduce the world's reliance on fossil fuels. In particular, if the international community was to contain the rise in carbon gases in the world's atmosphere, then emerging economies like China, the world's largest carbon dioxide emitter, and India would also have to contain the use of fossil fuels. One scholar has written that Kyoto is problematic precisely because it has fostered the illusion that serious progress is being made to confront climate change.[22]

Since the Kyoto accord expires in 2012, the United Nations Framework Convention on Climate Change (UNFCCC) has been working on extending Kyoto for an additional five or eight years. Extending the life of the protocol is difficult since Canada withdrew from the treaty in 2011, and both Japan and Russia have indicated that they are uninterested in extending Kyoto. Consequently, a major goal has been to develop a new approach to climate change to replace Kyoto altogether—one that is universally binding on all states but that makes provision for significant financial transfers from the rich, developed countries to the poor nations of Asia, Africa, and Latin America. To this end, government leaders from some 115 countries, supported by thousands of public officials and representatives from nongovernmental organizations, met in Copenhagen in December 2009 to devise a new global climate change framework. Government negotiators, however, were unsuccessful in developing an acceptable alternative.

Rather than devising a new regulatory system, leaders were able to agree on only some non-binding commitments, such as constraining carbon usage, containing the rise of global temperature to a maximum 2 degrees Celsius (roughly 3.7 degrees Fahrenheit) above preindustrial levels, and assisting poor countries that are vulnerable environmentally. Some countries, including the United States, have pledged nevertheless to reduce their carbon gases unilaterally.[23]

Subsequent UN climate change conferences in Cancún, Mexico, in 2010 and in Durban, South Africa, in 2011 achieved agreement on some modest initiatives. However, delegates were unable to achieve consensus on fundamental issues because of competing preconceptions and conflicting strategies on curbing the use of fossil fuels. In the meantime, the world's relentless demand for energy continues to require greater burning of oil and coal.

THE ETHICS OF CLIMATE CHANGE

The question of how best to confront the problem of global warming raises numerous moral concerns. One of the most important ethical issues is the conflict between economic development and environmental sustainability, between meeting current human needs and protecting the environment for future generations. Ideally, economic development should be sustainable—that is, conducive to the short- and long-term protection of the environment. But if a choice must be made between limiting economic growth and preventing global warming, job creation and protecting the environment, which goal should take precedence? This dispute is morally complex because it involves an intergenerational conflict between people's current wants and needs and the claims of future generations. Since fossil fuels have served as the principal energy source for industrialization and economic development, there is a significant incentive to continue using such fuels to promote further economic modernization. Although the burning of such fuels leads to immediate energy benefits, the costs of carbon emissions, the major cause of global warming, are transferred to the future. Indeed, since

the cumulative destructive impact of carbon dioxide is not felt immediately, there is little incentive for countries to restrict the use of such fuels. This is especially the case for low-income countries that are eager to increase their standard of living through modernization.

Besides the challenge of how best to reconcile the intergenerational trade-offs, devising a morally appropriate policy is inherently subjective and difficult because public policy making is probabilistic. The lack of consensus over which strategies are most conducive to achieving desired outcomes frequently derives from conflicting interpretations of scientific knowledge as well as uncertainty over the effects and results of different public policies. This uncertainty principle is clearly evident in the scientific and public policy debates over climate change.[24] For example, while there is a significant consensus over the fact of global warming, there is much less agreement over its causes, timing, and magnitude.[25] Thus, while public officials may agree that the spread of greenhouse gases is a harmful by-product of industrial pollution, they may hold radically different perspectives about how best to control and reduce emissions of greenhouse gases.

A second important ethical issue in the climate change debate is the trading of emissions rights. According to the Kyoto accord, industrial states with excessive levels of carbon emissions, such as Greece, Ireland, Norway, and the United States, may pay countries with low levels of emissions as a way of meeting Kyoto obligations. Although the introduction of market forces could possibly help reduce total world greenhouse emissions, the commercialization of pollution is itself a dubious ethical development. For one thing, it removes the stigma that is normally associated with pollution.[26] When an industry violates pollution regulations, a government agency fines the industry. Such a fine is not simply a financial cost to business but also represents a community's moral judgment that the industry's action (excessive pollution) was wrong. However, the commercialization of pollution destroys the moral stigma associated with unacceptable behaviors. Moreover, the trading of emissions rights is morally problematic because it weakens the communal solidarity required in the collective management of global resources. When some countries can fulfill their communal responsibilities toward the global warming regime by buying the right to pollute, global solidarity is weakened.

A third ethical concern is how to allocate the burden of pollution reduction among states. In particular, how should constraints on the burning of fossil fuels apply to the industrial nations of the North and the developing nations of the South? Should the costs of cutting carbon dioxide be borne by the North or by all states, including the South? What arrangement would be fair? One perspective—the one endorsed by the Kyoto framework—is that, since the North is overwhelmingly responsible for most existing greenhouse gas emissions,[27] it should be chiefly responsible for reducing the use of petroleum and carbon. Developing nations do not assert that climate change is solely the responsibility of the developed states. Instead, they claim that since current atmospheric pollution is a direct by-product of the North's industrialization, the high-income countries must bear the primary responsibility for reducing greenhouse emissions. Because poor countries with little pollution can sell emissions rights, the North can meet its Kyoto emissions targets by making payments to the South. The trading of emissions rights between the North and the South—which some environmentalists claim will exceed any previous international wealth transfer in modern history[28]—could result in a far more egalitarian international economic order.

The opposing perspective, the one endorsed by the United States, claims that, regardless of past responsibility, all nations must participate in curbing greenhouse emissions. This is especially the case for the emerging economies like Brazil, China, India, and Mexico, whose energy consumption has risen dramatically in recent decades. Indeed, China displaced the United States as the major emitter of greenhouse gases in 2010, producing roughly one-quarter of the world's carbon dioxide in 2012. The inadequacy of the Kyoto framework, which placed carbon limitations only on the developed industrial states, is illuminated by comparing the emissions reductions of industrial countries with the growth of emissions in the emerging economies. If all industrial countries subject to Kyoto meet their targets, the reduction in carbon dioxide through 2012 will be roughly 483 million tons. By contrast, the coal-burning power plants that have been built in China and India alone will have emitted some 2.5 billion tons of carbon dioxide into the atmosphere—or more than five times the carbon reduced under Kyoto.[29]

Finally, the shift to nuclear power as a way of curbing fossil fuel use raises important ethical and safety issues. Nuclear power plays an important role in a number of countries—notably France, Japan, Russia, Spain, South Korea, Sweden, and the United States. It is estimated that close to 80 percent of France's electricity is generated by nuclear power, while the United States' one hundred nuclear power plants generate roughly 20 percent of the country's electricity. In the absence of some 450 nuclear power plants throughout the world, global greenhouse emissions would be an estimated 10 percent higher.[30] The moral problem posed by increased reliance on nuclear energy is that nuclear power involves significant environmental dangers and risks. The dangers were amply demonstrated in March 2011 when a tsunami severely damaged the nuclear power plant at Fukushima, Japan, spreading deadly radiation throughout the region. As a result of this accident, Japan closed down nearly all of its fifty-four reactors for inspection and modification, and as of March 2012 only two of them were generating power.[31] More ominously, the accident increased the public concern over the safety of nuclear power plants and led the governments of Germany and Switzerland to announce a phaseout of nuclear energy.

MORAL REFLECTIONS

Global warming raises a number of important ethical issues.

- Ideally, development should be sustainable. But to the extent that economic development and reduction in carbon dioxide emissions conflict, which goal should take precedence—job creation or pollution control, economic growth or less global warming?

- Because developed countries are responsible for most of the existing greenhouse emissions, should they bear the principal cost of curbing greenhouse emissions, as established in the Kyoto framework? Or must climate change apply universally, with limited acknowledgment for past pollution?
- Because the developed countries have established high standards of living while implementing various types of policies and strategies that encourage environmental protection, should they transfer these technologies to the poor countries? Should developed countries pay developing nations in order to reduce their emissions?
- Is it moral to buy or sell pollution rights? Why or why not?
- Given the risks and dangers associated with nuclear power, is the shift from carbon-burning plants to nuclear power plants morally warranted?

PROMOTING LEGAL JUSTICE IN GLOBAL SOCIETY

Although states have ratified a large number of human rights conventions to deter human rights abuses, the protection of human rights is chiefly a responsibility of sovereign governments. Since each state has its own criminal justice system, legal accountability for human rights abuses, even for crimes against humanity, remains in the hands of each state. But when crimes against humanity occur during civil wars or when war crimes are committed in tribal, religious, or ethnic wars, what legal institution should prosecute such offenses? Often states that have been involved in bitter domestic wars are either too weak to pursue trials or more concerned with restoring domestic tranquility than with adjudicating guilt for past atrocities. Thus, when a state is unable or unwilling to prosecute political and military leaders for gross human rights abuses, should the international community undertake such tasks?

Since the end of the Cold War, human rights groups have sought to advance two initiatives to increase transnational legal accountability for gross human rights abuses committed in wartime. The first development is the claim of universal jurisdiction—the belief that some crimes, such as genocide and torture, are so offensive that any state may prosecute them. The second initiative, following the example of the Nuremburg War Crimes Tribunals, involves the creation of international criminal tribunals to prosecute leaders for atrocities and other crimes against humanity. The first two post–Cold War tribunals were established by the Security Council to prosecute atrocities committed in the Yugoslavian civil war of the early 1990s and the Rwandan genocide of 1994. Subsequently, the international community established a larger, permanent global criminal court to prosecute major human rights offenses. The International Criminal Court (ICC), a formal institution of the United Nations, began functioning in 2002 after sixty states ratified the 1998 Rome Treaty that created the court. Below I examine each of these two initiatives to extend legal accountability from sovereign states to the international community.

Universal Jurisdiction

Historically, courts have had jurisdiction over crimes committed in their territory. According to the *territorial principle*, state sovereignty within a specified territory allowed a government to exercise authority over all persons within that land. States have also claimed jurisdiction over nationals outside of their own territorial boundaries (*nationality principle*) and over harmful activities (e.g., currency counterfeiting) that threaten a nation's welfare (*protective principle*). More recently, some states have extended jurisdiction to cover two additional claims: first, to allow state courts to pursue justice against persons who, either as individuals or as public officials, carried out heinous crimes against its people (this principle is known as *"passive personality,"* to differentiate it from active or national personality); and second, to allow states to pursue legal accountability because the crime, such as genocide or slavery, is regarded as universally reprehensible (*universal jurisdiction*). This latter is the most controversial because the prosecuting state does not have to have any connection with the crime. As Stephen Macedo notes, "Universal jurisdiction is the principle that certain crimes are so heinous and so universally recognized and abhorred, that a state is entitled or even obliged to undertake legal proceedings without regard to where the crime was committed or the nationality of the perpetrators or the victims."[32] In short, the claim of universal jurisdiction is based solely on the nature of the crime, without consideration as to where the offense was committed or the nationality of the offender or victim.

The notion of universal jurisdiction, which has been strongly supported by human rights NGOs and even some governments, is a further manifestation of the extension of legal accountability beyond state boundaries. A number of countries, including Belgium, Spain, and Switzerland, have enacted laws giving national courts jurisdiction over certain types of crimes, like genocide and torture, regardless of where the crime occurs or who the victims are.[33] Writing about the efforts of Spanish courts to prosecute Argentine personnel for crimes committed in Argentina against Argentine nationals, Naomi Roht-Arriaza, a lawyer, asks, "How could a court have power to try people who were not even present in Spain, for crimes committed in far-off countries, against mostly non-Spaniards?"[34] This question, which highlights the tension between state sovereignty and the quest for a humane global order, raises profound issues about global governance and the role of national and transnational legal accountability.

There can be little doubt that the growth of international humanitarian law has heightened global concern for human rights. But universal jurisdiction is not simply about increasing the protection of human rights. Rather, it seeks to extend legal accountability from the home state to international courts and, most problematically, to other sovereign states. Such an extension of jurisdiction is not only inconsistent with the legal and political foundations of the contemporary neo-Westphalian global order but also contrary to the central postulate of the United Nations—namely, the sovereign equality of states. Moreover, since there is no established global civil society and no uniform transnational criminal justice system, the expansion of state court to foreign countries will inevitably politicize justice.

Advocates of universal jurisdiction do not seek to defend the existing political and legal order. Rather, their goal is to transform the world in accordance with a cosmopolitan worldview so that individuals are accorded moral precedence over states. Their aim is not to support the UN system rooted in the juridical equality of states, from which the principle of sovereign immunity emanates. Instead, their desire is to undermine sovereignty. Although sovereign equality may impede justice when dictatorial or totalitarian regimes abuse their own people's rights, sovereignty can also be a tool for securing human rights, promoting global justice, and maintaining international peace. Kissinger writes,

> The advocates of universal jurisdiction argue that the state is the basic cause of war and cannot be trusted to deliver justice. If law replaced politics, peace and justice would prevail. But even a cursory examination of history shows that there is no evidence to support such a theory. The role of the statesman is to choose the best option when seeking to advance peace and justice, realizing that there is frequently a tension between the two and that any reconciliation is likely to be partial.[35]

The tension between sovereignty and human rights is never more intense than when a former government official is sought by prosecutors from another state for alleged offenses committed while in office. According to the widely accepted principle of sovereign immunity, government officials are not subject to the legal jurisdiction of other states. Geoffrey Robertson, a leading British human rights lawyer, claims that when human rights and sovereign immunity conflict, the former must take precedence over the latter. "The reality," he writes, "is that states are not equal." In his view, governments that abuse human rights, like those in Cuba, North Korea, Sudan, and Syria, do not deserve "dignity" or "respect" and their leaders should not be entitled to immunity. This view is increasingly accepted in the post–Cold War world. For example, the ICC indicted General Omar al-Bashir, Sudan's president, in 2009 and Colonel Muammar Qaddafi of Libya in 2011, while a special UN war crimes tribunal prosecuted former Liberian president Charles Taylor for atrocities in Sierra Leone and subsequently found him guilty of "aiding and abetting" those crimes in 2012. He is the first former head of state to be found guilty by an international court. Nevertheless, it would be incorrect to suggest that senior government officials are no longer entitled to sovereign immunity. In 2002, the International Court of Justice (ICJ) reaffirmed sovereign immunity in the Yerodia case between the Democratic Republic of Congo and Belgium. In that case the ICJ ruled that Congo's foreign minister, despite his earlier alleged role in human rights crimes, was entitled to immunity as a senior official of a sovereign state.[36]

The Rise of International Tribunals

In the early 1990s, the UN Security Council established two war crimes tribunals—the International Criminal Tribunal for the former Yugoslavia (ICTY) and the International Criminal Tribunal for Rwanda (ICTR). The aim of these two courts was to prosecute leaders responsible for atrocities in the Bosnian civil war of the early 1990s and the Rwanda genocide of 1994.[37] The work of both tribunals was slow, legally cumbersome, and expensive. As of 2012, the ICTY had prosecuted some 126 offenders at a cost of more than $1.7 billion,[38] while the ICTR had prosecuted 62 offenders at a cost of more than $1.5 billion.[39]

As I noted earlier (in case 6-1 on the Rwandan trials), the ICTR had little impact on Rwandan society since the court was located in neighboring Tanzania, requiring two days to travel from Kigali to Arusha. The impact of the ICTY on the peoples of the former Yugoslavia as well as European nations was arguably much greater. This is the case not only because of the greater ease of travel to the tribunal but also because of greater interest in the fate of those responsible for atrocities committed during the three-year Bosnian war. Interest in the ICTY increased in 2001, when Slobodan Milosevic, Serbia's former president and arguably the architect of much human suffering in the Balkans, was arrested and transferred to The Hague to stand trial. After five years of litigation, Milosevic died of a heart attack in 2006 before the court could reach a verdict. More recently two other indicted Serb leaders have been arrested and transferred to The Hague. The first leader, Radovan Karadzic, was a Bosnian Serb politician who served as the first president of the Bosnian Serbian Republic from 1992 to 1996. He was captured in 2008, thirteen years after he was indicted by the ICTY. The second leader, Ratko Mladic, was a senior military officer of the Bosnian Serb Army. He was captured and transferred to The Hague in 2011 by Serb authorities who were motivated by the desire to increase the country's prospects for candidacy to the European Union. Both Karadzic and Mladic were indicted for war crimes and crimes against humanity committed during the three-year Bosnian war.[40]

In view of the perceived need to avoid impunity and hold military and political leaders accountable for atrocities, some one hundred world leaders signed the 1998 Rome Treaty to establish the International Criminal Court.[41] The treaty became binding international law in 2002 after sixty countries ratified it. The court, which describes itself as an "independent permanent international criminal court in relationship with the United Nations," began functioning a year later in The Hague with the appointment of Luis Moreno-Ocampo as chief prosecutor. Like the ICTY and ICTR, the aim of the ICC is to prosecute egregious human rights offenses, focusing on four types of crimes—genocide, crimes against humanity, war crimes, and aggression.

The ICC establishes jurisdiction in two ways. First, the Security Council can request that the court investigate a specific situation. Second, the court can gain jurisdiction when a crime occurs in the territory of a state that is party to the statute or where the suspect is a national of such a state. Unlike the two tribunals, however, the ICC enjoys a significant level of independence since it is not directly accountable to the Security Council. As a result, some critics argue that the ICC's major flaw is its "prosecutorial discretion without accountability."[42] A related criticism is that the court can be insensitive to political conditions and impair peacemaking and political reconciliation.[43]

The ICC's first case—against leaders of the Lord's Resistance Army (LRA), a guerrilla force in the Acholi territory of northern Uganda—commenced when Uganda, a member state of the court, referred the wartime atrocities to the ICC.[44] There can be little doubt that LRA guerrillas have inflicted enormous human suffering on the Acholi people in the past twenty years. According to one estimate, some two million people have been displaced from their homes and more than twenty thousand children have been kidnapped by insurgents.[45] When the court took on the LRA case, the chief prosecutor predicted that the principal offenders would be arrested by the end of 2004 and that trials would be under way by 2005. But once indictments were issued, political realities in Uganda brought the legal investigation to a near standstill.[46] As of 2012, the four LRA leaders were still at large.

Following its first indictments, the ICC charged leaders from four other African countries with crimes against humanity and war crimes: four from the Congo, one from the Central African Republic, three from Sudan (including Omar al-Bashir, the president of the country), and six from Kenya. In 2011, the court indicted Colonel Muammar Qaddafi and his son Saif, along with Abdullah al-Sanoussi, the regime's intelligence chief, for their role in the killings of hundreds of persons who were involved in the antigovernment rebellion in the spring of that year.[47] In March 2012, the ICC rendered its first verdict in a case against Thomas Lubanga Dyilo of the Congo. Lubanga was found guilty of war crimes for having conscripted children under the age of fifteen into tribal wars. He was sentenced to fourteen years in prison. As with war crimes tribunals, the work of the ICC is slow and expensive, having realized only one verdict in ten years at a cost of more than $900 million.

The fundamental limitation of the ICC's work is that it pursues legal justice divorced from political realities. It assumes that human rights can be best defended and protected by prosecuting egregious violations and thereby deterring future wrongdoing. IR scholar Robert Tucker writes that in most circumstances nonlegal approaches, such as amnesties and truth commissions, "hold out greater prospects for reconciliation and the building of democratic institutions than does the court."[48] Political scientist Stephen Krasner explains the reason for this: "Judicial procedures are designed to judge the guilt or innocence of individuals, but developing stable democratic societies and limiting the loss of human life require prudent political calculations, not judicial findings."[49]

Mahmood Mamdani, a scholar of African politics, criticizes the ICC for politicizing international justice. He claims that the law is being applied selectively, focusing only on a few poor African countries, thereby calling into question the ICC's universality. "When law is applied selectively," he writes, "the result is not a rule of law but a subordination of law to the dictates of power."[50] Additionally, Mamdani critiques the ICC for pursuing justice at the expense of peace. In his view justice and peace can be reconciled only if the needs of survivors are taken into account. The challenge for Africa is not to disregard justice but to explore forms of justice that can contribute to the resolution of political conflicts. In his view, such justice will prioritize peace over punishment and pursue justice that gives precedence to reconciliation. Mamdani writes, "The real danger of detaching the legal from the political regime and handing it over to human rights fundamentalists is that it will turn the pursuit of justice into revenge-seeking, thereby obstructing the search for reconciliation and a durable peace."[51] Since most atrocities are committed as part of political conflicts, achieving peace will be possible only if communal trust is restored through political reconciliation. Retributive justice is of course essential in a stable, humane world, but legalism alone is insufficient to heal a deeply divided community. In sum, peace and political healing are not inevitable outcomes of legal prosecution. If you want peace, focus on politics; if you want legal accountability, focus on prosecution; and if you desire a just peace, emphasize both political reconciliation and legal accountability.

To further illuminate challenges of transnational prosecution, I turn to the London detention of Augusto Pinochet, the former president of Chile.

CASE 12-2: THE DETENTION OF AUGUSTO PINOCHET

On September 11, 1973, Chile's armed forces toppled the elected government of Salvador Allende. Allende, a Marxist, had instituted radical reforms that resulted in economic recession and widespread unemployment and intensified political cleavages and social fragmentation. By 1973 ideological divisions had become so intense that the country was on the verge of civil war. Thus, few were surprised when Chile's armed forces took control of the state. Originally, there was substantial public support for the coup, especially from professional and business groups who were eager for an end to the chaos that had resulted from the experiment in socialist political economy. Even the center-left Christian Democratic Party (PDC), along with leaders of the Roman Catholic Church, regarded the coup as necessary. Of course the widespread support for the coup was based upon the belief that the military would return power to constitutional authorities as soon as public order had been restored. Few political or professional leaders ever expected that the effects of the coup would last seventeen years.

REGIME ATROCITIES

In carrying out the coup, military authorities imposed swift and total control over all sectors of society. Hundreds of government officials and radical political leaders were immediately imprisoned or killed and many simply disappeared. Of the more than three thousand persons who were killed during the era of military rule, more than one thousand were classified as disappeared detainees (*detenidos desaparecidos*).

Since Marxism was viewed as the cancer that had destroyed Chile's democratic values and traditions, military authorities determined that the only effective solution to this political disease was to eliminate groups committed to Marxist ideology. As Edgardo Boeninger, a former president of the University of Chile, has pointed out, "From the outset, the military government interpreted its mission as a war against Marxism."[52] Accordingly, the government banned the Communist Party and other leftist parties of Allende's UP coalition and sought to eradicate all radical organizations and movements through political repression, including widespread intelligence gathering, censorship of the media, and imprisonment, exile, and killings of leaders and militants. Subsequently, all political parties were suspended and the National Congress dissolved. Although an effort was made to respect judicial authority, the independence of courts was compromised with the imposition of martial law.

In 1974 Pinochet established a secret police force, DINA (Directorate for National Intelligence), to direct the gathering of intelligence and to carry out clandestine operations as a means to depoliticize society. In its first year of operation, DINA focused on the destruction of the MIR, an urban guerrilla organization, and in 1975 and 1976 it sought to eliminate socialist and communist militants.[53] In 1976 Orlando Letelier, Allende's foreign minister and ambassador to the United States, was killed in a Washington, D.C., car bombing. When U.S. law enforcement agents traced the crime to DINA agents, relations between the two countries deteriorated to the point where all U.S. military aid to Chile was suspended. In response to domestic and international criticisms of DINA, Pinochet abolished the covert operations organization in 1977, replacing it with the National Information Center (CNI).[54]

In 1985 opposition groups established an informal political alliance, or National Accord, and two years later created the *Concertación para la Democracia* (Alliance for Democracy)—a fourteen-party coalition whose goal was to restore democracy to Chile. As required by the 1980 constitution, a referendum was held in October 1988 to determine whether the electorate supported eight more years of military rule or whether they wished to end Pinochet's tenure and elect a new president. The referendum, which Pinochet was convinced he would win, resulted in a surprising but resounding victory for the prodemocracy political coalition, with the *Concertación* (the "no" vote) receiving nearly 55 percent of the vote and the pro-Pinochet coalition (the "yes" vote) 43 percent.[55] Because of these results, presidential elections took place a year later. In the elections, Patricio Aylwin, the leader of the Christian Democratic Party and the candidate of the *Concertación*, won a resounding victory with 55 percent of the vote. When Aylwin assumed office in March 1990, democracy was once again restored.

THE RESTORATION OF DEMOCRACY

Since the armed forces remained a powerful political force, the consolidation of democracy needed to proceed with care. Aylwin knew that it was impossible to overturn the 1978 amnesty law, which exempted state crimes from prosecution. He also knew that Pinochet, as head of the Chilean army and member of Chile's Senate, retained significant influence throughout Chilean society. As a result, he decided to pursue accountability through a truth commission. Established by presidential appointment, the eight-member National Commission on Truth and Reconciliation investigated the nature and scope of gross human rights violations, submitting its nine-hundred-page report in February 1991.[56]

A month later, Aylwin, in an important televised speech, disclosed the commission's central finding—namely, that the military regime had been responsible for carrying out a systematic

campaign of political repression that had resulted in the deaths or kidnappings (disappearance) of more than twenty-two hundred persons.[57] After acknowledging regime wrongdoing, the president expressed contrition and indicated that reparations would be granted as a symbol of the state's collective atonement. Aylwin also stressed the importance of focusing on the moral reconstruction of society and the consolidation of democratic institutions. In his view, Chileans should stop looking to the past to find blame and instead should focus on healing and restoration. "It is time for pardon and reconciliation," he said.[58]

In the early 1990s, as the composition of courts began to change, criminal prosecution for past crimes became more feasible. A major victory for human rights activists occurred in 1993 when General Contreras and Brigadier Espinoza, former leaders of DINA, were tried and found guilty.[59] Another pivotal ruling by the High Court was its 1999 decision that the amnesty law did not cover abductions and disappearances because such crimes were unresolved and therefore remained open. This judgment meant that the courts could continue to investigate and prosecute persons allegedly responsible for kidnappings and secret killings if the death of victims had not been certified.

PINOCHET'S LONDON DETENTION

On October 16, 1998, Spanish judge Baltazar Garzón issued an international warrant for the arrest of Senator Pinochet, who was in London recovering from back surgery. The warrant was based on evidence alleging that Pinochet was responsible for the deaths of Spanish citizens in Chile following the 1973 coup. When the Spanish judge was informed that the warrant did not comply with British extradition law, a second warrant was issued charging Pinochet with torture. When Chilean president Eduardo Frei was informed of the arrest, his immediate reaction was to ask why, if the Spanish were so eager to judge others for serious crimes, they had never prosecuted anyone for the crimes committed during the Spanish Civil War.[60] Although many officials in

Chile's government were pleased with Pinochet's arrest, the Chilean government itself was strongly opposed to the extradition, viewing this action as an affront to its political sovereignty. If Pinochet had committed crimes, he should be tried in the country where those crimes had occurred. Pinochet's lawyers for their part challenged the Scotland Yard arrest, claiming that as a former head of state he was immune. A High Court panel of three justices took up the case and ruled that Pinochet was entitled to immunity from civil and criminal proceedings. This decision was immediately appealed to the House of Lords.

In late November 1998, a five-judge panel issued its judgment, ruling 3–2 that there were legal grounds for extraditing Pinochet to Spain.[61] Because extradition is ultimately a process regulated by the British government, not its courts, the Pinochet case was now in the hands of the home secretary, Jack Straw. After carefully weighing legal and humanitarian issues, and keeping in mind the newly elected Labour Party's promise to pursue "an ethical foreign policy,"[62] Straw decided to allow the formal extradition process to commence.

No sooner had this process begun than the House of Lords unanimously set aside the November judgment because of possible bias. The Lords concluded that Lord Hoffman should not have participated in the case because of his close ties to Amnesty International, a human rights NGO. Accordingly, the Lords established a new panel of seven justices who had not participated in the earlier judgment. This new court issued its judgment to a packed House of Lords on March 24, 1999. The 6–1 decision affirmed the earlier judgment that Pinochet had committed extraditable crimes and that his immunity as a former head of state did not protect him from such judgment. With regard to the first claim, the Lords argued that since extraditable crimes had to be crimes under British law, this meant that the only legitimate offenses that were subject to prosecution were those committed after the UK had ratified the Convention against Torture in late 1988. As a result, nearly all of the charges

brought by the Spanish magistrate had to be dismissed, leading him to add thirty-four new cases to the indictment.

On the issue of immunity, the Lords asserted that Pinochet was not immune from prosecution for crimes against humanity. In coming to this conclusion, the justices distinguished between the immunity of a sitting head of state and the immunity of a former public official. An official holding office was entitled to full sovereign immunity (*personae*), a judgment that was as affirmed, as noted earlier, by the ICJ in its Yerodia judgment. However, once a person leaves office, he or she is entitled only to a restrictive immunity, applicable solely to an official's governmental actions. Since Pinochet no longer held public office, he enjoyed only limited immunity. The issue then was whether the crimes allegedly committed by Pinochet were actions that could be considered legitimate state functions. Although the justices provided different justifications and arguments for their answer to this issue, a majority claimed that torture was inconsistent with the office of head of state. Lord Browne-Wilkinson went so far as to argue that torture was a crime against humanity and was therefore a part of the *jus cogens* (a norm from which no state may deviate). He then claimed, "International law provides that offences *jus cogens* may be punished by any state because offenders are 'common enemies of mankind and all nations have an equal interest in their apprehension and prosecution.'"[63]

One month after the Lords issued their ruling, Mr. Straw announced again his decision to allow extradition. When a British court ordered the extradition, Pinochet's lawyers appealed the order, claiming that his health was failing. This led the home secretary to establish a medical panel to examine the senator's medical condition. In early January 2000 the medical panel issued its report, concluding that Pinochet was not fit to stand trial. After additional challenges from Spanish and Belgian authorities, Mr. Straw ruled on March 2 that Pinochet would not be extradited and that he could leave Britain. Pinochet immediately flew to Chile, thereby ending seventeen months of detention.

After Pinochet returned to Chile, judicial authorities led by judge Juan Guzmán sought to prosecute the former president along with senior military personnel.[64] Pinochet was first stripped of senatorial immunity by the country's Supreme Court and then indicted by judge Guzmán—an action that was overruled by the Supreme Court because he had not been deposed, as required by Chilean law. Thus, after being properly deposed and given medical tests, Judge Guzmán indicted Pinochet a second time, placing him under house arrest. This time Santiago's Appeals Court confirmed the indictment but reduced the charges from kidnapping and murder to concealment of the crimes. The quest for a trial finally came to an end in July 2001, when the Appeals Court ruled, based on medical tests, that Pinochet was too infirm to stand trial. Pinochet died in December 2006.

LEGAL ETHICS

It is incontestable that during and after the 1973 coup thousands of Chileans were detained, tortured, kidnapped, and killed. It is also clear that during the seventeen-year era of military rule, the armed forces carried out a campaign of political repression to pacify the country and depoliticize Chilean society, especially in the immediate aftermath of the coup. Following the restoration of democracy in 1990, Chileans remained divided over the nature, causes, and effects of military rule and how best to balance the quest for justice with the restoration of democracy. Foreign observers also differed over what strategy should be pursued to foster the multiple goals of consolidation of the rule of law, political reconciliation, and legal accountability. Who should determine how a society deals with its historical wounds? Should nations be responsible for their own healing, or should the international community intervene when egregious injustices have been committed? If external intervention is appropriate, which state, group of states, or international organization should assume this responsibility? Finally, what role should major powers, international governmental organizations, or leading international NGOs play in pursuing justice and structuring the processes of national healing and political reconciliation?

Although advocacy groups expressed a variety of arguments and views about the Pinochet case, fundamentally actors tended to converge around two alternative perspectives—cosmopolitanism and communitarianism. The cosmopolitans, represented by victims' groups and human rights NGOs, were interested primarily in holding offenders accountable for their crimes. Their focus was chiefly on rectifying past wrongs. Communitarians, by contrast, were more concerned with the restoration of a constitutional order. Their concern was to foster a future-oriented restoration of communal solidarity rooted in political reconciliation and the renewal of political society. Although these two views of how to address past wrongdoing continue to represent some political groups in contemporary Chile, most Chileans today identify with a worldview that combines the two perspectives.

The Pinochet case raises important questions about public policy goals. Does the development of an ethical world require a focus on punishment or prevention? Should the quest to overcome systemic atrocities pursue a forward-looking strategy of reconciliation or a backward-looking strategy of legal accountability? Or should regimes pursue a middle course, like South Africa's strategy of truth and reconciliation—a strategy that promised amnesty for offenders who confessed their guilt? In the Pinochet case, human rights groups were chiefly concerned with legal accountability. For them, impunity was abhorrent, and every effort needed to be made to punish offenders. But others have suggested that the most important task following the restoration of democratic rule was the consolidation of the rule of law to ensure that gross violations of human rights would never recur.

The Pinochet case also highlights the challenge of reconciling legal demands with political realities in global society. Courts normally adjudicate disputes only when they are justiciable— that is, when a conflict involves an alleged violation of law. Since courts in domestic societies are part of the sovereign authority of the state, the issue of politics versus law does not arise often. But in global society, where international law is weak and legal institutions are underdeveloped, identifying the legal dimensions of a conflict is often a difficult task. Indeed, since there is no central authority in the world, whether or not an issue is regarded as legal or political will inevitably be viewed as a political concern. Thus, who should decide which offenses are justiciable? Each member state? The Security Council? Any foreign state that has an interest in prosecuting an alleged offender?

Since legal concepts can be defined and applied in a wide variety of ways, some critics of global legalism argue that law can become an instrument of power politics, resulting not in justice but in "politicized justice." Indeed, the American opposition to universal jurisdiction and more specifically to the ICC is rooted in the fear that law could be used as a political weapon—as a way to prosecute officials who were engaged in actions that necessitated the use of force. Some judges, for example, would like to prosecute Henry Kissinger for war crimes in Southeast Asia, senior NATO officials for war crimes in the 1999 Kosovo war, and senior officials of the Bush administration for their participation in the "war on terror." Similarly, some question why a Spanish judge (Baltazar Garzón) would seek to prosecute General Pinochet when Spain itself had never prosecuted any person for human rights crimes committed during the Spanish civil war and the subsequent dictatorship of General Francisco Franco.[65] Mamdani expresses concern over the dangers of "politicized justice" resulting from the ascendance of the influence of human rights "fundamentalists." For example, he writes that since there is little to distinguish between mass violence unleashed against civilians in African countries like Congo, Liberia, Mozambique, the Ivory Coast, Sierra Leone, and northern Uganda, how are we to decide in which countries "genocide" has occurred? And most importantly, who is to decide this?[66] Since the ICC, as of 2012, has only indicted leaders from Africa, Mamdani questions the legal impartiality of the ICC.

Historically, sovereignty has acted as a barrier against the international prosecution of foreign crimes. Indeed, the act of state doctrine has prevented states from adjudicating offenses committed in other states. But since the Nuremburg and Tokyo military trials at the end of the Second World War, sovereign authority has slowly eroded. This erosion was especially evident in the Pinochet case, when some justices argued that crimes like genocide and torture are offenses against the moral foundations of the world (*jus cogens*) and that every state is bound to prosecute such crimes, regardless of where they occur. But good governance is not secured only by the goals that it pursues. Indeed, constitutional government is a means, not an end. Universal jurisdiction over crimes against humanity may contribute to a just world order, but such a system needs important constraints if it is to succeed. Kissinger has wisely observed, "Any universal system should contain procedures not only to punish the wicked but also to constrain the righteous. It must not allow legal principles to be used as weapons to settle political scores."[67]

If the integrity and impartiality of the law are to be protected, it is important to distinguish between the two realms and to avoid the overuse of law in global society. Barry Gewen wisely notes, "Some issues are simply not adjudicative; courts are inadequate vehicles for dealing with decisions taken at the highest levels, even involving the most heinous of crimes; and much stands to be lost from the increasing inclination to place all political judgment into a legal or pseudo-legal straitjacket."[68] As World War II was ending, Justice Robert Jackson, the chief judge of the Nuremberg Tribunal, agreed with President Truman that it was the executive's responsibility to determine if Nazi leaders should be tried or killed. But he also believed that it was unwise to have show trials simply to give the impression of legal impartiality. Judge Jackson wrote, "We must not use the forms of judicial proceedings to carry out or rationalize previously settled political or military policy."[69] In the final analysis, statesmen should use caution in relying on international courts to address complex, deeply political issues.

MORAL REFLECTIONS

Pinochet's detention represents one of the most important developments in international humanitarian law. The detention was significant because it illustrated the moral conflict between the sovereign authority of states and the promotion and protection of international human rights. The Pinochet case did not resolve the sovereignty–human rights tension, but it did illuminate the important arena of human rights protection. Following are key moral issues relating to this case:

- Confronting regime wrongdoing is a difficult responsibility. In seeking to pursue legal accountability, national reconciliation, and the consolidation of the rule of law and democratic government, how should a nation pursue these multiple goals? Should a government pursue all simultaneously or should it give precedence to one or more?

- When states are incapable or unwilling to prosecute offenders of gross human rights crimes, should this responsibility devolve to other states or to international organizations?
- Are some crimes so offensive to global human values that any state should be entitled to prosecute them? Given the existing institutions in global society, is universal jurisdiction desirable? Is it likely to advance justice and peace? Why or why not?
- Robertson writes, "The Pinochet case was momentous because—for the first time—sovereign immunity was not allowed to become sovereign impunity."[70] Did the detention of Pinochet advance the cause of human rights? Why or why not?

SUMMARY

Even though the scope of global governance has expanded rapidly in recent decades, the international community's institutions remain politically underdeveloped. The world remains a decentralized community where states—not IGOs, NGOs, religious movements, or advocacy networks—are the primary actors. Consequently, promoting the global common good ultimately involves cooperative action among states, especially the largest, most powerful, and most economically developed countries. But devising shared strategies on environmental protection or any other important global good is especially challenging since it demands that statesmen balance national interests with global goods, or short-term needs with long-terms concerns.

The limitations of global governance are especially evident in promoting human dignity. Despite an expansion in humanitarian international law, gross human rights abuses persist, especially when ethnic and religious groups compete for political power or when regimes pursue political repression. In order to address continued human rights abuses, a growing number of groups and states have supported the expansion of international criminal law. This expansion, expressed most recently in the doctrine of universal jurisdiction and the creation of the ICC, is receiving growing international support. But these legal innovations may be premature. Until states cede more sovereignty and create institutions to make and enforce law, the international adjudication of crime will have only a marginal impact on global society.

Conclusion

Ethics Matters

Politics will, to the end of history, be an area where conscience and power meet, where the ethical and coercive factors of human life will interpenetrate and work out their tentative and uneasy compromises.[1]
—REINHOLD NIEBUHR

Saints can be pure, but statesmen, alas, must be responsible.[2]
—ARTHUR SCHLESINGER

There is no single operational international code of behavior. There are competing codes, rival philosophical traditions, clashing conceptions of morality. . . . It is true, as some point out, that all statesmen use the same moral language. . . . Unfortunately, from the point of view of moral harmony, this is meaningless. A community of vocabulary is not the same thing as a community of values.[3]
—STANLEY HOFFMANN

E THICS MATTERS. Although most international relations are carried out by complex entities called states, these political communities bear moral responsibilities domestically and internationally. Domestically, states are just and legitimate to the extent that they fulfill widely accepted international moral obligations, such as the protection of human rights and the promotion of the social and economic well-being of persons. Internationally, states are morally legitimate to the extent that they fulfill their legal and ethical responsibilities as members of global society. These duties include honoring the sovereignty and territorial integrity of other states, the pursuit of peaceful foreign relations, the promotion of international stability and global justice, and the protection of the global environment.

The realist tradition has commonly regarded international relations as an arena dominated by the quest for security and by the instruments of power and force. Although security is a core national interest, survival is not the only goal of states. Indeed, most global politics involves the pursuit of many different individual and collective interests through a variety of means other than power. Because the conceptualization of national interests and the development and implementation of policies are based on moral values and ethical judgments, political decision making is of necessity a moral enterprise—a truth that is regularly confirmed by contemporary international events. For example, after India and Pakistan carried out nuclear tests in mid-1998, thereby confirming their status as nuclear powers, the U.S. government was faced with the challenge of responding to this dangerous development. Political calculations were involved in determining how the U.S. government should confront India and Pakistan in their violation of the nonproliferation regime. However, moral reasoning was also involved as decision makers pondered the short- and long-term implications of these developments. The U.S. government's decisions to provide famine relief to North Korea in 1997 and 1998 and to continue comprehensive economic sanctions against Iraq in the aftermath of the Persian Gulf War were similarly rooted in moral judgments. Clearly, the claim of moral skeptics that power and necessity alone dictate international politics is unpersuasive.

As Reinhold Niebuhr's statement at the beginning of this chapter suggests, political decision making is a domain in which morality and power coalesce. This study has sought to defend the Niebuhrian claim by exploring the nature and role of moral values in international relations. The aim has not been to provide "moral" solutions to major international issues. Rather, the goal has been to define concepts, strategies, and ethical traditions that facilitate moral reflection about international relations and to illustrate the role of political morality in global politics with case studies in five major problem areas: human rights, force, intervention, economic sanctions, and global issues.

As noted throughout this study, moral values are essential in developing a sound foreign policy and creating norms and structures that are conducive to a more peaceful and just global society. As ancient philosophers long ago observed, the good life (*summum bonum*) is based on individual and communal justice. A major aim of international ethics is to foster political justice within and among states by illuminating relevant moral norms and structuring moral reasoning. This task is especially daunting because global society is comprised of many states, each with its own cultural norms and conceptions of morality. However, the existence of cultural pluralism does not invalidate either the quest for international justice or the legitimacy of political morality. Rather, the reality of competing cultures and moral traditions provides an environment for encouraging a deeper, more reflective political morality and a more self-critical application of such morality to international affairs.

One of the reasons for scholars' and decision makers' limited concern with international ethics is the belief that politics and moral reasoning are two distinct realms that should not be integrated: politics is a domain of power and communitywide decision making, whereas ethics, as a branch of philosophy, is a domain of speculative reasoning. It is commonly assumed that whereas the task of the moral philosopher is to explore the nature of morality and the basis of moral obligation, the task of the statesman is to foster global order, facilitate transnational cooperation, and promote peaceful conflict resolution. These two tasks, it is sometimes argued, should not be combined if analysis and decision making are to remain logical and internally consistent. However, applied ethics, by definition, seeks to develop moral reasoning in specific areas of public and private life. Thus, international ethics is concerned with the interrelationship of moral values and foreign policy, ethics and international politics.

Of course, not all issues, claims, and arguments in international relations are concerned with ethics. As noted in chapter 1, ethics involves the identification, critique, and application of moral values to human life. International ethics is thus concerned solely with the normative realm, that is, with choices and actions involving right and wrong, good and evil. Nonmoral concerns—such as historical facts about territorial boundary claims or the international law of the sea or empirical facts about the balance of trade, weapons development programs, or environmental protection rules—are not a central focus of international ethics because descriptive issues do not involve normative judgments. Thus, in bringing moral reasoning to bear on international affairs, it is important to distinguish between the empirical and normative realms and then to identify and apply political morality to particular foreign policy issues or global concerns.

The challenge of differentiating between the empirical and normative realms is illustrated by the phenomenon of global warming, a development brought about partly by human-made greenhouse gases that trap solar heat. Knowledge about the nature, causes, and potential effects of global warming is based on science and thus is not subject to moral judgment. By contrast, defining the nature and extent of states' responsibilities for global warming is a normative issue because the individual and collective behaviors of states are partly responsible for the earth's climate. In view of the effects of greenhouse emissions on the earth's temperature, continued industrialization is likely to encourage further climate change. Thus, the potential adverse effects of increased global warming pose major moral concerns about states' individual and collective responsibility for past greenhouse emissions and for curbing future pollution.

In fostering moral reasoning and ethical decision making, statesmen and moralists employ a variety of approaches that rely on different methodologies, strategies, and ethical traditions. In classifying moral decision making, it is helpful to distinguish between those approaches that apply political morality deductively and those that do so inductively. The first approach is essentially a "top-down" methodology, bringing first principles to bear on specific issues and problems. Fundamentally, it is a rule-based strategy and is characterized by a highly structured decision-making process, relying heavily on moral theories. This approach is deductive because it begins with core norms and then applies them to particular issues and problems.

The application of the just war tradition to issues of war and peace illustrates this approach. As one of the most sophisticated and comprehensive moral theories in international relations, the just war tradition defines norms by which to assess when and how states may employ force in pursuing political justice. As a moral theory of decision making, the just war tradition provides an understanding of statecraft in which the use of force in the service of justice is "both permitted and restrained."[4] Because the just war doctrine is based on the quest for interstate justice, the doctrine's concepts and propositions are useful in assessing not only issues of war and peace but also other international relations concerns, such as economic sanctions and humanitarian intervention.[5]

The second approach to ethical decision making is inductive and informal, relying on a variety of concepts and strategies. It is a "bottom-up" methodology that applies morality flexibly to the goals, means, and results of decisions, relying mainly on the ends-based and tridimensional strategies described in chapter 4. Because this approach is less structured than the deductive model, it relies on prudence to integrate morality into foreign policy decision making. According to realist scholars, this inductive, prudential approach to decision making is politically and morally superior to an approach based on a priori guidelines because it permits flexibility in addressing the dynamic, ever-changing events of global society.

Both the deductive and the inductive decision-making models are ideal types, representing extremes along a continuum. Because most moral reasoning and decision making in international affairs involve elements from both models, most international ethical analysis will be found in the middle of the continuum. In implementing decision making rooted in both deductive and inductive approaches, it is desirable to adhere to procedural rules that ensure moral accountability. As noted in chapter 4, a flexible, inductive approach can quickly lead to consequentialism if the integrity of decision making is not protected.

Regardless of which decision-making approaches and ethical traditions are applied to international affairs, it is clear that virtually all important foreign policy issues and global concerns involve moral values. Although politically salient issues such as disarmament, Third World poverty, gross human rights abuses, air and water pollution, and war clearly involve political morality, even technical problems and politically neutral issues might involve moral judgments. Indeed, because political life is based on human choices, few national and international concerns can bypass normative judgments. Moreover, in bringing political morality to bear on public policies, decision makers must judge moral action not only in terms of outcomes, as is commonly the case, but also in terms of the intended goals and methods used. Thus, developing a moral foreign policy is challenging precisely because few issues are likely to be fully moral at the three dimensions of policy making—that is, at the levels of goals, means, and outcomes.

Given the complexity of most global issues, ethical reasoning in international affairs seldom results in simple moral verdicts. Indeed, the explicit integration of political morality with the development and implementation of foreign policies rarely results in consensus among public officials and citizens. However, this lack of agreement does not imply (as some cynics have suggested) that moral standards do not exist in global politics, that moral analysis is unnecessary in foreign affairs, or that ethical decision making is a wholly subjective, relativistic enterprise. To be sure, the absence of agreement in international ethics is sometimes due to the underdeveloped nature of global morality. However, the lack of consensus in international ethics is often based on disputes over facts and interests, not moral values. As a result, what appears to be a dispute over political ethics might be, in reality, a conflict over different interpretations of facts or different assessments of political strategies.

For example, the mid-1980s global debate over the moral appropriateness of economic sanctions against South Africa was rooted mainly in different views of the political effectiveness of such statecraft, not in different perspectives on apartheid. Some apartheid critics favored sanctions in the belief that they would hasten democratic reform in South Africa; others opposed sanctions because they believed that isolating South Africa would only delay political change. Similarly, the failure of the United

States and other major Western powers to respond to ethnic cleansing in the Bosnian war was partly due to strategic calculations about the costs, feasibility, and likely consequences of military intervention and partly due to a lack of moral courage to act on behalf of the common good. However, the international community's inaction toward the Bosnian genocide was also influenced by the widely disparate interpretations about the nature and causes of the war and the nature, sources, and scope of ethnic violence. Some viewed ethnic cleansing mainly as a Serb strategy to destroy the Muslim people and their culture; others viewed ethnic violence as part of a war among Croats, Muslims, and Serbs over whether and how to construct a multiethnic Bosnian state.[6] Although most Western observers viewed Serbs as the major perpetrators of Bosnian violence, by 1995 it was evident that Croats and Muslims had also been involved in widespread ethnic killing. Thus, the reticence and ineffectiveness of the United Nations in halting Bosnian violence was based in part on the perceived complexity and ambiguity of the conflict itself.

Although lack of knowledge might inhibit people from confronting gross evil in global society, the main obstacle to a vigorous application of international political ethics is behavioral, not intellectual. It is not the absence of empirical and moral knowledge that contributes to injustice and instability in global society; rather, leaders themselves fail to fulfill perceived moral obligations. One scholar has observed that in moral life "ignorance isn't all that common; dishonesty is far more so."[7] Thus, in developing a more humane and just global society, the great challenge is to develop both moral knowledge and personal character that leads to the fulfillment of foundational moral obligations. Applying international ethics will require knowledge of relevant concepts, strategies, and theories of international political morality. However, it will also involve the cultivation of moral character and human virtue that are essential in the moral life. If international ethics is to contribute to a more humane and just world order, citizens and leaders must possess the wisdom to define international justice and the courage to fulfill its moral obligations.

Notes

INTRODUCTION

1. Edward Hallett Carr, *The Twenty Years' Crisis, 1919–1939: An Introduction to the Study of International Relations* (New York: Harper Torchbooks, 1964), 146.

2. George F. Kennan, "Morality and Foreign Policy," *Foreign Affairs* 64 (Winter 1985/1986): 206.

3. Arnold Wolfers, *Discord and Collaboration: Essays on International Politics* (Baltimore, Md.: Johns Hopkins University Press, 1962), 58.

4. In 2011, the United Nations appointed its former secretary-general Kofi Annan as special envoy to Syria to help broker a peace accord. Annan, however, was unable to halt the fighting or facilitate political accommodation between the antagonists. Because of the lack of international support and the unwillingness of the government and rebels to pursue a peaceful compromise, Annan terminated his peace-seeking mission in August 2012.

CHAPTER 1: MORALITY AND FOREIGN POLICY

1. Arnold Wolfers, *Discord and Collaboration: Essays on International Politics* (Baltimore, Md.: Johns Hopkins University Press, 1962), 58.

2. James Q. Wilson, "What Is Moral and How Do We Know It?" *Commentary* (June 1993): 43.

3. Sir Harold Nicolson, *Diplomacy*, 3rd ed. (New York: Oxford University Press, 1973), 147.

4. Dean Acheson, "Ethics in International Relations Today: Our Standard of Conduct," *Vital Speeches of the Day* 31 (February 1, 1965): 227.

5. Thomas Donaldson, "Kant's Global Rationalism," in *Traditions of International Ethics*, ed. Terry Nardin and David R. Mapel (Cambridge: Cambridge University Press, 1992), 137.

6. R. M. Hare, *Freedom and Reason* (Oxford: Oxford University Press, 1963), 15.

7. John Rawls, *A Theory of Justice* (Cambridge, Mass.: Harvard University Press, 1971). For a further elaboration of Rawls's conceptualization of morality, see "The Nature and Bases of Political Morality" in this chapter.

8. Lord Moulton of Bank, "Law and Manners," quoted in Rushworth M. Kidder, *How Good People Make Tough Choices* (New York: Morrow, 1995), 67.

9. For a discussion of the distinction between moral and nonmoral decision-making realms, see William Frankena, *Ethics*, 2nd ed. (Englewood Cliffs, N.J.: Prentice Hall, 1973).

10. Lea Brilmayer, *American Hegemony: Political Morality in a One Superpower World* (New Haven, Conn.: Yale University Press, 1994), 25.

11. It is interesting to note that a major aim of normative political theory has been to define the nature, scope, methods, duties, and constraints involved in just or legitimate political rule. Political thinkers have given many different justifications for political hierarchies, including knowledge, power, consent, social class, and religious fidelity.

12. For an example of how personal morality can be integrated in political life, see Mark Amstutz, *The Healing of Nations: The Promise and Limits of Political Forgiveness* (Boulder, Colo.: Rowman & Littlefield, 2005).

13. Michael Walzer, *Just and Unjust Wars: A Moral Argument with Historical Illustrations* (New York: Basic Books, 1977).

14. Charles Beitz, *Political Theory and International Relations* (Princeton, N.J.: Princeton University Press, 1979).

15. George Kennan, *Realities of American Foreign Policy* (New York: Norton, 1966), 48.

16. John Rawls, *The Law of Peoples* (Cambridge, Mass.: Harvard University Press, 1999). Rawls first presented his ideas in a lecture titled "The Law of Peoples," published in *On Human Rights: The Oxford Amnesty Lectures, 1993*, ed. Stephen Shute and Susan Hurley (New York: Basic Books, 1993), 41–82. For a penetrating critique of Rawls's argument, see Stanley Hoffmann, "Dreams of a Just World," *New York Review of Books*, November 2, 1995, 52–56.

17. See, for example, David Gauthier, *Morals by Agreement* (Oxford: Oxford University Press, 1986).

18. Terry Nardin, "Ethical Traditions in International Affairs" in *Traditions*, ed. Nardin and Mapel, 12–13.

19. Dorothy V. Jones, *Code of Peace: Ethics and Security in the World of Warlord States* (Chicago: University of Chicago Press, 1992).

20. Michael Walzer, *Thick and Thin: Moral Argument at Home and Abroad* (Notre Dame, Ind.: University of Notre Dame Press, 1994), 1–19.

21. Walzer, *Thick and Thin*, 8.

22. Francis V. Harbour, "Basic Moral Values: A Shared Core," *Ethics & International Affairs* 9 (1995): 155–70.

23. A. J. M. Milne, "Human Rights and the Diversity of Morals: A Philosophical Analysis of Rights and Obligations in the Global System," in *Rights and Obligations in North–South Relations: Ethical Dimensions of Global Problems*, ed. Moorehead Wright (New York: St. Martin's, 1986), 21.

24. Walzer, *Just and Unjust Wars*, 19.

25. Thomas Donaldson, *The Ethics of International Business* (New York: Oxford University Press, 1989), 1.

26. John C. Bennett, *Foreign Policy in Christian Perspective* (New York: Scribner, 1966), 36.

27. David Halloran Lumsdaine, *Moral Vision in International Politics: The Foreign Aid Regime, 1949–1989* (Princeton, N.J.: Princeton University Press, 1993), 283.

28. Lumsdaine, *Moral Vision*, 287.

29. Robert W. McElroy, *Morality and American Foreign Policy* (Princeton, N.J.: Princeton University Press, 1992), 30.

30. William Wilberforce labored for nearly fifteen years in the House of Commons before the slave trade was outlawed in 1807; he then devoted his remaining eighteen years in Parliament to the emancipation of slaves within the British Empire. On July 29, 1833, eight years after Wilberforce retired from Parliament, the House of Commons passed a bill abolishing slavery.

31. See Stuart Eizenstat, *Imperfect Justice: Looted Assets, Slave Labor, and the Unfinished Business of World War II* (New York: PublicAffairs, 2006).

32. Robert Kennedy, *Thirteen Days* (New York: Norton, 1968), 27.

33. Arthur Schlesinger Jr., "The Necessary Amorality of Foreign Affairs," *Harper's Magazine*, August 1971, 73.

34. Stanley Hoffmann, *Duties beyond Borders* (Syracuse, N.Y.: Syracuse University Press, 1981), 33.

35. For a description of the nature and effect of the Serb conquest of Kosovo, see Noel Malcolm, *Kosovo: A Short History* (New York: Harper Perennial, 1999), 238–63.

36. Warren Zimmerman, "Milosevic's Final Solution," *New York Review of Books*, June 10, 1999, 41.

37. Misha Glenny, *The Fall of Yugoslavia: The Third Balkans War*, 3rd rev. ed. (New York: Penguin, 1996), 67.

38. The disintegration of Albania occurred in response to the collapse of the nation's economy after citizens discovered that their retirement savings had been squandered in fictitious, pyramid-type (Ponzi) investment schemes.

39. It is estimated that when war erupted in March 1999, there were more than forty thousand Serb military and police personnel in Kosovo.

40. Stanley Hoffmann, "What Is to Be Done?" *New York Review of Books*, May 6, 1999, 17.

41. Besides the United States, this group included Britain, France, Germany, Italy, and Russia.

42. The Rambouillet accord was based in great part on a plan developed by Christopher Hill, the U.S. ambassador to Macedonia. The plan, which was rooted in the Serb–Kosovar negotiations that he had carried out in 1998, called for Kosovo's autonomy but left the issue of sovereignty undefined. See Malcolm, *Kosovo*, "Preface."

43. See Michael Mandelbaum, "Leave Kosovo Issue on the Table," *Newsday*, March 9, 1999, 35.

44. Zimmerman, "Milosevic's Final Solution," 41.

45. Tim Judah, *Kosovo: War and Revenge* (New Haven, Conn.: Yale University Press, 2000), 84.

46. Quoted in Mark Danner, "Kosovo: The Meaning of Victory," *New York Review of Books*, July 15, 1999, 53.

47. Michael Ignatieff, "Annals of Diplomacy: Balkan Physics," *New Yorker*, May 10, 1999, 78.

48. Vaclav Havel, "Kosovo and the End of the Nation-State," *New York Review of Books*, June 10, 1999, 6.

49. Havel, "Kosovo and the End of the Nation-State," 6.

50. Henry A. Kissinger, "New World Disorder," *Newsweek*, May 31, 1999, 43.

51. Some have argued that Operation Horseshoe was part of a Serbian long-term strategy of forcefully deporting Albanians from Kosovo in order to make the province a more homogenous ethnic community and thereby prepare it to be incorporated into an ethnically pure community prior to its integration into a Greater Serbia. While Serbia may have planned to carry out this operation irrespective of NATO action, it is clear, nevertheless, that if NATO's air war did not initiate widespread ethnic cleansing, it at least greatly accelerated the systematic deportation of hundreds of thousands of Kosovars.

52. Judah, *Kosovo*, 250.

53. Leon Wieseltier, "Force without Force: Saving NATO, Losing Kosovo," *New Republic*, April 26 and May 3, 1999, 29.

54. Paul W. Kahn, "War and Sacrifice in Kosovo," *Report from the Institute for Philosophy & Public Policy*, Spring/Summer 1999, 4.

55. Kissinger, "New World Disorder," 43.

56. Havel, "Kosovo and the End of the Nation-State," 6.

CHAPTER 2: ETHICS AND GLOBAL SOCIETY

1. Michael Ignatieff, "The Return of Sovereignty," *New Republic*, February 16, 2012, 28.

2. Brad R. Roth, *Sovereign Equality and Moral Disagreement: Premises of a Pluralist International Legal Order* (New York: Oxford University Press, 2011), 143.

3. Peter Singer, *One World: The Ethics of Globalization*, 2nd ed. (New Haven, Conn.: Yale University Press, 2002), 148.

4. Hedley Bull, *The Anarchical Society: A Study in Order in World Politics* (New York: Columbia University Press, 2002).

5. Stanley Hoffmann, "The Crisis of Liberal Internationalism," *Foreign Policy*, no. 98 (Spring 1995): 160.

6. The domestic analogy is based on the comparison of international society to domestic order. The a priori rights and duties of states are viewed as comparable to the rights and duties of citizens in prepolitical society, that is, the state of nature.

7. Examples of communitarian thinkers include seventeenth-century German international lawyer Samuel Pufendorf, eighteenth-century Swiss jurist Emmerich de Vattel, nineteenth-century British political theorist John Stuart Mill, and contemporary political philosopher Michael Walzer. For a recent normative justification of the existing international system, see Mervyn Frost, *Ethics in International Relations: A Constitutive Theory* (Cambridge: Cambridge University Press, 1996). Frost's "constitutive theory" provides a normative justification for the communitarian perspective.

8. Examples of cosmopolitan thinkers include sixteenth-century Spanish theologian Francisco Suarez, nineteenth-century German philosopher Immanuel Kant, and contemporary political philosopher Henry Shue. One of the most influential contemporary expositions of this perspective is Charles Beitz, *Political Theory and International Relations* (Princeton, N.J.: Princeton University Press, 1979). For a more recent comprehensive account of the cosmopolitan perspective, see Allen Buchanan, *Justice, Legitimacy, and Self-Determination: Moral Foundations for International Law* (New York: Oxford University Press, 2004).

9. Kwame Anthony Appiah, *Cosmopolitanism: Ethics in a World of Strangers* (New York: Norton, 2006), xv.

10. For a comparative assessment of cosmopolitan and communitarian perspectives, see Chris Brown, *International Relations Theory: New Normative Approaches* (New York: Columbia University Press, 1992).

11. Brown, *International Relations Theory*, 110.

12. For a full exposition of this position, see Beitz, *Political Theory and International Relations*, which applies John Rawls's theory of justice to international affairs.

13. Anne-Marie Slaughter, "The New Foreign Policy Frontier," *The Atlantic*, July 27, 2011. Available at http://www.theatlantic.com/international/archive/2011/07/the-new-foreign-policy-frontier/242593.

14. John Rawls, *A Theory of Justice* (Cambridge, Mass.: Harvard University Press, 1971). The theory is based on impartiality (or what Rawls terms "the veil of ignorance") and structured around two core principles. The first he calls Maximum Equal Liberty and the second Equal Opportunity and Difference. Rawls argues that the principle of liberty, which is affirmed through civil rights and constitutional norms, is fundamental because it ensures that individuals have the maximum freedom to fulfill their wants. His second principle suggests that social and economic benefits should be the result of fair competition and distributed so that all receive equal gain, unless differences helped those at the bottom of the social ladder. In effect, income inequalities are justified only to the extent that the poorest people also benefit from transactions.

15. John Rawls, *The Law of Peoples* (Cambridge, Mass.: Harvard University Press, 1999).

16. Rawls, *Law of Peoples*, 83.

17. Rawls, *Law of Peoples*, 35.

18. Rawls, *Law of Peoples*, 37.

19. Singer, *One World*, 12.

20. Singer, *One World*, 9.

21. Singer, *One World*, 199.

22. Peter Singer, *The Life You Can Save* (New York: Random House, 2010), 12.

23. Singer, *The Life You Can Save*, 152.

24. According to the *Economist*, the number of people who have been lifted out of poverty from 1981 to 2010 is 660 million. This unprecedented reduction in Chinese poverty has helped to meet the UN Millennium Development Goal of halving world poverty in 2010—five years ahead of schedule. See "A Fall to Cheer," *Economist*, March 3, 2012, 81.

25. Paul Collier, *The Bottom Billion: Why the Poorest Countries Are Failing and What Can Be Done about It* (New York: Oxford University Press, 2007).

26. Robert McNamara, *One Hundred Countries, Two Billion People* (New York: Praeger, 1973), 6–8.

27. United Nations Development Programme, *Human Development Report, 1990*, chap. 2. See http://hdr.undp.org/en/reports/global/hdr1990.

28. The index is a numerical coefficient between 0 and 1, with low numbers suggesting poverty and high numbers suggesting prosperity.

29. United Nations, *Human Development Report, 2011*. The data are from "Human Development Index Trends, 1980–2011." Available at http://hdr.undp.org/en.

30. According to economist Martin Wolf, the ratio of per capita income between the richest and poorest countries in 1913 was fifteen to one, by 1950 the ratio had increased to twenty-six to one, and by 2000 it had grown to seventy-one to one. See Martin Wolf, *Why Globalization Works* (New Haven, Conn.: Yale University Press, 2004), 44.

31. Wolf, *Why Globalization Works*, 172.

32. Collier, *The Bottom Billion*, 3.

33. Andre Gunder Frank, *Latin America Underdevelopment or Revolution* (New York: Monthly Review Press, 1969), chap. 1.

34. See Singer, *A Life You Can Save*, noted previously; see also Thomas Pogge, *World Poverty and Human Rights: Cosmopolitan Responsibilities and Reforms*, 2nd ed. (Malden, Mass.: Polity Press, 2008) and Thomas Pogge, *Politics as Usual: What Lies behind the Pro-Poor Rhetoric* (Malden, Mass.: Polity Press, 2010).

35. Robert Heilbroner, "The Triumph of Capitalism," *New Yorker* (January 23, 1989), 98.

36. United Nations Development Programme, *Human Development Report, 2007/2008* (New York: Palgrave Macmillan, 2007), 280.

37. Henry Shue, *Basic Rights: Subsistence, Affluence, and U.S. Foreign Policy* (Princeton, N.J.: Princeton University Press, 1980).

38. Pogge, *World Poverty and Human Rights*, and Pogge, *Politics as Usual*.

39. Singer first articulated this perspective in an influential essay published in response to the massive famine in Bangladesh. In the essay Singer argued that societies with resources had a moral obligation to relieve human suffering when they were able to do so. See Peter Singer, "Famine, Affluence, and Morality," *Philosophy and Public Affairs* 1 (Spring 1972): 229–43.

40. According to the parable, a traveler was attacked, robbed, and injured severely. Subsequently, a priest and a Levite passed by the victim but they did not help; only a Samaritan—a member of an outcast group—stopped and assisted the injured victim. See Luke 10:29–37.

41. Rawls, *The Law of Peoples*, 106.

42. Amartya Sen, *Development as Freedom* (New York: Knopf, 1999). See, especially, the introduction and chaps. 1 and 2.

43. Don Eberly, *The Rise of Global Civil Society: Building Communities and Nations from the Bottom Up* (New York: Encounter Books, 2008), 58–61.

44. Singer, *One World*, 180.

CHAPTER 3: THE ROLE OF ETHICAL TRADITIONS

1. Charles R. Beitz, "The Reagan Doctrine in Nicaragua," in *Problems of International Justice*, ed. Steven Luper-Foy (Boulder, Colo.: Westview Press, 1988), 194.

2. Joseph S. Nye Jr., "Redefining the National Interest," *Foreign Affairs* 78 (July/August 1999): 24.

3. Peter Berger, "Moral Judgment and Political Action," *Vital Speeches of the Day* 56 (December 1, 1987): 120.

4. Gordon A. Craig and Alexander L. George, *Force and Statecraft: Diplomatic Problems of Our Time*, 2nd ed. (New York: Oxford University Press, 1990), 275–88.

5. Terry Nardin, "Ethical Traditions in International Affairs," in *Traditions of International Ethics*, ed. Terry Nardin and David R. Mapel (Cambridge: Cambridge University Press, 1992), 6.

6. Nardin, "Ethical Traditions," 6.

7. Nardin, "Ethical Traditions," 6. Interestingly, the tradition of prudence, rooted in the political thought of Aristotle and Aquinas and developed subsequently by Edmund Burke and others, is omitted in this study.

8. David A. Welch, "Can We Think Systematically about Ethics and Statecraft?" *Ethics & International Affairs* 8 (1994): 26–27.

9. Welch, "Can We Think Systematically about Ethics and Statecraft?" 33.

10. See J. L. Mackie, *Ethics: Inventing Right and Wrong* (New York: Penguin, 1977), 64.

11. Hans J. Morgenthau, *Politics among Nations: The Struggle for Power and Peace*, 5th ed., rev. (New York: Random House, 1978).

12. Morgenthau, *Politics among Nations*, 5.

13. Kenneth Waltz, *Theory of International Politics* (Reading, Pa.: Addison-Wesley, 1979), 118.

14. Steven Forde, "Classical Realism," in *Traditions of International Ethics*, ed. Nardin and Mapel, 63.

15. Jack Donnelly, "Twentieth-Century Realism," in *Traditions of International Ethics*, ed. Nardin and Mapel, 93.

16. George F. Kennan, "Morality and Foreign Policy," *Foreign Affairs* 64 (Winter 1985/1986): 206.

17. Morgenthau, *Politics among Nations*, 12.

18. For a clear articulation of these three justifications, see U.S. Department of State, Bureau of Public Affairs, "The Decision to Assist Grenada," January 24, 1984. In this statement, Langhorne Motley, the assistant secretary of state for inter-American affairs, explains to the House Armed Services Committee why the United States intervened in Grenada.

19. The U.S. government deemed this request for collective defense as consistent with Article 52 of the UN Charter, Articles 22 and 28 of the OAS Charter, and Article 8 of the OECS Treaty.

20. See, for example, John Norton Moore, "Grenada and the International Double Standard," *American Journal of International Law* 78 (January 1984): 148–49.

21. Alberto R. Coll, "Why Grenada Was Important," *Naval War College Review* 40 (Summer 1987): 4–13.

22. Terry Nardin and Kathleen D. Pritchard, "Ethics and Intervention: The United States in Grenada, 1983," *Case Studies in Ethics and International Affairs*, no. 2 (New York: Carnegie Council on Ethics and International Affairs, 1990), 7.

23. Coll, "Why Grenada Was Important," 7–8.

24. See, for example, Christopher C. Joyner, "The United States Action in Grenada," *American Journal of International Law* 78 (January 1984): 131–44, and Francis A. Boyle et al., "International Lawlessness in Grenada," *American Journal of International Law* 78 (January 1984): 172–75.

25. According to Chapter VII of the UN Charter, the Security Council is the institution responsible for determining when threats to international security exist and what actions are to be taken in response to those threats. When the United States intervened in Somalia in December 1992 to halt starvation and in Haiti in October 1994 to restore to power the elected president, Jean-Bertrand Aristide, it did so with the approval of the Security Council. Similarly, in 2012 NATO intervened militarily in Libya to protect civilians with the authorization of the Security Council.

26. Michael W. Doyle, *Ways of War and Peace: Realism, Liberalism, and Socialism* (New York: Norton, 1997), 415.

27. Doyle, *Ways of War and Peace*, 413.

28. For an excellent overview of the ideas and implementation of the Reagan Doctrine, see James M. Scott, *Deciding to Intervene: The Reagan Doctrine and American Foreign Policy* (Durham, N.C.: Duke University Press, 1996).

29. For an overview of different types of liberalism, see Doyle, *Ways of War and Peace*, pt. 2. Doyle differentiates among three types of liberalism in international relations thought: first, institutionalists, such as Locke and Bentham, who emphasize the role of human nature and the necessity of institutions to constrain human passions; second, commercial pacifists, such as Adam Smith and Joseph Schumpeter, who believe that trade is conducive to peace; and third, internationalists, such as Kant and Hume, who emphasize the pacific nature of international relations among constitutional regimes.

30. For a discussion of Kant's system, see Doyle, *Ways of Peace and War*, 252–58.

31. For a discussion of political idealism in international affairs, see Michael Joseph Smith, "Liberalism and International Reform," in *Traditions of International Ethics*, ed. Nardin and Mapel, 201–24.

32. Smith, "Liberalism and International Reform," 203.

33. E. H. Carr, *The Twenty Years' Crisis, 1919–1939: An Introduction to the Study of International Relations* (New York: Harper Torchbooks, 1964), 41–60.

34. Zbigniew Brzezinski, *Power and Principle: Memoirs of the National Security Adviser, 1977–1981* (New York: Farrar, Straus & Giroux), 49.

35. R. J. Vincent, "The Response of Europe and the Third World to United States Human Rights Diplomacy," in *The Diplomacy of Human Rights*, ed. David D. Newsom (Lanham, Md.: University Press of America, 1986), 36.

36. For a description and assessment of congressional human rights initiatives throughout the 1970s, see John P. Salzberg, "A View from the Hill: U.S. Legislation and Human Rights," in *The Diplomacy of Human Rights*, ed. Newsom, 13–20.

37. Jimmy Carter, "Power for Humane Purposes," in *Morality and Foreign Policy: A Symposium on President Carter's Stance*, ed. Ernest Lefever (Washington, D.C.: Ethics and Public Policy Center, 1977), 4–5.

38. Hendrik Hertzberg, quoted in Joshua Muravchik, *The Uncertain Crusade: Jimmy Carter and the Dilemmas of Human Rights Policy* (New York: Hamilton Press, 1986), 1.

39. The increased importance of the report is partly evident by its expanded breadth and depth, growing from about 137 pages in 1977 to more than 1,100 pages in 1981.

40. Quoted in Muravchik, *The Uncertain Crusade*, 24.

41. Irving Kristol, "Morality, Liberalism, and Foreign Policy," in *Morality and Foreign Policy*, ed. Lefever, 69.

42. Brzezinski, *Power and Principle*, 126.

43. Brzezinski, *Power and Principle*, 528.

44. Muravchik, *The Uncertain Crusade*, 53–73.

45. Jeane Kirkpatrick, "Human Rights and American Foreign Policy: A Symposium," *Commentary*, November 1981, 43.

46. Carr, *The Twenty Years' Crisis*, 93.

47. Hans J. Morgenthau, *Scientific Man versus Power Politics* (Chicago: University of Chicago Press, 1965), 203.

48. Charles Krauthammer, *Democratic Realism: An American Foreign Policy for a Unipolar World* (Washington, D.C.: American Enterprise Institute, 2004). For further comments on Krauthammer's 2004 Irving Kristol Lecture, see Francis Fukuyama, "The Neoconservative Moment," *National Interest*, Summer 2004, 57–68; Charles Krauthammer, "In Defense of Democratic Realism," *National Interest*, Fall 2004, 15–22; and Robert Cooper, "Imperial Liberalism," *National Interest*, Spring 2005, 25–34.

49. Anatol Lieven and John Hulsman, *Ethical Realism: A Vision for America's Role in the World* (New York: Pantheon, 2006), 67–83.

50. *National Security Strategy of the United States of America* (The White House: September 2002). Available at georgewbush-whitehouse.archives.gov/nsc/nss/2002.

51. Robert Jervis, for example, argues that the doctrine involves four elements: a belief that the nature of government determines foreign policy; threats from nonstate actors necessitate new strategies, including preventive war; the possible need for unilateral action; and the need for American primacy to maintain international order. See Robert Jervis, "Understanding the Bush Doctrine," *Political Science Quarterly* 118, no. 3 (2003): 365–88. In a subsequent article, Jervis eliminates the demand for U.S. primacy and instead highlights the danger posed by terrorism, especially when linked to tyrannical regimes and WMD. Although one of the distinctive features of the Bush Doctrine is its integration of power and morality, Jervis's conceptualization of the doctrine focuses completely on power and security, neglecting altogether the role of political morality in promoting human dignity and fostering political democracy. See Robert Jervis, "Why the Bush Doctrine Cannot Be Sustained," *Political Science Quarterly* 120, no. 3 (2005): 351–77. Ethicist Peter Singer also has a limited view of the BD. He conceives of the doctrine as involving two elements: the belief that no distinction will be made between terrorists and those who support and harbor them and the commitment to preemptive force. See Peter Singer, *The President of Good & Evil: The Ethics of George W. Bush* (New York: Dutton, 2004), 144–45.

52. Norman Podhoretz, "In Praise of the Bush Doctrine," *Commentary*, September 2002, 28.

53. Jervis, "Why the Bush Doctrine Cannot Be Sustained," 351.

54. Ironically, the Bush administration has conflated preemptive force with preventive force. Preemption involves the use of coercive power when clear evidence exists of an imminent attack; preventive force, by contrast, is the use of coercive power to eliminate danger before a threat can emerge. The war with Iraq was an example of preventive military action.

55. Podhoretz, "In Praise of the Bush Doctrine," 22.

56. John Gaddis, "The Past and Future of American Grand Strategy," Charles S. Grant Lecture, Middlebury College, April 21, 2005.

57. Podhoretz, "In Praise of the Bush Doctrine," 20.

58. Philip Zelikow, "The Transformation of National Security: Five Redefinitions," *National Interest*, Spring 2003, 17–28.

CHAPTER 4: STRATEGIES OF ETHICAL DECISION MAKING

1. Peter Berger, "Moral Judgment and Political Action," *Vital Speeches of the Day* 54 (December 1, 1987): 179.

2. Owen Harries, "First Kosovo. Then Russia. Now China," *New York Times*, May 16, 1999, 17.

3. Stanley Hoffmann, *Duties beyond Borders: On the Limits and Possibilities of Ethical International Relations* (Syracuse, N.Y.: Syracuse University Press, 1981), 143–44.

4. Jeremy Bentham, *Principles of Morals and Legislation*, in *Great Political Thinkers: Plato to the Present*, ed. William Ebenstein, 4th ed. (Hinsdale, Ill.: Dryden Press, 1969), 515.

5. Jonathan Schell, *The Fate of the Earth* (New York: Avon Books), 152.

6. Bernard Brodie, "Implications for Military Policy," in *The Absolute Weapon: Atomic Power and World Order*, ed. Bernard Brodie (New York: Harcourt Brace, 1946), 76.

7. Henry Kissinger, *The Necessity for Choice: Prospects of American Foreign Policy* (Garden City, N.Y.: Doubleday, 1962), 12.

8. George F. Kennan, *The Nuclear Delusion* (New York: Pantheon, 1982), 202.

9. Michael Walzer, *Just and Unjust Wars: A Moral Argument with Historical Illustrations* (New York: Basic Books, 1977), 282.

10. Such conditions can involve norms for going to war (e.g., pursuit of a just cause, limited wartime goals, and exhaustion of alternatives before resorting to war) and norms for conducting the war (e.g., the use of proportional violence and the protection of civilians).

11. Michael Mandelbaum, *The Nuclear Revolution* (Cambridge: Cambridge University Press, 1981), 4.

12. National Conference of Catholic Bishops, *The Challenge of Peace: God's Peace and Our Response* (Washington, D.C.: United States Catholic Conference, 1983), 41–42.

13. The concept of firebreak, used by firefighters to denote land that is cleared to prevent the escalation of forest fires, refers to the physical and psychological area of demarcation between conventional and nuclear arms.

14. During the 1970s and 1980s, U.S. military strategists debated the relative merits of limited, nuclear war-fighting threats versus massive assured destruction threats. The first strategy, known as counterforce, or nuclear utilization theory (NUT), emphasized the actions that would be taken in the event of a failure in deterrence; the other strategy, known as countervalue, or MADvocy, emphasized the prevention of nuclear conflict altogether by emphasizing the unacceptability of nuclear conflict and by opposing nuclear war-fighting options that made retaliation more credible.

15. John Mearsheimer, "Why We Will Soon Miss the Cold War," *Atlantic Monthly*, August 1990, 37.

16. Thomas Schelling, "What Went Wrong with Arms Control," *Foreign Affairs* 64 (Winter 1985/1986): 233.

17. Walzer, *Just and Unjust Wars*, 382.

18. National Conference of Catholic Bishops, *The Challenge of Peace*, 54–55.

19. John Lewis Gaddis, *The United States and the End of the Cold War* (New York: Oxford University Press, 1992), chap. 10.

20. Schelling, "What Went Wrong with Arms Control," 233.

21. See, for example, John Mueller, "The Essential Irrelevance of Nuclear Weapons: Stability in the Postwar World," *International Security* 13 (Fall 1988): 55–79, and John A. Vasquez, "The Deterrence Myth: Nuclear Weapons and the Prevention of Nuclear War," in *The Long Postwar Peace: Contending Explanations and Projections*, ed. Charles W. Kegley Jr. (New York: HarperCollins, 1991), 205–23.

22. Thomas Donaldson, "Kant's Global Rationalism," in *Traditions of International Ethics*, ed. Terry Nardin and David R. Mapel (Cambridge: Cambridge University Press, 1992), 137–38.

23. David Halloran Lumsdaine, *Moral Vision in International Politics: The Foreign Aid Regime, 1949–1989* (New Haven, Conn.: Yale University Press, 1993), 283.

24. Frederick Lewis Schuman, *American Policy toward Russia since 1917* (New York: International Publishers, 1928), 277.

25. Thomas A. Bailey, *America Faces Russia: Russian-American Relations from Early Times to Our Day* (Ithaca, N.Y.: Cornell University Press, 1950), 253.

26. For an analysis of Herbert Hoover's role in the Russian famine relief, see Benjamin M. Weissman, *Herbert Hoover and Famine Relief to Soviet Russia: 1921–1923* (Stanford, Calif.: Hoover Institution Press, 1974). The most thorough description and assessment of the American relief expedition in 1921 is Bertrand M. Patenaude, *The Big Show in Bololand: The American Relief Expedition to Soviet Russia in the Famine of 1921* (Stanford, Calif.: Stanford University Press, 2002).

27. Schuman, *American Policy toward Russia*, 204.

28. Weissman, *Herbert Hoover and Famine Relief*, 199.

29. Robert W. McElroy, *Morality and American Foreign Policy* (Princeton, N.J.: Princeton University Press, 1992), 86.

30. George F. Kennan, *Russia and the West under Lenin and Stalin* (Boston: Little, Brown, 1960), 180.

31. Hoffmann, *Duties beyond Borders*, 190–91.

32. Alberto R. Coll, "Normative Prudence as a Tradition of Statecraft," *Ethics & International Affairs* 5 (1991): 33.

33. Joseph S. Nye Jr., *Nuclear Ethics* (New York: Free Press, 1986), 22.

34. Ronald Reagan, "Launching the SDI," in *Promise or Peril: The Strategic Defense Initiative*, ed. Zbigniew Brzezinski (Washington, D.C.: Ethics and Public Policy Center, 1986), 49.

35. William E. Burrows, "Ballistic Missile Defense: The Illusion of Security," *Foreign Affairs* 62 (Spring 1984): 844.

36. McGeorge Bundy, George F. Kennan, Robert S. McNamara, and Gerard Smith, "The President's Choice: Star Wars or Arms Control," *Foreign Affairs* 63 (Winter 1984/1985): 265.

37. Leon Wieseltier, "The Ungrand Compromise," *New Republic* 16 (1986): 31.

38. David Halberstam, *The Best and the Brightest* (New York: Ballantine Books, 1993).

39. For further discussion of the role of these alternative approaches to moral decision making, see Rushworth Kidder, *How Good People Make Tough Choices: Resolving Dilemmas of Ethical Living* (New York: Simon & Schuster, 1995).

40. Graham Allison and Philip Zelikow, *Essence of Decision: Explaining the Cuban Missile Crisis*, 2nd ed. (New York: Longman, 1999).

CHAPTER 5: THE ETHICS OF INTERNATIONAL
HUMAN RIGHTS

1. R. J. Vincent, "The Idea of Rights in International Ethics," in *Traditions of International Ethics*, ed. Terry Nardin and David R. Mapel (Cambridge: Cambridge University Press, 1992), 267.

2. Richard N. Haass, *The Reluctant Sheriff: The United States after the Cold War* (New York: Council on Foreign Relations), 69.

3. Charles Krauthammer, "Morality and the Reagan Doctrine," *New Republic*, September 8, 1986, 20.

4. See Pew Research Center study titled "Global Restrictions on Religion, 2009." Available at http://www.pewforum.org/Government/Global-Restrictions-on-Religion.aspx. For an analysis of the nature and impact of restrictions on religious freedom, see also Brian J. Grim and Roger Finke, *The Price of Freedom Denied: Religious Persecution and Conflict in the Twenty-First Century* (Cambridge: Cambridge University Press, 2011).

5. For further discussion of this distinction, see Maurice Cranston, *What Are Human Rights?* (New York: Basic Books, 1962), 8–12.

6. Alan Gewirth, "Common Morality and the Community of Rights," in *Prospects for a Common Morality*, ed. Gene Outka and John P. Reeder Jr. (Princeton, N.J.: Princeton University Press, 1993), 30–31.

7. Gewirth, "Common Morality and the Community of Rights," 30–31.

8. Rhoda E. Howard and Jack Donnelly, "Human Dignity, Human Rights, and Political Regimes," *American Political Science Review* 80 (September 1986): 802.

9. Howard and Donnelly, "Human Dignity, Human Rights, and Political Regimes," 804.

10. R. J. Vincent, *Human Rights and International Relations* (Cambridge: Cambridge University Press, 1986), 21.

11. For a contrary view, see Arthur Schlesinger Jr., "Human Rights and the American Tradition," *Foreign Affairs* 57, no. 3 (1979): 504. Schlesinger argues that because religion had traditionally rejected the notion that people were entitled to earthly happiness, Christianity had little to do with the rise of the idea of human rights.

12. For an excellent overview of the meaning of the human rights doctrine, see Jack Donnelly, *Universal Human Rights in Theory and Practice* (Ithaca, N.Y.: Cornell University Press, 1989), 9–27.

13. Vincent, *Human Rights and International Relations*, 7.

14. According to the philosophy of utilitarianism, decisions should seek to maximize "utility" by making choices that provide "the greatest good for the greatest number."

15. Christian Bay, "Self-Respect as a Human Right: Thoughts on the Dialectics of Wants and Needs in the Struggle for Human Community," *Human Rights Quarterly* 4 (February 1982): 53–75.

16. Charles R. Beitz, "Human Rights and Social Justice," in *Human Rights and U.S. Foreign Policy*, ed. Peter G. Brown and Douglas MacLean (Lexington, Mass.: Lexington Books, 1979), 45–63.

17. Henry Shue, *Basic Rights: Subsistence, Affluence, and U.S. Foreign Policy* (Princeton, N.J.: Princeton University Press, 1980), 13–34.

18. Michael Ignatieff, *Human Rights as Politics and Idolatry* (Princeton: Princeton University Press, 2001), 57.

19. A. J. M. Milne, "Human Rights and the Diversity of Morals: A Philosophical Analysis of Rights and Obligations in the Global System," in *Rights and Obligations in North-South Relations*, ed. Moorehead Wright (New York: St. Martin's, 1986), 21.

20. Vincent, *Human Rights and International Relations*, 54–55.

21. Donnelly, *Universal Human Rights in Theory and Practice*, 112–14.

22. James Finn, ed., *Freedom in the World: The Annual Survey of Political Rights and Civil Liberties, 1994–1995* (New York: Freedom House, 1995), 505–8.

23. Michael Elliott, "The Caning Debate: Should America Be More Like Singapore?" *Newsweek*, April 18, 1994, 22.

24. Kishore Mahbubani, "The United States: 'Go East, Young Man,'" *Washington Quarterly* 17 (Spring 1994): 11.

25. Mahbubani, "The United States," 21.

26. A different but related question concerns capital punishment. Most European countries have outlawed such punishment, while the criminal justice system of the United States provides for its continued use. Is death by lethal injection or electrocution a barbaric practice, as European human rights leaders claim, or is it a legitimate deterrent to violent crime?

27. Jack Donnelly, *International Human Rights* (Boulder, Colo.: Westview Press, 1993), 7.

28. Louis Henkin, *The Age of Rights* (New York: Columbia University Press, 1990), 19.

29. Other important international human rights agreements include the International Convention on the Prevention and Punishment of the Crime of Genocide (1948); the International

Convention on the Elimination of All Forms of Racial Discrimination (1965); the Convention against Torture and Other Cruel, Inhuman or Degrading Treatment or Punishment (1984); and the Convention on the Rights of the Child (1989).

30. The right to development became an official part of the UN lexicon in 1986 when the General Assembly adopted the Declaration on the Right to Development. Among other things, the statement proclaims that "the right to development is an inalienable human right by virtue of which every human person and all peoples are entitled to participate in, contribute to, and enjoy economic, social, cultural and political development, in which all human rights and fundamental freedoms can be fully realized."

31. Charles J. Brown, "In the Trenches: The Battle over Rights," *Freedom Review*, September–October 1993, 9.

32. Since the Vienna meeting, several other conferences have reinforced the growing cultural and political pluralism in the international community. The three most important were the International Conference on Population and Development in Cairo (1994), the World Summit on Social Development in Copenhagen (1995), and the Fourth International Conference on Women in Beijing (1995).

33. Helen Stacy, "Relational Sovereignty," *Stanford Law Review* 55 (May 2003): 2048. Available at http://staff.jccc.net/bwright1/New_Folder/relational%20sovereignty.htm.

34. Mary Robinson, foreword to *In Our Own Best Interest: How Defending Human Rights Benefits Us All*, by William F. Schulz (Boston: Beacon Press, 2001), xi.

35. Julie A. Mertus, *Bait and Switch: Human Rights and U.S. Foreign Policy*, 2nd ed. (New York: Routledge, 2008), 2.

36. James Peck, *Ideal Illusions: How the U.S. Government Co-opted Human Rights* (New York: Metropolitan Books, 2010), 3.

37. C. William Walldorf Jr., *Just Politics: Human Rights and the Foreign Policy of Great Powers* (Ithaca, NY: Cornell University Press, 2008).

38. Vincent, *Human Rights and International Relations*, 142.

39. George F. Kennan, "Ethics and Foreign Policy: An Approach to the Problem," in *Foreign Policy and Morality: Framework for a Moral Audit*, ed. Theodore M. Hesburgh and Louis J. Halle (New York: Council on Religion and International Affairs, 1979), 44.

40. Stanley Hoffmann, "Reaching for the Most Difficult: Human Rights as a Foreign Policy Goal," *Daedalus* 112 (Fall 1983): 33.

41. Robert Goldwin, "Human Rights and American Policy, Part IV—Arguments and Afterwords," *The Center Magazine*, July–August 1984, 59.

42. For a criticism of the Carter administration's human rights policy, see Joshua Muravchik, *The Uncertain Crusade: Jimmy Carter and the Dilemmas of Human Rights Policy* (New York: Hamilton Press, 1986).

43. William H. Gleysteen Jr., "Korea: A Special Target of American Concern," in *The Diplomacy of Human Rights*, ed. David D. Newsom (Lanham, Md.: University Press of America, 1986), 99.

44. Michael Ignatieff, "The Return of Sovereignty," *New Republic*, February 16, 2012, 28.

45. George F. Kennan, *The Cloud of Danger: Current Realities of American Foreign Policy* (Boston: Little, Brown, 1977), 43.

46. Herbert Butterfield, *History and Human Relations* (London: Collins, 1951), 110.

47. Hoffman, "Reaching for the Most Difficult," 28.

48. R. J. Rummel, *Death by Government* (New Brunswick, N.J.: Transaction Publishers, 1994), 15.

49. Hoffmann, "Reaching for the Most Difficult," 4.

50. Interestingly, the United States did not formally ratify the Genocide Convention until 1988, some nineteen years after Senator William Proxmire of Wisconsin began to call for its senatorial endorsement.

51. For a compelling account of the United States' failure to respond to genocide, see Samantha Power, *"A Problem from Hell": America and the Age of Genocide* (New York: Basic Books, 2002).

52. Although it can be argued that the U.S.-led wars against the Taliban in Afghanistan in 2001 and the Baathist regime in Iraq in 2003 were undertaken to end tyrannical governments, the fundamental purpose of both wars was to eliminate the direct and indirect threat of terrorism.

53. Power, *"A Problem from Hell,"* 508.

54. Power, *"A Problem from Hell,"* 504.

55. The most thorough account of the genocide is Alison Des Forges, *Leave None to Tell the Story: Genocide in Rwanda* (New York: Human Rights Watch, 1999). See also Gérard Prunier, *The Rwanda Crisis: History of a Genocide* (New York: Columbia University Press, 1995); Philip Gourevitch, *We Wish to Inform You That Tomorrow We Will Be Killed with Our Families: Stories from Rwanda* (New York: Farrar, Straus & Giroux, 1998); and Linda R. Melvern, *A People Betrayed: The Role of the West in Rwanda's Genocide* (New York: Zed Books, 2000). For an interpretive historical account of the factors that contributed to the origins and evolution of Hutu-Tutsi animosity, see Mahmood Mamdani, *When Victims Become Killers: Colonialism, Nativism, and the Genocide in Rwanda* (Princeton, N.J.: Princeton University Press, 2001).

56. The ineffectiveness of UNAMIR after the genocide began was also due to the fact that the original mission was an observer force. Even after evidence became available that a major genocide was under way, the Security Council refused to increase the size of UNAMIR or to expand its mandate. For an overview of the establishment, role, and ultimate failure of the UN peacekeeping mission in Rwanda, see Lt. Gen. Roméo Dallaire, *Shake Hands with the Devil: The Failure of Humanity in Rwanda* (New York: Carroll & Graf, 2003).

57. David Rieff, "The Age of Genocide," *New Republic*, January 26, 1996, 31.

58. Rieff, "The Age of Genocide," 31.

59. Milton Leitenberg, "Anatomy of a Massacre," *New York Times*, July 31, 1994, sec. 4, 15.

60. Michael Barnett, *Eyewitness to a Genocide: The United Nations and Rwanda* (Ithaca, N.Y.: Cornell University Press, 2002), 155.

61. One of the moral ambiguities about this humanitarian aid was that it gave assistance and protection to Hutu leaders and fighters who had inspired and carried out the genocide.

62. Barnett, *Eyewitness to a Genocide*, 155.

63. Power, *"A Problem from Hell,"* 334.

CHAPTER 6: THE ETHICS OF POLITICAL RECONCILIATION

1. Walter Wink, *When the Powers Fall: Reconciliation in the Healing of Nations* (Minneapolis, Minn.: Fortress Press, 1998), 54.

2. Pope John Paul II, "Offer Forgiveness and Receive Peace," Message for World Day of Peace, January 1, 1997.

3. Carlos Santiago Nino, *Radical Evil on Trial* (New Haven, Conn.: Yale University Press, 1996), 187–88.

4. The inquiry into this topic has spawned extensive scholarly literature. The best general introduction to this subject is the three-volume study titled *Transitional Justice: How Emerging Democracies Reckon with Former Regimes*, edited by Neil J. Kritz and published by the United States Institute of Peace Press. Volume 1 deals with general considerations, volume 2 concerns country studies, and volume 3 covers relevant laws, rulings, and reports.

5. José Zalaquett, "Balancing Ethical Imperatives and Political Constraints: The Dilemma of New Democracies Confronting Past Human Rights Violations," in *Transitional Justice: How Emerging Democracies Reckon with Former Regimes*, ed. Neil J. Kritz, vol. 2, *Country Studies* (Washington, D.C.: United States Institute of Peace Press, 1995), 496.

6. Timothy Garton Ash, "The Truth about Dictatorship," *New York Review of Books* 45 (February 19, 1998): 35.

7. For a discussion of this point, see Miroslav Volf, "The Social Meaning of Reconciliation," *Interpretation* 54 (April 2000): 158–68.

8. Daniel Philpott, *Just and Unjust Peace: An Ethic of Political Reconciliation* (New York: Oxford University Press, 2012), 5.

9. Trudy Govier and Wilhelm Verwoerd, "Trust and the Problem of National Reconciliation," unpublished paper.

10. Francis Fukuyama, *Trust: The Social Virtues and the Creation of Prosperity* (New York: Free Press, 1995).

11. For an excellent overview of the nature and role of truth commissions, see Priscilla B. Hayner, *Unspeakable Truths: Transitional Justice and the Challenge of Truth Commissions* (New York: Routledge, 2011). See also Tristan Anne Borer, ed., *Telling the Truths: Truth Telling and Peace Building in Post-Conflict Societies* (Notre Dame, Ind.: University of Notre Dame Press, 2006).

12. Michael Feher, "Terms of Reconciliation," in *Human Rights in Political Transitions: Gettysburg to Bosnia*, ed. Carla Hesse and Robert Post (New York: Zone Books, 1999), 325–28.

13. Abraham Lincoln, "Second Inaugural," in *Lend Me Your Ears: Great Speeches in History*, ed. William Safire (New York: Norton, 1992), 441.

14. George Weigel argues that St. Augustine's conception of *tranquillitas ordinis* provides a helpful account of a stable and just political order. For a discussion of this moral order, see George Weigel, *Tranquillitas Ordinis: The Present Failure and Future Promise of American Catholic Thought on War and Peace* (New York: Oxford University Press, 1987).

15. Diane F. Orentlicher, "Settling Accounts: The Duty to Prosecute Human Rights Violations of a Prior Regime," *Yale Law Journal* 100 (1991): 2542–44.

16. "Argentina: Presidential Pardons" in *Transitional Justice: How Emerging Democracies Reckon with Former Regimes*, ed. Neil J. Kritz, vol. 3, *Laws, Rulings, and Reports* (Washington, D.C.: United States Institute of Peace Press, 1995), 528–32.

17. The genocide began after Rwandan president Juvenal Habyarimana was killed when his jet was downed by missiles as it was landing in Kigali.

18. David Rieff, "The Age of Genocide," *New Republic*, January 26, 1996, 31.

19. It is estimated that in 1996 Rwanda had less than seventy-five trained lawyers.

20. Peter Uvin, "Difficult Choices in the New Post-conflict Agenda: The International Community in Rwanda after the Genocide," *Third World Quarterly* 22 (2001): 181.

21. Conditional release has been typically granted to prisoners of lower-level crimes who are thought to have served roughly half their presumed sentence.

22. In 1996 Rwanda adopted a genocide law that classified crimes in terms of four categories. Category 1 involves persons who helped plan and execute the genocide, including those who perpetrated rape and sexual torture. Categories 2 to 4 apply to less serious offenses—to perpetrators and conspirators of homicide, accomplices of intentional killing, and those who committed property crimes.

23. Rwanda opposed the tribunal for three reasons. First, it believed that justice and political reconciliation would be advanced more effectively if the court were located in Kigali rather than in Arusha, Tanzania. Not only was Arusha difficult to reach for most Rwandans, but trials in a

foreign land would greatly impair dissemination of the judicial proceedings. Second, Rwanda opposed the ICTR because its jurisdiction covered only crimes committed in 1994, not in the years preceding the genocide. Since the Tutsis assumed that the massacres of 1990 and 1991 had created a basis for the 1994 genocide, they believed that those atrocities needed to be investigated and prosecuted. Finally, Rwanda opposed the ICTR because the tribunal statute excluded the death penalty. Since Rwanda's penal code allowed for death sentences, Rwandans believed that death was an appropriate punishment for those most responsible for the dehumanizing and killing of hundreds of thousands of people.

24. For information on the ICTR, see http://www.unictr.org.

25. Although the aim of the ICTR is to prosecute offenders bearing the greatest responsibility for the genocide, of the forty-nine trials that had been completed by 2011, ten alleged offenders had been acquitted and twelve had received prison sentences of fifteen or fewer years.

26. In that time it prosecuted twenty-two senior German leaders responsible for war crimes and crimes against peace, and to a lesser extent crimes against humanity. The tribunal found nineteen of the leaders guilty and sentenced twelve to death. For a review of the nature and work of the Military War Tribunal at Nuremberg, see Howard Ball, *Prosecuting War Crimes and Genocide: The Twentieth-Century Experience* (Lawrence: University of Kansas Press, 1999), 44–61.

27. One of the provisions in the ICTR's founding UN act (Security Council Resolution 955) states, "The prosecution of persons responsible for serious violations of international humanitarian law would enable this aim to be achieved and would *contribute to the process of national reconciliation* [emphasis by author] and to the restoration and maintenance of peace."

28. Helena Cobban, "The Legacies of Collective Violence," *Boston Review*, April/May 2002. For a critique of Cobban's argument see Kenneth Roth and Alison Des Forges, "Justice or Therapy?" *Boston Review: A Political and Literary Forum* 27 (Summer 2002), http://www.bostonreview.net/BR27.3/rothdesForges.html. See also "Helena Cobban Replies" in the same *Boston Review* issue.

29. Cobban, "The Legacies of Collective Violence."

30. According to Elizabeth Kiss, restorative justice is an approach that emphasizes the healing of victims, legal accountability for offenders, preventing future human rights abuses, and promoting reconciliation. Since the first three norms are also given priority in retribution, the distinctive feature of the restorative approach is reconciliation. See Elizabeth Kiss, "Moral Ambition within and beyond Political Constraints: Reflections on Restorative Justice," in *Truth v. Justice: The Morality of Truth Commissions*, ed. Robert I. Rotberg and Dennis Thompson (Princeton, N.J.: Princeton University Press, 2000), 79.

31. Robert Meister, "Forgiving and Forgetting: Lincoln and the Politics of National Recovery," in *Human Rights in Political Transitions*, ed. Hesse and Post.

32. Mahmood Mamdani, *When Victims Become Killers: Colonialism, Nativism, and the Genocide in Rwanda* (Princeton, N.J.: Princeton University Press, 2001), 272–73.

33. "Argentina: *Nunca Más*—Report of the Argentine Commission on the Disappeared" in *Transitional Justice*, vol. 3, 6.

34. Some of the most important legislation fostering racial segregation in the early twentieth century included a 1913 law defining where blacks and whites could live and work, the 1913 Pass Laws that regulated the movement of blacks, and the 1923 Native (Urban Areas) Act that extended the principle of racial segregation to urban areas. For a comprehensive overview of all major South African statutes enacted from 1910 through the early 1980s that institutionalized racial segregation, see Truth and Reconciliation Commission, *Truth and Reconciliation Commission of South Africa Report*, vol. 1 (London: Macmillan Reference, 1999), 450–66.

35. Some of these included the Mixed Marriages Act (1949), which made interracial marriage illegal; the Population Registration Act (1950), which required that all persons be classified by

race; the Group Areas Act (1950), which specified where members of each race could live; the Reservation of Separate Amenities Act (1953), which required that public facilities be racially segregated; and the Black Authorities Act (1951), which, together with subsequent legislation, established black homelands. For a discussion of the apartheid ideology and its practices, see Leonard Thompson, *A History of South Africa*, 3rd ed. (New Haven, Conn.: Yale University Press, 2000).

36. One of the most important of these was the creation of a tricameral parliament, giving Indians and "Coloureds," but not Africans, their own legislature along with some participation in executive power sharing.

37. Piet Meiring, *Chronicle of the Truth Commission: A Journey through the Past and Present—into the Future of South Africa* (Vanderbijlpark, S.A.: Carpe Diem, 1999), 146.

38. Alex Boraine, "Truth and Reconciliation in South Africa: The Third Way," in *Truth v. Justice*, ed. Rotberg and Thompson, 143.

39. According to the TRC Report, *ubuntu* is generally translated as "humaneness," and expresses itself in the phrase "People are people through other people."

40. Desmond Tutu, *No Future without Forgiveness* (New York: Doubleday, 1999), 19.

41. Tutu, *No Future without Forgiveness*, 23.

42. As conceptualized by the TRC, the approach of restorative justice involves a number of distinctive features. First, it calls for a redefinition of crime that focuses on personal injuries and human suffering rather than on impersonal rule breaking. Second, it emphasizes reparations for victims in order to facilitate their restoration into the fabric of communal life, while also emphasizing the rehabilitation of perpetrators based on full accountability for past offenses. Third, it encourages direct conflict resolution among victims, offenders, and the community. And finally, it calls for "a spirit of understanding" between victims and offenders, without mitigating or undermining offenders' accountability for wrongdoing. Such accountability is not only legal and political but also moral. TRC, *Commission Report*, vol. 1, 126–31.

43. The commission's specific tasks were to (1) uncover the truth about gross human rights violations perpetrated from March 1, 1960, to May 10, 1994; (2) establish the fate or whereabouts of victims; (3) assist in restoring the dignity of victims by giving them an opportunity to testify about their suffering; (4) recommend a set of measures of reparation that would help restore the human dignity of victims; (5) grant amnesty to those who confessed their crimes; (6) prepare and disseminate a comprehensive report on the commission's findings; and (7) make recommendations that contribute to the establishment of a humane society and prevent future violations of human rights. TRC, *Commission Report*, vol. 1, 55.

44. The members represented a broad cross-section of South African society and included seven women, ten men, seven Africans, two Indians, two "Coloureds," six whites, six lawyers, and four church ministers. Most had been strongly identified as opponents of the apartheid regime.

45. According to the TRC process, amnesty depended solely on three conditions: (1) full confession of crimes; (2) crimes had to be a part of the political struggle over apartheid; and (3) the crimes must have been carried out during the legally prescribed time frame specified by parliament (March 1960 to May 1994).

46. More than one-third of these applications were rejected because they failed to fulfill the objective criteria necessary for eligibility.

47. The TRC officially began its work in December 1995 and concluded most of its operations in July 1998, when three of its four offices (Johannesburg, East London, and Durban) were closed. After the TRC's final report was published in October 1998, the Cape Town office continued to function with a small staff to support the ongoing amnesty hearings and the drafting of a supplementary report, released in early 2003.

48. Since victims' testimony was not subject to cross-examination, a South African court ruled that the TRC could not arbitrarily identify alleged offenders without first warning them of the charge and allowing sufficient time to contest it in court.

49. John Dugard, "Retrospective Justice: International Law and the South African Model," in *Transitional Justice and the Rule of Law in New Democracies*, ed. A. James McAdams (South Bend, Ind.: University of Notre Dame Press, 1997), 284–86.

50. McAdams, *Transitional Justice and the Rule of Law in New Democracies*, 23.

51. Rajeev Bhargava, "Restoring Decency to Barbaric Societies," in *Truth v. Justice*, ed. Rotberg and Thompson, 60.

52. David A. Crocker, "Retribution and Reconciliation," *Report from the Institute for Philosophy & Public Policy* 20 (Winter/Spring 2000): 6.

53. Fareed Zakaria, *The Future of Freedom: Liberal Democracy at Home and Abroad* (New York: Norton, 2003).

54. D. A. Rustow has observed that the first step in establishing a democratic regime is the development of national unity. He argues that communal solidarity must precede the other three phases of democratization—namely, the acceptance of political conflict, the institutionalization of rules governing political conflict, and the habituation of political struggle. See D. A. Rustow, "How Does a Democracy Come into Existence?" in *The Practice of Comparative Politics: A Reader*, ed. Paul G. Lewis and David C. Potter (Bristol: Open University Press, 1973), 120–30.

55. Michael Ignatieff, *The Warrior's Honor: Ethnic War and the Modern Conscience* (New York: Henry Holt, 1997), 168.

56. The name of the revolutionary group means "spear of the nation."

57. Following the just war doctrine, the laws of war comprise two dimensions—the principles of going to war (justice of war) and the rules of war (justice in war). A war may be morally legitimate but prosecuted in a criminal manner. Similarly, an unjust war can be carried out legally and justly by, for example, targeting only military personnel or using only the minimum force to achieve military objectives. Thus, the ANC's military purposes (the destruction of the apartheid regime) may have been just, but the resort to terror, indiscriminate bombings, and the killing or torture of informants was contrary to the laws of war.

58. Alex Boraine, *A Country Unmasked* (Oxford: Oxford University Press, 2000), 326.

59. Quoted in Boraine, *A Country Unmasked*, 317.

60. The court justified its ruling based on the postamble of the interim constitution, which set forth the argument for the political and moral reconstruction of the nation. The court argued that amnesty for civil and criminal liability was justified by the postamble's claim that amnesty would encourage truth telling and by the promise of reparations to victims. Additionally, the court found that the amnesty provision was not inconsistent with international law, nor did it violate the country's treaty obligations. For a further discussion of the court's ruling, see Boraine, *A Country Unmasked*, 118–21.

61. Boraine, *A Country Unmasked*, 341.

62. *New York Times*, November 1, 1998.

63. Hannah Arendt, *The Human Condition* (Chicago: University of Chicago Press, 1958), 238–40.

64. Patrick Glynn, "Toward a New Peace: Forgiveness as Politics," *Current* (March/April 1995): 19.

65. For an illuminating study of the potential role of forgiveness in politics, see Donald W. Shriver Jr., *An Ethic for Enemies: Forgiveness in Politics* (New York: Oxford University Press, 1995).

66. Elie Wiesel, "Remarks of Elie Wiesel at Ceremony for Jewish Heritage Week," in *Bitburg: In Moral and Political Perspective*, ed. Geoffrey Hartman (Bloomington: Indiana University Press, 1986), 243.

67. Lance Morrow, "Forgiveness to the Injured Doth Belong," *Time*, May 20, 1985, 90.

68. Wiesel, "Remarks," 242.

69. Wiesel, "Remarks," 243–44.

70. "Interview of President Reagan by Representatives of Foreign Radio and Television," in *Bitburg*, ed. Hartman, 250–51.

71. William Safire, "'I Am a Jew . . .'" in *Bitburg*, ed. Hartman, 214.

72. Quoted in Shriver, *An Ethic for Enemies*, 110.

CHAPTER 7: THE ETHICS OF WAR

1. Quoted in James G. Blight and Janet M. Lang, *The Fog of War: Lessons from the life of Robert S. McNamara* (Boulder, Colo.: Rowman & Littlefield, 2005), 113.

2. Carl von Clausewitz, *On War*, trans. Michael Howard and Peter Paret (Princeton, N.J.: Princeton University Press, 1976), 370.

3. Stanley Hoffmann, *Duties beyond Borders: On the Limits and Possibilities of Ethical International Politics* (Syracuse, N.Y.: Syracuse University Press, 1981), 81.

4. Quoted in James Turner Johnson, "Threats, Values, and Defense: Does the Defense of Values by Force Remain a Moral Possibility?" in *The Nuclear Dilemma and the Just War Tradition*, ed. William V. O'Brien and John Langan (Lexington, Ky.: Lexington Books, 1986), 36.

5. Thucydides, *The Peloponnesian War*, trans. Rex Warner (New York: Penguin, 1954), 402.

6. Since *Islam* is used to denote "the faithful," *House of Islam* thus means the "house of the faithful," whereas those opposed to Islam are part of the "house of the unfaithful."

7. Bernard Lewis, *The Political Language of Islam* (Chicago: University of Chicago Press, 1988), 73.

8. Bernard Lewis, "The Roots of Muslim Rage," *Atlantic Monthly*, September 1990.

9. See, for example, John Kelsay, *Islam and War: The Gulf War and Beyond* (Louisville, Ky.: John Knox Press, 1993), chap. 4.

10. Roland H. Bainton, *Christian Attitudes toward War and Peace: A Historical Survey and Critical Re-evaluation* (New York: Abingdon Press, 1960), 148.

11. Bainton, *Christian Attitudes*, 45.

12. Will Durant and Ariel Durant, *The Story of Civilization: Part III. The Age of Louis XIV* (New York: Simon & Schuster, 1963), 195.

13. For a comprehensive account of this theory, see Paul Ramsey, *The Just War: Force and Political Responsibility* (New York: Scribner, 1968). For a historical account of the origins and development of this theory, see James Turner Johnson, *Ideology, Reason, and the Limitation of War: Religious and Secular Concepts, 1200–1740* (Princeton, N.J.: Princeton University Press, 1975), and James Turner Johnson, *Just War Tradition and the Restraint of War: A Moral and Historical Inquiry* (Princeton, N.J.: Princeton University Press, 1981).

14. James Turner Johnson, "The Concept of Just Cause," *American Purpose* 10 (Spring 1996): 4; see also James Turner Johnson, "The Broken Tradition," *National Interest*, Fall 1996, 27–30.

15. George Weigel, "Moral Clarity in a Time of War," *First Things* (January 2003): 22. Rowan Williams, the archbishop of Canterbury, has critiqued some of Weigel's arguments, and the author responds with a vigorous defense of his claims. See "War & Statecraft: An Exchange," *First Things* (January 2004): 14–21.

16. William V. O'Brien, *The Conduct of Just and Limited War* (New York: Praeger, 1981).

17. For a discussion of this emerging element of just war theory, see Louis Iasiello, "The Moral Responsibilities of Victors in War," *Naval War College Review*, Summer/Autumn 2004, 33–52, and Robert E. Williams Jr. and Dan Caldwell, "Jus Post Bellum: Just War Theory and the Principles of Just Peace," *International Studies Perspectives* 7 (2006): 309–20.

18. James Turner Johnson, "The Just War Tradition and the American Military," in *Just War and the Gulf War*, ed. James Turner Johnson and George Weigel (Washington, D.C.: Ethics and Public Policy Center, 1991), 22.

19. This evil became especially apparent when Iraq used civilians as protective shields during the air war, dumped large quantities of petroleum into the Persian Gulf, and destroyed nearly a thousand Kuwaiti oil fields.

20. Michael Walzer, "Perplexed," *New Republic*, January 28, 1991, 14.

21. Michael Walzer, "Justice and Injustice in the Gulf War," in *But Was It Just? Reflections on the Morality of the Persian Gulf War*, ed. David E. DeCosse (New York: Doubleday, 1992), 3.

22. Quoted in George Weigel, "The Churches and War in the Gulf," *First Things* 11 (March 1990): 39.

23. "Message from Thirty-Two Church Leaders to President Bush," in *Just War and the Gulf War*, ed. James Turner Johnson and George Weigel (Washington, D.C.: Ethics and Public Policy Center, 1991), 137.

24. Walzer, "Perplexed," 13.

25. See, for example, Walzer, "Justice and Injustice," 12–13.

26. Robert W. Tucker, "Justice and the War," *National Interest*, Fall 1991, 111–12.

27. Jean Bethke Elshtain, "Just War and American Politics," *Christian Century*, January 15, 1992, 43.

28. Francis X. Winters, "Justice and the Gulf War," *National Interest*, Winter 1991/1992, 104.

29. Eliot A. Cohen, "A Strange War," *National Interest*, Thanksgiving 2001, 12.

30. The NSS is available on the Web at www.whitehouse.gov/nsc/nss.html. For an analysis and assessment of the NSS, see John Lewis Gaddis, "A Grand Strategy," *Foreign Policy* (November/December 2002): 50–57, and Philip Zelikow, "The Transformation of National Security: Five Redefinitions," *National Interest*, Spring 2003, 17–28.

31. *National Security Strategy of the United States*, Section V.

32. Ivo Daalder and James Steinberg, "The Future of Preemption," *American Interest*, Winter 2005, 32.

33. Quoted in Alan M. Dershowitz, *Preemption: A Knife That Cuts Both Ways* (New York: Norton, 2006), 163–64.

34. Michael Walzer, *Just and Unjust Wars: A Moral Argument with Historical Illustrations* (New York: Basic Books, 1977), 81.

35. For an ethical defense of preventive war in the post–Cold War era, see Whitley Kaufman, "What's Wrong with Preventive War? The Moral and Legal Basis for the Preventive Use of Force," *Ethics & International Affairs* 19 (2005): 23–38.

36. *A More Secure World: Our Shared Responsibility*, Report of the Secretary-General's high-level Panel on Threats, Challenges and Change. Available at www.un.org/secureworld.

37. Daalder and Steinberg, "The Future of Preemption," 34.

38. Daalder and Steinberg, "The Future of Preemption," 35.

39. For an excellent overview of the nature and evolution of economic sanctions on Iraq after the Persian Gulf War, see Erik D. K. Melby, "Iraq," in *Economic Sanctions and American Diplomacy*, ed. Richard N. Haass (New York: Council on Foreign Relations, 1998), 107–28.

40. After the fall of the Hussein regime, U.S. officials discovered significant graft in the Oil-for-Food Program. As a result UN secretary-general Kofi Annan established an Independent

Inquiry Committee (IIC), headed by Paul Volcker, former chairman of the U.S. Federal Reserve, to determine the nature and scope of the illegal activities. The IIC found that Hussein had gained about $1.8 billion in illicit revenue by manipulating the program. Even more significant, however, the IIC found that the revenues from smuggling oil outside the UN program generated nearly $11 billion, or more than five times the revenues from within the program. See the IIC's reports at www.iic-offp.org/documents.htm.

41. The enforcement of no-fly zones, which involved some 350,000 sorties during the twelve years that they were in force, cost the U.S. some $20 billion.

42. Michael R. Gordon and David E. Sanger, "Powell Says U.S. Is Weighing Ways to Topple Hussein," *New York Times*, February 13, 2002, A1.

43. Michael J. Glennon, "Why the Security Council Failed," *Foreign Affairs* 82 (May/June 2003): 26–27.

44. Todd S. Purdum, *A Time of Our Choosing: America's War in Iraq* (New York: Times Books, 2003), 65.

45. It was expected that the war would begin several days later, thereby allowing time so that more Special Forces teams could secretly enter Iraq to make preparations for combat. But the CIA received current intelligence indicating that Saddam Hussein would be meeting in a particular building on that same night. On the advice of Secretary of Defense Donald Rumsfeld and CIA director George Tenet, the president authorized a bombing attack on the Baghdad site that evening.

46. Weigel, "Moral Clarity in a Time of War," 25.

47. John J. Mearsheimer and Stephen M. Walt, "An Unnecessary War," *Foreign Policy* (January/February 2003): 59.

48. Of course, the only reason Iraq had accepted the resumption of UN inspection teams in December 2002 was that the United States, along with Britain and Spain, had begun making preparations for war. It was the growing threat of war that had compelled Saddam Hussein to take seriously Security Council Resolution 1441.

49. Michael Walzer, "The Right Way," *New York Review of Books* (March 13, 2003), 4.

50. Jimmy Carter, "Just War—or a Just War?" *New York Times*, March 9, 2003.

51. Anne-Marie Slaughter, "Good Reasons for Going around the U.N.," *New York Times*, March 18, 2003, 31.

CHAPTER 8: THE ETHICS OF IRREGULAR WAR

1. "Is Torture Ever Justified?" *Economist*, January 11, 2003, 9.

2. Michael L. Gross, *Moral Dilemmas of Modern War: Torture, Assassination and Blackmail in an Age of Asymmetric Conflict* (Cambridge: Cambridge University Press, 2010), 139.

3. Richard A. Posner, "The Best Offense," *New Republic*, September 2, 2002, 30.

4. Michael Walzer, *Just and Unjust Wars: A Moral Argument with Historical Illustrations* (New York: Basic Books, 1977), 179–96.

5. Charles Krauthammer, "Morality and the Reagan Doctrine," *New Republic*, September 8, 1986, 23.

6. Carl von Clausewitz, *On War*, trans. Michael Howard and Peter Paret (Princeton, N.J.: Princeton University Press, 1976), 87.

7. Bruce Hoffman, "Rethinking Terrorism and Counterterrorism since 9/11," *Studies in Conflict & Terrorism* 25 (2002): 313.

8. Walzer, *Just and Unjust Wars*, 197.

9. Michael Ignatieff, *The Lesser Evil: Political Ethics in an Age of Terror* (Princeton, N.J.: Princeton University Press, 2004), 111.

10. Quoted in Walzer, *Just and Unjust Wars*, 199.

11. Ignatieff, *The Lesser Evil*, 110.

12. Historian Timothy Garton Ash has identified four criteria by which to judge and classify terrorists. He suggests that in evaluating the moral and political legitimacy of alleged terrorists, we should focus on biography, goals, methods, and context. See Timothy Garton Ash, "Is There a Good Terrorist?" *New York Review of Books*, November 29, 2001, 30–33.

13. The following insights are taken from Russell D. Howard, "Preface," in Russell D. Howard and Reid L. Sawyer, *Defeating Terrorism: Shaping the New Security Environment* (Guildford, CT: McGraw-Hill, 2004), ix–xi.

14. A "dirty bomb," also called a radiological weapon, is a conventional explosive containing radioactive material that is dispersed when the bomb explodes. Such a weapon kills or injures in both the initial blast and the residual radiation and dispersed contamination.

15. For an illuminating assessment of U.S. counterterror policies in light of just war principles, see Neta C. Crawford, "Just War Theory and the U.S. Counterterror War," *Perspectives on Politics* 1 (March 2003): 5–25.

16. Argentina's truth commission, established to investigate the fate of the missing after democracy was restored in 1983, disclosed that nearly four thousand people had been killed by the military and security services and that nearly nine thousand others were missing after they had been kidnapped or arrested. The commission's report, titled *Nunca Más* (Never Again), confirmed what many Argentine citizens had surmised—namely, that the government authorities had carried out a brutal, covert, and illegal counterterror campaign.

17. John H. Langbein, "The Legal History of Torture," in *Torture: A Collection*, ed., Sanford Levinson (New York: Oxford University Press, 2004), 101.

18. In ratifying the torture convention, the U.S. Senate declared, "The United States understands that, in order to constitute torture, an act must be *specifically intended* to inflict severe physical or mental pain or suffering and that mental pain or suffering refers to *prolonged* mental harm."

19. Sanford Levinson, "Contemplating Torture: An Introduction," in *Torture: A Collection*, 23.

20. Henry Shue, "Torture," *Philosophy & Public Policy* 7 (Winter 1978): 124.

21. "Ends, Means and Barbarity," *Economist*, January 11, 2003, 20.

22. It is estimated that this war resulted in the death of about 400,000 to 500,000 Algerians, 27,500 French soldiers, and between 3,000 and 9,000 French civilians. Although the French were able to destroy much of the FLN organization through a counterinsurgency campaign involving torture, in the end the brutal tactics of the French failed to prevent the Algerians from gaining independence. See David Rieff, "The Bureaucrat of Terror," *World Policy Journal*, Spring 2002, 105.

23. Bruce Hoffman, "A Nasty Business," *Atlantic Monthly*, January 2002, 51.

24. For an uncommonly thoughtful description and defense of the legal and moral challenges involved in the U.S. counterterror campaign, see William Shawcross, *Justice and the Enemy: Nuremberg, 9/11, and the Trial of Khalid Sheikh Mohammed* (New York: PublicAffairs, 2011).

25. This reasoning was declared invalid by the U.S. Supreme Court in 2006. In the *Hamden v. Rumsfeld* case, the court ruled that even though terrorists were not a party to the 1949 Geneva Convention, the United States was nevertheless bound to treat prisoners humanely in accordance with Article 3 of the convention. In particular, prisoners were entitled to minimal legal protections.

26. Keith Pavlischek, "Human Rights and Justice in an Age of Terror: An Evangelical Critique of an Evangelical Declaration against Torture." Available at http://www.booksandculture.com/articles/webexclusives/2007/september/ept24a.html.

27. Mark Bowden, "The Dark Art of Interrogation," *Atlantic Monthly*, October 2003, 56.

28. For a detailed overview of the Abu Ghraib scandal, see Seymour M. Hersh, *Chain of Command: The Road from 9/11 to Abu Ghraib* (New York: HarperCollins, 2004).

29. Mark Danner, "The Logic of Torture," *New York Review of Books*, June 24, 2004, 74. For a more complete overview of allegations of torture by U.S. military forces, see Mark Danner, *Torture and Truth: America, Abu Ghraib, and the War on Terror* (New York: New York Review of Books, 2004).

30. When U.S. military authorities first learned of prisoner abuses at Abu Ghraib in January 2004, they immediately established a task force, headed by Major General Antonio Taguba, to investigate the allegations. In his secret report issued at the end of February, General Taguba found that military personnel had committed "sadistic, blatant, and wanton criminal abuses"—a conclusion that led to the removal of the general in charge of prison security and to the court martial of several soldiers charged with criminal wrongdoing. For a brief discussion of the Taguba report, see Mark Danner, "Torture and Truth," *New York Review of Books*, June 10, 2004, 46–50. In July 2004 the army's inspector-general, Lieutenant General Paul T. Mikolashek, issued a detailed report on Iraqi prisoner abuses. In his report, General Mikolashek argued that, contrary to General Taguba's conclusions, the mistreatment of prisoners was not due to systemic problems. Instead, he claimed that the abuses were the result of "unauthorized actions taken by a few individuals, coupled with the failure of a few leaders to provide adequate monitoring, supervision, and leadership over those soldiers." While acknowledging that U.S. military detention operations in Iraq and Afghanistan were plagued with poor training, haphazard organization, and outmoded policies, General Mikolashek claimed that those flaws did not directly contribute to the mistreatment of prisoners at Abu Ghraib (*New York Times*, July 23, 2004, 1 and 9).

31. For a discussion of the struggle over interrogation techniques, see Anthony Lewis, "Making Torture Legal," *New York Review of Books*, July 15, 2004, 4–8; and Dana Priest and Bradley Graham, "A Struggle over Interrogation Tactics," *Washington Post National Weekly Edition*, June 28–July 11, 2004, 15.

32. James Turner Johnson, "Torture: A Just War Perspective," *Review of Faith & International Affairs*, Summer 2007, 31.

33. Richard A. Posner, "Torture, Terrorism, and Interrogation," in *Torture: A Collection*, ed. Sanford Levinson, 291.

34. Jean Bethke Elshtain, "Reflection on the Problem of 'Dirty Hands,'" in *Torture: A Collection*, ed. Levinson, 79.

35. Stephen L. Carter, *The Violence of Peace: America's Wars in the Age of Obama* (New York: Beast Books, 2011), 41.

36. Paul W. Kahn, *Sacred Violence: Torture, Terror, and Sovereignty* (Ann Arbor: University of Michigan Press, 2008), 13 and 21–41.

37. Alan M. Dershowitz, *Why Terrorism Works: Understanding the Threat, Responding to the Challenge* (New Haven, Conn.: Yale University Press, 2002), 137.

38. Hoffman, "A Nasty Business," 51.

39. Dershowitz, *Why Terrorism Works*, 141.

40. Richard A. Posner, "The Best Offense," *New Republic*, September 2, 2002, 30.

41. Gross, *Moral Dilemmas of Modern War*, 122–31.

42. Gross, *Moral Dilemmas of Modern War*, 134.

43. Zachary R. Calo, "Torture, Necessity, and Supreme Emergency: Law and Morality at the End of Law," *Valparaiso University Law Review* 43 (2009): 1612.

44. Eric Metaxas, *Bonhoeffer: Pastor, Martyr, Prophet, Spy* (Nashville: Thomas Nelson, 2011), 323.

45. Quoted in Calo, "Torture, Necessity, and Supreme Emergency," 1598–99.

46. Ignatieff, *The Lesser Evil*, 137.

47. Ward Thomas, "Norms and Security: The Case of International Assassination," *International Security* 25 (Summer 2000): 110.

48. Philip II of Spain, for example, ardently supported the assassination of Protestant leaders, sponsoring numerous plots against William of Orange in Holland and Queen Elizabeth I in England. Indeed, in the 1570s and 1580s the English queen was subject to at least twenty assassination plots, while she herself plotted assassinations in Ireland.

49. Hugo Grotius, the distinguished seventeenth-century Dutch jurist, for example, believed that it made no difference where an enemy was killed.

50. Thomas, "Norms and Security," 113.

51. Political philosopher Michael Gross follows the logic of this view and concludes that TK is morally unacceptable when it personalizes violence. See Michael L. Gross, "Fighting by Other Means in the Mideast: A Critical Analysis of Israel's Assassination Policy," *Political Studies* 51 (2003): 350–68. Daniel Statman critiques this argument, claiming that TK is just because it focuses violence on individuals bearing the greatest culpability. See Daniel Statman, "The Morality of Assassination: a Response to Gross," *Political Studies* 51 (2003): 775–79.

52. Journalist Seymour Hersh argues that the aim of the U.S. bombing mission was to kill Colonel Qaddafi. See Seymour Hersh, "Target Qaddafi," *New York Times Magazine*, February 22, 1987, 17–26.

53. Evan Thomas and Daniel Klaidman, "The War Room," *Newsweek*, March 31, 2003, 26.

54. Gross, *Moral Dilemmas of Modern War*, 118.

55. These data are from the Long War Journal website on the war on terror. Available at http://www.longwarjournal.org/pakistan-strikes.php.

56. Tom Junod, "The Lethal Presidency of Barack Obama," *Esquire Magazine*, August 2012.

57. In December 2009 a strike occurred against al-Awlaki in Yemen, but, although thirty others were killed, his life was spared. A day after this strike, a Nigerian bomber tried to blow up a Northwest jumbo jet, but the bomb failed to detonate. When interrogated, the Nigerian bomber confessed that he had tried to bring the plane down at al-Awlaki's direction.

58. The memorandum issued by the Office of Legal Counsel declared that al-Awlaki, an enemy combatant participating in armed conflict, could be killed if capture was not possible. The U.S. prohibition against assassinations did not apply to him, the memorandum asserted. See "Secret U.S. Memo Made Legal Case to Kill a Citizen," *New York Times*, October 9, 2011, 1.

59. Junod, "The Lethal Presidency of Barack Obama."

60. Quoted in Jane Mayer, "The Predator War," *New Yorker*, October 26, 2009, 42.

61. Harold Koh, "The Obama Administration and International Law," March 25, 2010. Available at www.state.gov/s/l/releases/remarks/139119.htm.

62. Jo Becker and Scott Shane, "Secret 'Kill List' Proves a Test of Obama's Principles and Will," *New York Times*, May 29, 2012.

63. Becker and Shane, "Secret 'Kill List.'"

64. David Cortright, "License to Kill," *Cato Unbound*, January 9, 2012. Available at http://www.cato-unbound.org/2012/01/09/david-cortright/license-to-kill.

65. Ritika Singh and Benjamin Wittes, "Drones Are a Challenge—and an Opportunity," Brookings Institution, January 11, 2012. Available at http://www.brookings.edu/research/opinions/2012/01/11-drones-wittes.

66. This is the argument made by Jack Goldsmith, a former official of the Department of Justice under the Bush administration, in his *Power and Constraint: The Accountable President after 9/11* (New York: Norton, 2012). See also Charles Krauthammer, "Obama Adopts the Bush Approach to the War on Terrorism," *Washington Post*, May 22, 2009.

67. See Michael B. Mukasey, "What Could We Have Learned from Awlaki?" *Wall Street Journal*, October 5, 2011, 17.

68. Laura Blumenfeld, "In Israel, a Divisive Struggle over Targeted Killing," *Washington Post*, August 27, 2006.

69. Blumenfeld, "In Israel, a Divisive Struggle over Targeted Killing."

70. Dan Izenberg, "High Court Allows Conditional Targeted Killings," *Jerusalem Post*, December 14, 2006.

71. David Cole, "Obama and Terror: The Hovering Questions," *New York Review of Books*, July 12, 2012, 34.

72. Ignatieff, *The Lesser Evil*. 144.

CHAPTER 9: THE ETHICS OF FOREIGN INTERVENTION

1. Lea Brilmayer, *American Hegemony: Political Morality in a One-Superpower World* (New Haven, Conn.: Yale University Press, 1994), 154.

2. Charles Krauthammer, "Morality and the Reagan Doctrine," *New Republic*, September 8, 1986, 21.

3. Quoted in Drew Christiansen and Gerard F. Powers, "The Duty to Intervene: Ethics and the Varieties of Humanitarian Intervention," in *Close Calls: Intervention, Terrorism, Missile Defense, and "Just War" Today*, ed. Elliott Abrams (Washington, D.C.: Ethics and Public Policy Center, 1998), 183.

4. Gary J. Bass, *Freedom's Battle: The Origins of Humanitarian Intervention* (New York: Knopf, 2008), 382.

5. Quoted in Kelly Kate Pease and David P. Forsythe, "Human Rights, Humanitarian Intervention, and World Politics," *Human Rights Quarterly* 15 (1993): 292.

6. According to Chapter VII, the Security Council can take whatever political and military actions it designates to respond to "a threat to peace, breach of the peace or act of aggression." In effect, the United Nations can intervene against the wishes of a member state when the Security Council so decides. Such action was undertaken in 1992 when the United Nations authorized U.S. military intervention in Somalia.

7. Michael Mandelbaum, "The Reluctance to Intervene," *Foreign Policy*, no. 95 (Summer 1994): 14.

8. Mandelbaum, "The Reluctance to Intervene," 8.

9. Michal Ignatieff, "The Return of Sovereignty," *New Republic*, February 16, 2012, 26.

10. Ignatieff, "The Return of Sovereignty," 26.

11. Stephen D. Krasner, *Sovereignty: Organized Hypocrisy* (Princeton, N.J.: Princeton University Press, 1999).

12. Mandelbaum, "The Reluctance to Intervene," 6.

13. For an informative collection of essays on emerging norms governing international boundaries, see Laura W. Reed and Carl Kaysen, eds., *Emerging Norms of Justified Intervention* (Cambridge, Mass.: Committee on International Security Studies, American Academy of Arts and Sciences, 1993).

14. Michael Walzer calls this approach the "domestic analogy." For a discussion of this argument, see Michael Walzer, *Just and Unjust Wars: A Moral Argument with Historical Illustrations* (New York: Basic Books, 1977), 58.

15. Walzer, *Just and Unjust Wars*, 101.

16. Walzer, *Just and Unjust Wars*, 88.

17. Michael Walzer, "The Moral Standing of States: A Response to Four Critics," *Philosophy & Public Affairs* 9, no. 3 (Spring 1980): 214.

18. Walzer, *Just and Unjust Wars*, 54.

19. Jefferson McMahan, "The Ethics of International Intervention," in *Political Realism and International Morality: Ethics in the Nuclear Age*, ed. Kenneth Kipnis and Diana T. Meyers (Boulder, Colo.: Westview Press, 1987), 82–83.

20. McMahan, "The Ethics of International Intervention," 85.

21. Stanley Hoffmann, *Duties beyond Borders: On the Limits and Possibilities of Ethical International Politics* (Syracuse, N.Y.: Syracuse University Press, 1981), 58.

22. Dorothy Jones, *Code of Peace: Ethics and Security in the World of Warlord States* (Chicago: University of Chicago Press, 1992).

23. Jones, *Code of Peace*, xii, 163–64.

24. Walzer, *Just and Unjust Wars*, 61–63.

25. Walzer, *Just and Unjust Wars*, 90–108. A number of scholars have challenged Walzer's international relations paradigm as being too statist and insufficiently sensitive to the injustices that arise within states. For a critique of Walzer's argument, see Gerald Doppelt, "Walzer's Theory of Morality in International Relations," *Philosophy & Public Affairs* 8, no. 1 (1978): 2–26; Charles R. Beitz, "Bounded Morality: Justice and the State in World Politics," *International Organization* 33 (Summer 1979): 405–24; and David Luban, "Just War and Human Rights," *Philosophy & Public Affairs* 9, no. 2 (1979): 161–81. For Walzer's response to his critics, see Michael Walzer, "The Moral Standing of States: A Response to Four Critics," *Philosophy & Public Affairs* 9, no. 3 (1980): 209–29.

26. At the outset of the Cold War, President Harry Truman announced that the United States would provide material support to Greece and Turkey so that they could fight rising communist revolutionary forces in their countries. This declaration—known as the Truman doctrine—guided U.S. strategy throughout the forty-five years of superpower conflict.

27. For a discussion of the role and relevance of the just war doctrine to military intervention, see Kenneth R. Himes, "Just War, Pacifism and Humanitarian Intervention," *America*, August 14, 1993, 15, 28–29.

28. Charles Krauthammer, "When to Intervene," *New Republic*, May 6, 1985, 11.

29. International Commission on Intervention and State Sovereignty, *Responsibility to Protect: Report of the International Commission on Intervention and State Sovereignty*. See www.idrc.ca.

30. According to the ICISS, the principle of protection demands that (1) the assessment of humanitarian needs should be undertaken from the perspective of the victim, not the concerns of the intervening state; (2) the primary responsibility for meeting human needs should rest with each state concerned; and (3) *the duty to protect* means not only to respond and react but also to prevent and rebuild. ICISS, *Responsibility to Protect*, 17.

31. ICISS, *Responsibility to Protect*, xi.

32. ICISS, *Responsibility to Protect*, xii.

33. See Matthew C. Waxman, *Intervention to Stop Genocide and Mass Atrocities* (New York: Council on Foreign Relations, 2009).

34. For a preliminary assessment of R2P, see Alex J. Bellamy, "The Responsibility to Protect—Five Years On," *Ethics & International Affairs* 24 (Summer 2010): 143–69; and Edward C. Luck, "The Responsibility to Protect: Growing Pains or Early Promise?" *Ethics & International Affairs* 24 (Winter 2010): 349–65.

35. The report, which was commissioned by the UN Human Rights Council, used the R2P doctrine as a benchmark. It concluded that Sudan had manifestly failed to protect the people of Darfur from large-scale international crimes and that it was therefore "the solemn obligation of the international community to exercise its *responsibility to protect*." See Alex J. Bellamy, "Realizing the Responsibility to Protect," *International Studies Perspectives* 10 (2009): 117–19.

36. It is unclear to what degree the R2P principle influenced leaders' perceptions of how to respond to developments in Libya. For a discussion of alternative perceptions of R2P and the Libyan revolt, see "Roundtable: Libya, RtoP, and Humanitarian Intervention," *Ethics & International Affairs* 25 (Fall 2011): 251–313.

37. It is significant that five states abstained on the Security Council vote: China, Russia, Germany, Brazil, and India. China and Russia avoided using their veto because many Arab countries supported the resolution. The African Union, by contrast, was staunchly opposed to the UN's involvement.

38. By the time that the Security Council adopted its resolution, the U.S. government had frozen financial assets worth $33 billion in American financial institutions.

39. Walzer claims that few Arab countries supported the NATO initiative, while Russia and China, although opposed to the action, refrained from vetoing the Security Council resolution.

40. Michael Walzer, "The Case against Our Attack on Libya," *New Republic*, March 20, 2011.

41. William Galston, "Necessary and Sufficient: The Case against Libyan Intervention is Philosophically Flawed," *New Republic*, March 24, 2011.

42. The Editors, "Some Questions about Obama's Speech," *New Republic*, March 28, 2011.

43. For a description of the fragmented nature of power, see Joshua Hammer, "Vengeance in Libya," *New York Review of Books*, January 12, 2012.

44. Galston, "Necessary and Sufficient."

45. The NTC estimates that during the Libyan civil war some thirty thousand persons were killed, fifty thousand were seriously injured, and four thousand were missing.

46. Anne-Marie Slaughter, "Why Libya Sceptics Were Proved Badly Wrong," *Financial Times*, August 24, 2011.

47. Jack Donnelly, "Human Rights, Humanitarian Intervention and American Foreign Policy: Law, Morality and Politics," *Journal of International Affairs* 37 (Winter 1984): 313.

48. Stanley Hoffmann, "Delusions of World Order," *New York Review of Books*, May 28, 1992, 37–43.

49. Waxman, *Intervention to Stop Genocide and Mass Atrocities*, 9.

50. For an excellent discussion of the U.S. military and diplomatic operation in Somalia, see John L. Hirsch and Robert B. Oakley, *Somalia and Operation Restore Hope: Reflections on Peacemaking and Peacekeeping* (Washington, D.C.: U.S. Institute of Peace Press, 1995).

51. Hirsch and Oakley, *Somalia and Operation Restore Hope*, 145.

52. It is important to emphasize that the Security Council authorized this action in great part because of the total breakdown of government authority. Because there was no effective government in Somalia, the UN Charter's prohibitions against UN intervention in the domestic affairs of states (Article 2.7) were not applicable.

53. Alberto R. Coll, "Somalia and the Problems of Doing Good: A Perspective from the Defense Department," in *Close Calls: Intervention, Terrorism, Missile Defense, and 'Just War' Today*, ed. Elliott Abrams (Washington, D.C.: Ethics and Public Policy Center, 1998), 177–81.

54. John R. Bolton, "Somalia and the Problems of Doing Good: a Perspective from the Department of State," in *Close Calls*, ed. Abrams, 157.

55. Coll, "Somalia and the Problems of Doing Good," 179.

56. Chester Crocker, "The Lessons of Somalia," *Foreign Affairs* 74 (May/June 1995): 7.

CHAPTER 10: THE ETHICS OF INTERNATIONAL ECONOMIC RELATIONS

1. Dani Rodrick, *The Globalization Paradox: Democracy and the Future of the World Economy* (New York: Norton, 2011), 208.

2. Joseph E. Stiglitz, *Making Globalization Work* (New York: Norton, 2007), 266.

3. Jeffrey A. Frieden, *Global Capitalism: Its Rise and Fall in the Twentieth Century* (New York: Norton, 2006), 476.

4. This argument is taken from Jagdish Bhagwati, *In Defense of Globalization* (New York: Oxford University Press, 2004), 11.

5. Thomas L. Friedman, *The Lexus and the Olive Tree: Understanding Globalization* (New York: Anchor Books, 2000), 9.

6. For a discussion of the negative effects of globalization, see Moisés Naím, "The Five Wars of Globalization," *Foreign Policy*, January/February 2003, 29–37.

7. See Thomas L. Friedman, *The World Is Flat: A Brief History of the Twenty-First Century* (New York: Farrar, Strauss & Giroux, 2005).

8. Friedman, *The Lexus and the Olive Tree*.

9. Clive Crook, "A Survey of Globalisation: Globalisation and Its Critics," *Economist*, September 29, 2001, 6.

10. Martin Wolf, *Why Globalization Works* (New Haven: Yale University Press, 2004), 44.

11. Stiglitz, *Making Globalization Work*, 8–9.

12. Wolf, *Why Globalization Works*, 141–42.

13. "A Place for Capital Controls," *Economist*, May 1, 2003.

14. This definition is taken from Martin Wolf, *Fixing Global Finance* (Baltimore, Md.: Johns Hopkins University Press, 2008), 10.

15. Michael Lewis, *Boomerang: Travels in the New Third World* (New York: Norton, 2011), 97.

16. Stiglitz, *Making Globalization Work*, 266.

17. Examples of such speculative investments include contracts to purchase currencies in the future at a given time at a given price. They also include options to exchange a currency at a given exchange rate at a specified date.

18. Gary Clyde Hufbauer and Kati Suominen, *Globalization at Risk: Challenges to Finance and Trade* (New Haven, Conn.: Yale University Press, 2010), 27.

19. Wolf, *Fixing Global Finance*, 21–22.

20. The net effect of this action, however, was to compromise the foundational principle of capitalism—which is that risking capital can result in gains as well as losses. When the U.S. government bailed out banks to shore up the financial system, it compromised the core capitalist ethic, contributing to what economists call "moral hazard"—that is, encouraging undue risks because people don't have to bear the consequences of their actions.

21. The seventeen members of the eurozone are Austria, Belgium, Cyprus, Estonia, Finland, France, Germany, Greece, Ireland, Italy, Luxembourg, Malta, the Netherlands, Portugal, Slovakia, Slovenia, and Spain. Denmark and the United Kingdom are members of the EU but chose not to adopt the euro. Eight other EU countries are under consideration for euro membership.

22. Subsequently, EU authorities examined Greece's accounts and concluded that Greece's deficit was even higher—13.6 percent of GDP.

23. These data are from Bill Marsh, "It's All Connected: A Spectator's Guide to the Euro Crisis," *New York Times*, October 23, 2011.

24. "Eurozone Crisis Explained," *BBC News—Business*, June 19, 2012.

25. Martin Wolf, "There Is No Sunlit Future for the Euro," *Financial Times*, October 18, 2011.

26. Howard Schneider, "IMF: Euro Zone in 'Significant' Jeopardy from Threat of Deflation," *Washington Post*, July 18, 2012.

27. Following a tradition dating to the sixteenth century, merchants haggle over the price of large mounds of Gouda and Edam cheese, and once a price is agreed to, the merchants seal the

agreement with a hand clap—the visible promise that the farmer will deliver the cheese and the trader will make full payment. A guild of colorfully dressed cheese carriers moves and weighs the cheese in a medieval weighing house in the market square.

28. Wolf, *Fixing Global Finance*, 26.

29. David A. Baldwin, *Economic Statecraft* (Princeton, N.J.: Princeton University Press, 1985).

30. See, for example, Roger Fisher, *Conflict for Beginners* (New York: Harper & Row, 1969).

31. James M. Lindsay, "Trade Sanctions as Policy Instruments: A Reexamination," *International Studies Quarterly*, no. 30 (June 1986): 155–56.

32. Kim Richard Nossal, "International Sanctions as International Punishment," *International Organization* 43 (Spring 1989): 313–14.

33. Baldwin, *Economic Statecraft*, 57.

34. M. S. Daoudi and J. S. Dajani, *Economic Sanctions: Ideals and Experience* (London: Routledge & Kegan Paul, 1983).

35. For a discussion of the relationship between private and public actors, see Kenneth A. Rodman, "Public and Private Sanctions against South Africa," *Political Science Quarterly* 109 (Summer 1994): 313–34.

36. Gary C. Hufbauer, Jeffrey J. Schott, and Kimberly Ann Elliott, *Economic Sanctions Reconsidered: History and Current Policy*, 2nd ed. (Washington, D.C.: Institute for International Economics, 1990), 49–73.

37. Hufbauer, Schott, and Elliott, *Economic Sanctions Reconsidered*.

38. Robert A. Pape, "Why Economic Sanctions Do Not Work," *International Security* 22 (Fall 1997): 90–136.

39. Baldwin, *Economic Statecraft*, 96–114.

40. Lisa Martin, *Coercive Cooperation: Explaining Multilateral Economic Sanctions* (Princeton, N.J.: Princeton University Press, 1992).

41. William Kaempfer and Anton Lowenberg, *International Economic Sanctions: A Public Choice Perspective* (Boulder, Colo.: Westview Press, 1992), 133.

42. For a discussion of this point with reference to selective cases (the Megarian decree, the League of Nations sanctions against Italy, and the trans-Siberian pipeline sanctions), see Stefanie Ann Lenway, "Between War and Commerce: Economic Sanctions as a Tool of Statecraft," *International Organization* 42 (Spring 1988): 409–19.

43. Joy Gordon, "Reply to George A. Lopez's 'More Ethical than Not,'" *Ethics & International Affairs* 13 (1999): 150.

44. Quoted in Richard E. Sincere Jr., *The Politics of Sentiment: Churches and Foreign Investment in South Africa* (Washington, D.C.: Ethics and Public Policy Center, 1984), v.

45. Drew Christiansen and Gerard F. Powers, "Economic Sanctions and the Just War Doctrine," in *Economic Sanctions: Panacea or Peacebuilding in a Post–Cold War World?*, ed. David Cortright and George A. Lopez (Boulder, Colo.: Westview Press, 1995), 102.

46. Albert C. Pierce, "Just War Principles and Economic Sanctions," *Ethics & International Affairs* 10 (1996): 99–113.

47. See, for example, Kenneth A. Rodman, "Public and Private Sanctions against South Africa," *Political Science Quarterly* 109 (Summer 1994).

48. The principle of double effect provides that civilians may be killed in war but only if their death is the by-product of the destruction and violence directly intended against military targets.

49. Pierce, "Just War Principles and Economic Sanctions," 100–101.

50. Drew Christiansen and Gerard F. Powers, "Sanctions: Unintended Consequences," *Bulletin of the Atomic Scientists*, November 1993, 43.

51. For an excellent overview of the nature and evolution of economic sanctions on Iraq following the Persian Gulf War, see Erik D. K. Melby, "Iraq," in *Economic Sanctions and American Diplomacy*, ed. Richard N. Haass (New York: Council on Foreign Relations, 1998), 107–28.

52. "Why War Would Be Justified," *Economist*, February 22, 2003, 13.

53. For an overview of this initiative, see David Cortright and George A. Lopez, *Smart Sanctions: Targeting Economic Statecraft* (Lanham, Md.: Rowman & Littlefield, 2002).

54. Michael Walzer, "Justice and Injustice in the Gulf War," in *But Was It Just? Reflections on the Morality of the Persian Gulf War*, ed. David DeCosse (New York: Doubleday, 1992), 3.

55. Christiansen and Powers, "Economic Sanctions and the Just-War Doctrine," 102.

56. William H. Kaempfer, James A. Lehman, and Anton D. Lowenberg, "Divestment, Investment Sanctions, and Disinvestment: An Evaluation of Anti-Apartheid Policy Instruments," *International Organization* 41 (Summer 1987): 461.

57. Jennifer Davis, "Sanctions and Apartheid: The Economic Challenge to Discrimination," in *Economic Sanctions*, ed. Cortright and Lopez, 178.

58. Rodman, "Public and Private Sanctions against South Africa," 323.

59. Thomas W. Hazlett, "Did Sanctions Matter?" *New York Times*, July 22, 1991, A5.

60. Helen Suzman, "Sanctions Won't End Apartheid," *New York Times*, October 4, 1987, sec. IV, 23.

61. Alan Paton, *Cry, the Beloved Country* (Cape Town: Hans Strydom Publishers, 1987), 7.

62. Federated Chamber of Industries, *The Effect of Sanctions on Unemployment and Production in South Africa* (Pretoria: FCI Information Services, 1986).

63. Neta C. Crawford, "The Humanitarian Consequences of Sanctioning South Africa: A Preliminary Assessment," in *Political Gain and Civilian Pain: Humanitarian Impacts of Economic Sanctions*, ed. Thomas G. Weiss et al. (Lanham, Md.: Rowman & Littlefield, 1997), 77.

64. The Anglo-American Corporation paid about 20 percent less than the value of traded stock, and it did so with undervalued South African currency (rand).

65. Merle Lipton, *Sanctions and South Africa: The Dynamics of Economic Isolation*, Special Report No. 1119 (London: Economist Intelligence Unit, January 1988), 92.

66. Crawford, "Humanitarian Consequences of Sanctioning South Africa," 73.

67. Crawford, "Humanitarian Consequences of Sanctioning South Africa," 77.

68. F. W. de Klerk, "The Bull in the Garden," *Civilization* 5 (April/May 1998): 61.

CHAPTER 11: PURSUING INTERNATIONAL JUSTICE

1. Peter B. Kapstein, *Economic Justice in an Unfair World: Toward a Level Playing Field* (Princeton, N.J.: Princeton University Press, 2006), 14.

2. "Opening the Door," *Economist*, November 2, 2002, 11.

3. Alan Dowty, *Closed Borders: The Contemporary Assault on Freedom of Movement* (New Haven, Conn.: Yale University Press, 1987), 226.

4. Stanley Hoffmann, *Duties beyond Borders: On the Limits and Possibilities of Ethical International Politics* (Syracuse, N.Y.: Syracuse University Press, 1981), 164–65.

5. For a review of this procedural perspective of international justice, see Chris Brown, *International Relations Theory: New Normative Approaches* (New York: Columbia University Press, 1992), 170–88.

6. Terry Nardin, *Law, Morality and the Relations of States* (Princeton, N.J.: Princeton University Press, 1983), 267–68.

7. The HDI is an index based on three criteria: longevity (measured by life expectancy), knowledge (based on adult literacy and mean years of schooling), and standard of living (measured by per capita income adjusted for purchasing power parity). For the 2006 rankings, see

United Nations Development Programme, *Human Development Report, 2006* (New York: Palgrave Macmillan, 2006), 283–86.

8. Carol C. Adelman, "The Privatization of Foreign Aid," *Foreign Affairs* 82 (November/December 2003): 10–11. See also Devesh Kapur and John McHale, "Migration's New Payoff," *Foreign Policy*, November/December 2003, 49–57.

9. John Cassidy, "Helping Hands: How Foreign Aid Could Benefit Everybody," *New Yorker*, March 18, 2002, 63.

10. William Easterly, *The Elusive Quest for Growth: Economists' Adventures and Misadventures in the Tropics* (Cambridge, Mass.: MIT Press, 2002), 42.

11. The eight MDG initiatives include (1) halve the proportion of people living on less than a dollar a day; (2) ensure that all children complete primary school; (3) educate boys and girls equally; (4) reduce the mortality rate among children under five by two-thirds; (5) reduce the maternal mortality rate by three-quarters; (6) halt and begin to reverse the spread of HIV/AIDS, malaria, and other major diseases; (7) halve the proportion of people without access to safe water and sanitation; and (8) increase aid and improve governance.

12. Jeffrey D. Sachs, *The End of Poverty: Economic Possibilities for Our Time* (New York: Penguin, 2005), 301–2.

13. Sachs, *The End of Poverty*, 360.

14. P. T. Bauer, *Reality and Rhetoric* (Cambridge, Mass.: Harvard University Press, 1984), 38–62. See also P. T. Bauer, *Equality, the Third World, and Economic Delusion* (Cambridge, Mass.: Harvard University Press, 1981).

15. William Easterly, *The White Man's Burden: Why the West's Efforts to Aid the Rest Have Done So Much Ill and So Little Good* (New York: Penguin, 2006), 11.

16. David Halloran Lumsdaine, *Moral Vision in International Politics: The Foreign Aid Regime, 1949–1989* (Princeton, N.J.: Princeton University Press, 1993), 3.

17. First diagnosed in 1981 in the United States, AIDS (acquired immune deficiency syndrome) is a disease of the immune system caused by a virus known as HIV (human immunodeficiency virus). The disease impairs people's immune systems, making them far more likely to get infections and tumors.

18. HIV can also be spread through other means—such as direct contact with the blood or fluids of an HIV-positive person, tainted needles, or breast-feeding.

19. In February 2002, for example, Graham convened an international conference in Washington, D.C., for some eight hundred Christian leaders to mobilize support for an anti-AIDS campaign. Prior to that event Graham had been in touch with Senator Jesse Helms (R-NC) and challenged Helms to use his position as U.S. senator to promote humanitarian assistance to AIDS victims. On one occasion, Senator Helms told Graham, "Well, Franklin, I'm going to have to change some of the positions I've had in the past." Thus, when Helms addressed the 2002 conference, he declared his support for increased government aid to African victims, declaring, "I was wrong, and I'm going to take the latter days of my time in the Senate to do everything I can to help push this [comprehensive anti-AIDS initiative]." See "The Age of AIDS: Interview with Franklin Graham," *Frontline*, May 30, 2006. Available at http://www.pbs.org/wgbh/pages/frontline/aids/interviews/graham.html.

20. George W. Bush, *Decision Points* (New York: Crown, 2010), 335.

21. Bush, *Decision Points*, 338.

22. Bush, *Decision Points*, 340.

23. "President Discusses the Fight against Global and Domestic HIV/AIDS," January 31, 2003. Available at http://georgewbush-whitehouse.archives.gov/news/releases/2003/01/20030131-4.html.

24. The focus countries included Botswana, Cote d'Ivoire, Ethiopia, Guyana, Haiti, Kenya, Mozambique, Namibia, Niger, Rwanda, South Africa, Tanzania, Uganda, and Zambia. Vietnam was added in mid-2004, bringing the total to fifteen countries.

25. John W. Dietrich, "The Politics of PEPFAR: The President's Emergency Plan for AIDS Relief," *Ethics & International Affairs* 21 (Fall 2007): 280.

26. Rochelle Walensky and Daniel Kuritzkes, "The Impact of the President's Emergency Plan for AIDS Relief (PEPFAR) beyond HIV and Why It Remains Essential," *Clinical Infectious Diseases* 50 (January 2010): 272–75.

27. Condoleezza Rice, *No Higher Honor: A Memoir of My Years in Washington* (New York: Crown, 2011), 229.

28. See Garrett Hardin, *Living within Limits: Ecology, Economics and Population Taboos* (New York: Oxford University Press, 1993), esp. 276–93.

29. See, for example, Joseph H. Carens, "Aliens and Citizens: The Case for Open Borders," *Review of Politics* 49 (Spring 1987): 251–73; Joseph H. Carens, "Migration and Morality: A Liberal Egalitarian Perspective, in *Free Movement: Ethical Issues in the Transnational Migration of People and of Money*, ed. Brian Barry and Robert E. Goodin (University Park: Pennsylvania State University Press, 1992), 25–47; and Peter Singer and Renata Singer, "The Ethics of Refugee Policy," in *Open Borders? Closed Societies? The Ethical and Political Issues*, ed. Mark Gibney (New York: Greenwood Press, 1988), 111–30.

30. Dowty, *Closed Borders*, 15.

31. The right of return is a delimited claim for admission. The right of return applies mainly to peoples seeking to return to their nation's homeland on the basis of historic ties of prior membership. For a discussion of how this right applies to Palestinian and Jewish people within Israel, see W. Gunther Plaut, *Asylum: A Moral Dilemma* (Westport, Conn.: Praeger, 1995), 82–88.

32. Brian Barry, "The Quest for Consistency: A Skeptical View," in *Free Movement*, ed. Barry and Goodin, 284.

33. Michael Walzer, *Spheres of Justice: A Defense of Pluralism and Equality* (New York: Basic Books, 1983), 62.

34. Walzer, *Spheres of Justice*, 9–10.

35. Myron Weiner, "Ethics, National Sovereignty and the Control of Immigration," *International Migration Review* 30 (Spring 1996): 192.

36. According to the 1951 UN Convention on the Status of Refugees, a refugee is a person "who owing to well-founded fear of being persecuted for reasons of race, religion, nationality, membership of a particular social group or political opinion, is outside the country of his nationality and is unable, or owing to such fear, is unwilling to avail himself of the protection of that country."

37. U.S. Committee on Refugees and Immigration, "Key Statistics," *World Refugee Survey*, 2007. Available at www.refugees.org/site/Survey.

38. For an illuminating analysis of the ethics of asylum, see Matthew J. Gibney, *The Ethics and Politics of Asylum: Liberal Democracy and the Response to Refugees* (Cambridge: Cambridge University Press, 2004). See also Gil Loescher, *Beyond Charity: International Cooperation and the Global Refugee Crisis* (New York: Oxford University Press, 1993).

39. Louis Henkin, *The Age of Rights* (New York: Columbia University Press, 1990), 48.

40. For an analysis of the ethics of immigration policies, see Joseph H. Carens, "Who Should Get In? The Ethics of Immigration Admissions," *Ethics & International Affairs* 17, no. 1 (2003): 95–110.

41. For example, Peter Singer and Renata Singer, following the principle of "equal consideration of interests," argue for greatly increasing the number of refugees resettled in rich countries. See Singer and Singer, "The Ethics of Refugee Policy," in *Open Borders?*, ed. Gibney, 122–28.

42. Weiner, "Ethics, National Sovereignty and the Control of Immigration," 175.

43. IND (Immigration and Naturalization Service), "The Organization for Entry into the Netherlands, Naturalization," November 2006. Available at www.nd.nl.

44. Department of Homeland Security, *Yearbook of Immigration Statistics: 2005* (Washington, D.C.: U.S. Department of Homeland Security, Office of Immigration Statistics, 2006), 91.

45. Congressional Budget Office, "Immigration Policy of the United States," February 2006, viii.

46. *New York Times*, March 24, 2012, A14.

47. "News Release," Immigration and Customs Enforcement," October 18, 2011.

48. For a critique of the continuing mass migration of Hispanics to the United States, see Samuel P. Huntington, *Who Are We?: The Challenges to America's National Identity* (New York: Simon & Schuster, 2004).

49. According to the proposed act, applicants for legalization had to be high school graduates, have arrived prior to their sixteenth birthday, have lived for at least five consecutive years in the United States, and be under thirty years of age at the time of application.

50. During the 1990s, average annual refugee arrivals were one hundred thousand, or double the number in the more recent period. Part of the explanation for the decrease is related to increased security procedures and other policy changes in the aftermath of the 9/11 terrorist attacks. See Office of Immigration Statistics, Policy Directorate, "Annual Flow Report, March 2007: U.S. Legal Permanent Residents: 2006."

51. Weiner, "Ethics, National Sovereignty and the Control of Immigration," 195.

52. Singer and Singer, "The Ethics of Refugee Policy, in *Open Borders?*, ed. Gibney, 116.

53. *New York Times*, June 14, 1996, sec. A, 1, 13.

54. The Mariel boatlift occurred in the spring of 1980 after Fidel Castro announced that anyone wishing to leave Cuba could do so. As a result, some 125,000 Cubans, with the help of more than a thousand Florida boats, migrated to the United States during a two-month period. Because U.S. law would not allow such a large number of immigrants or refugees, the U.S. government classified such persons as "special entrants."

55. To inhibit illegal Cuban migration to the United States and to deter airplane and boat hijackings, U.S. and Cuban officials signed a similar bilateral agreement that called for the repatriation of Cubans seeking unauthorized entry into the United States.

56. This decision was contested in court. Human rights advocates filed a legal suit arguing that the executive decision was unconstitutional because it violated the 1951 Convention on Refugees. A district court affirmed the decision, and a federal appeals court overturned the lower court ruling. The Justice Department immediately filed an appeal with the U.S. Supreme Court. After granting the Bush administration temporary authority to continue forced repatriation, the high court ruled that the original executive order was not unconstitutional.

57. Walzer, *Spheres of Justice*, 18–21.

58. Weiner, "Ethics, National Sovereignty and the Control of Immigration," 179.

CHAPTER 12: PROMOTING GLOBAL JUSTICE

1. Peter Singer, *One World: The Ethics of Globalization* (New Haven, Conn.: Yale University Press, 2002), 13.

2. Michael Ignatieff, "We're So Exceptional," *New York Review of Books*, April 4, 2012, 8.

3. Brad R. Roth, *Sovereign Equality and Moral Disagreement: Premises of a Pluralist International Legal Order* (New York: Oxford University Press, 2011), 289.

4. Charles R. Beitz, *Political Theory and International Relations* (Princeton, N.J.: Princeton University Press, 1979), 151.

5. Governments vary greatly in their nature and capacity. Some, like the democratic states of Europe, are benevolent and humane, while others, like the dictatorships of Belarus and Zimbabwe, are corrupt and abusive. Still others are strong, like Chile and the Netherlands, while others, like Congo and Haiti, are fragile and incapable of maintaining domestic order and providing essential public goods, such as education and basic health care.

6. To be sure, moral obligations may supersede a government's authority when it carries out actions that contravene a basic moral principle, such as the sanctity of life or the gross abuse of human rights.

7. Since the development of institutions frequently results in the creation of international governmental organizations, some thinkers have used institutions and organizations interchangeably. But this is incorrect since an institution is a broader, more inclusive concept based on norms, tacit practices, formal rules, and governmental structures.

8. For a discussion of this concept, see Robert D. Putnam, *Making Democracy Work: Civic Tradition in Modern Italy* (Princeton, N.J.: Princeton University Press, 1993), chap. 6; see also Robert D. Putnam, "Bowling Alone: America's Declining Social Capital," *Journal of Democracy* 6 (1995): 65–78.

9. Since democratic structures do not exist in the world, some scholars argue that global governance need not fulfill the domestic standards of democratic consent. For a proposal on how global governance can be reconciled with democratic legitimacy, see Allen Buchanan and Robert O. Keohane, "The Legitimacy of Global Governance Institutions," *Ethics & International Affairs* 20 (2006): 405–37.

10. Francis Fukuyama, *State-Building: Governance and World Order in the 21st Century* (Ithaca, N.Y.: Cornell University Press, 2004).

11. Amartya Sen, *Development as Freedom* (New York: Knopf, 1999), 160–88.

12. Michael Mandelbaum, *The Case for Goliath: How America Acts as the World's Government in the Twenty-First Century* (New York: PublicAffairs, 2005).

13. "The New Titans: A Survey of the World Economy," *Economist*, September 16, 2006, 12.

14. This is Adam Smith's argument in *The Wealth of Nations*, in which he argues that a free enterprise system would contribute to the general interest of society. According to Smith, the actions of individuals would lead to the general prosperity of society as if an "invisible hand" had guided production.

15. For a mid-twentieth-century application of Lloyd's metaphor, see Garrett Hardin, "The Tragedy of the Commons," *Science*, December 13, 1968, 1243–48.

16. For a discussion of the regulation of the earth's collective goods, see Per Magnus Wijkman, "Managing the Global Commons," *International Organization* 36 (Summer 1982): 511–36.

17. Some major treaties designed to protect the environment include the Convention on Fishing and Conservation of Living Resources of the High Seas (1958); the Convention on the International Trade in Endangered Species of Wild Flora and Fauna—CITES (1973); the London Convention on the Prevention of Marine Pollution (1972); the Montreal Protocol on Substances that Deplete the Ozone Layer (1987); and the Basel Convention on the Control of Transboundary Movements of Hazardous Wastes and Their Disposal (1989).

18. For the science of global warming, see the IPCC Assessment Reports (1990, 1996, 2001, 2007), which are available at www.ipcc.ch.

19. The next (fifth) IPCC report will be issued in 2014.

20. U.S. opposition to Kyoto was fueled in part by the fear that the failure to involve the emerging economies was not only "unfair" but would cancel whatever gains were realized by the North's emissions reductions. Not surprisingly, the U.S. Senate overwhelmingly passed a resolution (95–0) that required developing nations to accept binding emission targets before it would consider ratification.

21. According to Kyoto guidelines, the protocol would become a binding convention when fifty-five countries accounting for at least 55 percent of the world's 1990 greenhouse emissions had ratified it. Thus, even though nearly eighty countries had ratified the treaty by the beginning of the new millennium, the emissions threshold had not been met. Only when the Russian Duma ratified the accord in 2004 was this condition fulfilled.

22. Stephen M. Gardiner, "The Global Warming Tragedy and the Dangerous Illusion of the Kyoto Protocol," *Ethics & International Affairs* 18, no. 1 (2004): 36.

23. For example, President Obama has pledged to reduce American emissions 17 percent below 2005 levels by 2020.

24. For a brief summary of the science of climate change, see Donald A. Brown, *American Heat: Ethical Problems with the United States' Response to Global Warming* (Boulder, Colo.: Rowman & Littlefield, 2002), chap. 6; and Scott Barrett, *Environment and Statecraft: The Strategy of Environmental Treaty-Making* (New York: Oxford University Press, 2003), 362–66. For an overview and critique of widely held views about climate change, see Aaron Wildavsky, *But Is It True? A Citizen's Guide to Environmental Health and Safety Issues* (Cambridge, Mass.: Harvard University Press, 1995), chap. 11. For a more recent illustration of contrasting views on climate change, see the following exchange: "No Need to Panic about Global Warming," *Wall Street Journal*, January 27, 2012; William Norhaus, "Why the Global Warming Skeptics Are Wrong," *New York Review of Books*, March 22, 2012, 32–34; "In the Climate Casino: An Exchange," *New York Review of Books*, April 26, 2012, 55–57.

25. For contrasting perspectives on climate change, see, for example, Marvin S. Soroos, *The Endangered Atmosphere: Preserving the Global Commons* (Columbia, S.C.: University of South Carolina Press, 1997); and Bjorn Lomborg, *The Skeptical Environmentalist* (Cambridge: Cambridge University Press, 2001).

26. For a moral assessment of "emissions rights," see Michael J. Sandel, "It's Immoral to Buy the Right to Pollute," *New York Times*, December 15, 1997, A15.

27. According to one estimate, the richest 20 percent of the world's population is responsible for more than 60 percent of current global greenhouse gas emissions. Since carbon dioxide, the main contributor to the greenhouse effect, remains in the atmosphere for more than a hundred years, the total responsibility for the richest countries is likely to be more than 80 percent. J. Timmons Roberts and Bradley C. Parks, *A Climate of Injustice: Global Inequality, North-South Politics, and Climate Policy* (Cambridge, Mass.: MIT Press, 2007), 10.

28. Henry D. Jacoby, Ronald G. Prinn, and Richard Schmalensee, "Kyoto's Unfinished Business," *Foreign Affairs* 77 (July/August 1998): 60.

29. Fareed Zakaria, "The Case for a Global Carbon Tax," *Newsweek*, April 16, 2007, 94.

30. Brian Tucker, "Science Friction: The Politics of Global Warming," *National Interest*, Fall 1997, 84.

31. For an excellent overview of the prospects for nuclear energy after the Fukushima accident, see "Special Report: The Dream That Failed," *Economist*, March 10, 2012.

32. Stephen Macedo, "Introduction," in *Universal Jurisdiction*, ed. Stephen Macedo (Philadelphia: University of Pennsylvania Press, 2004), 4.

33. When a Brussels court, using the principle of universal jurisdiction, threatened to indict General Tommy Franks for crimes committed by U.S. forces during the 2003 invasion of Iraq,

the U.S. government responded by threatening to move NATO headquarters from Belgium to another country. See William Shawcross, *Justice and the Enemy: Nuremberg, 9/11, and the Trial of Khalid Sheikh Mohammed* (New York: PublicAffairs, 2011), 103–4.

34. Naomi Roht-Arriaza, *The Pinochet Effect: Transnational Justice in the Age of Human Rights* (Philadelphia: University of Pennsylvania Press, 2005), 7.

35. Henry A. Kissinger, "The Pitfalls of Universal Jurisdiction," *Foreign Affairs* 80 (July/August 2001): 95.

36. In April 2000, a Belgian judge issued a warrant for the arrest of Abdulaye Yerodia, a political leader of the Democratic Republic of Congo (DRC) for allegedly committing war crimes and crimes against humanity against Tutsi rebels in the eastern part of the country. By the time the warrant was issued, Yerodia was foreign minister of the DRC. The Congolese government filed a complaint with the ICJ accusing Belgium of violating the principle of sovereign immunity. In February 2002, the ICJ ruled that Belgium had indeed overstepped its authority and ordered Belgium to rescind the arrest warrant for Mr. Yerodia.

37. For an overview of the role of the United States in setting up and overseeing the work of these tribunals, see David Scheffer, *All the Missing Souls: A Personal History of the War Crimes Tribunals* (Princeton, N.J.: Princeton University Press, 2012).

38. Of the 161 persons indicted by the ICTY, 126 cases had been completed by 2012 with these results: 64 persons were sentenced, 13 were acquitted, 20 indictments were withdrawn, 16 persons died in custody or before their arrest, and 13 prisoners were returned to national jurisdiction. Seventeen persons were appealing their sentences. For more information on the ICTY, see http://www.icty.org/sections/TheCases/KeyFigures.

39. Of the seventy-two persons indicted by the ICTR, the court had sentenced thirty-eight offenders and acquitted ten. Two cases had been withdrawn and four cases were returned to national jurisdiction. As 2011, sixteen persons were appealing their verdicts. For more data on the ICTR cases, see http://www.unictr.org/Cases/StatusofCases/tabid/204/Default.aspx.

40. The principal crimes that the two leaders committed were carried out during the long siege of Sarajevo and the mass killing of eight thousand men and boys at Srebrenica, an area that the United Nations had declared a "safe area" under the protection of four hundred Dutch peacekeepers.

41. For an excellent overview and critique of the ICC, see Geoffrey Robertson, *Crimes against Humanity: The Struggle for Global Justice*, 3rd ed. (New York: New Press, 2006), 419–67.

42. Kissinger, "The Pitfalls of Universal Jurisdiction," 94.

43. For a discussion of the politics of the ICC, see "Roundtable: The Political Ethics of the International Criminal Court," *Ethics & International Affairs* 26 (Spring 2012): 53–101.

44. For an overview of the politics and legal aspects of the ICC's Uganda case, see Adam Branch, "Uganda's Civil War and the Politics of ICC Intervention," *Ethics & International Affairs* 21 (Summer 2007): 179–98.

45. Jess Bravin, "Justice Delayed: For Global Court, Ugandan Rebels Prove Tough Test," *Wall Street Journal*, June 8, 2006, 1 and 14.

46. Once the court began its investigation and issued its indictments, the LRA responded with increased violence. In 2005, a delegation of Acholi people traveled to the court's headquarters to plead that the ICC drop its case in order to facilitate peace negotiations and relegate justice to the sidelines. More significantly, in 2006 Uganda's government and LRA representatives engaged in secret talks that culminated with the country's president, Yoweri Museveni, offering to shield Joseph Kony, the top LRA leader, from ICC prosecution if he surrendered. Museveni's effort to place reconciliation above legal accountability points to a central tension between the quest for peace and the quest for justice. Since the ICC is concerned solely with justice, it is not prepared to address the political adjustments that might be necessary to achieve national reconciliation.

47. Colonel Qaddafi was captured and killed in October 2011, while his son Saif was captured in early 2012. Saif is being detained by militia in Zintan, a town in southern Libya. A special jail was being built in Tripoli so that Saif could be transferred and tried in a national court. The ICC would also like to try Saif, but the Libyan government has refused its request. Sanoussi was captured in mid-2012 in Mauritania and was extradited to Libya several months later.

48. Robert W. Tucker, "The International Criminal Court Controversy," *World Policy Journal* 18 (Summer 2001): 80.

49. Stephen D. Krasner, "A World Court That Could Backfire," *New York Times*, June 15, 2001, 19.

50. Mahmood Mamdani, *Saviors and Survivors: Darfur, Politics and the War on Terror* (New York: Doubleday, 2009), 284.

51. Mamdani, *Saviors and Survivors*, 286.

52. Edgardo Boeninger, "The Chilean Road to Democracy," *Foreign Affairs* 64 (Spring 1986): 813.

53. Of the 2,279 persons killed during the era of military rule, 18 percent were socialist, 17 percent were MIR, and 16 percent were communist. See Lois Hecht Oppenheim, *Politics in Chile: Democracy, Authoritarianism, and the Search for Development*, 2nd ed. (Boulder, Colo.: Westview Press, 1999), 119.

54. Subsequently, the U.S. government requested the extradition of Colonel Manuel Contreras, the head of DINA when Letelier was killed. Chile's Supreme Court, however, refused the request on technical grounds. After democracy returned in 1990, courts were allowed to proceed with the trials of both Contreras and his DINA deputy, Pedro Espinoza, for ordering the killing of Letelier and a coworker. This trial was ultimately possible because it was specifically exempted from the 1978 amnesty law. It is also important that, in response to U.S. pressures, the Chilean government agreed to make financial reparations to the Letelier family, which an Organization of American States tribunal set at $2.6 million in 1992. A year later Contreras and Espinoza were found guilty and sentenced to prison terms of seven and six years, respectively. They entered prison in 1995 after the Supreme Court upheld these judgments.

55. Although voluntarily relinquishing the presidency would no doubt be difficult, Pinochet knew that he would nevertheless retain enormous political influence since he was constitutionally able to serve another eight years as the chief of the army and to serve as a member of the Chilean Senate for life.

56. Even though the truth disclosed by the commission was deemed useful by a large majority of Chilean political moderates, political partisans of the left and right criticized the report, questioning its fairness and historical accuracy. Victims' groups were disappointed that the commission had not been more successful in identifying perpetrators and in disclosing the remains of missing detainees. Military authorities, for their part, felt that the commission had not fully appreciated the chaotic conditions that existed in mid-1973—conditions that had forced them to topple the Allende regime.

57. *Report of the National Commission on Truth and Reconciliation*, vol. 2, trans. Phillip E. Berryman (Notre Dame: University of Notre Dame Press, 1993), 900.

58. Neil J. Kritz, ed., *Transitional Justice: How Emerging Democracies Reckon with Former Regimes*, vol. 3 (Washington, D.C.: U.S. Institute of Peace Press, 1995), 170.

59. This trial was possible because the 1978 amnesty law had specifically exempted General Contreras and Brigadier Espinoza.

60. Naomi Roht-Arriaza, *The Pinochet Effect*, 37.

61. The justices made several important claims: first, since Chile was a signatory to the 1984 Convention against Torture, it implicitly recognized the right of other states to either prosecute

or extradite persons that had allegedly committed torture; second, absolute immunity afforded by the 1978 State Immunity Act did not extend to criminal proceedings and therefore did not apply to extradition proceedings; third, since crimes like torture and kidnapping were contrary to fundamental law, they were not protected actions by a state official; and fourth, the act of state doctrine—which prevents one state from legally judging the actions of another state—does not protect foreign leaders from gross crimes like hostage taking because British statutes expressly permit jurisdiction when addressing some gross human rights offenses. Diana Woodhouse, ed., *The Pinochet Case: A Legal and Constitutional Analysis* (Portland, Ore.: Hart Publishing, 2000), 5.

62. Naomi Roht-Arriaza, *The Pinochet Effect*, 36.

63. Robertson, *Crimes against Humanity*, 266–67.

64. For an overview of the judicial investigations after Pinochet's return to Chile, see Naomi Roht-Arriaza, *The Pinochet Effect*, chap. 3.

65. Interestingly, the flamboyant Judge Garzón, who sought to prosecute other world leaders for human rights abuses, was himself found guilty in 2012 of misusing the law and was disbarred from Spanish courts for eleven years.

66. Mamdani, *Saviors and Survivors*, 281.

67. Kissinger, "The Pitfalls of Universal Jurisdiction," 88.

68. Barry Gewen, "What Is a War Crime?" *American Interest*, Summer 2006, 145–46.

69. Quoted in Shawcross, *Justice and the Enemy*, 200.

70. Robertson, *Crimes against Humanity*, 339.

CONCLUSION

1. Reinhold Niebuhr, *Moral Man and Immoral Society* (New York: Charles Scribner's Sons, 1960), 4.

2. Arthur Schlesinger Jr., "The Necessary Amorality of Foreign Affairs," *Harper's Magazine*, August 1971, 72.

3. Stanley Hoffmann, *Duties beyond Borders: On the Limits and Possibilities of Ethical International Politics* (Syracuse, N.Y.: Syracuse University Press, 1981), 19.

4. James Turner Johnson, "Just Cause Revisited," in *Close Calls: Intervention, Terrorism, Missile Defense, and "Just War" Today*, ed. Elliot Abrams (Washington, D.C.: Ethics and Public Policy Center, 1998), 38.

5. Drew Christiansen and Gerard F. Powers, "The Duty to Intervene: Ethics and the Varieties of Humanitarian Intervention," in *Close Calls*, ed. Abrams, 183–208.

6. G. Scott Davis, "Interpreting Contemporary Conflicts," in *Religion and Justice in the War over Bosnia*, ed. G. Scott Davis (New York: Routledge, 1996), 4–5. See also Michael Sells, "Religion, History, and Genocide in Bosnia-Herzegovina," in *Religion and Justice in the War over Bosnia*, ed. Davis, 25–28.

7. Michael Walzer, *Just and Unjust Wars: A Moral Argument with Historical Illustrations* (New York: Basic Books, 1977), 19.

Index

211–212; trust in, 211–212

force, 136; moral perspectives on, 136–142

foreign policy: application of moral norms to, 18–22; and human rights, 103–107

foundationalism, 14–15

France, 27, 152, 237; humanitarian intervention in Rwanda, 111; opposition to war in Iraq, 151; reliance on nuclear energy, 254; war against Algeria, 163

Fraser, Donald, 57

free-rider problem, 248

Frei, Eduardo, 261–262

Frieden, Jeffrey A., 201

Friedman, Thomas, 202

Front de Libération Nationale (FLN), 163, 166

Fukushima nuclear power plan, 254

Fukuyama, Francis, 61, 116, 246

gacaca, 121

Gaddis, John Lewis, 64, 73

Galston, William, 191

genocide, 108; prevention of, 107–109

Germany, 119, 131–133, 237

Gerson, Michael, 231

Gilpin, Robert, 48

Gladstone, William E., 45

Glennon, Michael, 151

Glenny, Misha, 22

global governance, 244–245; impediments to, 246–248

global poverty, 37–38; ethics of, 42–44; nature of, 38–40

global public goods, 205, 244; characteristics of, 248; provision of, 248

global society: alternative conceptions of, 30–32;

and individuals, 233–238; justice in, 32–35, 255

global warming, 251–253. See also climate change

globalization, 37, 202–205; criticisms of, 203–204; definition of, 202; in finance, 205–208

Goldwin, Robert, 106

Good Samaritan, 42, 76

government, 244

Govier, Trudy, 116

Greece, 208–210

greenhouse emissions, 253–254

Grenada, 50–52, 68

Gross, Michael, 157, 166–167

Grotius, Hugo, 31

Guantánamo, Cuba, 165, 240

Haass, Richard, 91

Habyarimana, Juvenal, 110

Haiti, 227–228, 240

Hamas, 160

Hardin, Garrett, 233

Harding, Warren, 77

Havel, Vaclav, 25, 27

Heilbroner, Robert, 41

HIV/AIDS, 230–232

Hobbes, Thomas, 30, 50

Hoffman, Bruce, 166

Hoffmann, Stanley, 21, 23, 32, 67, 68, 107, 135

Holbrooke, Richard, 23, 24

Holocaust, 20, 132

holy war, 137

Hoover, Herbert, 77

House of Lords, 262

Human Development Index (HDI), 39, 41–42

human equality, 25

humanitarian intervention, 193–195; justification of, 194–195

human rights: Carter's policy of, 57–59; foreign policy and, 103–107; idea of,

93–94; promotion of, 105–107; theories of, 94–96

Hume, David, 47

Hussein, Saddam, 18, 142–143, 150–151, 169

Hutu people, 110, 120

hypocrisy, 107, 180

idealism, 46, 54–56

Ignatieff, Michael, 29, 32, 95, 106, 160, 175, 178, 243

immigration, 238–239; ethics of, 239–241

India, 38, 39, 41, 181, 248

Indonesia, 41

Institutions, 245

insurgency, 158

intelligence, 166

interahamwe, 120

Intergovernmental Panel on Climate Change (IPCC), 251

International Atomic Energy Agency (IAEA), 151

International Commission on Intervention and State Sovereignty (ICISS), 187–188

International Covenant on Civil and Political Rights, 92, 100–101

International Covenant on Economic, Social, and Cultural Rights, 100–101

International Criminal Court (ICC), 119, 247, 255, 258; critics of, 259–260; limitations of, 259

International Criminal Tribunal for Rwanda (ICTR), 120, 121, 257

International Criminal Tribunal for the Former Yugoslavia (ICTY), 257–258

internationalism, 54

international justice, 31, 33–34, 226–229; and foreign

Mladic, Ratko, 258
Mohammed, Khalid Sheikh (KSM), 174
Montenegro, 25
moralism, 21
morality, 9, 18; moral courage, 86–88; moral decision making, 84–86; moral hypocrisy, 107; moral imagination, 84; moral judgment, 79; moral minimalism, 17; moral relativism, 4; moral self righteousness, 107; nature of, 10–11. *See also* political morality
More, Sir Thomas, 168
Morgenthau, Hans, 48–49, 50, 60, 62
Moulton, John Fletcher, 10
Mukasey, Michael, 173
mutual assured destruction (MAD), 71, 81–82
mutual assured security (MAS), 81–82

Nardin, Terry, 15, 47
National Commission on Truth and Reconciliation, 113, 261
National Conference of Catholic Bishops: pastoral letter on nuclear arms, 72, 73
National Council of Churches (NCC), 145
National Party (NP), 125
National Security Strategy of the United States (NSS), 62–63, 147
Netherlands, 19, 237
New Jewel Movement (NJM), 50–51
Nicaragua, 61
Nicolson, Harold, 9
Niebuhr, Reinhold, 48, 62
Nino, Carlos, 113, 119
nonintervention, 178–180; preconditions for, 186

North Atlantic Treaty Organization (NATO), 3, 23, 26; ethics of Libyan intervention, 191–192; military intervention in Kosovo, 23–26; military intervention in Libya, 189–192; war against Serbia, 21
North Korea, 75
nuclear deterrence: ethics of, 71–72, 85; nature of, 72
nuclear energy, 254
nuclear war, 72, 81
nuclear weapons, 70
Nunca Más (Argentina), 124
Nuremburg Tribunal, 117, 121, 255
Nye, Joseph S. Jr., 45, 80

Obama, Barack, 86, 172, 173, 190; and drone warfare, 171
official development assistance (ODA), 228
Oil-for-Food Program, 150, 218
Operation Horseshoe, 25
Operation Restore Hope, 196–197
Orentlicher, Diane, 118
Organization of American States (OAS), 178
Organization of Eastern Caribbean States (OECS), 51, 52, 53

pacifism, 136–137
Pakistan, 86, 170, 173, 181
Papandreou, George, 208
pardon, 114, 128
passive personality, 256
Paton, Alan, 216, 221
Pavlischek, Keith, 164
Peck, James, 104
Persian Gulf War, 142–146
Philpott, Daniel, 116
Pinochet, Augusto, 260; death of, 263; legal case

against, 261–263; London detention of, 261–265
Podhoretz, Norman, 61, 64
Pogge, Thomas, 41, 42
political autonomy, 24
political ethics, 79
political forgiveness: applied to Germany, 131–133; definition of, 130
political liberalism, 54
political morality, 4, 21, 130; misuse of, 20–21; nature and bases of, 12–16
political reconciliation, 87, 131, 134
political self-determination, 23–24
politics, 245
Pope John Paul II, 113
Pope Urban II, 138
Posner, Richard, 157, 166
poverty: absolute, 39; nature of, 38; strategies for reducing it, 40–41
Powell, Colin, 151–152
Power, Samantha, 108–109, 111
preemption, 147–148
President's Emergency Plan for AIDS Relief (PEPFAR), 231–232; tridimensional analysis of, 232
preventive war against Iraq, 150–152
principled realism, 46–47, 60–62
procedural justice, 226
promise keeping, 116
prudence, 50, 79, 80
public opinion, role in foreign affairs, 19–20

Qaddafi, Muammar, 3, 169, 189, 257

Rambouillet Accord, 23, 24
Rawls, John, 10, 15, 30, 35–36, 43
Reagan Doctrine, 53, 61

Reagan, Ronald, 51–52, 103, 131–135, 220; Bitburg controversy, 131–133; economic sanctions against South Africa, 219–220; military intervention in Grenada, 50–53; moral ambiguity of U.S. economic sanctions, 220–222; Strategic Defense Initiative, 80–82. *See also* Reagan Doctrine
realism, 46, 48–50
reconciliation, 115, 116, 123
refugees, 226; caring for, 236–237; repatriation of, 237
reparations, 115, 122
responsibility to protect (R2P), 103, 188, 195, 199
restitution, 115, 122
restorative justice, 122, 124, 127
retributive justice, 118, 123
Robertson, Geoffrey, 257, 265
Robinson, Mary, 104
Rodrick, Dani, 201
Roht-Arriaza, Naomi, 256
Roth, Brad, 29, 243
Rousseau, Jean Jacques, 32, 54
rule-based analysis, 74
rule utilitarianism, 68–69
Russia, 24, 27, 76–78, 151, 152, 188, 248
Rwanda: genocide in, 103, 108, 110–111; prosecution of genocide offenders, 119–122
Rwandan Patriotic Front (RPF), 110, 120

Sábato, Ernesto, 124
Sachs, Jeffrey, 229
Safire, William, 133
Sakharov, Andrei, 58
Sarkozy, Nicolas, 189, 209

Schell, Jonathan, 70
Schelling, Thomas, 73
Schlessinger, Arthur, Jr., 21
self-defense, 53
self-determination, 52, 55
Sen, Amartya, 43, 247
September 11 (2001) terrorist attacks, 2, 87, 147, 164, 173
Serbia, 26
Sermon on the Mount, 50
Shue, Henry, 42, 163
Sierra, Leone, 257
Singapore, caning in, 97–98
Singer, Peter, 29, 30, 36–38, 42–43, 211, 233, 243
Slaughter, Anne-Marie, 35, 192
Smith, Adam, 54
Smith, Michael, 55
social capital, 246
Somalia, 181, 193, 195–198
Somali National Alliance (SNA), 197
South Africa, 19, 213; apartheid regime in, 124; economic sanctions against, 219–220; multiracial democracy of, 125–126; political reconciliation in, 126; truth commission (TRC) of, 114, 117, 124, 126–128
sovereignty, 31, 178–180
Soviet Union, 41, 58, 100, 180, 185. *See also* Russia
Spain, 152, 209, 237–238, 261–262
Stacy, Helen, 103
state, moral legitimacy of, 29
Stiglitz, Joseph, 201, 205
Strategic Defense Initiative (SDI), 80–81; ethics of, 81–82
Straw, Jack, 262
structural realism, 48
subprime mortgage crisis, 207
Sudan, 189, 259

suicide bombings, 161
supreme emergency, 167
Suzman, Helen, 220
Syria, 4; revolt in, 83, 84, 91
Switzerland, 20

Taliban, 2, 170
Tanzania, 181
targeted killing (TK), 164, 168, 171, 174
Ten Commandments, 12
Terrorism, 159–161; antiterrorism, 161; counterterrorism, 162; U.S. war on, 164–165
Thatcher, Margaret, 220
Thucydides, 48, 137
ticking bomb, 166
torture, 163; French use in Algeria, 163; use in Argentina, 162. *See also* coercive interrogation
"tragedy of the commons" metaphor, 249
transgovernmentalism, 34
tridimensional ethics, 78–80, 167; application to economic sanctions, 217; application to PEPFAR, 232; assessment of the Kosovo war, 25–26; assessment of NATO's intervention in Libya, 191–192; assessment of SDI, 81–82
trust, 116, 130
truth commissions, 114
Truth and Reconciliation Commission (TRC), 126
truth telling, 116, 125
Tunisia, 3
Tutsi people, 110, 119, 120
Tutu, Desmond, 125, 220
tyrannicide, 168

ubuntu, 125, 126
Uganda, 25
Umkhonto we Sizwe (MK), 127

UN Assistance Mission in Rwanda (UNAMIR), 111, 120
UN Conference on Environment and Development (Earth Summit), 250
UN Framework Convention on Climate Change (Climate Treaty), 250–252
UN Operation in Somalia (UNOSOM), 196–198
Unified Task Force (UNITAF), 196–198
United Nations (UN): charter of, 52, 99–100, 146, 149, 169, 178 196; General Assembly, 27, 52, 100, 124, 178, 219; Security Council, 4, 27, 111, 120, 143, 150–151, 154, 188, 196–197, 219, 247; peacekeeping missions of, 25; trade sanctions against South Africa, 215
United States, 100, 185; assistance to AIDS victims, 230–232; famine relief to Soviet Russia, 76–78; immigration policies of, 238–241; intervention in Grenada, 50–52; preventive war against Iraq, 150–154; response to genocide, 109; war on terror, 164–165
U.S. Army Field Manual, 169
U.S. Army Lieber Code, 168
Universal Declaration of Human Rights, 92, 234, 237
universal jurisdiction, 255, 256–257
unlawful combatants, 164
utilitarianism, 68
Uvin, Peter, 120

Vance, Cyrus, 58
Verwoerd, Wilhelm, 116
Vienna Declaration, 102
Vincent, R. J., 57, 91, 94
virtue ethics, 87

Walldorf, C. William, Jr., 104
Walt, Stephen, 127, 153
Waltz, Kenneth, 49
Walzer, Michael, 13, 17, 71, 148, 153, 159, 184, 190–191, 218, 234–235
war: classical war, 185; irregular war, 185–159; preemptive and preventive war, 146–149

wealth creation, 40–41
weapons of mass destruction (WMD), 147, 151–152, 154, 160
Weigel, George, 140, 153
Weiner, Myron, 235
Weizsäcker, Richard von, 134
Welch, David, 47
Westphalian system, 181
Wiesel, Elie, 134
Wieseltier, Leon, 25
Wilberforce, William, 19
Wilson, James Q., 7, 9
Wilson, Woodrow, 21, 32, 54–55, 76
Wolf, Martin, 40, 210–211
Wolfers, Arnold, 2, 9, 14
world justice, 36–37. *See also* cosmopolitanism

Yew, Lee Kwan, 98
Yugoslavia, post–Cold War dissolution of, 22–23, 91

Zakaria, Fareed, 127
Zambia, 228
Zelikow, Philip, 64
Zimbabwe, 228
Zimmerman, Warren, 22, 24

About the Author

MARK R. AMSTUTZ is professor of political science at Wheaton College (Illinois), where he teaches courses in international relations, U.S. foreign policy, international ethics, and Third World politics and development. He is the author of numerous articles and books, including *Christian Ethics and U.S. Foreign Policy* (1987); *International Conflict and Cooperation: An Introduction to World Politics*, 2nd ed. (1999); *The Healing of Nations: The Promise and Limits of Political Forgiveness* (2004); and *The Rules of the Game: A Primer on International Relations* (2008). His book *Evangelicals and American Foreign Policy* will be published in 2013.